THE LIFE OF
SIR PHILIP SIDNEY

THE LIFE OF
SIR PHILIP SIDNEY

BY

MALCOLM WILLIAM WALLACE

1967
OCTAGON BOOKS, INC.
New York

Originally published 1915 by Cambridge University Press

Reprinted 1967

by permission of the Cambridge University Press

OCTAGON BOOKS, INC.
175 FIFTH AVENUE
NEW YORK, N. Y. 10010

Printed in U.S.A. by
NOBLE OFFSET PRINTERS, INC.
NEW YORK 3, N. Y.

PREFACE

IT is more than fifty years since Mr Fox-Bourne published his excellent *Memoir of Sir Philip Sidney*. Although many books have since been published on the subject no one of them represents a first-hand attempt to examine the sources of information; their authors have simply availed themselves of Mr Fox-Bourne's labours. An exception should be noted in the case of Professor Flügel's *Einleitung* to his edition of the *Apologie* and *Astrophel and Stella*, but this is a collection of notes rather than a detailed 'Life.' Some twenty-five years ago Mr Fox-Bourne re-wrote his *Memoir* in a briefer and more popular form for the Heroes of the Nation series of biographies, and in this edition he was able to incorporate some new facts regarding Sidney's life which the lapse of time had brought to light.

Under these circumstances it may be unnecessary to offer any apology for another study of the life of a man whose character and achievements have always possessed a peculiar fascination for his countrymen. I have attempted to make a thorough examination of the manuscript and published sources of information, and to estimate Sidney's significance by studying him in his relation to his contemporaries and to the history of his time. To what has been previously known of his life I have been able to add some significant details, notably the account of his school-days based on Marshall's manuscript— a document of very unusual interest which I was so fortunate as to discover at Penshurst. The story of his more intimate relation to the Prince of Orange is also of real significance. In addition I have discovered a number of facts which are interesting rather than significant, for example, the identity of H. S., and the name of one of Sidney's translations which had been forgotten. And finally I have incorporated in this account of his life many new facts of very slight importance, and I am afraid that my desire to tell everything that a student of Sidney's life might wish to know has sometimes had the effect of obscuring the wood by the multitude of the trees.

In telling the story, however, I have constantly tried to remember that details find their chief value in the degree in which they throw new light on the character or amplify the conceptions which we have already formed. In one of his letters. Mr George Meredith writes: "We cannot come to the right judgment in Biography unless we are grounded in History. It is knowledge of the world for the knowing of men. Question the character, whether he worked, in humanity's mixed motives, for great ends, on the whole: or whether he inclined to be merely adroit, a juggler for his purposes. Many of the famous are only clever interpreters of the popular wishes. Real greatness must be based on morality. These platitudes are worth keeping in mind." I have tried to keep in mind similar considerations and to deduce as just an estimate from the facts as possible.

To my late colleague and friend, Professor George S. Stevenson, I am indebted for the deep interest which he took in my work, for many helpful suggestions, and for reading the proof of the first half of the book. It is a melancholy pleasure to record here my sense of the supreme loss which his death means to his friends and to the university.

In preparing the Notes on Sidney's Portraits I am much indebted to the courtesy and wide knowledge of Mr Milner of the National Portrait Gallery.

This account of Sidney's life was completed before the outbreak of war in August last. When we are able once more to turn to books that deal with themes not directly related to the one all-engrossing subject, the life of Sidney may possess a new interest for us, for he, too, died in the Netherlands in defence of ideals strangely similar to those for which the British nation is to-day engaged in a life-and-death struggle.

M. W. W.

UNIVERSITY COLLEGE,
TORONTO.
June 26, 1915.

CONTENTS

CHAPTER I

BIRTH AND PARENTAGE

PHILIP SIDNEY was born " on Friday the last of November being St Andrew's day, a quarter before five in the morning " in the year 1554, according to an entry made by his father, Sir Henry Sidney, in a family psalter[1]. Both his father and his mother were closely related to many of the noblest English families of the time. By his mother, Mary, the eldest daughter of John Dudley, Duke of Northumberland, and Jane Guilford, his wife, he was descended from the great houses of Grey, Talbot, Beauchamp and Berkeley; his father was the son of that Sir William Sidney who had commanded the right wing of the English army at Flodden, who had later become Tutor and Chamberlain and Steward of the Household to King Edward the Sixth, and who was related to the Brandon Dukes of Suffolk. It was in his mother's lineage, however, that Philip himself always felt the greatest pride.

" Though, in all truth," he once declared, " I may justly affirm that I am by my father's side of ancient and always well-esteemed and well-matched gentry, yet I do acknowledge, I say, that my chiefest honour is to be a Dudley[2]."

[1] A large folio preserved in the library of Trinity College, Cambridge. It contains 155 leaves and each page is richly illuminated. The volume is bound in oak boards with leather back and brass corners.

[2] In his reply to the author of *Leicester's Commonwealth*. Printed by Collins in his *Memoirs of the Lives and Actions of the Sidneys, etc.* (p. 64), prefixed to his *Letters and Memorials of State....written and collected by Sir Henry Sidney ....the famous Sir Philip Sidney, etc.*, and otherwise known as the *Sidney Papers*. (2 vols., London, 1746.)

and Sir Henry Sidney, wishing to impress on his young son the moral obligations imposed by noble birth, wrote to him,

" Remember, my son, the noble blood you are descended of by your mother's side, and think that only by virtuous life and good action you may be an ornament to that illustrious family[1]."

The Dudleys traced their descent from Robert de L'Isle, one of the barons who rebelled against King John.　He was the son of Ralph de L'Isle, who was the grandson and heir of another Ralph de L'Isle.　Throughout the 13th, 14th and 15th centuries the family was represented by men who played conspicuous parts in English history.　Robert de L'Isle in 1265 was in rebellion against Henry III under Simon de Montfort's leadership ; Warine de L'Isle, his son, followed his father's example by taking up arms in protest against the supremacy of the Spencers, Edward II's favourites, and suffered a traitor's death.　Gerard de L'Isle, his son, having been restored in blood, won an honourable reputation as a soldier in the Scottish and French wars of Edward III, as did also his son, Warine, both during the lifetime of his father and after his death.　This Warine was survived by an only daughter, Margaret (1361–1392), the wife of Thomas, Lord Berkeley, and from this union there was an only daughter, Elizabeth, who was born in 1388 and who married Richard Beauchamp, Earl of Warwick. The three daughters of this marriage all made great matches: Margaret (1404–1468) became Countess of Shrewsbury, Eleanore, Duchess of Somerset, and Elizabeth, Lady Latimer.　The Earl of Shrewsbury and his son John Talbot, who had been created Baron L'Isle in 1444 and Viscount L'Isle in 1452, were both killed at the battle of Chastilion in 1453.　Thomas Talbot, son of John Talbot, succeeded to his father's dignities, but he died without issue in 1471.　His sister Elizabeth had married Sir Edward Grey, who was created Baron L'Isle in 1476 and Viscount L'Isle in 1486.　It was their daughter Elizabeth who became the wife of Edmund Dudley, Esq., Henry VII's infamous minister, and mother of John Dudley, afterwards Duke of Northumberland, who was Philip Sidney's grandfather[2].

[1] *Sidney Papers*, vol. i, p. 9.　　　　[2] See genealogical tree, p. 3.

Ralph de L'Isle, grandson and heir of Ralph de L'Isle

Robert de L'Isle, m. Alice, daughter and heir of Henry, Lord of Heyford-Warine

Hugh de L'Isle

Cassandra, m. Richard de Argenten

Brian de L'Isle

Robert de L'Isle

Robert de L'Isle de Rugemont

Warine de L'Isle, Constable of Windsor Castle, 1312, died 1322; m. Alice, sister and heir of Henry le Tyes

Gerard de L'Isle (1299—1360), m. Elizabeth, daughter of Lord Strange of Blackmere

Warine de L'Isle, d. June 6, 1383; m. Margaret, daughter and heir of William Pipard, Knight

Margaret (1361—1392), m. Thomas, Lord Berkeley, who died 1418

Gerard de L'Isle, m. Anne, daughter of Sir Michael de la Pool

Elizabeth, m., in 1388, Richard Beauchamp, Earl of Warwick; d. 1439

Elizabeth, m. George Nevile, Lord Latimer

Margaret (1404—1468), m. John Talbot, Earl of Shrewsbury, who d. 1453

Eleanore, b. 1408; m. (1) Lord Roos, (2) Duke of Somerset

John Talbot, created Baron L'Isle 1444, Viscount L'Isle 1452, d. 1453; m. Joan, daughter of Thomas Chedder

Thomas Talbot, Viscount L'Isle, 1443—1471

Elizabeth, m. Sir Edward Grey, who was created Baron L'Isle in 1476, Viscount L'Isle in 1486 and d. 1492

Margaret, died s.p.

Anne, m. Sir John Willoughby

Elizabeth, m. Edmund Dudley, Esq. (1463—1510)

John, Viscount L'Isle, m. Muriel, daughter of Thomas Howard, Duke of Norfolk. He died in 1504

Margaret, m. Henry Stafford, Earl of Wiltshire

John Dudley, Duke of Northumberland, m. Lady Jane Guilford

Elizabeth, died s.p.

Henry, died at battle of St Quintin's, 1557

John, Earl of Warwick, died at Penshurst, 1554

Ambrose, Earl of Warwick (1530—1590)

Robert, Earl of Leicester (1532—1588)

Guilford, m. Lady Jane Grey

Mary, m. Sir Henry Sidney

Catherine, m. Henry Hastings, Earl of Huntingdon

Sir Philip Sidney

The Sidneys traced their descent in unbroken male succession from the time of King Stephen or Henry II. A charter is still preserved at Penshurst in which Henry II before his accession to the throne of England grants to William de Sidne (who had accompanied him from Anjou and who later became his Chamberlain) the manor of Sutton in Surrey, and from this fact the name of the family has sometimes been derived[1].

Throughout the centuries they were well-esteemed and well-matched gentry, but no alliance with the greatest families is recorded until the marriage of Nicholas Sidney, Esquire (Philip's great-grandfather) with Anne, daughter of Sir William Brandon, and cousin and one of the heirs of Charles Brandon, Duke of Suffolk. The Brandons traced their descent from the Conqueror and also from Alexander, King of Scotland, and Nicholas Sidney's son, Sir William, inherited from his mother lands in Lincolnshire, Yorkshire and Lancashire, the extent of which was further increased by purchase and lease by Sir Henry Sidney[2].

Sir William Sidney (1482–1554), Philip's grandfather, was a man of great note throughout the reign of Henry VIII. In 1510, being then an Esquire of the King's House, he saw service against the Moors in Spain ; two years later he held command in the French war under Lord Edward Howard, High Admiral of England, and was knighted for his bravery at the burning of Conquest. In the battle of Flodden he commanded the right wing of the English army, and was then for his valour

---

[1] " The name of Sidney is said to be a corruption of Saint Denis but without any probability afforded by circumstances. The first on record, Sir William Sidney, Chamberlain to Henry II, had a grant from that monarch of Sutton in Surrey ; and as Stepney, near Blackwall, is a proved corruption of Stephen's Heath, analogy would more safely derive Sidney from Sutton Heath." Nichols, *Topographer and Genealogist*, vol. III, p. 393.

[2] Among the Penshurst documents delivered to Sir Francis Walsingham on May 26, 1589, "for the use of Mrs Elizabeth Sidney" (Sir Philip's daughter), parcel 17 contained " A deed of feoffment by Sir Wm. Stanley, Knight, unto Sir Henry Sidney, Knight, and others, of his third part of the fee simple land of Charles the elder, late Duke of Suffolk in York, Lincoln," etc. The document is dated February 19th, but the year is torn off. The parcel also contained " thirteen obligations concerning the Duke of Suffolk's lands in Lincolnshire," " An indenture of lease to Sir Henry Sidney of the fifth part of the late Duke of Suffolk's lands," etc. *Penshurst MS.*

made Knight Banneret[1]. He took part in Henry's later French wars and from that monarch received many tokens of his favour. He was made a Knight of the Garter, a member of the Privy Council, and Lieutenant of the Tower, and received from the King several grants of land, the most extensive of which were the monastery or abbey of Robertsbridge in Sussex in 1539[2] and Penshurst in 1552. Most of these marks of royal favour were conferred upon Sir William in direct recognition of the services which he and the Lady Anne, his wife (the daughter of Sir Hugh Pagenham), had rendered to Prince Edward, who had been committed almost exclusively to their care. Sir William was his tutor, and Chamberlain and Steward of the Household, Lady Anne his governess ; her sister was

" in such place as among meaner personages is called a dry nurse, for from the time he left sucking she continually lay in bed with him so long as he remained in woman's government[3]."

When the Prince was but two years old Henry Sidney, then ten years of age and a henchman of King Henry (his godfather), was formally appointed to be henchman to Prince Edward— " the first boy that ever he had[4]." A pretty story is told of Sir William, on one occasion when Edward was six or seven years old, summoning his granddaughter, Jane Dormer, who was of about the same age, to be the Prince's playfellow, and of their " reading, playing or dancing and such like pastimes answerable to their spirits and innocence of years." They also played cards, and the Prince is credited with having remarked at one stage of the game, " Now, Jane, your King is gone, I shall be good enough for you[5]." Two of Sir William's daughters, Mabell and Elizabeth, were members of the household of the Lady Mary, Edward's sister, by whom they were

[1] Collins, *Memoirs*, p. 77. *The Pedigree of Sir Philip Sidney, compiled by Rob't Cooke, Clarencieux King of Arms temp. Eliz.* London, privately printed, 1869.

[2] *Letters and Papers—Foreign and Domestic—Henry VIII*, vol. XIV, Pt. 1, April, 1539.

[3] Sir Henry Sidney to Sir Francis Walsingham, March 1, 1583.

[4] *Ibid.*

[5] Henry Clifford, *Life of Jane Dormer, Duchess of Feria*, p. 59.

much beloved " for their rare virtue and zeal in Catholic religion[1]." They died unmarried in her service.

Lady Sidney died in 1544 and Sir William ten years later. Of their family of two sons and seven daughters one son, Henry, and four daughters, survived their father. Mary was the wife of Sir William Dormer, who had been considered a great enough match for Jane Seymour, but whose mother, preferring to have him " matched in a kindred of good fame," had arranged the marriage with Lady Sidney[2]; from this union there were two daughters—Anne, who married Sir Walter Hungerford, and Jane, who married the great Spanish Count de Feria. Lucy was the wife of Sir James Harrington, and became the mother of three sons—Sir John, Sir Henry and Sir James, and eight daughters. Anne was the wife of Sir William FitzWilliam, and had one son, Sir William, and three daughters. Frances was to become the wife of Thomas Ratcliffe, Earl of Sussex, and to die without issue.

Henry Sidney was born, probably at Baynard's Castle in London, where his father chiefly lived, on July 20, 1529[3], and during his childhood and early manhood was closely associated with the Court. Wood records that he " became a student in New College (as it seems) in 1543 or thereabouts, but making no long stay there[4]." Edward VI, whose bedfellow he had often been, distinguished him with his very special favour throughout his life, and Molyneux tells us that when Sir Henry was one of the principal gentlemen of Edward's privy chamber " he was then reputed for comeliness of person, gallantness and liveliness of spirit, virtue, quality, beauty and good composition of body, the only odd man and paragon of the Court[5]." When

---

[1] Henry Clifford, *Life of Jane Dormer, Duchess of Feria*, p. 13.

[2] *Ibid.*, p. 42.

[3] " The nativity of Henry Sidney was on Tuesday the twenty day of July upon St Margaret's day in the morning a quarter after one of the clock, the twenty-one year of Henry the Eight and in the year of our Lord one thousand five hundred twenty and nine. His god-father was King Henry the Eight : his other god-father was Sir William Fitzwilliam after Earl of Southampton and Lord Privy Seal : his godmother was the Lady Kingston wife to Sir Wm. Kingston, Knt of the most noble order, and controller of King Henry the Eight his household." *Sidney Psalter.*

[4] *Athenae Oxonienses*, ed. Bliss, 3rd ed. 1813, vol. i, col. 513.

[5] *Holinshed's Chronicle*, vol. iii, p. 1548.

it is remembered that the Duke of Northumberland counted on nothing more than on the marriages of his children to secure the stability of his family, that he married his son John to the daughter of the Protector Somerset, his son Guilford to the Lady Jane Grey and his daughter Catherine to Henry, Lord Hastings, another possible claimant to the English throne, the marriage of his eldest daughter Lady Mary to Henry Sidney is a testimony that Northumberland anticipated a brilliant career for the young King's favourite. The marriage took place at Asser on March 29, 1551, and was "afterward most publicly and honourably solemnized in Ely Place in Holborn in the Whitsuntide holidays next following[1]." The marriage covenants between the Earl of Warwick (he was created Duke of Northumberland some months later) and Sir William Sidney, by which the Earl conveys to Sir Henry and Lady Mary the manor of Halden in Kent, are dated May, 1551[2]. At the beginning of June, attended by four servants, Sir Henry accompanied the Marquis of Northampton on his mission to the French King, Henry II, to whom he carried the habit of the Order of the Garter, and on July 17th he set out for England bearing despatches from Northampton to the Privy Council[3]. On October 11th his father-in-law was created Duke of Northumberland, and on the same day Henry Sidney and William Cecil were knighted, a fact which Sir Henry in his later life was fond of recalling. During the remaining years of Edward's reign honours and rewards came thick and fast upon Sir Henry. On December 26, 1552, he was again sent on a French embassy[4], and Sir William Pickering, English ambassador at Paris, wrote to the Privy Council commending Sidney's dexterity and his discreet and wise handling of the matter confided to him, and to Sir William Cecil of Sir Henry's great wisdom and circumspection[5].

Sir Henry also held many offices—Chief Cup-bearer to the King for life, Chief Cypherer to the King for life, and Chief Steward of various royal manors, mansions and parks[6].

[1] *Sidney Psalter.*
[2] Collins, *Memoirs*, p. 83.
[3] *State Papers—Foreign—Edward VI.*
[4] *Acts of the Privy Council*, Dec. 26, 1552.
[5] *State Papers—Foreign—Edward VI*, Jan. 17, 1553.
[6] Collins, *Memoirs*, p. 83.

The boy-king seemed to delight in doing him honour, and Sir Henry himself has given us this account of their relationship :

" As that sweet prince grew in years and discretion, so grew I in favour and liking of him, in such sort as by that time I was twenty-two years old he made me one of the four principal gentlemen of his bedchamber. While I was present with him he would always be cheerful and pleasant with me, and in my absence gave me such words of praise as far exceeded my desert. Sundry times he bountifully rewarded me ; finally he always made too much of me ; once he sent me into France and once into Scotland. . . .Lastly not only to my own still felt grief but also to the universal woe of England he died in my arms[1]."

During the last two years of Edward's reign Sir Henry was one of the chief lieutenants of Northumberland. We find him in the company of his father-in-law at Court[2], and in the north of England repressing the rebels in the summer of 1552, whence he is despatched post-haste with messages to the Council and King, which he must deliver before going to his wife, as Northumberland awaits an answer at Newcastle[3]. In December of the same year there was talk of his being sent as ambassador to the Emperor[4].

Immediately before Edward's death there can have been few young noblemen in England whose worldly prospects were more brilliant, or who enjoyed a greater measure of domestic happiness than Sir Henry Sidney. Many years later when his estate was much decayed he estimated that he was worth £30,000 less than at the death of King Edward[5]. If we multiply this sum by six or seven to reduce it to the terms of its value in our own day it becomes obvious that Sir Henry was a very wealthy man in his own right, besides being prospective heir to the vast estates of his father in several English counties. Moreover, we have every reason to believe that his great match with the daughter of Northumberland was not merely a *mariage*

[1] Sir Henry to Walsingham, March 1, 1583.
[2] *State Papers—Dom.—Edward VI*, vol. xiv, June 4, 1552.
[3] *State Papers—Dom.—Addenda—Edward VI*, vol. iv, July 25, 1552.
[4] *State Papers—Dom.—Edward VI*, vol. xv, Dec. 28, 1552.
[5] " If I die tomorrow next I should leave them [his sons] worse than my father left me by £20000. . . .yea and £30000 worse than I was at the death of my most dear King and master King Edward the VIth." Sir Henry to Walsingham, March 1, 1583.

de convenance.   Practically all marriages in sixteenth century
English society were arranged by parents and for worldly
reasons, but we know that Sir Henry and Lady Mary were
bound together throughout their lives of sorrow and disappointment by ties of the warmest affection and admiration.   Of
their relation to each other before the time of their marriage
we know nothing, but there still remains a curious bit of evidence
regarding the happiness of their early married life.   In a copy
of Hall and Grafton's *Chronicle* which is still extant, there are
manuscript Latin verses written by Sir Henry, and the following
moralizing lines by Lady Mary, in which it would surely be
an excess of caution to refuse to recognize Lady Sidney's
sense of insecurity on the dizzy heights to which her family
had attained, and of fear lest a sword of Damocles was suspended
over the Sidney household :

> " To whyshe the best and fere the worst
>   are to points of the wyese
>   to suffer then whatt happen shall
>   that man is happy thryese.   1551
>
>   Mary Sidney
>   fere god."

> " Upon the good daye have
>   thou in mind the unware
>   who that may come behind
>   Is not for to sped thou think a pain
>   Will not the thing that thou maeist not attain
>   for thou and none other art cause of thy let
>   if that which thou mayest not thou travel
>   to get.   Scriptum manu felix.
>
>   M. S."

> " Of al thinges the newest is the best
>   saue of loue and frinship which
>   the elder it waxeth is euer the better
>   Escript par la maine d'un
>   femme heuruse assavoir
>
>   [Mary Sid]ney[1]."

[1] Catalogue of the Anderson Auction Co., New York—Tuesday and Wednesday, Feb. 1 and 2, 1910 (Selections from the library of George G. Tillotson):
" Edward Hall and Richard Grafton—The Union of the two noble and illustre famelies of Lancastre and Yorke etc.   Londini : Richard Grafton, 1548."
The volume was bought by Dodd, Mead and Co., of New York City.

In her later life Lady Mary was to find need of the stoicism which she here seems to invoke. The lines thus carelessly jotted down form a dramatic background to her future experience of tragic sorrow, ill-health, isolation and petty trouble. To her husband she was to remain " a full fair lady, in mine eye at least the fairest " ; she was to find in him the " noble and careful father " of her children, whom she honoured for his uprightness and unswerving devotion to whatsoever things were of good report, and if pride in the character of their offspring is one of the truest sources of happiness for mature men and women, the mother of Sir Philip Sidney and the Countess of Pembroke was not denied one of the greatest consolations of life. In spite of these things there was probably no period after the death of Edward VI when Lady Sidney would have felt impelled to subscribe herself a happy woman without many qualifications.

To what extent Sir Henry Sidney was involved in the conspiracy of his father-in-law to secure the throne for Lady Jane Grey we do not know. He was a witness to Edward's will[1] on June 21st, and on July 4th, only two days before his death, Edward bestowed on him a manor in Wiltshire—the last of many gifts. On July 21st or 22nd he received his pardon from Queen Mary[2]. It would be interesting to know the story of Sir Henry's life during the intervening days. He was on terms of the closest intimacy with the Duke and Duchess of Northumberland and Sir Andrew Dudley, Northumberland's brother ; Lord Hastings and Ambrose Dudley were his warm friends, and all of these were deeply involved. Moreover, in a letter to Queen Mary, the authenticity of which there seems little reason to doubt, Lady Jane says that the news of her accession was communicated to her by Lady Sidney.

" The person by whom this news was brought unto me was the Lady Sidney, my sister-in-law, daughter of the duchess of Northumberland ; she told me with seriousness more than common that it was needful I should go with her and I did so[3]."

[1] *Queen Jane and Queen Mary*, p. 91.
[2] Froude, *History of England*, vol. VI, p. 48. *Queen Jane and Queen Mary*, p. 13.
[3] Pollino.

At first sight it seems strange that Sir Henry should have escaped a lodging in the Tower. It is not difficult, however, to conjecture an explanation. In the first place his strong common sense may have forewarned him of the futility of the whole scheme, and he may have been able to view the feverish activity of the whole Dudley family as the intoxication of ambition. He must have found it, however, an almost impossible rôle not to come out definitely for the one side or the other, and he can never have been in greater need of the circumspection which characterized his whole life than he was at this juncture. One circumstance which must have told strongly in his favour with Queen Mary was the fact that two of his sisters, Mabell and Elizabeth, had long been members of her household, and were so entirely devoted to her that

" when the Queens (the wives of King Henry) had sought with much importunity to have them in their service they would by no means leave the Lady Mary although the King himself requested it[1]."

These ladies were much beloved by Mary for their rare virtue and zeal in the Catholic religion. And Sir Henry had at least one other friend at Court. His father had not only placed his own daughters in Lady Mary's household; it was he who persuaded his granddaughter Jane Dormer to accept a similar service, and for this child of his dead sister Sir Henry had always had an especially warm feeling. When we remember further that it did not need Northumberland's dying message to persuade Mary that his children were rebels by his commandment and not of their own free wills, and that she sincerely wished to be merciful wherever it was possible to show mercy, it is not strange that the Sidneys were able to avoid the full force of the blow when it descended.

What is perhaps stranger is the fact that Sir Henry, although neither liking nor liked as he had been, to use his own phrase, found employment under the new sovereign within a few months and was even shown unusual favours. On March 13, 1554, he started on a journey to Spain, having been appointed a member

---

[1] Clifford, *Life of Jane Dormer*, p. 62.

of the deputation sent thither to escort King Philip to England, where he was to wed the English Queen[1]. The ambassadors, among whom were the Earl of Bedford and Lord Fitzwalter, had a formal audience with Philip on June 23rd[2], and returned with him to England on July 19th[3]. During his absence Queen Mary had granted to Sir Henry the wardship of Robert Pakenham, probably one of his young cousins, on May 28th, and on November 8th she ratified all the letters patent which had been granted to him and his father by the late King, and confirmed Sir Henry in all his offices such as Chief Cypherer, Serjeaunt of the Otter Hounds, etc.[4] Ten days later Sir Henry was ordered to attend upon the Lord Cobham, who had gone to welcome Cardinal Pole and to accompany him from Rochester to Gravesend, and when on November 30th Sir Henry's first son was born King Philip himself was godfather and gave the boy his own name. In the multifarious business of governing Spain and her possessions the Spanish King never forgot the occasion ; many years later when the news of Sir Philip Sidney's death reached him he scribbled on the despatch in the laconic manner which characterized him : " He was my godson[5]."

The magnificence of the christening festivities at Penshurst must have seemed in strange contrast to the immediately preceding events of death and tragedy which had taken place in the Dudley and Sidney families. The second god-father on the occasion was John Russell, Earl of Bedford, now an old man with but a few months to live. Under Henry VIII he had been in high favour, was Lord Privy Seal during the reigns of both Edward VI and Mary, and had headed the English deputation which was sent to Spain to arrange Philip's marriage with Queen Mary. He was a devoted friend of the Dudleys, and his granddaughter was later to become the wife of Ambrose Dudley. The godmother was Jane, Duchess of Northumberland, now within a few weeks of her death, an old woman, though but forty-six years of age. Few human beings can have had a more

[1] *Queen Jane and Queen Mary*, p. 68.
[2] Hume, *Two English Queens and Philip*, p. 56.
[3] *Queen Jane and Queen Mary*, p. 77.   [4] Collins, *Memoirs*, p. 84.
[5] *State Papers—Spanish*, ed. Martin A. S. Hume, 1892. Advices from Deventer (Paris Archives), Nov. 9, 1586.

bitter experience of the vicissitudes of life than this unhappy woman. She had given herself absolutely to the furtherance of her husband's ambitious schemes, and during the weeks preceding and following Edward's death we find her very active in the work of bending Lady Jane to her will and of securing for her son the title of King. Then came the sudden collapse of all her hopes. On August 22nd her husband was beheaded, and on February 12th her son, Guilford, and her daughter-in-law, Lady Jane, met a similar fate. Her four surviving sons, John, Ambrose, Robert and Henry, had lain in the Tower for more than a year under condemnation of death for treason. They had been released, though still standing attainted of high treason, on October 18, 1554, and John, the eldest, went directly to Penshurst, where three days later he died—some five weeks before Philip Sidney was born. The Duchess herself had been turned out of her house, and her furniture and household goods had been confiscated. Of her thirteen children only three sons and two daughters remained, and she now desired nothing but that her surviving children should be restored in blood and that she should be granted a speedy release from the cares of this world. She had been successful in securing the friendship of the Duchess of Alva and several Spanish lords now in England, who had already " done her sons good," and no doubt she welcomed King Philip's presence at Penshurst as a sign of good omen. Her will[1], written entirely with her own hand a short time after this event, although " with great weakness," is a remarkable composition. She forbade

" any pomp to be showed upon my wretched carcass that hath had at times too much in this world full of all vanities, deceits and guiles ; and whoever doth trust to this transitory world as I did may happen to have an overthrow as I had. Therefore to the worms will I go as I have afore written in all points ; as you will answer it afore God and you break any jot of it your wills hereafter may chance be as well broken."

Bitterly remembering that "none of my children shall inherit the degree I die in," she expresses the hope that the Queen's Highness will be good and gracious lady to them. This document

---

[1] Collins, *Memoirs*, p. 33.

contains the first reference we have to Philip Sidney after his birth. The Duchess bequeaths

"to her daughter Mary Sidney 200 marks, and 200 marks to her little son, but if he chance to die the money to go to his mother, and she chance to die the money to go to her son, and if they both die to go to her son Sidney."

Worn out by her sorrows she died at her manor of Chelsea on January 22, 1555, and was buried in the church there with great solemnity on February 1st[1].

The trouble in which the Dudleys found themselves involved had made most serious inroads on the possessions of Sir Henry Sidney in spite of the fact that he was confirmed in his offices and escaped the dangers of confiscation. In the seven months which elapsed between the death of Edward VI and that of Sir William Sidney[2], Sir Henry spent some £10,000, largely no doubt for the purpose of mitigating the calamities that had overtaken his wife's family. He continued to find employment, however, under Mary, and the kindly feelings which in his later life he entertained toward Spain, and King Philip in particular, make it probable that he was one of the many Englishmen for whom the Spanish king performed friendly offices in pursuance of his deliberate policy of conciliation. When in April, 1555, Sir Henry's sister Frances became the wife of Thomas Ratcliffe, Lord Fitzwalter, and afterwards Earl of Sussex, King Philip honoured the occasion by his presence[3]. During the whole of the succeeding month the Court was on the *qui vive* expecting daily to hear that Queen Mary had given birth to a child, and messengers who were to announce the happy

[1] *Machyn's Diary*, p. 81. Her monument, much defaced, may still be seen. The inscription is quoted by Collins, p. 36.

[2] Sir William died at Penshurst Feb. 10, 1554, and was buried in the church there on Feb. 26th. A magnificent raised tomb was erected to his memory by Sir Henry Sidney, the inscription on which is given by Collins, p. 82. An account of the funeral is preserved in a MS. in the British Museum (*Add.* 26676, f. 89).

[3] *Calendar of State Papers—Venetian*, No. 67 (April 29, 1555). In his will the Earl of Sussex makes very special mention of the five precious stones given him by King Philip "when I was sent in commission into Spain for the concluding of the marriage between Queen Mary and him and to bring him into England." *Lansdowne MSS.* vol. xxxix, f. 50.

event to the various princes of the continent were ordered
to hold themselves in readiness to start. Sir Henry was appointed to go to the King of the Romans and the King of
Bohemia ; his passport was signed by Philip and Mary[1], and
on May 6th he received 500 marks in prest toward his expenses[2].

It was, however, only one of the many occasions on which
the poor Queen was doomed to disappointment, and no ambassadors were needed. On March 14, 1556, Sir Henry was ordered
by the Council " to repair hither to-morrow," and on April
28th he was appointed Vice-Treasurer and General Governor
of all the King and Queen's revenues in the Kingdom of Ireland.
In company with Lord Fitzwalter, his brother-in-law, who was
Lord Deputy of Ireland, Sir Henry set out at once and reached
Dublin on Whitsunday. His first duties were those of the
soldier ; he " had the leading both of horsemen and footmen,
and served as ordinarily with them as any other private captain
did there," and within two months of his arrival proved his
soldiership in a great battle by killing with his own hand
James MacConnell, a mighty captain of the Scots who had
invaded Ulster. Later he was appointed Lord Justice, and
in April, 1557, he returned to England to seek money for the
Irish enterprise. He was in Ireland again in July, and was not
to see England for over two years—when the dream of Spanish
ascendancy had passed away and a new queen had for nearly
a year been seated on the throne. They were strenuous years
for Sir Henry. On four different occasions, during the absences
of Sussex, he acted in his stead as Deputy. On one occasion
Queen Mary sent him £200 for his own use by way of reward
for his services, but inadequate funds, forces and munitions
made his task a hopeless one, and he longed for nothing more
than to be recalled.

During the years of Sir Henry Sidney's first employment
in Ireland it is probable that Lady Sidney continued to live at
Penshurst. They must have been sad and lonely years for the
young wife, beset with the bitter memories of recent events,
deprived of her husband's society, and living in a part of the

---

[1] *State Papers—Dom.—Mary*, vol. IV.
[2] *Acts of the Privy Council*, May 6, 1555.

country rather remote from her friends.   Nor had she yet drained
her cup of sorrows.   In August, 1557, while the bells of the
churches in London and every English shire were ringing and
bonfires were blazing to express the nation's joy because the
English cause had triumphed in the battle of St Quintin's in
France, Lady Mary learned that her young brother, Harry
Dudley, was amongst the slain on the English side[1].   The next
year death visited Penshurst itself.   A little daughter, Margaret,
had been born about the time of Sir Henry's departure in 1556,
but she lived less than two years, and was buried at Penshurst,
April 13, 1558[2].   We have almost no definite information as
to Lady Sidney's life at this time ; the only event that has been
recorded was the passing of an Act of Parliament in 1558
whereby Ambrose Dudley and Robert Dudley, Knights, and
Lady Mary Sidney and Lady Catherine Hastings were restored and enabled in blood and name[3].

When Sir Henry returned to England Philip was almost
five years old.   We can imagine with what watchful care his
mother had tended him during the years when he was her chief
solace.   Both now and until he was ten years of age her sweet
and noble character, not yet warped by years of disappointment
and petty cares, must have been the chief force in shaping his
development.   We know that during these years he had the
best possible tutors[4], but we may assume that of these the best
was his mother.   Unfortunately we have only the most fragmentary information regarding Lady Mary's acquirements,
but there is reason to believe that she may have belonged to
the group of famous women scholars of her day, among whom
her sister-in-law Lady Jane Grey and Queen Elizabeth were
conspicuous.   Her interest in contemporary literature is attested
by Geffraie Fenton's dedication to her in 1567 of *Certaine
Tragicall Discourses*.   In 1552 when Hoby was translating his
Courtier in Paris he sent to Sir Henry an *Epitome of the Italian
Tongue* which he had compiled for this special purpose—about

---

[1] *Machyn's Diary*, pp. 147, 150.
[2] British Museum MSS. *Add*. 34891. Her epitaph is quoted in Collins,
Memoirs, p. 97.
[3] Collins, *Memoirs*, p. 37.   [4] Aubrey, *Brief Lives, etc.*, vol. II, p. 247.

a year after the marriage of Sir Henry and Lady Mary. Lady
Cecil, Lady Bacon and Lady Hoby[1], three of the brilliant
daughters of Sir Anthony Coke, were among Lady Mary's
most intimate friends, and we know that she conversed easily
in Italian. The scraps of Latin and French in her handwriting
in the Sidney copy of Grafton's Chronicle suggest that she had
received an education in languages. Her beautiful handwriting
can hardly be paralleled in the sixteenth century collections
in the Public Record Office except by that of her son Philip.
Lady Mary was well qualified both by her character and by
a liberal education to have almost exclusive charge of her boy
during the first ten years of his life, and of this there is no better
evidence than the only letter which has survived of the many
she must have written him[2].

Another important influence in Philip's early environment,
which we must not forget, was exercised by the noble old castle
in which he lived. Few of the stately homes of England would
have been better calculated than was Penshurst to instil into
the mind of a sensitive boy ideals of dignity and simple beauty
and a feeling for the historic. The manor had come into the
possession of the Sidneys only some two years before Philip
was born, when Edward VI granted it to Sir William Sidney[3].
The name is derived

" from the old British word *Pen*, the height or top of anything, and *hyrst*,
a woods. It is called in some ancient records Pencestre and more
vulgarly Penchester, from some fortified camp or fortress anciently situated there[4]."

In the Doomsday Book we learn that it was in the possession
of a family who took their name from the place. Sir Stephen
de Penchester, who was Constable of Dover Castle and Warden
of the Cinque Ports under Henry III and Edward I, was buried
in Penshurst church, where the recumbent effigy from his tomb,
now standing erect, still remains. Under Edward II the manor
passed to John de Pulteney, who was afterwards knighted

---

[1] *State Papers—Dom.—Eliz.* Lady Mary to Burleigh, April, 1573.
[2] *V.* p. 70.
[3] The letters patent are quoted by Collins—*Memoirs*, p. 81.
[4] Hasted, *History of Kent*, vol. ɪ, p. 408.

W. L. S.

and who was four times Lord Mayor of London ; in 1322 he
had license to embattle his mansion house of Penshurst. A
similar license was granted to Sir John Devereux, the owner
of the manor under Richard II. From the time of Henry VI
Penshurst passed successively into many hands. It was purchased by the Duke of Bedford and by him bequeathed to
his brother, Humphrey, Duke of Gloucester, at whose death it
reverted to the Crown. Henry VI bestowed it on Humphrey
Stafford, Duke of Buckingham, in whose family it remained for
a long time. Once more it reverted to the Crown, however,
and on March 24, 1547, John, Earl of Warwick (Lady Sidney's
father), applied for a grant of Warwick Castle, park, etc., or of
Tonbridge and Penshurst together with Hawlden and Canon-
bury[1]. His application was successful, but on July 18, 1551,
he gave Penshurst to the King again in exchange for other
property. Edward immediately bestowed it on Sir Ralph
Fane, but he, a few months later, was accused of being an
accomplice with the Duke of Somerset and was beheaded on
February 26th. His estates were forfeited, and on April 25,
1552, Penshurst passed into the possession of Sir William Sidney,
in whose family it still remains.

At first sight the castle impresses one with a sense of
austerity and bareness. Its grey walls encrusted with moss
and lichen, black and yellow and brown, and its battlemented
towers suggest an ancient fortress. This impression is emphasized by the absence of great trees in close proximity to the
building. But the exquisite beauty of colour in the walls,
and the atmosphere of antiquity which pervades the rather
heterogeneous pile give to Penshurst a unique charm among
English manor-houses. The oldest part of the castle (and also
of the neighbouring church) probably dates from the year 1200,
but the greater part was the work of John de Pulteney in the
first half of the fourteenth century. Later additions were
made by the Duke of Bedford, Sir Henry Sidney in 1579 and
1585, his son Robert, Earl of Leicester, and others. The most
distinctive feature is the great Hall—one of the few remaining
in England. The steep roof is supported by massive oak

---

[1] *State Papers—Dom.—Edward VI*, vol. i.

timbers springing from grotesquely carved human figures. At one end is the Screens—split oaken panels which separate the Porch from the Hall proper ; immediately above is the Minstrels' Gallery, and above this a beautiful window filled with very ancient glass. In the midst of the Hall is the great fire-place ; in the roof above it was an opening through which the smoke escaped. At the farther end of the Hall is the dais where the lord of the manor dined with his family and friends. From the dais a stone staircase leads to an upper chamber, a narrow slit in the wall of which allowed the lord to keep an eye on the revelry of his retainers in the Hall below.

Before the Sidneys inhabited Penshurst its chief association with literature was in the person of the great scholar and human-ist, Humphrey of Gloucester. On a manuscript written by Capgrave, the historian, and still preserved in the library of Oriel College, Oxford, is an inscription written in French to the effect that " This book belongs to me, Humphrey, Duke of Gloucester, the gift of brother John Capgrave, who presented it to me at my manor of Penshurst, New Year's Day, 1438[1]." Since Sir Philip Sidney's time many poets have celebrated the beauties of Penshurst and the virtues of the Sidneys, and among these Ben Jonson and Waller are only the most notable.

Jonson's lines have often been quoted :

> " Thou art not, Penshurst, built to envious show
> Of touch or marble ; nor canst boast a row
> Of polished pillars or a roof of gold :
> Thou hast no lantern whereof tales are told ;
> Or stair, or courts ; but stand'st an ancient pile,
> And these grudged at, art reverenced the while."

Jonson also refers to

> " That taller tree, which of a nut was set,
> At his great birth where all the muses met "—

in allusion to " Sir Philip Sidney's Oak," the tree which had been planted to commemorate his birth and which survived until 1768.

[1] *Penshurst*, the Hon. Mary Sidney, 1903, p. 7.

During Philip's early boyhood there must have been long
periods during which he saw but little of his parents, for on
Elizabeth's accession Lady Mary became one of the principal
ladies-in-waiting on her Majesty, and Sir Henry was in constant
attendance at the Court. Lady Mary had probably known
Elizabeth from childhood, and she now shared in the prosperity
which had suddenly become the portion of the surviving
members of the Dudley family. The Sidneys were on terms
of special intimacy with the Spanish ambassadors at Elizabeth's
Court, and they served as intermediaries in many delicate
negotiations. In the autumn of 1559, for instance, when the
ambassador of the Emperor and De Quadra, the ambassador
of Spain, were attempting to bring about a marriage between
the Archduke Charles of Austria and the English Queen, Lady
Sidney was the intermediary between Elizabeth and the
ambassadors, and her share in the elaborate fencing which was
considered necessary may be read in great detail in De Quadra's
reports to his master, printed in the Spanish State Papers.
A year later, again, it was Sir Henry and Lady Sidney who
were the chief agents in attempting to consummate a scheme
whereby the Queen with the approval of Philip of Spain was to
marry Lord Robert Dudley and undertake to re-establish
Catholicism in England. After some months the Queen
decided that the power of Philip could not be made use of
in bringing about her marriage with Dudley, and the close of
these negotiations was definitely marked by the Council's
refusal to admit the Papal Nuncio to England. There is nothing
surprising in this friendliness of the Sidneys toward Spain and
toward Catholicism. To King Philip they were bound by
ties of gratitude. Moreover, Sir Henry believed, as did almost
all of Elizabeth's advisers, including Cecil and Bacon, that the
Queen's safety depended on the friendship of Spain, and
although, many years later, he came to regard Catholicism
and patriotism as incompatible professions in England, at this
time he probably regarded the distinction between the new
religion and the old as a matter of slight importance. De
Quadra wrote to his master that Sir Henry was "not at all
well informed on religious questions." His virtues were

primarily those of the soldier and administrator ; for politics and diplomacy, as also for theology, he had neither aptitude nor taste.

Early in 1560 Sir Henry was appointed Lord President of the Council in the Marches of Wales and continued in this office for the rest of his life. The holding of the Welsh presidency did not preclude the accepting of other and more important duties, and Sir Henry was frequently recalled from his post to undertake special missions. Early in 1562 he was despatched to France, where he was to co-operate with Throgmorton, the resident English ambassador, in labouring " to procure peace betwixt the French King and his subjects." In August he was sent to Edinburgh to express to the Queen of Scots Elizabeth's deep regret that as a result of " the extreme and cruel proceedings of the Duke of Guise's party in France," the proposed meeting between the two Queens in the north of England must be postponed for at least a year. In Edinburgh Sir Henry spent two busy weeks in conferences with the Scottish Queen. He also saw much of John Knox, with whom he afterwards carried on a friendly correspondence. In future years Sir Henry must often have remembered as one of the most interesting experiences of his life the fortnight during which he was in frequent and intimate intercourse with the two most striking figures in the Scotland of his day.

In October Elizabeth sent English troops to the support of the French Protestants, under the command of the Earl of Warwick, and Sir Henry accompanied his brother-in-law as military adviser. He was in London again to report to the Queen and Council in less than a month, but momentous events had taken place there during his absence. The Queen had suddenly fallen ill of small-pox and for some days her life was despaired of. Should she die it was hardly possible that England could escape the horrors of civil war. The crisis passed, however, and before Sir Henry reached London Mary Stuart was able to send her congratulations to Elizabeth on her perfect recovery and to express her joy "que ce beau visage neu diminura rien de sa perfection[1]."

[1] *State Papers—Scottish—Eliz.*, Nov. 2, 1562.

Elizabeth had been more fortunate than at least one of her faithful attendants. Lady Mary Sidney, while helping to nurse the Queen back to health, had herself contracted the disease, and when she recovered it was to find that her face was permanently marked. To the proud, sensitive woman it was an unspeakable calamity.

"When I went to Newhaven," Sir Henry afterwards wrote[1], "I left her a full fair lady, in mine eye at least the fairest, and when I returned I found her as foul a lady as the small-pox could make her, which she did take by continual attendance of her Majesty's most precious person (sick of the same disease), the scars of which (to her resolute discomfort) ever since hath done and doth remain in her face, so as she liveth solitarily *sicut nicticorax in domicilio suo*."

Henceforth she frequented the Court only when Elizabeth commanded her presence, and she was denied even the satisfaction of knowing that any feelings of gratitude stirred her mistress' heart. In future years her husband's long absences from the country made her presence in London imperative in order that she might look after his interests, but whenever it was possible she retired to Penshurst and devoted herself to her children. Besides Philip, there were now two little daughters, Elizabeth, who was born at the beginning of October, 1560, and who was the godchild of the Queen[2], and Mary, who was born at Ticknell, near Bewdley in Wales, on October 27, 1561[3]. On November 19, 1563, a second son was born who was named after Lady Sidney's brother, Lord Robert[3].

During the winter months of 1563 Sir Henry was occupied with his duties in Wales. In the spring he was summoned home to assist in the wretched conclusion of the English intervention in France. While Warwick was making his noble but hopeless defence of Havre, Sir Henry was employed in the work of sending him reinforcements. When Warwick was elected a Knight of the Garter, Sir Henry, in his absence, was installed at Windsor in his stead. On April 23rd of the following year he was himself made a Knight of the Most Noble Order and was

[1] Letter to Walsingham, March 1, 1583.

[2] *State Papers—Foreign—Eliz.* Henry Kelligrew to Throgmorton, Oct. 10, 1560.

[3] *Sidney Psalter.*

installed on Sunday, May 14th[1]. The remainder of this year he spent in his Presidency from whence in November he wrote the Council that if they wished to put into the provincial governments men of the new religion they must send them from England, as there were none in Wales. None of his duties was more repugnant to him than the persecution of recusants.

Meanwhile a larger sphere of activity was opening up for Sir Henry. The anarchy that existed in Ireland and the failure of the Earl of Sussex to improve the situation had made some change imperative, and from the beginning Sir Henry's previous experience and his generally recognized abilities both in military affairs and in administration had marked him out for the office. As early as 1562 it was rumoured that he would be given the appointment, but Elizabeth then needed Sir Henry's services elsewhere, and she forced Sussex to remain at a post for which he had shown his utter incapacity. In Ulster the O'Neills had crushed their hereditary enemies, the O'Donnells, and their chief, Shan, had made himself so powerful that it seemed not unlikely that he would establish his sovereignty over the whole island. Summoned to England, he had come under an elaborate safe-conduct, and after treating with Elizabeth much as one sovereign with another, and intriguing with De Quadra, he had returned to Ireland to make himself more powerful and dangerous than ever. The ambiguous loyalty of Kildare and Desmond, the great Earls of the South, did not prevent their occasionally corresponding with Shan ; Ormond, the head of the Butler clan and a friend of Elizabeth from their childhood, was prosecuting his long feud with Desmond, and by his presence at Elizabeth's Court was doing much to thwart all consistent justice in English dealings with Ireland. The English Pale was, if possible, in a more wretched condition than the rest of the country. Sussex had failed to have Shan poisoned, and in the field he was no match for him. Finally

[1] In the British Museum there is preserved a beautifully illuminated full page manuscript (*Add.* 30808)—" the Arms and Styles of the Knights and Companions of the most honourable Order of the Garter, made and set forth at the present installation of the right worshipful Sir Henry Sidney, Knight, Lord President of Wales, who was installed at Windsor on Sunday, the 14th day of May, 1564, in the 6th year of our Sovereign lady, Queen Elizabeth."

he secured his recall in 1564, and Sir Nicholas Arnold was left
with limited authority and more limited means. He did all
that it was in blood and iron to do, but he was powerless to
move beyond the Pale or even to protect it adequately from
Shan's incursions. Desperate as to whether she should recognize Shan's authority or make a fresh attempt to crush him,
Elizabeth turned to Sir Henry Sidney.

No wonder he shrank from the task and declared that if
the Queen would but grant him leave to serve her in England,
or in any place in the world else saving Ireland, or to live private,
it should be more joyous to him than to enjoy all the rest and
to go thither. He knew the details of the Irish problem better
than any statesman of the day, he had no faith in any solution
except in a large policy of firm dealing and uniform justice,
and he had no hope that such a policy would be adequately
supported. To crush Shan O'Neill seemed to him no impossible
task if men and money were provided in sufficient quantity,
but he knew that half the explanation of his predecessors'
failures was to be found in the wretched support which had
been granted them from England. Moreover, the ancient
feud between Desmond and Ormond regarding the boundaries
of their jurisdiction and also regarding certain prize wines,
promised to be a greater obstacle to good government in Ireland
than Shan's pride of place. Only recently when Desmond
was in London Sir Henry had been employed on the controversy,
and he knew that the Queen was determined that Ormond should
have what he wished, and that she was indifferent to the right
or wrong of the matter. A bitter feud between Sussex and
Leicester constituted one more reason calculated to give Sir
Henry pause. During Mary's reign he and Sussex had been
on excellent terms, and the latter had held a high opinion of
Sir Henry's abilities, but he resented the appointment of
Leicester's brother-in-law to the office in which he had so signally
failed. Nevertheless a desperate situation had to be faced,
and Sir Henry yielded when the Queen showed an unwonted
willingness to accept the conditions which he laid down. He
reminded her that until the country was reduced to order it
was fatuous to be concerned primarily as to the expense, and

made the following stipulations before he would go : He should
retain his Presidency of Wales, and carry with him £12,000
to pay the debts which had already been incurred, he should
have power to levy what troops he considered necessary and
should be supplied with the money to pay them, his appointment should be for a maximum period of three years, and he
should be at liberty to return to England at any time if he deemed
it necessary for the good of the service. These conditions he
submitted to the Queen on May 20th[1], and on June 22nd the
Council announced his appointment to Arnold. A similar
letter was sent to Shan O'Neill, who had the effrontery to
reply praising Arnold's government and expressing the hope
that Sidney would do as well. On July 4th his instructions
were drawn, and after he had himself modified them they
were revised on July 9th. Still he delayed his departure, for
the money which he insisted on taking with him was not forthcoming, and the necessity of doling out a certain amount to
the Scottish nobles who were in rebellion against Queen Mary
increased the difficulty of finding the Irish funds. On October
13th Sir Henry was reappointed Lord President of Wales[2].
Meanwhile reports came in steadily of O'Neill's capture of forts
and castles which he manned with his own followers, and at
length on October 25th the Lord High Treasurer Winchester
was able to inform Sir Henry that he had paid to his servant,
Owen More, £11,000 parcel of the £12,000 contained in his
privy seal. Events at Court during these months were not
calculated to raise his hopes. The Desmond-Ormond feud
became more acute, and Sussex and Sir Henry were interrogated
as to their opinions on the subject by the Privy Council. Lady
Sidney's health was so bad that there seemed no likelihood of
her being able to go with her husband, but when Sir Henry
reached Chester in the middle of November she was able to
accompany him. There for more than six weeks they were
stayed by contrary winds, and Cecil strove in vain to write
comforting letters telling Sir Henry of his own sympathy and
that of the Queen, and reporting an " atonement " made between

[1] *State Papers—Ireland—Eliz.*
[2] Wright, I, 210.

Sussex and Leicester.   One of Sir Henry's vessels in attempting to put to sea was wrecked with most of his household stuff and utensils, the whole of Lady Sidney's apparel and all her jewels, many horses, stable stuff, etc.   Sir Henry estimated the loss at much more than £1500.   It was with a sad heart that he finally reached Dublin on January 13, 1566.

CHAPTER II

CHURCH PREFERMENT

ELIZABETH's settlement of the religious question was far from satisfactory to a majority of her more zealous Protestant subjects. It was not only that the Marian bishops—" the caged wolves "—were not brought to the block forthwith; the Marian priests, they bitterly complained, were to a great extent left undisturbed. It is impossible now to determine at all accurately the number of deprivations during the early years of Elizabeth's reign; the estimates vary from 200[1] to 1875[2]. What is certain, however, is that Elizabeth was most anxious to conciliate the Catholics, and to place no unnecessary obstacles in the way of those inclined to conform, and that deprivation was by no means confined to Catholics but extended even to those who had been in exile during Mary's reign and whose consciences would not allow them to accept the " popish abominations" which were retained in the English establishment. The controversy regarding vestments raged throughout the first decade of the reign, and this together with the many abuses that were countenanced in the new church stirred the anxious fears as well as the indignation of the professors at Zurich and Geneva. Their point of view is seen in a letter written by Beza to Bullinger in 1566 on " this most distressing subject."

" What must we say," he asks, " when not only the papists are left in possession of the revenues of their benefices but even of their ecclesiastical offices upon merely taking an oath to maintain the reformation; so that godly brethren are for the most part placed under the authority,

[1] Dr Gee in *The Elizabethan Clergy.*
[2] Father Birt in *The Elizabethan Religious Settlement.*

and compelled to submit to the jurisdiction of those who are in general both unlearned and in their hearts the most bitter enemies of true religion? What must we say when there are openly sold in the court of the metropolitan dispensations for non-residence, for plurality of benefices...and even for obtaining a benefice during childhood, and other things of this kind than which Rome herself has nothing more disgraceful or abominable[1] ? "

George Withers in a letter to the Elector Palatine complains bitterly of the same abuses :

" the ministry is in fact nothing at all nor is there any discipline. For those persons cannot be said to be ministers of Christ but servants of men, who can do nothing according to the prescript of the word, but are obliged to act in every respect at the nod of the Queen and the bishops. What must we say when most of them are popish priests, consecrated to perform mass ; and the far greater part of the remainder are most ignorant persons, appointed at the will of the people not to the ministry of the word but to repeat the office of the day or festival which almost any child might do without difficulty ? What must we say when those who preside over the churches are allowed to be absent from them for the sake of study or attendance on other things[2] ?"

As a matter of fact traffic in benefices of all kinds was common, pluralism and absenteeism were widespread. That children frequently held benefices does not seem to have been true, and the statement of Perceval Wiburn[3] (one of the Marian exiles who had become prebendary of Winchester and Rochester but who had been deprived for nonconformity) that " even boys, and others not in holy orders, may be capable of holding ecclesiastical preferment" seems to refer to exceptional cases. Even then the boy was supposed to be at the time a student in the University where he was preparing himself for the duties of his office. It is somewhat surprising, then, to say the least, that the first event which it is possible to chronicle in the life of Philip Sidney after the date of his birth is his institution as incumbent of the parsonage of Whitford in the parish of Skyveog by the reverend father in God, Thomas, Bishop of St Asaph. This event occurred in May, 1564, when Philip was nine years of age. A few months later took place his induction as prebend

[1] *Zurich Letters* (Parker Soc.), 2nd Series, p. 130.
[2] *Ibid.*, p. 163.   [3] *Ibid.*, p. 360.

of Llangunlo in the diocese of St Davids, and at some date which I have not been able to discover he was installed as prebend of Hereford[1].

The history of Whitford parsonage in the reigns of Edward and Mary reflects strangely the unsettled and mercenary character of the times. On October 21, 1547, Hugh Whitford, the incumbent, devised, granted, etc., to Roger Chaloner and John Whitford

" this his charge and parsonage of Whitford with the mansion place belonging to the same and also all glebe land...and the emoluments, advantages and appurtenances to the said parsonage and mansion place in any wise pertaining or belonging "

for the term of twenty-one years from the feast of St Michael last past. During this period they are to keep the place in good repair and to make an annual payment to the said Hugh of £30. If they fail to make due payment he is to have his parsonage again. The indenture is signed " By me Hugh Whitford Clerk," and attached to it is a Latin parchment in two parts beginning respectively *Et nos Robertus* and *Et nos Richardus* in which the bishop and the dean of St Asaph sanction the bargain[2]. After a number of years Chaloner assigned his moiety, and various persons became successively the owners of the benefice. Finally, however, their rights were impugned on the ground that

" the supposed dean of the Church of St Asa[ph was] not by the law of the church dean, for that he obtained t[he same] by simony which also appeareth by sentence,"

and the question was raised as to the legality of a grant made by a priest who had obtained a deanery of a Cathedral church by simony[3].

---

[1] In a modern list (probably compiled by the Honourable Miss Mary Sidney) of the documents preserved at Penshurst, the " Installation of Philip as Prebend of Hereford " is number twenty-eight. I have not found the original document. Molineux mentions Sir Henry Sidney's especial good will to the church at Hereford and his friendly gift to it. (*Holinshed's Chronicle*, vol. III, p. 1552.)

[2] *Penshurst MS.*

[3] *Penshurst MS.*, consisting of a single sheet nearly half of which is gone and the rest falling to pieces. On one side is the " Byll," on the other the " Rebuttal."

I have not discovered either the date or the outcome of this suit, but the legal deprivation of Hugh Whitford by Thomas, Bishop of St Asaph, and the sequestration of the fruits of the benefice in 1564 seemed at first to nullify all claims which were based on the original assignment of interest.

"Upon consideration of the towardness and virtuous qualities conceived in the said Philip Sidney he was admitted, collated, instituted and thereto inducted...in the same charge and parsonage with all issues, profits, commodities and advantages to the same belonging or in any wise growing or appertaining."

On May 6, 1564, in a *Pateat universis per presentes*[1] Philip Sidney, Clerk, announces that he has chosen Gruff Jones, Clerk, rector during his absence, although the documents in which Thomas, Bishop of St Asaph, announces his institution[2] and induction[3] are dated May 7th, and May 8th respectively. Immediately on the deprivation of Hugh Whitford the bishop had committed all the fruits of the benefice to the custody of William Mostyn and Gruff Jones, and on June 4th by an indenture of covenant Philip Sidney and William Mostyn "his surety, factor and friend" bind themselves

"that if it shall fortune at any time hereafter the title of the said Philip to be repealed or annulled, and any other title claim or interest justly presented by any person or persons approved, and by order of law allowed,"

that then the said Philip shall resign into the hands of the bishop all his claims to the parsonage. Moreover, in that event he and Mostyn covenant

"to sustain, bear and pay all manner of costs and charges sustained and borne as well by him [the bishop] and his officers and other ministers and sequesters in and upon the same benefice and parsonage of Whitford by reason of the depriving, sequestration or any other process from all manner of costs and charges ordinary and extraordinary rising and growing upon the same and at all times during the incumbency of the said Philip in the said parsonage."

---

[1] *Penshurst MS.* The appointment of Gruff Jones as rector in the absence of Philip Sidney.

[2] *Penshurst MS.* A parchment with the large dependent seal of the Bishop of St Asaph.

[3] *Penshurst MS.* The induction of Philip Sidney as rector.

As though the bishop were not yet sufficiently hedged about, Philip and Mostyn further agree to

" keep harmless the said reverend father, his heirs, executors and administrators from all damages, costs, charges, trouble and expense as well for and concerning the deprivation, sequestration, collation, induction and admission, as other things done and executed about the said rectory and parsonage of Whitford before the day of making hereof or that may hereafter happen or ensue by reason or occasion of the same[1]."

The cold-blooded spirit of bargaining is probably somewhat heightened by the precise legal phraseology, but the whole transaction contains little to admire unless it be the business-like qualities of the bishop. All the parties to the contract were probably aware that the new incumbent was not likely to be left in undisturbed possession. Both Gruff Jones and William Mostyn had claims on the benefice quite apart from the fact that the bishop had recently committed its revenues to their custody. On August 14, 1563, Griffith ap ed ap John, whom I identify with Gruff Jones, had bound himself with others for the true payment of £65. 6s. 8d. to Robert Johns and John Thomas ap Holl ap —— of Skyveog for the last year's tithes of Whitford parsonage. These gentlemen, whose rights were based on the original assignment to Chaloner and John Whitford, agreed on August 6, 1564, to deliver Gruff Jones' obligation to Philip Sidney on the feast of Candlemas next coming, provided that Hugh Whitford had not before that time established his claim by due process of law[2]. Hugh Whitford did not succeed in re-establishing himself, and we may assume that the tithes were paid to Philip Sidney, but one of the claimants at least— Robert Johns—did not for that reason resign his interest in the benefice. As we shall see, he, William Mostyn and Hugh Whitford had each to be bought off eventually before Philip Sidney was left unmolested in the enjoyment of his sinecure.

Meanwhile he had become possessed of another benefice. In the register of the diocese of St Davids it is recorded that in 1565 Philip Sidney, Scholar, was instituted prebend of

[1] *Penshurst MS.* An Indenture of Covenant made the 4th day of June, 1564.
[2] *Penshurst MS.*

Llangunlo in place of T. Bulkley, who had been deprived[1], and there are still in existence at Penshurst two Latin parchments dealing with the fact. The first of these records his induction on January 14, 1565, and refers to the deprivation of Thomas Bulkley; the second announces the installation of Harry Tannar, Clerk, in the prebend, for and in the behalf of Mr Philip Sidney, on the 9th day of November, 1565.

We may assume that up to this time Sir Henry Sidney himself had conducted the negotiations regarding Philip's appointments both at Whitford and Llangunlo, but on November 17, 1565, a few days after Harry Tannar's installation at Llangunlo, Sir Henry reached Chester on his way to Ireland to assume his duties as Lord Deputy, and in his absence Philip's interests were looked after by his uncle, the Earl of Leicester. William Mostyn's claims on Whitford parsonage were the first to be disposed of. It will be remembered that on October 21, 1547, Hugh Whitford had granted a moiety of his rights to John Whitford for a period of twenty-one years. John Whitford entered into and enjoyed the premises, and by a deed of assignment dated October 7, 1559, he

" for due consideration granted the same to William Mostyn of Mostyn within the County of Flint, Esquire, for the residue of the said term of years by force whereof the said William Mostyn into the premises entered, and was and is thereof possessed."

We have here the explanation of the fact that on Philip Sidney's appointment Mostyn figures as his surety, factor and friend. On November 26, 1566, however, William Mostyn " for due consideration " assigns to Philip Sidney, Esquire, son of Sir Henry Sidney, all his rights to the benefice absolutely[2].

The claims of Robert Jones and Hugh Whitford were not so easily disposed of, and finally the various suits depending between the said parties were by common consent handed over to the arbitration of William, Earl of Pembroke, and Robert, Earl of Leicester. As a result of this arbitration Robert Jones was paid £100 by Philip Sidney, in consideration of which he on April 30, 1567, gave a quit-claim resigning absolutely

---

[1] Henry Gee, *The Elizabethan Clergy*, p. 291.
[2] *Penshurst MS.* Parchment with seal attached.

his rights in the benefice and promising to give up all actions and quarrels with a large number of people[1]. The arbitrators gave absolute judgment against Hugh Whitford and in favour of Philip, who, however, must pay to Hugh Whitford during his natural life an annuity of £30. On April 20, 1567, Robert Mason of Ludlow and William Mostyn of Whitford became sureties for the payment of this annuity in the sum of £500. Nevertheless an attempt was made at once to compound with Hugh Whitford for this annuity by the payment of a lump sum, and on April 27, 1567, in consideration of 100 marks paid to him by Philip Sidney, he resigned all right, title and interest that he had in the benefice to Gryffith Jones, clerk, and his successors, and unto the said Philip Sidney, Esquire. He further agreed

" to forsake and revoke all and all manner of actions, quarrels, trespasses, appeals and demands whatsoever unto the reverend father in God now Bishop of St. Asaph, Gryffith Jones, clerk, Philip Sidney, Esquire, and unto William Mostyn, Esquire, and to any of them severally by these presents all and all manner of actions, such quarrels, debts, trespasses, appeals and demands whatsoever now hanging and depended, moved, or stirred between me and the said parties or any of them, as well in all and every cause ecclesiastical as temporal from the beginning of the world unto the day of the date hereof[2]."

One would suppose that this document, with its beautiful dependent seal ornamented with skull and cross-bones, would have bound the militant Hugh in chains of iron, but he was not yet to cease from troubling. When Sir Henry returned to England in April, 1568, he found Hugh still stirring about his rights in the benefice, and the story is closed by an indenture dated June 10, 1568, between Sir Henry and Philip of the one part and Hugh ap Howell alias Whitford of the other, in which, in consideration of £100 now paid to him by Sir Henry, the said Hugh gives up all claims on his annuity and everything else connected with the benefice, and agrees that henceforth Philip Sidney is to have quiet possession of Whitford parsonage[3].

[1] *Penshurst MS.* Quit-claim of Robert Jones.
[2] *Penshurst MS.* Quit-claim of Hugh Whitford.
[3] *Penshurst MS.* Indenture between Sir Henry and Philip of the one part and Hugh Whitford of the other.

W. L. S.

I have thought it worth while to give this long account of comparatively unimportant events in the life of Philip Sidney because it furnishes us in its detail with what is perhaps a unique example of the trafficking in benefices which was common during the early years of Elizabeth's reign, and, to a lesser extent, much later. Leicester was referred to by his most malicious detractor as " he that sweepeth away the glebe from so many benefices throughout the land and compoundeth with the parson for the rest[1]," and in his will the Earl gives authority to his executrix and overseers to sell " the parsonage of Warrington which I have in Lancashire[2]." Elizabeth frequently drew upon church funds for the relief of her impoverished pensioners, and at some undetermined period she granted to Philip Sidney a Welsh sinecure worth £120 per annum which was many years later held by George Herbert, the poet. Unprincipled as these transactions seem when viewed from a modern point of view we must remember that the public conscience was only awaking to the objectionableness of the practice in Elizabeth's day, and that unqualified condemnation of those who enjoyed the revenues flowing from such sources would be beside the point. In contemporary France conditions were probably much worse. There,

" benefices were but a form of royal revenue; it was by them that services in war, or diplomacy at court, merit in art or literature or dancing, were rewarded. Non-residence was almost universal. Benefices were dealt in, says a Venetian ambassador, like stock at Venice[3]."

We shall probably not be far wrong in assuming that throughout his life Philip Sidney's slender purse was chiefly replenished with moneys derived from his various benefices.

---

[1] *Leicester's Commonwealth* (1st edition, 1584, p. 69).
[2] Collins' *Sidney Papers*, vol. I, p. 72.
[3] Armstrong, *The French Wars of Religion*, pp. 10–11.

CHAPTER III

OF Philip's school-days we are able to relate more events and to give more detailed minutiae than of any other period of his life. This is due to the discovery of a manuscript at Penshurst which has hitherto been unaccountably overlooked. It is an " old mouse-eaten record " stitched together in book form, and contains, besides the covers, twenty pages, of which the last two are blank. On the outside of the front cover is written, " The Account of Mr. Philip Sidney's Expenses since the 3rd of December, 1565, until the Feast of St. Michael the Archangel, 1566." Page 1 records those

" Sums of money received by me, Thomas Marshall, your Lordship's humble servant, to the use of my young master Mr. Philip Sidney since your honour's departure with my Lady from Westchester towards Ireland, namely Monday the 3rd of December, 1565, until Michaelmas next ensuing, anno 1566."

Pages 2 to 18 inclusive are devoted to

" The Account of such sums of money as I Thomas Marshall have disbursed for my young master Mr. Philip Sidney beginning upon Tuesday the 4th of December 1565 and ending at Michaelmas next ensuing anno 1566."

Philip had been enrolled as a student of Shrewsbury School on October 17, 1564—the same day on which Fulke Greville, who was to become his most intimate friend during the remainder of his life, and James Harrington, his first cousin, became students of the same institution. The period covered by the accounts, then, is approximately that of the boy's second year in the school. The manuscript is literally falling to pieces as a result of damp, and a large irregular section, somewhat triangular in shape, has been eaten out of the bottom of each sheet. Fortunately, the number of items that are irrecoverable is comparatively small. Before proceeding to examine the contents in detail, however, it will be necessary to know something of the school which Philip was attending.

One or more grammar schools had probably existed in Shrewsbury from very early times. A Guild School had been kept by the Drapers' Company[1], and it is almost certain that the collegiate churches of St Mary and St Chad—both of which are mentioned in Doomsday—each had a grammar school ; otherwise they would have failed to perform one of the essential functions of such institutions. Moreover, from the Chantry certificates of Edward VI we know that the neighbouring Salop parishes of Wellington, Oswestry, St Leonard's in Bridgenorth, Madelay, and Newport each had its grammar school taught by a schoolmaster or priest[2]. But the Chantries Acts of 1545 and 1547 had swept away most if not all of these foundations, and in the first three years of Edward VI's reign the failure of the Protector and the Council to carry out their good intentions regarding new institutions had caused a cry of protest to go up from every part of England. Under the Duke of Northumberland a considerable number of schools were re-founded, and of this number Shrewsbury was one. It is a significant fact that the chief credit for this happy issue was accorded to a draper and bailiff of the town, and that the endowment of the new school was derived from the tithes of the dissolved collegiate churches of St Mary and St Chad.

The charter of the "Free Grammar School of King Edward VI in Shrewsbury" was granted on February 10, 1552, in response to the earnest petitions of the bailiffs and burgesses of the town and of many people in the surrounding country. A small endowment had been settled upon the new seat of learning, a timber building was purchased by the bailiffs for £20, some adjacent houses were rented, and under the

---

[1] Leach, *English Schools at the Reformation*, p. 34.
[2] *Ibid.*, pp. 187–9.

head-mastership of a certain " Sir Morys " work was begun at
once. During the next ten years we know almost nothing of the
school. Sir Morys was succeeded after a few months by John
Eyton, who had to be "avoided"; the name of his successor
is not known. The real history of Shrewsbury School begins
with the appointment to the head-mastership, on June 21,
1561, of Thomas Ashton, a fellow of Trinity College, Cambridge.
In the year 1562 he enrolled 289 boys, and in each of the
succeeding five years the admissions averaged about 100[1].
In other words, there were probably about 400 boys under
Ashton's charge at any one time during Philip Sidney's residence in Shrewsbury, and so great was the reputation of the
school that Camden, writing in 1586, could call it " the largest
school in all England for the education of youth."   Of Ashton's
two assistants, Thomas Wylton, who resigned in 1568, and
Richard Atkys, who held the position until his death in 1587,
we know little more than the names, and we have no reason
for assuming even that they were graduates of Oxford or
Cambridge, although Atkys continued to hold his place for ten
years after the promulgation of the ordinances of 1577 which
required the third master to be a B.A. at least.   At any rate,
Ashton's personality towered far above that of his colleagues,
and it was his ideals that shaped the character of the school.
When he resigned the head-mastership in 1571 to enter the
service of the Earl of Essex his continued interest in the welfare of the institution which he had virtually founded showed
itself in many ways.   He continued to watch over its finances ;
he secured a sufficient additional endowment from the Crown
to place the school on a stable basis, and, most important of
all, he drew up ordinances which were to remain in force for
more than two hundred years, and which gave him the opportunity not only of determining the path which was to be
followed in the present but also of suggesting incidentally
ideals for the future.   In his last years Ashton had earned the
admiration of the Queen, of Burleigh, Leicester and Bedford,
in his conduct of the affairs—political and private—of the
Earls of Essex, and the first Earl showed his appreciation of

---

[1] Owen and Blakeway, *History of Shrewsbury*, vol. II, p. 96.

the schoolmaster's worth by leaving him an annuity of £40.
He died in 1578. " He is a man, God be blessed for him,
that hath done much good in Shropshire," wrote a certain
Shrewsbury draper when Ashton resigned his charge[1]. What
Philip Sidney's estimate of his schoolmaster was is not recorded,
but we may feel fairly sure that he shared the sentiments
expressed some thirty years later by one of his schoolfellows,
Andrew Downes, then Regius Professor of Greek in the University of Cambridge. Referring to Ashton, Downes says :

"I name this gentleman who has now been long dead, that I may do
honour to his memory, for after God and my parents he is the person to
whom I am most indebted for all the literature I possess. Whatever I
have of humanity, or of any good in me, proceeds from him ; nor do
I feel so grateful to the Almighty for anything else as for this, that by his
providence I enjoyed the advantage of a preceptor of whom all his scholars
may be justly proud. Amid all the misfortunes of my life, of which I
have had an ample share, I consider it as a supreme, indeed an unparalleled
felicity that my father put me when a boy under the care of this most
excellent person[2]."

It is not strange that Philip Sidney's father was anxious
to place his son under the care of such a master. Sir Henry
had been appointed Lord President of Wales in 1560, and
almost every year his official duties led him to spend some
time in Shrewsbury, where his residence, the Council House,
was just opposite the school. For instance, in 1562, we read
in the Corporation Accounts :

" Paid for wine, an ox, feeding of horses, and other necessaries given to
Sir Henry Sidney, Knight, Lord President in the Marches of Wales while
he was here in the town in the month of August, on account of his favour
to the town—£12. s10. d8[3]."

In this way he would become acquainted with the character of
the school, and it is just possible that he had known the schoolmaster even before this time, as there is some reason to believe
that Ashton had previously acted as tutor to the sons of Sir
Andrew Corbet, a member of the Council, and a warm friend

[1] Owen and Blakeway, vol. i, p. 365.
[2] Quoted in the Blakeway MSS. printed in *A History of Shrewsbury School*.
By Alfred Rimmer.
[3] Owen and Blakeway, vol. i, p. 354.

of Sir Henry. No doubt the possibility of having his son within easy reach of Ludlow, the chief seat of the Lord President, was also an argument in determining Sir Henry's choice of a school.

When Philip Sidney entered Shrewsbury the growing fame of the institution and the excellence of the instruction were in striking contrast to the external equipment. The timber building in Ratonyslone[1]—still called the School Lane—which had been purchased by the bailiffs in 1551, together with the adjoining houses which were rented, constituted the entire school premises until 1582, and although an anonymous chronicler of Shrewsbury refers to them as " Situate near unto the Castle gate of the said town upon a goodly prospect[2]," Thomas Ashton, writing to his bailiffs in 1574 and urging the necessity of more substantial and commodious quarters, has to refer to the existing building as " old and inclining to ruin " and its location as " an evil place[3]." To reach the school the boys had to pass the common gaol of the town. In the ruinous timber houses the danger from fire was so great that one of Ashton's ordinances forbade the use of candles. Sanitary arrangements, if we may judge from the letter just referred to, were almost entirely lacking. There were no residences either for masters or boys ; there was neither chapel nor library ; the students were " tabled " by the householders of the town, who were given rather extensive authority over their young charges. In spite of all defects, however, as we have seen, the school flourished.

Ashton's ordinances, to which reference has already been made, did not come into force formally until February 11, 1578, but negotiations on the subject between the ex-headmaster and the bailiffs had extended over a period of seven years, and we shall not be far wrong in assuming that the picture of the school-life which may be drawn from the ordinances is substantially that of a few years earlier, when Philip Sidney was one of the scholars[4]. His schoolmates were

[1] Rimmer, *op. cit.*, p. 29.   [2] *Taylor MS.* Quoted by Rimmer, p. 20.
[3] Fisher, *Annals of Shrewsbury School*, p. 425.
[4] For a full list of the ordinances see Baker's *History of St John's College, Cambridge,* vol. I, pp. 407–413.

drawn from every rank of society. The majority were from the middle classes, but there were also sons of lords, knights, and gentlemen. Shrewsbury was a free grammar school, that is there was no charge for tuition (except a graduated scale of entrance fees); and elementary instruction was not given, although at a somewhat later period " an accidens schole for begynners " was established. Most of the scholars had no doubt passed through the song schools and writing schools of the time. The boys who came from a distance—the great majority—boarded about the town suburbs, and their " hosts " were obliged to " cause and see all suche their children or tablers to resorte to their parishe churche everie sondaie and holidaie to heare devine service, at morninge and eveninge praier." In a general way they were probably expected to stand *in loco parentis* to their " tablers "; for example, in 1582 the bailiffs made a proclamation

" that no scholars, boys nor prentices should that night (election evening) go abroad to disquiet the town with unreasonable noises, fightings, and disorders which were wont usually to proceed as that night,"

under penalty of £5 fine to each householder who let them out[1].

" No slogardie a-night " was permitted in Ashton's school. From the Purification (February 2nd) until All Saints' Day (November 1st) the boys were required to be in their places at the school by six o'clock in the morning, of the approach of which hour they received warning by the ringing of a bell for fifteen minutes. During the rest of the year school began at seven o'clock, but was closed an hour later in the afternoon. The boys probably had their breakfast before coming to the school; for the statutes make no mention of an interval for this purpose, and in a non-residential school an interval would not have been practicable[2]. As soon as the bell ceased ringing prayers were " sung and said every morning devoutly upon their knees." The second and third schoolmasters conducted this service each for one week in turn. The roll was then called and absentees were punished by the master " according to his discretion and their deserts." The head schoolmaster

[1] Rimmer, p. 75.
[2] The boys at Eton rose at 5 a.m.

began his work an hour later. One is not surprised to find among Philip Sidney's expenses the item " For wax sises to burn in the school a-mornings before day...4*d*.," although the later ordinances prescribed that " no candle shall be used in the said school for breeding diseases and danger and peril otherwise." Eleven o'clock was the hour for dinner and work was resumed at a quarter to one, the school bell having again been rung for·fifteen minutes. Again there were prayers and roll-call, and the afternoon session in winter closed at half-past four, " if daylight will serve thereunto," in summer at half-past five. Nor were these long hours relieved by extended vacations ; the school broke up only at Christmas for eighteen days, at Easter for twelve days, and at Whitsuntide for nine days. The weekly holiday was on Thursday, when " the scholars of the first form before they go to play shall for exercise declaim and play one act of a comedy." On Sunday, as we have seen, the boys attended their various parish churches ; if in any particular church, however, a sermon was to be preached, they were all expected to hear it. Several monitors were appointed for each church " to note as well their absence as misbehaviour in anything." There is no reference in the statutes to any wider extension of the monitorial system as it was known in several other English schools of the time, at Eton and Westminster, for example[1]. Failure to return promptly after vacation, wilfulness or obstinacy concerning the laws of the school, and betting, open or covert, were all severely punished, usually by expelling the offender. To what extent the rod was used we have no information ; at Eton we know that Udall's severity constituted one of his claims to fame.

Of the school sports our only information is contained in one of the statutes to the effect that " the scholars' play shall be shooting in the long bow and chess play, and no other games except it be running, wrestling, or leaping, and no game to be above one penny or match above four pence." It was

[1] At Eton there were eighteen praepostors. At Saffron Walden in Henry VIII's reign they had " prepositores in the field when they play, for fyghtyng, rent clothes, blew eyes, or siche like " (*v*. Maxwell Lyte, *History of Eton College*, p. 136).

the renaissance period in the popularity of archery as of many other things, and Ashton was probably of the same mind as his great contemporary schoolmaster, Roger Ascham, that "if a man would have a pastime wholesome and equal for every part of the body, pleasant and full of courage for the mind... let him seek chiefly of all other for shooting[1]." Evidently he did not share Ascham's enthusiasm for cock-fighting—a sport which seems to have been popular at Eton. One of Philip Sidney's expenditures was " for certain bird bolts for to shoot at birds." The Severn flowed close by the school, and we may suppose that the young Salopians were accustomed to cleave with pliant arm the glassy wave.

The course of instruction for Shrewsbury boys, like that provided in all other grammar schools of the period, was almost exclusively in the classics. The statutes prescribed the study of Cicero, Caesar's Commentaries, Sallust, Livy and "two little books of Dialogues drawn out of Tully's Offices and Lodovicus Vives by Mr Thomas Ashton" for prose, and for verse, Virgil, Horace, Ovid and Terence; in Greek the text-books were Cleonarde's grammar, the Greek Testament, Isocrates ad Demonicum, or Xenophon's Cyrus. The head-master was given discretion to depart somewhat from the prescription, however, by substituting for these authors " some of them mentioned in the table for manner of teaching to be read in the school," a document the discovery of which would surely prove interesting. In which of the seven classes of the school these various authors were read we are not told[2], but Thomas Marshall's accounts record the purchase by Philip Sidney, in his second year, of " Ashton's doing of Tully's Offices and Lodovicus, Virgil, Sallust and Cato." Other items show us that the boy's studies were not confined to the books mentioned in the statute. The purchase of a French grammar and of " example-books for phrases and sentences in Latin and French" points to his study of at least one modern language, in which we also know that he could write a letter to his father ; he

---

[1] *Toxophilus* (Arber's reprint), p. 46.

[2] For the apportionment of a very similar list of authors to each of the seven forms at Eton and Winchester, see Maxwell Lyte, *op. cit.*, p. 139, and Sargeaunt, *Annals of Westminster School*, p. 39.

had probably begun the study before coming to Shrewsbury,
for Aubrey tells us that as a child he had the best tutors procurable, and we know that his sister Mary had a French tutor
at Penshurst before she was eight years of age. " Example-
books for the secretary hand " suggests the origin of the beautiful handwriting which distinguishes his letters from all those
of his contemporaries. Unlike the gentlemen—and statists—
of the sixteenth century, he did not hold it a baseness to write
fair ; on the contrary, he esteemed the writing of a legible hand
a matter of great importance. " I would, by the way, your
worship would learn a better hand," he wrote to his brother
Robert in 1580 ; " you write worse than I, and I write evil
enough." " Radolphus Gualterus Tigurinus " was a text-book
on quantity and prosody[1]. The well-known Puritanism of
Ashton and Atkys, as also of Lawrence (who became a master
at Shrewsbury in 1568), is attested by Philip's purchase of
Calvin's Catechism[2]. That there is no mention of Greek books
is not surprising, for they would be studied only in the last
two years. It is probable, however, that Philip never acquired
more than a smattering of that language. Writing to Languet
in 1574, he says that "there are some things also which I wish
to learn of the Greeks which hitherto I have but skimmed
on the surface." Languet answered :

" About the Greek language I cannot advise you. It is a beautiful
study but I fear you will have no time to carry it through, and all the time
you give to it will be lost to your Latin, which though it is considered a
less interesting language than the Greek is yet much more important
for you to know."

---

[1] *De Syllabarum et Carminum ratione*, Libri duo, Authore Radolpho Gual-
thero Tigurino. The first edition was published at Zurich in 1542. A sentence
from the introduction to the second book defines the scope of the whole work :
"Superiori libro quantum et necessitas postulavit et instituta permisit brevitas
Syllabarum quantitatem absoluimus : nunc quo modo eaedem in pedes hi
vero in certum ordinem et compositionem legitimam adeoq ; carmen dis-
ponendi sint, docebimus." A copy is in the British Museum.

[2] Calvin's Catechism was also used in Rivingston School, founded in 1568
by Pilkington, the Puritan Bishop of Durham, where both governors and
schoolmasters were required to express their abhorrence of " Romish super-
stition, doctrine and idolatry " (*v.* Works of Bp. Pilkington, p. 663. Parker
Society).

To this Sidney replied :

" Of Greek literature I wish to learn only so much as shall suffice for the perfect understanding of Aristotle.   For though translations are made almost daily still I suspect they do not declare the meaning of the author plainly or aptly enough ; and besides I am utterly ashamed to be following the stream, as Cicero says, and not go to the fountain head[1]."

It would seem clear that neither at Shrewsbury nor Oxford had he given much attention to Greek.   Of music, to which two hours a week were devoted at Westminster, there is no mention, and it is not probable that it was included in the curriculum, for in later years we find Philip bitterly regretting the deficiency of his education in this respect.

It remains substantially true, then, that the education of a Shrewsbury boy was almost entirely confined to Latin.   The " versifying " and writing of themes or epistles which constituted part of the regular Saturday programme, and, indeed, during school hours all exercises—oral or written—were in Latin.   "All men covet to have their children speak Latin," wrote Ascham in the *Schoolmaster*, and the practice of restricting young children to its use, which he condemns, was, we know, all but universal.   Colloquial Latin was learned chiefly from the comedies of Terence, and at Shrewsbury the weekly exercise in declamation from one of his plays was no doubt looked on, in part, as a preparation for the yearly Whitsuntide play.   It was performed in the " Quarrel," a piece of land near the Severn, and under Ashton's superintendence acquired a great reputation.   Both the Shrewsbury Corporation and the Drapers' Company contributed at times to the expense of the performance, which on one occasion at least was repeated throughout the Whitsun holidays, and attracted large numbers of people to Shrewsbury.   It is probable that Ashton's interest in his boys' Latinity was not his primary concern in the giving of the Shrewsbury play, in which work he seems to have been engaged even before his appointment to the head-mastership.

Any attempt to estimate the influence which his Shrewsbury days exercised on Philip Sidney's later life must necessarily

---

[1] *The Correspondence of Sir Philip Sidney and Hubert Languet*, ed. Pears, pp 24, 26, 28.

be tentative, but it is surely not fanciful to ascribe something of the insatiable desire of learning which characterized his brief career to his former head-master's similar enthusiasm and to the atmosphere which pervaded the school. " The principal care, then," wrote Ashton to the bailiffs in the letter from which quotation has already been made, " is to make provision for those which shall go out from this school, for their further learning and study," and in announcing his determination to have scholarships established in Oxford and Cambridge, he reminds them

" how the poor are forced to give over this learning and study for that they can have no place in neither university, in any college, in default neither the shire nor the school aforetime hath made provision therefor."

It speaks well for the scholarship of the school that among Philip Sidney's companions were Fulke Greville, Andrew Downes, and John Meighen, who was to occupy the position of head-master for more than half a century, that Lawrence on resigning his post in 1583 could boast that within twelve years he had sent over one hundred students to Oxford and Cambridge, and that Camden in 1586 could refer to Shrewsbury as " the largest school in all England for the education of youth." We may also assume that the pronounced Puritan atmosphere made a strong impression on the boy. We can picture him at this time as he appears in the beautiful Penshurst portrait of himself and his brother Robert, a serious, thoughtful boy, perhaps too much devoted to his studies and meditation, too little given to mirth, religious more than boy beseemed, and withal somewhat haughty and reserved, conscious of the noble blood from which he was descended on the mother's side, and proud of his high-minded father, who was Lord Deputy of Ireland.

" Though I lived with him and knew him from a child," says Fulke Greville, " yet I never knew him other than a man : with such staiednesse of mind, lovely, and familiar gravity, as carried grace, and reverence above greater years. His talk ever of knowledge, and his very play tending to enrich his mind : So as even his teachers found something in him to observe and learn above that which they had usually read, or taught."

From Thomas Marshall's book of accounts we know many of the details of Philip's life during the greater part of the second year that he spent at Shrewsbury. In the early summer of 1565 Sir Henry Sidney had been appointed Lord Deputy of Ireland, and on November 17th he reached Chester. Lady Mary accompanied him, though the earlier plan had been that she should wait in England until her lord was established in Dublin. For nearly two months the Lord Deputy and his wife were prevented by contrary winds from crossing. Always prone to melancholy, Sir Henry wrote to Cecil on December 3rd that he had no mind for Ireland, and that he had never been so weary of any place as of this in which he was stayed, where neither meat, drink nor good lodging was procurable. Perhaps his spirits were the more depressed by the fact that on this very day he had parted for an indefinite period from the boy whom he styled *lumen familiae suae*. Philip, accompanied by two schoolboy friends, had come up from Shrewsbury to bid farewell to his father and mother, and they left him at Westchester on Monday, December 3rd, when they started for the coast in the hope of effecting a passage. On January 9th they were still in Holyhead, but at length on January 13th they reached Dublin.

Philip, together with his friends and Thomas Marshall, a servant under whose supervision he had been left, remained in Westchester for two days and a half. That he had been ill a short time previously we learn from one of the first of Marshall's entries :

> "Item, for a yard of cloth to make Mr. Philip a pair of
> boot hose, having none but a pair of linen which were
> to thin to ride in after his disease   ..   ..   ..   3s. 4d."

On Wednesday the little nags which the boys rode had all been shod, various bills had been paid, and in the afternoon the party set out. That night they spent at Chirke, at " one Mr. Ed[war]ds," and the next day they were back in Shrewsbury[1]. Several items representing Philip's expenditures immediately after coming back to school are not recoverable

---

[1] His Shrewsbury laundry bills are reckoned from December 6th.

because of the mutilation of the manuscript, but the following suggest the resumption of his studies after an absence of some duration, possibly caused by the "disease" already referred to:

"Item, upon Monday the 10th day for the mending of the lock of Mr. Philip's coffer, and for an iron bolt for his chamber door .. .. 12*d*.

Item, upon Thursday the 13th day for black silk buttons 8*d*, for quills 2*d*, for a black silk lace 2*d* .. .. 12*d*.

Item, for gum, gall and copperas to make ink, and a pot for same .. .. 6*d*.

Item, for a pen and inkhorn and sealing-wax .. .. .. 6*d*.

Item, for two quire of paper for example-books, phrases and sentences in Latin and French .. .. 8*d*.

Item, for wax sises to burn in the school a-mornings before day 4*d*.

Item, for mending a glass window in his chamber .. .. 4*d*."

Another December entry introduces us to Philip's *famulus* :

"Item, for a pair of shoes for Randal Calcott who attendeth on Mr. Philip with me, who since he came hath not put your lordship greatly to further charges besides his diet, shoes and washing .. .. 12*d*."

Randal seems to have been hard on shoes, for between Christmas and Michaelmas Marshall had to buy seven pairs for him, each costing 12*d*., whereas Philip's ordinary shoes cost but 10*d*. His washing amounted to 2*s*. 6*d*. for each three months —just half the cost of Philip's. The accounts furnish us no information as to the cost of " diet," but a total expenditure of 14*s*. 6*d*. for shoes and washing for nine months does not seem extravagant, even if we make allowance for the much greater value of money at that time.

Philip, meanwhile, was making preparations for spending his Christmas vacation away from Shrewsbury. He was " polled " by the barber, he bought three dozen silk points and "certain bird bolts for to shoot at birds," and Marshall bought cloth " to make him a coat to wear w[ith] his cape against Christmas, not hav[ing a]ny fit garment to go in." He spent the holiday at Eton near Wroxeter, the beautiful seat of Sir Richard Newport. Sir Richard was the son of Thomas Newport of High Ercall, High Sheriff of Shropshire, and Lady

Newport was the only daughter of Chief Justice Bromley.
Their daughter Magdalen[1] was later to become famous as the
mother of two famous sons—Edward, Lord Herbert of Cherbury
(who was born at Eton), and George Herbert, the poet. Sir
Richard's son Francis was born in the same year as Philip,
although he did not enter Shrewsbury School until 1569. Of
Philip's visit to the Newports at this time we have no details,
unless we are to conjecture from the following entry that the
bird-shooting of the boys had resulted in a slight accident to
Philip :

> " Item, the 11th day (of January) for an ounce of oil of roses
> and another of camomell to supple his knee that he could
> not ply or bend   ..   .. *6d.*"

The only interesting information to be derived from Marshall's accounts during the winter and spring months has to
do with the books purchased by Philip, and these we have
already mentioned. The Whitsuntide play for the year was
Julian the Apostate, and it is recorded that " Queen Elizabeth
made progress as far as Coventry intending for Salop to see
Mr. Ashton's play but it was ended[2]." Perhaps the pre-
sentations were brought to an abrupt conclusion on account
of an outbreak of plague in the school referred to by Marshall
on May 30th :

> " Item, for..........when we went [to the house of] Sir
> Andrew Co[rbet and that of Sir] Richard Newpo[rt when
> the scholar]s were sick   ..   .. *4d.*"

The entry which immediately follows is lost, but from the
next two items we know that three weeks later Philip had
returned to Shrewsbury :

> " Imprimis, the 21st day, for a Sallust for him ..   ..   .. *14d.*
> Item, for perfumes to air the chamber with when we came forth
> of the country after the young gentlemen were recovered.. *12d.*"

Shrewsbury's experience of these epidemics was as frequent
as that of other English towns. In 1563 by a resolution of
the Corporation it was

---

[1] *V.* Lord Herbert of Cherbury's *Autobiography*, ed. Lee, p. 9.
[2] Rimmer, *op. cit.*, p. 56.

"Agreed that a proclamation shall be made...that if any person inhabiting within the town or franchise do go or ride to London, or any other place where plague doth remain, that he shall not return and come within 4 miles to this town or franchise before 2 months be fully ended... and that no person inhabiting within the said town or franchise do receive or lodge any person that cometh from any place where the plague doth reign, nor receive into their custody any wares apparel or household stuff that cometh from any such place upon pain of disfranchisement[1]."

I have found no reference, except Marshall's, to the plague in 1566, and we may assume that it was of short duration. In 1575, however, the MS. chronicle records that " the Queen's Majesty went a progress towards Shrewsbury, but because of death within a four miles of the same she came no further than Lichfield," and there was a very serious outbreak in August and September of 1576[2]. So seriously did these constantly recurring plagues interfere with the work of the school that one of Ashton's ordinances required that " a house shall be provided within the county for the masters and scholars to resort to in time of plague," and during Meighen's headmastership a country house for this purpose was built at Grinshill, a few miles from Shrewsbury. As we have seen, Philip Sidney spent the three weeks during which the school was closed in June, 1568, partly with the Newports, partly at the home of Sir Andrew Corbet of Moreton Corbet, Shropshire. Sir Andrew was a special friend of Ashton and of Sir Henry Sidney, and was a member of the Council in the Marches of Wales. Of his numerous family of boys, Vincent, the third son, had been born in the same year as Philip Sidney, and was at this time at school in Shrewsbury ; Robert, the eldest son, was later Philip's companion in Venice, and in a letter introducing him to Languet, Philip refers to him as his cousin and " my very greatest friend, a man of high birth, but one who, as Buchanan says, 'In excellence of parts outdoes his birth.' " We may be sure that Philip found his enforced vacation a not intolerable experience.

Toward the end of June Marshall was much occupied with providing a very unusually elaborate addition to the rather

[1] Owen and Blakeway, *op. cit.*, p. 354.
[2] *Ibid.*, pp. 362 and 370.

meagre wardrobe of his young charge, as the following extracts
from his accounts will show :

> "Item, the 25th day, for making of his green coat whereof the
> cloth came from my fellow Knight[1] .. .. 2*s.*
> Item, for a quarter of green sarcenet for the collar and to
> face it .. .. 14*d.*
> Item, for a yard of fustian to line the body of the same .. 10*d.*
> Item, for a yard and an half of cotton to line the skirts .. 12*d.*
> Item, for buttons thereto .. .. 8*d.*
> Item, for 14 yards of lace to compass it about .. .. .. 22*d.*
> Item, for 4 skeins of silk .. .. 8*d.*
> Item, for canvas for the collar .. .. 1*d.*"

Such an unusual expenditure for dress pointed to coming
events of unusual importance. The first of these took place
early in July. Philip was a " tabler " in the home of Mr
George Leigh, a Shrewsbury gentleman, and was now invited
by his host to stand in a kind of boy-godfather relation to
his son. Marshall's account is as follows :

> "Imprimis, upon Thursday the 11th day, at the christening of
> a son of Mr. Leigh's who beareth his name, given to the
> midwife 20*d.* and to the nurse 20*d.*, and more money was
> offered to the mother but it would not be taken—My Lady
> Newport being godmother .. .. 3*s.* 4*d.*"

In later years Philip's name was to be borne by many infants
ranging in dignity from the sons of William of Orange and the
Earl of Pembroke to the son of Tarleton, the jester, but Philip
Leigh was surely the first of those who were thus made immortal.

---

[1] A servant of Sir Henry Sidney whose name occurs several times in Marshall's accounts. Writing to Leicester on Dec. 13, 1565, before starting for Ireland, Sir Henry refers to Ralph Knight as " a foul baby" to whom Leicester may safely entrust any commissions.

CHAPTER IV

A VISIT TO OXFORD

THE remaining pages of Marshall's manuscript (more than half of the total) are filled with the details of Philip's visit to Kenilworth and Oxford on the occasion of the Queen's famous visit to the University in August and September, 1566. This was probably the most memorable of the boy's experiences at this period of his life, and it is a piece of great good fortune that a record of it should have been preserved even though it be of a fragmentary character.

At Shrewsbury, as we have seen, there were very few holidays, and from Whitsuntide until Christmas there were none unless a visit to the school of some great personage procured the boys a day's freedom, or an outbreak of the plague drove them to seek greater security in the country. We may be sure, then, that when about noon on July 24th, Philip, with a little company of his friends and attendants, rode out of Shrewsbury to pay a visit to his uncle, the great Earl of Leicester, at Kenilworth Castle and at the University of Oxford, the boy was nothing loath to vary the quiet monotony of his school life by seeing something of the world in which his nearest relatives were playing conspicuous rôles. Besides, his beloved studies were not to be entirely suspended, for his books had been packed in two canvas alum bags for the journey, and Mr Ashton was one of the party. Already the Earl of Leicester had singled out his promising nephew for his special favour, a favour which was to continue throughout Philip's life, and which in its spontaneousness and singleness was to do much toward redeeming a character essentially selfish and unprincipled. No doubt the Earl was desirous that Philip should not be allowed to degenerate into a mere student, and had summoned him to be a spectator of the events which were about to take place. In these the great Queen herself was to be the central figure, and Leicester, the Chancellor of the University of Oxford, was to be the official host of his Sovereign.

His uncle's greatness might well have made a deep impression on the boy. On Robert Dudley the royal favour was now bestowed in an unparalleled fashion. He had all the qualities which Elizabeth prized—youth, good looks, good manners, and a genius for flattery. There can be little doubt that if Elizabeth ever wished to marry anyone it was the handsome, reckless, unprincipled man whom she had distinguished with her special favour from the days when, as boy and girl, they had studied Latin together under Roger Ascham. During the years immediately following Lady Dudley's death their intimacy scandalized the English people, from the Puritans to the members of the Privy Council. Honours came thick and fast upon the favourite, and he was in constant and close attendance upon Elizabeth. Kenilworth Castle was only the most magnificent of the gifts she lavished upon him. On two successive days of September, 1564, she created him Baron Denbigh and Earl of Leicester ; while on progress in 1565 she honoured him by a visit to Kenilworth. He had become Chancellor of the University of Oxford on December 31, 1564, and in a burst of magnanimity Elizabeth had attempted in 1565 to bring about his marriage with Mary, Queen of Scots. The negotiations for a marriage between Elizabeth and the Archduke Charles of Austria, which Cecil and the other members of the Council were now earnestly seeking to bring to a conclusion, caused no change in the relations of the Queen and Leicester. Philip Sidney might well be impressed by his uncle's greatness.

The little cavalcade which we have seen leaving Shrewsbury on a July afternoon consisted of ten persons. Philip Sidney was attended by Thomas Marshall and Randal Calcott, his Shrewsbury *famulus*, a boy probably about his own age. Philip rode a nag which had been presented to him by Viscount

Hereford, Lord Ferrers of Chartley, afterwards the first Earl of Essex, already a friend of the boy to whom he became later so warmly attached; his saddle, covered with French skins, had been bought for the occasion. Another member of the party was Edward Onslow, a Shrewsbury boy and a friend of Philip. His father, Richard Onslow, had been Recorder of London since 1563, and a few weeks before the time of our story had been made Solicitor-General to the Queen; in the same year he was to become Speaker of the House of Commons[1]. Edward Onslow, on the present occasion, was attended by two servants. Mr George Leigh, at whose home in Shrewsbury Philip was a "tabler," and to whose son he had recently stood as god-father, was also of the party, as was Mr Ashton, the head-master; they were each attended by one man. At Shifnal, a few miles from Shrewsbury, the company halted for "afternoon drinking," and reached Wolverhampton for supper, where they passed the night. On Thursday they dined at Brumegeame, and the afternoon pause was made at Hampton-on-the-Hill. But disappointment was in store for our travellers. At this point Marshall's manuscript is mutilated to such an extent that four or five entries are irrecoverable—entries which might possibly have contained an explanation of what follows. Perhaps a messenger met them at Hampton-on-the-Hill, or possibly at Coventry, where they would have spent the night, with the information that a change of plans had necessitated their return to Shrewsbury. At any rate, on Saturday we find the following entry:

"Item, upon Saturday, the 27th day at Boningall, an inn
 5 miles on this side Wolverhampton for dinner .. .. 6s."

The same night they reached Shrewsbury. The three-and-a-half days of continuous riding in July had told disastrously on Philip,

[1] Roger Onslow, Edward's grandfather, was at this time Sheriff of Salop. A member of the Mercers' Company of Shrewsbury, he had lived most of his life in London, and was a special friend of Sir Henry Sidney, to whom he was somewhat distantly related. Richard Onslow's great-great-grandson and the latter's nephew, Arthur, were also Speakers of the House of Commons. Edward Onslow, Philip Sidney's friend, "was knighted at some uncertain time, married Isabel, daughter of Sir Thomas Shirley of Preston Place, Sussex, and died 2 April, 1615" (*Dict. Nat. Biog.*).

who was sorely chafed and "breaking-forth through heat."
Two of Marshall's purchases on their return were as follows:

> "Item, upon Monday, the 29th day, for a yard of Holland
> for two pair of linen hose for Mr. Philip after he came from
> Killingworth because of his merrygalls[1] and breaking-forth
> through heat   ..   ..   18*d.*
> Item for a box of ointment for his merrygalls and after that for
> another to have with us to Killingworth if the like should hap   2*s.*"

Elizabeth's movements when on progress were always
uncertain. From Lord Burghley's diary we learn that on
August 3rd she was at Collyweston in Northamptonshire,
and on August 5th at Stamford. It was more than two weeks
before Philip was once more advised to set out for Kenilworth.
On August 14th he again left Shrewsbury. This time there
were only six in the party—Philip, attended by Thomas
Marshall and Randal Calcott, Mr Ashton and his man, and
Davy Long. Long is probably to be identified with David
Longdon, a shoemaker by trade, who was at this time a servant
of Ashton but who afterwards became the first bailiff of
Shrewsbury School and a serjeant of the town. The travellers
spent the first night with Sir Richard Newport at Arcole[2],
where Philip had frequently visited before. The next morning,
accompanied by their host, they set out again, and that night
they reached Wolverhampton ; on Friday, the 16th, they
proceeded by way of Brumegeame and Hampton-on-the-Hill
to Coventry, where the Earl of Leicester was staying. Philip
and Mr Ashton spent the night as the guests of the Earl, and
on Saturday the party reached Kenilworth.

The next morning Marshall and Davy Long rode over to
Coventry " to speak with my Lord of Leicester for the knowledge
of Mr. Philip's apparel." Before setting out from Shrewsbury
the first time Marshall had evidently been concerned that his
young charge should be attired in a manner befitting his rank
and the occasion. Hitherto, Philip's wardrobe had been of

---

[1] " Merry-galls, a sore produced by chafing " (N. E. D.).

[2] " Ercall was the Caput of those vast estates which formed the heritage
of the Newports—a heritage than which none greater has accrued to any single
Shropshire family since the advent of the Normans " (Eyton, *Antiquities of
Shropshire*, vol. IX, p. 63).

the most modest proportions. Sometimes Robert Wright, a servant of his father at Ludlow, sent a garment or some cloth ; sometimes Marshall had to convert old doublets into new hose. The sums expended for clothing were always small. On the present occasion, for instance, Philip was provided, amongst other things, with a canvas doublet, pinked, the collar and facing of which were of white sarcenet, a pair of velvet shoes, a white leather jerkin " whereof the skin came from my fellow Knight," two dozen of silk points, etc., but the only serious outlay on which Marshall had ventured was the following :

"Item, a pair of velvet overstocks that I made him of his
    old black velvet gown, the charges whereof followeth :
Imprimis for a yard of double sarcenet to line them with ..   6s.
Item, for two yards two nails and a half of satin of Bruges to
    line the panes[1] of his hose .. .. 5s. 7d.
Item, for half a yard of white lining and half a quarter ..   8d.
Item, for a yard of cotton for an outer lining .. .. 12d.
Item, for half a yard and a nail of Holland to line the hose
    inwardly .. .. 8d.
Item, for a quarter pennyweight of jean fustian for two
    pockets in his hose .. .. 4d.
Item, for five ounces of lace and a yard, for the panes of his
    hose .. .. 11s. 7d.
Item, for an ounce and a pennyweight of silk to sew them .. 12d.
Item, for the making of them .. .. 4s."

Perhaps Marshall had misgivings lest the great Earl should not approve of his preparations ; more probably Leicester had summoned him to discuss the subject. None of Elizabeth's nobles was so addicted to dress as was the favourite, and that was one of the reasons why Elizabeth approved of him. When in 1571 he kept the feast of St Michael at Warwick the magnificence of his attire quite overwhelmed the spectators. Had poor Marshall been acquainted with the Earl's predilections he might well have feared a rebuke at the interview. He might have justly pleaded that he had done all he could with the money at his disposal, for before beginning the first journey to Kenilworth he had been compelled to borrow £6

[1] " Panes, strips made by cutting or slashing a garment longitudinally for ornamental purposes " (N. E. D.).

from Mr Leigh, and on the second journey he had to appeal
to Sir Richard Newport at Coventry for £3 1s. and some two
weeks later to the Earl himself at Oxford for a loan of £3 20d.
Marshall made no record as to the outcome of the interview,
but, fortunately, he set down an exact list of the apparel " that
the Earl of Leicester vouchsafed to bestow " on his nephew,
and which was immediately ordered from Whittell, Leicester's
tailor in London.   The inventory is as follows :

> "Imprimis a short damask gown guarded[1] with velvet and laid on
> with lace.
>
> Item, a double taffeta coat guarded throughout with the same and
> covered with lace.
>
> Item, a crimson satin doublet, cut.
>
> Item, a green taffeta doublet, cut.
>
> Item, a canvas doublet streaked with blue.
>
> Item, a canvas doublet streaked with red and silver.
>
> Item, a plain canvas doublet not yet received, which is to be sent
> by Whittell, the Earl's tailor.
>
> Item, a pair of crimson velvet hose with silk netherstocks.
>
> Item, a pair of hose of stamell[2] of carnation colour, with netherstocks
> of the same.
>
> Item, a pair of green leather, laid on with lace and netherstocks
> of crewel.
>
> Item, a pair of blue leather, laid on with lace and netherstocks
> of crewel.
>
> Item, a white leat[her] jerkin compassed with parchm[ent] lace
> of gold.
>
> Item, a red leat[her] jerkin.
>
> Item, a black leat[her je]rkin.
>
> Item, six pair of [double so]led shoes, two white, [two black, and]
> two blue.
>
> Item, a shir[t........] With black silk and sil[ver........].
>
> Item, a sh[irt........] black silk.
>
> Item, two........"

The rest of the page is completely eaten away, but we have
read enough to be sure that in the great Oxford celebrations
the gorgeous attire of the serious-faced, handsome boy who

---

[1] " Guard—to ornament (a garment, etc.) with 'guards'   to trim as with
lace, braid, etc." (N. E. D.).

[2] Florio gives as one definition of the word " stame," " Also a kind of
cloth as our Penystone or Stammell is."

rode beside the Chancellor made him a conspicuous figure. He was to meet his Sovereign probably for the first time, and Leicester, who was determined that he should make a good impression, believed in assisting nature by art.

From Saturday until the following Thursday (August 22nd) Philip remained at Kenilworth Castle. How he occupied himself we do not know. The following is the only entry of any interest that is not hopelessly mutilated in Marshall's manuscript:

> " Item, upon Wednesday the 21st day, given in reward [to] Mr.
> Spilsberie a French crown, for his gen[tle]ness showed at all
> times to Mr. [P]hilip and his Master and all yo[ur] Lordship's
> servants that the[re w]ere attending on him, as my[self,]
> Sterry, Whitton, Pope and Pavy, [there be]ing no place else
> with........to plant his fo[ot........a]bode there ..   .. 6s."

The latter part of the item suggests that Kenilworth was crowded with visitors, and it would seem clear that certain of Sir Henry Sidney's servants had been summoned, perhaps from Ludlow, Penshurst or London, to attend Philip at Oxford. No doubt Philip did some reading with Mr Ashton, and he would almost certainly visit Warwick Castle, five miles to the southeast, now the seat of his uncle Ambrose, Earl of Warwick. Like Kenilworth, it dated from the time of the Normans, and had long been intimately associated with the history of the Dudleys. He may even have ridden somewhat farther in the opposite direction to Dudley Castle—but of all this we know nothing. On Thursday afternoon he set out for Oxford, under the conduct of Dr Wilson[1], whom Leicester had specially appointed

---

[1] Thomas Wilson is best known to students of English as the author of *The Arte of Rhetorique* (1553) and *The Rule of Reason containyng the Arte of Logique* (1551). At Cambridge, where he took his B.A. (1545–6) and M.A. (1549), he was a student of Sir John Cheke and Sir Thomas Smith, and became a friend of Roger Ascham. He had long been attached to the Dudley family, and on the fall of Northumberland had gone abroad. At Ferrara he took the degree of LL.D. in 1559, and in 1561 was made Master of Requests to Elizabeth. He was now under Leicester's patronage and was a friend of Lady Sidney. During the present celebrations at Oxford he was incorporated as a doctor on September 6th ; five years later Cambridge conferred on him a similar honour. After serving on various missions to Portugal and the Netherlands he was made a member of the Privy Council in 1577, when he succeeded Sir Thomas Smith as Secretary of State, and in 1580 he became Dean of Durham. He died in 1586.

to take charge of his nephew on the way. The first night was spent " at one Mr. Ranles beyond Warwick " ; the next day the party stopped for dinner at Tuddington, and the same night they reached Oxford. It is little wonder that Philip was again suffering from " merry-galls."

On arriving at Oxford Philip, with the other members of the party, went to an inn, where they stayed two days, but on Sunday (August 25th) he took up his abode in one of the colleges and remained there during the whole of his visit. Marshall's entry reads :

> "Item, the same day at night supper at Lincoln College with Mr. Bridgewater[1], one of my Lord of Leicester's chaplains and rector of the same College, and so continued at his table during our abode there with the whole train, and partly lodged there also, the space of 15 days, viz. from the said Sunday at supper inclusive until the 8th of September being Sunday at after dinner.'

Philip had a full week in which to become acquainted with Oxford and the colleges before the arrival of the Queen —and his new finery—were to engross his whole attention. Unfortunately our book of accounts gives us no information as to how he spent the time : the items set down for this week are not very suggestive even for a vivid imagination. Marshall records expenditures for shoeing and pasturing the horses and mending saddles and bridles, for the purchase of scaling-hose, garters and " a pair of doublesoled shoes for Mr. Philip and another for Randall," " for mending Mr. Philip's double taffeta coat and for making his blue streaked canvas doublet meet for him," for paper and ink, but as to how the boy occupied himself from day to day we have no hint. Nevertheless we may be sure that under the guidance of Mr Ashton, Mr Bridgewater

---

[1] John Bridgewater, or Aquaepontanus, as he styled himself, had been elected rector of Lincoln College on April 14, 1563, on the resignation of Dr Francis Babington. He had previously (May 1, 1562) been admitted to the rectory of Wolton Courtney in the diocese of Wells. He took his M.A. from Brasenose College in 1566. In 1574 he resigned his rectory-ship of Lincoln College to prevent expulsion, because he was actually, or very near it, a Roman Catholic. At Rheims he was said to have entered the Society of Jesus, and he published several pro-Catholic Latin works on the Continent. He was living in great esteem at Friers in Germany in 1594. Wood says he was " a good scholar and well read in several languages " (*v.* Wood's *Athenae*).

and Dr Wilson he explored many of the beautiful buildings and quadrangles which his father had often described to him, and looked on the strangely picturesque student-world, of which he was soon to become a member, with wonderment mingled with a sense of eager anticipation.

Even in 1566 Oxford was a great University. In the sixteen colleges and eight halls there were some seventeen hundred students, distinguished for their modesty, taciturnity, obedience and devotion to their studies, if we may believe a contemporary writer[1]. From all parts of England, he informs us, they came hither, such famous schools as Winchester, Eton, Durham and London sending the greater number. So perfect was the discipline and so great the zeal for learning that Erasmus had compared the colleges to well-ordered monasteries. The students assembled for morning chapel at five o'clock, after which they spent their day in serious pursuit of knowledge—of rhetoric, logic, philosophy, etc., or of Latin, Greek and Hebrew—under the tuition of University professors or of their tutors in the individual colleges. The college gates were closed for the night at eight o'clock in winter and nine in summer, and woe to the student who was found without after these hours, for the Proctors would accept "hardly any excuse." Nor does our author fail to mention the beauty of the city situated in the midst of cultivated fields, rich pastures and wooded hills, the salubrity of the air, and the healthfulness of the region. The colleges, he reminds us, were enduring monuments of beauty calculated to raise the mind from low-thoughted care to noble resolves and aspirations.

To Philip Sidney, accustomed as he was to the painfully meagre equipment of Shrewsbury School, this somewhat idealized picture would scarcely have seemed overdrawn as he wandered about the streets or investigated the various quadrangles. From Lincoln College, by following the lane which separates it from Exeter (now Brasenose Lane), he would have easy access, by an entrance from St Mary's, into

---

[1] Fierbertus: *Descriptio Oxoniensis Academiae* (Ox. Hist. Soc.), p. 16. Fierbertus, or Nicholas Fitzherbert, was a student of Exeter College during the whole of the time spent by Philip Sidney at Christ Church.

the "common schools"—twelve in number—where the pre-cocious boy who was never "other than a man" may have chosen to hear his first lectures. Or, walking along Jesus College Lane (now Market Street), he could reach North Gate Street (Cornmarket) in two or three minutes, and High Street was equally accessible along Allhallows Street. We may be sure that it was with very special interest that he visited Christ Church—*amplissimum sane omniumque augustissimum Collegium*—of which he was soon to be enrolled as a member.

On Saturday, the last day of August, the Queen arrived, attended by a numerous company—the Spanish Ambassador, the Marquis of Northampton, the Earls of Warwick, Ormond, Sussex, Rutland and Oxford, Sir William Cecil and many other noblemen. Roger Marbeck, the University Orator, welcomed her in a Latin oration—the first of many to which she was to listen during the coming week—in which he made public confession of the incredible joy which the University had recently experienced when they received the Earl of Leicester as their new Chancellor. He expatiated on the wonders of Elizabeth's scholarship and on the indebtedness of the University to her, and when he concluded the Queen was well pleased and gave him her hand to kiss. About a mile from the town the royal company was met by Mayor Williams, the Aldermen and certain burgesses, all in scarlet gowns. The Mayor delivered up to the Queen his mace, received it again from her with a silver cup, double gilt, worth £10 and containing sixty angels.

From this point to the city the procession was a most formal one, and was calculated to impress the multitude from Oxford and the surrounding country who thronged the Woodstock road, with a sense of the greatness and magnificence of England's Queen. The Clarenceux king-at-arms was present, and the procession was formed under his direction ; Clarenceux himself wore a military uniform richly decorated with the national and royal heraldic devices. The three Esquire Bedells led the way on horseback, bearing aloft their golden staves. Then came the Chancellor of the University and the Mayor of the city, followed by the chief members of the nobility. As they rode they gave free vent to their high spirits, and the magnificence of their dress and of their horses' trappings was unparalleled in the experience of the spectators. Next in order rode the royal lictors bearing huge sceptres, and then the Earl of Sussex, who carried a sword the hilt of which was richly decorated with gold work and gems, in an elaborately chased scabbard. A short distance behind came the chariot of the Queen, slowly drawn by beautiful horses decorated with scarlet trappings. The chariot was open on all sides, and on a gilded seat in the height of regal magnificence reposed the Queen. Her head-dress was a marvel of woven gold, and glittered with pearls and other wonderful gems ; her gown was of the most brilliant scarlet silk inwoven with gold, partly concealed by a purple cloak lined with ermine after the manner of a triumphal robe. Beside the chariot rode the royal cursitors, resplendent in coats of cloth of gold, and the marshals, who were kept busy preventing the crowds from pressing too near to the person of the Queen. Immediately behind the chariot came the royal attendants and women-in-waiting, who were no less striking either in regard to the beauty of their dress or the caparisons of their horses than were the more noble attendants of Her Majesty. Then followed a number of high-bred Spanish jennets decorated with silk and gold trappings ; these were led and had no riders. The royal guard, magnificent in gold and scarlet silk, brought up the rear of the procession. Of these there were about two hundred—not to forestall danger but *honoris causa*—and on their shoulders they bore huge bows and iron clubs like battle-axes. As the procession approached the city gate, the visitors were received with a universal shout of welcome which ceased only when they had reached the enclosure of Christ Church.

They entered the city by the north gate, called Bocardo, which was richly ornamented for the occasion and bore the inscription, in great capital letters, *Decet Regem regere Legem.* Here Robert Deale of New College welcomed the Queen in the name of the scholars, who, in academic garb, lined both sides of North Gate Street from Bocardo to Carfax. As the Queen passed they knelt and cried *Vivat Regina Elizabetha*, and the shout was taken up by the multitude of men and women, boys and girls, who had secured seats in the windows or were standing on the roofs of the houses. The Queen was much pleased, and replied from time to time, *Gratias ago, Gratias ago.* At Carfax, Giles Lawrence, the Regius Professor of Greek, pronounced an oration to Her Majesty in Greek, which she, replying in the same language, declared to be the best she had ever heard in that kind. From Carfax to Christ Church she passed along Fish Street between the ranks of the Bachelors, Masters of Arts and Doctors, all wearing their distinctive academic costumes, and at the door of the Hall she listened to another oration by Mr Kingsmill, whom she thanked and assured that he would have done well had he had good matter. Beneath a canopy carried by four senior Doctors the Queen entered the Cathedral. She knelt in prayer in the choir while Dr Godwin, the Dean, offered up thanksgiving for Her Majesty's safe arrival in Oxford, and the choir sang the Te Deum accompanied by cornets, after which the Queen went through the gardens to the apartments which had been prepared for her in the wing facing the east. The students of the college had all vacated their rooms in order that the various noblemen might be accommodated; the Spanish Ambassador occupied the lodgings of the Warden of Merton.

We can give only the most cursory account of the busy week which followed the arrival of the Queen. On Sunday morning she was indisposed and did not attend the Cathedral service, but she was present in the afternoon when Mr Thomas Harris of New College preached. At night the nobility assembled in the Hall of Christ Church, where the students gave a Latin play, *Marcus Geminus,* and the audience was so enthusiastic that when the Queen heard an account of the evening's entertainment she decided that she would " lose no more sport hereafter." Indeed the University had spared no pains to make the occasion unique among dramatic performances. The walls and ceiling of the noble hall were decorated with gilded panelling, the stage " set about with stately lights of wax variously wrought," extended across one end, and at the other end and along the sides banks of seats rising one above the other had been constructed. The seat prepared for the

Queen was directly opposite the stage—a veritable bower covered with golden hangings and furnished with tapestries and cushions. So magnificent was the improvised theatre, says one who was present, that you might have thought you were in one of the ancient Roman palaces.

Dramatic performances in the evening, and lectures and disputations in the afternoon and occasionally in the morning, constituted the programme of the week. On Monday and Wednesday evenings were given the first and second parts respectively of *Palamon and Arcite*, a play by Richard Edwards, the Master of the Children of the Chapel Royal. The enthusiasm of the Queen and the nobles was unbounded, and their enjoyment of the play would have been unalloyed but for an unfortunate accident at the performance of the first part of the play, when, owing to the press of the multitude, the wall of a staircase formed of huge square stones fell and killed three persons—a scholar, a college servant and a townsman. On Thursday night was played a Latin tragedy, *Progne*, composed by Dr James Calfhill, Canon of Christ Church. The disputations were held for the most part in St Mary's, and in none was the Queen more interested than in that on the subject " The moon is the cause of the ebb and flow of the tide " ; Mr Edmund Campion of St John's College was respondent, and managed before concluding his speech to connect the names of the Queen and Leicester in a fashion sufficiently deft to please Her Majesty. On Thursday afternoon she " made a very comfortable and eloquent oration in Latin " in St Mary's before the whole University, an oration which was received with such shouts of applause that the very walls resounded.

On Friday the Queen's visit was to come to an end, and the sorrow of the great crowds that thronged the city was to be read in their sad faces and quiet demeanour. In the morning a special Convocation was held, at which the degree of Master of Arts was conferred on many of the noblemen who were present, and certain Masters and Doctors of Cambridge were admitted to the same degree in the sister University. Presents of gloves were given by the University to Her Majesty and to certain of the nobles and officers of the royal household, and after dinner Mr Toby Matthew, in the name of the members of the college, bade the Queen farewell. He did not fail to commemorate the eloquence of her oration of the preceding day and to thank her for the honour which she had conferred on the University, and the Queen was so well pleased that she nominated him her Scholar. Then the procession which had entered the quadrangle six days before was re-formed, and proceeded by way of Carfax to St Mary's and thence along High Street to the East Gate. The students who lined both sides of High Street shouted *Vivat Regina* as the procession passed, but the innumerable " schedes of verses " which were pasted on the fronts of St Mary's, All Souls', and University College expressed the poignancy of the grief experienced by the University in being compelled to part from Her Majesty. At the head of the procession rode four Doctors in scarlet gowns and hoods, followed by four Masters in black gowns and hoods, and then came the Mayor and about fifteen of the Aldermen—also in their scarlets. The representatives of the city took leave of the Queen at Magdalen Bridge, where their liberties ended, and Her Majesty proceeded on her way to Ricot, some eight miles distant, where she was to be the guest of Mr Norris. The representatives of the University accompanied her to Shotover, some two miles from the city limits and the boundary of the University liberties. Here she listened graciously to the last of many orations, again delivered by Roger Marbeck, the University Orator, and took final leave of the city with the words : " Farewell, the worthy University of Oxford ; farewell, my good subjects there ; farewell, my dear Scholars, and pray God prosper your studies ; farewell—farewell[1]."

What share Philip Sidney took in the events of this famous week we do not know. We may be sure that Elizabeth and Cecil would look on him with special interest, not only as Leicester's nephew, but as the son of the Lord Deputy of Ireland. To many of those most prominent in the celebration Philip was closely related, and with many others he was to come into intimate contact in the immediate future. Leicester

[1] The narrative has been compiled from the various accounts given in *Elizabethan Oxford* (Ox. Hist. Soc.) and Nichol's *Progresses*.

and Warwick were his uncles, Huntingdon and Sussex his uncles by marriage. Don Guzman de Silva, the Spanish ambassador, was a warm friend of Sir Henry Sidney; the Earl of Ormond was his inveterate enemy. The Earl of Oxford, now about twenty-one years of age, was a few years later to be Philip's successful rival for the hand of Anne Cecil. Among those who took part in the disputations were Mr Thornton, afterwards Philip's tutor, Toby Matthew, who was to become Canon and Dean of Christ Church and Archbishop of York, and Edmund Campion, " the protomartyr of the English Jesuits," who was now a *protégé* of Sir Henry Sidney, and who more than ten years later was to entertain high hopes of persuading Philip Sidney to enter the fold of the Catholic Church. If for speculation we could substitute actual information regarding Philip's actions during this week it would be an interesting chapter in the story of his life.

For two days after the departure of the Queen Philip tarried in Oxford. He had given rewards to the Earl of Leicester's servants, and " to one Oliver, a Frenchman, preferred to your Lordship's service by the Earl of Warwick," and there were still other matters to attend to, notably to provide for the carrying to Shrewsbury of his new wardrobe. For this purpose Marshall purchased a trunk and also " a saddle either to carry a trunk on or to ride in, with girths, surcingle, leatherings and Warwick Staff[1]." A certain Mr Yates of Gloucestershire loaned his horse for the occasion, and on Sunday afternoon, September 8th, Philip turned his back on the city of romance, as it must have seemed to him, and began the journey toward Shrewsbury. One of the events of that Sunday afternoon ride between Woodstock and Chipping Norton—or perhaps the scene was the inn at Chipping Norton—where they spent the night, is pleasant to remember :

" Item, given by Mr. Philip's commandment to a blind harper
who is Sir William Holles' man of Nottinghamshire   .. 12d.[2]"

[1] The badge of the Dudleys.
[2] Sir William Holles of Haughton, Nottinghamshire, was the second son of Sir William Holles, Lord Mayor of London. In 1547 he married Anna daughter and heiress of John Densell. Their son, Denzil Holles, was the father

W. L. S.

Many years afterwards it was perhaps this very scene which Sidney had in his mind when he wrote :

" Certainly, I must confess my own barbarousness. I never heard the old song of Percy and Douglas that I found not my heart moved more than with a trumpet, and yet is it sung but by some blind crowder with no rougher voice than rude style ; which, being so evil apparelled in the dust and cobwebs of that uncivil age, what would it work trimmed in the gorgeous eloquence of Pindar ? "

On Monday (September 9th) the travellers reached Strat-ford-on-Avon in time for dinner, and those sentimentally inclined may speculate on the possibility of Master Philip's having here caught sight of a child, at this time aged two years and some four months, who was to become even more famous than the hero of our story. That night they reached the home of a Mr Sheldon at Belie, whose son, Greg, had accom-panied them from Oxford. Here they remained all day Tues-day, and on Wednesday they dined and spent the night with " Mr. Blunt at Kittermaster." On Thursday they reached Bewdley—a seat of the Council of the Marches—where they were the guests of Sir George and Lady Blount. Sir George was a member of the Welsh Council and an old friend of Philip's father. Some time before Monday (September 16th) they reached Shrewsbury.

Once more the nephew of the Earl of Leicester was a " tabler " in the home of Mr George Leigh, and one of the boys of a great public school. The old town on the western confines of England where he could lift his eyes to the Welsh hills was far remote from those channels in which flowed the more striking political and social events of the day, and must have seemed strangely quiet and retired to Philip after his excursion into the realms of pomp and pageantry. Some of Marshall's entries after their return remind us that his charge is once more merely a student—the son of the poor Lord Deputy of Ireland.

" Item, upon Saturday the 21st day for a yard and a nail
    of housewife's cloth to make him 4 pair of socks   ..   4*d*.

of John Holles, first Earl of Clare (1564?–1637), whose daughter Arabella married Thomas Wentworth, Earl of Strafford, and whose son Denzil was the famous parliamentarian.

Item, for two yards and an half of shop cloth to make him
ten handkerchers .. .. 5*s.*
Item, the 24th day for two quires of paper .. .. .. 8*d.*
Item, for a Cato, his former being lost, and a French grammar 12*d.*
Item, for ink .. .. 4*d.*"

There are other entries—" for mending his gown of changeable
taffeta," for shoes, boots, gloves, needles, thread, etc., and,
as if to emphasize the fact that the day of silk points, crimson
velvet hose and doublets of many colours had gone by, the
last item in the manuscript, on Michaelmas Day, reads:

"Item, for two dozen of *thread* points .. .. 6*d.*"

No account of Philip's school-days can be in any sense of
the word adequate if it ignores the influence exerted on him
in this formative period by the characters of his father and
mother. Serious, high-minded, upright in all their acts and
thoughts, they coveted no good thing for their son so much
as that he should grow up to be a God-fearing, self-respecting
man, a worthy scion of the great families from whom he was
descended. Of Lady Sidney's relations to her eldest-born we
know little. At the end of Marshall's book she has signed
her name " M. Sidney"—probably to indicate that she has
examined the accounts and found them satisfactory. On
the same page is written in her own handwriting in two
successive lines, " [G]od grant me grace to——" and " God
grant me grace——": the succeeding prayer has completely
faded from the manuscript, but it requires no great effort of
the imagination to conjure up the scene of the pious mother
dedicating herself anew to the task of instilling into her young
son those ideals which alone could give lasting happiness, as
she had learned during her own short life of tragedy and
sorrow. To the late spring or early summer of this same year
we may with a fair degree of certainty assign the following
letter—the first written by Sir Henry to his son[1]. If we
remember that the Lord Deputy's efforts to crush the rebellion

[1] (*a*) It was first printed by T. Dawson, London, 1591. Referring to the
copy which is preserved in Shrewsbury School Library, Fisher says: " It appears
from the title-page that the letter was written in 1566."

(*b*) Collins prints the letter " Ex Autog. apud Penshurst," and gives it
the caption " Sir Henry Sidney to his son Sir Philip Sydney, at School at

of Shan O'Neill were being constantly thwarted by intrigues at Court and by Elizabeth's continual upbraidings, that he was writing to Leicester to express his "hope of a speedy redemption from this my miserable thraldom," and that his health was so seriously undermined that he was in physical pain a great part of the time, the letter takes on a peculiar interest. It reads as follows :

"SON PHILIP :
          I have received two letters from you, one written in Latin, the other in French ; which I take in good part, and will you to exercise that practice of learning often ; for that will stand you in most stead in that profession of life that you are born to live in. And now, since this is my first letter that ever I did write to you, I will not that it be all empty of some advices which my natural care of you provoketh me to wish you to follow, as documents to you in this your tender age.

Let your first action be the lifting up of your mind to Almighty God by hearty prayer ; and feelingly digest the words you speak in prayer, with continual meditation and thinking of Him to whom you pray, and of the matter for which you pray. And use this as an ordinary act, and at an ordinary hour ; whereby the time itself shall put you in remembrance to do that you are accustomed to do in that time.

Apply your study to such hours as your discreet master doth assign you, earnestly ; and the time I know he will so limit as shall be both sufficient for your learning and safe for your health. And mark the sense and the matter of that you do read, as well as the words ; so shall you both enrich your tongue with words and your wit with matter, and judgment will grow as years grow in you.

Be humble and obedient to your masters, for, unless you frame yourself to obey others—yea, and feel in yourself what obedience is, you shall never be able to teach others how to obey you.

Be courteous of gesture and affable to all men, with diversity of reverence according to the dignity of the person. There is nothing that winneth so much with so little cost.

Use moderate diet so as, after your meal, you may find your wit fresher and not duller, and your body more lively and not more heavy.

Shrewsbury, An. 1566. 9 Eliz. then being of the age of XII years." (Philip was not twelve years old until November 30, 1566.)

(c) In that year " Old Master Onslow " was Sheriff of Salop and " Master Justice Corbet," a Justice of the King's Bench, was Recorder of Shrewsbury. Both would have official apartments in the Council House (*v.* Fisher, *op. cit.*, p. 11). The opening sentences of Sir Henry's letter suggest a period a few months after his arrival in Ireland, and Lady Sidney's hope that Philip's good master might govern him " yet many years " almost precludes the possibility of assigning the letter to a later period.

Seldom drink wine, and yet sometimes do, lest, being enforced to drink upon the sudden, you should find yourself enflamed. Use exercise of body, yet such as is without peril to your bones or joints ; it will increase your force and enlarge your breath. Delight to be cleanly as well in all parts of your body as in your garments ; it shall make you grateful in each company—and otherwise loathsome.

Give yourself to be merry ; for you degenerate from your father if you find not yourself most able in wit and body to do anything when you are most merry. But let your mirth be ever void of all scurrility and biting words to any man ; for a wound given by a word is oftentimes harder to be cured than that which is given by the sword.

Be you rather a hearer and bearer away of other men's talk than a beginner and procurer of speech ; otherwise you shall be accounted to delight to hear yourself speak. If you hear a wise sentence or an apt phrase, commit it to your memory with respect of the circumstances when you shall speak it. Let never oath be heard to come out of your mouth, nor word of ribaldry ; so shall custom make to yourself a law against it in yourself. Be modest in each assembly, and rather be rebuked of light fellows for maidenlike shamefastness than of your sad friends for pert boldness. Think upon every word that you will speak before you utter it, and remember how nature hath ramparted up, as it were, the tongue with teeth, lips—yea, and hair without the lips, and all betokening reins and bridles for the loose use of that member.

Above all things tell no untruth ; no, not in trifles. The custom of it is naughty. And let it not satisfy you that for a time the hearers take it for a truth ; for after it will be known as it is to your shame. For there cannot be a greater reproach to a gentleman than to be accounted a liar.

Study and endeavour yourself to be virtuously occupied. So shall you make such a habit of well-doing in you as you shall not know how to do evil, though you would. Remember, my son, the noble blood you are descended of by your mother's side ; and think that only by virtuous life and good action you may be an ornament to that illustrious family. Otherwise, through vice and sloth, you may be counted *labes generis,* one of the greatest curses that can happen to man.

Well, my little Philip, this is enough for me, and too much, I fear, for you. But if I find that this light meal of digestion nourish in anything the weak stomach of your capacity, I will, as I find the same grow stronger, feed it with other food.

Commend me most heartily unto Master Justice Corbet, old Master Onslow, and my cousin, his son. Farewell! Your mother and I send you our blessings, and Almighty God grant you His, nourish you with His fear, govern you with His grace, and make you a good servant to your prince and country !

Your loving father, so long as you live in the fear of God,

H. SIDNEY."

" A postscript by my Lady Sidney, in the skirts of my Lord President's letter " was appended as follows :

"Your noble, careful father hath taken pains with his own hand to give you, in this his letter, so wise, so learned and most requisite precepts for you to follow with a diligent and humble, thankful mind, as I will not withdraw your eyes from beholding and reverent honouring the same—no, not so long as to read any letter from me. And therefore, at this time, I will write unto you no other letter than this ; whereby I first bless you, with my desire to God to plant in you His grace, and, secondarily, warn you to have always before the eyes of your mind these excellent counsels of my lord, your dear father, and that you fail not continually, once in four or five days, to read them over.

And for a final leave-taking for this time, see that you show yourself as a loving, obedient scholar to your good master, to govern you yet many years, and that my lord and I may hear that you profit so in your learning as thereby you may increase our loving care of you, and deserve at his hands the continuance of his great joy, to have him often witness with his own hands the hope he hath in your well-doing.

Farewell, my little Philip, and once again the Lord bless you !

Your loving mother,

MARY SIDNEY."

The beauty of the family relationship which is suggested in this letter is perhaps unique in the sixteenth century. Lady Jane Grey's account of her relations to her parents[1] furnishes us with a strange contrast to the picture given above.

"When I am in presence either of father or mother," she says, "whether I speak, keep silence, sit, stand, or go, eat, drink, be merry, or sad, be sewing, playing, dancing, or doing anything else, I must do it, as it were, in such weight, measure and manner, even so perfectly, as God made the world, or else I am so sharply taunted, so cruelly threatened, yea, presently sometimes with pinches, nips and bobs, and other ways, which I will not name for the honour I bear them, so without measure misordered, that I think myself in hell...." And again she declares: "whatsoever I do else, but learning, is full of grief, trouble, fear, and whole misliking unto me."

It has been suggested that the disingenuousness which characterized so many of even the best men of Elizabeth's day traced its origin in no slight degree to the prevailingly harsh discipline to which children were subjected. From such an unhappy

---

[1] Quoted by Ascham in *The Schoolmaster* (ed. Arber), p. 47.

experience Philip Sidney was spared. It is a thousand pities
that we know so little of his relations to his mother ; to his
father, however, we know that from his youth up he was an
intimate companion and friend. *Noblesse oblige* became early
the master-light of the son's life as it was that of the father's.
To a remarkable degree we find the dominant traits of Sir
Henry's character reproduced in his son—his pride of family,
his engrossing conviction that only in disinterested service for
prince and country could a man find a worthy end toward
the achieving of which he could bend the whole of his energies,
his enthusiastic belief in the elevating influences of art and
literature and the study of antiquity, his uniform kindliness
toward all those of whatsoever degree with whom he came in
contact, his high, religious seriousness. When Philip concluded his schoolboy days at Shrewsbury he might justly have
been accounted a fortunate youth—fortunate in his birth, in
his parentage, and in the ideals of character, of religion, and
of scholarship which had constituted his early environment.

CHAPTER V

SIR HENRY IN IRELAND, 1566—1571

THE imagination fails to conjure up an adequate picture of the miseries of Ireland at this time. Within the narrow confines of the English Pale, where, alone, English rule was more than nominal, the country was desolate, and the rule and oppression of the stronger obtained everywhere. Outside the Pale a multitude of feudal chieftains reigned each in his small principality. The people lived like savages. Many had no clothing but the skins of wild beasts and no houses but holes in the earth. Marriage rites had fallen into disuse or were scoffed at. Warfare more or less petty was almost constantly waged, and if in an interval of peace some district began to show the good effect of cultivation it was soon reduced to its wonted desolation by a fresh outbreak of hostilities or by the cruel exactions known as " coin and livery " which the chieftains practised on their churls.

"Coin and livery," says a gentleman living in Ireland at the time, "is this. There will come a kern or Gallowglas, which be the Irish soldiers, to lie in the churl's house. Whiles he is there he will be master of the house ; he will not only have meat but money also allowed him, and at his departure the best things he shall see in the churl's house be it linen cloth, a shirt, mantle or such-like. Thus is the churl eaten up, so that if dearth fall in the country where he dwelleth he should be the first starved, not being master of his own[1]."

Of consistent administration of justice there was nowhere a pretence. " Surely," wrote Sir Henry to the Queen, " there was never people that lived in more misery than they do— such misery as in troth hardly any Christian with dry eyes could behold."

[1] *Censura Literaria*, vol. IV, p. 83.

Deeply conscious of the heavy responsibility resting upon him for the settlement of this chaos, Sir Henry attacked the problem with energy, clear-headed common sense and high-minded devotion which have given him a unique place among the English governors of Ireland. He was a very plain man and he had no elaborate theories regarding the problem. The solution at which he proposed to arrive was very simple. Ireland was a dependency of England, and the first step to be taken was to reduce it from a state of anarchy to one of order: rebellion whether formidable or petty must be stamped out. In the second place, law and justice must be evenly administered, even to the remotest corners of the realm, and justice must be assured to the churl as absolutely as to the feudal lord. When we remember Sir Henry's remarkable ability as a soldier and as an administrator and his unswerving devotion to unselfish ends, we are forced to the conclusion that had he received adequate support from Elizabeth he would have added to the annals of her reign one of its most creditable chapters. But he never learned how to adapt himself to a policy of compromise and half-measures, and to his wily, double-dealing mistress his forthright, transparent honesty always savoured of simplicity.

On his arrival he first addressed himself to Shan O'Neill as the most immediate danger that threatened English rule. This "monarchical tyrant" showed himself now humble, now insolent, but to all Sir Henry's attempts to come into personal contact with him Shan replied by reminding the Deputy that Sussex had tried to poison him, and that he had narrowly escaped perpetual imprisonment in London when under safe-conduct he had gone thither to visit the Queen. With the Council Sir Henry had at once grown into much favour, and he used the money he had brought to pay outstanding debts. But his desire to begin a constructive programme was negatived by Elizabeth's indecision. Sir Henry's plan of administration, according to which a President and Council were to be established in each of the four provinces, had been allowed by the English Privy Council and by the Queen, and he now pressed for the appointment of Sir Warham St Leger in Munster—

" an honest and a sufficient man." But Elizabeth chose to listen to Ormond's insinuations. A Council in Munster would shorten his feudal authority, Elizabeth suspected Sir Henry of affection to Desmond, she objected to the choice of Sir Warham St Leger, she objected because the country could not bear the cost of the Munster experiment. She was not sure that she wished to launch on so large a project as the " extirpation " of Shan was sure to prove. By Ormond's procurement copies of her letters to the Lord Deputy were in circulation in Dublin before Sir Henry received them, and popular reports that he was in disgrace paralyzed his power. Almost maddened by the treatment he was receiving, he begged Cecil and Leicester to have him recalled. He informed the Council of a great confederacy between Shan and the Earl of Argyle, and he predicted that Shan would soon invade the English Pale. He begged them that if the disgrace of Calais was to be repeated in Ireland they would spare him the shame of having it happen in his government.

By July the Queen's letters were more favourable. Although upbraiding him for the querulous expressions he used in his reports and commanding him not only to be favourable to Ormond, but to allow him to practise one " kind " of coin and livery, which Sir Henry had abolished, she promised that money and troops would be sent to wage war on Shan. On September 22nd Sir Henry with some 2000 men marched out of Drogheda and entered Shan's country. Meanwhile Shan had decided to attack Drogheda in the absence of Sir Henry, and to carry off Lady Sidney. Sarsfield, the Mayor of Dublin, hurried up with troops in response to a message from Lady Sidney, and was able to give such assistance to St Leger and Heron, who had been left in command by Sir Henry, that Shan was repulsed with great loss[1]. He turned north to Derry and was again driven back. Sir Henry followed up his advantage, and in all made eight or nine raids upon Shan, moving so swiftly and unexpectedly that when Shan received news of the approach of the bear and the ragged staff[2] he was usually incredulous.

[1] Campion, *History of Ireland* (1571).   [2] The badge of the Dudleys.

Not for many years had there been such an exhibition of
English power in Ireland, nor of power so beneficently exer
cised toward everyone except Shan and his followers.   But to
Elizabeth it seemed a small thing.   When Sir Henry returned
to the Pale it was to receive letters of sharp reproof and a
command to proceed into Munster to determine the Ormond-
Desmond cause.   Accordingly Shan received a new lease of
life, and from January to April the Deputy travelled through
all parts of the south and west of the island.

Into the minute details of this long journey we cannot
follow him[1].   His long report to Elizabeth (April 20, 1567)
constitutes one of the most vivid pictures of the miserable
state of Ireland in the sixteenth century which has come down
to us.   It was a hard and painful journey for Sir Henry.   Though
sorely troubled with the disease of the country, the stone, he
was indefatigable in seeking to restore order.   Jenyson, the
English auditor, visited him in Munster, and he wrote Cecil that
it pitied his heart to see the Lord Deputy so continually busied
in the causes from six in the morning till nine at night[2].   Everywhere Elizabeth's complaining and reproachful letters pursued
him, and with one disastrous result, according to Sir Henry's
own testimony.

" Thereupon received I many a bitter letter which indeed tired me, and
so perplexed my most dear wife as she fell most grievously sick upon the
same, and in that sickness remained once in trance above fifty-two hours.
Upon whose recovery I sent her into England where she lived till my
coming over[3]."

Of Lady Sidney's life at this time few details have survived:
we hear of her being present at a communion service in Dublin
Cathedral, and in her husband's letters she occasionally sends
commendations to Lady Cecil and Lady Bacon, but excepting
her share in the defence of Drogheda we know little of how
she passed her days.   She probably had her children, Elizabeth, Mary, Robert and Ambrosia, with her.   Lady Sidney's

---

[1] *V.* Letter to Walsingham, March 1, 1583, and Sir Henry's report to Elizabeth, Collins' *State Papers*, p. 18.

[2] *State Papers—Irish—Eliz.*, March 16, 1567.

[3] Sir Henry to Walsingham, March 1, 1583.

ill-health had now become chronic, and when she left for Eng-
land she was probably too weak to take her children with her.
A few months later, and just about the time that Sir Henry
joined her in London, Elizabeth died at Kilmainham, the
Deputy's residence in Dublin. Her death took place on
November 8, 1567, and she was buried in the Cathedral
Church at Dublin[1].

On reaching Dublin Sir Henry prepared at once to resume
the campaign against Shan O'Neill, and before the end of
April he was in Ulster. His harrying the country three months
previously had not been in vain. Shan, realizing that the
end was at hand, had sought to make peace, but the Deputy
answered none of his letters. Shan's old enemies, the
O'Donnells, had joined with Sir Henry, and while the latter
was ravaging Tyrone the O'Donnells overwhelmed Shan in a
great battle near Derry. He fled to the Irish Scots in the far
north-east of Antrim. They were now led by Allaster
McConnell ; their pent-up grievances burst forth during a
drunken brawl, and from the slaughter which followed only
two or three of Shan's followers escaped. Of the death of their
great leader, Campion says that Gillespie (Allaster McConnell's
nephew)

"mangled him cruelly, lapped him in an old Irish shirt, and tumbled
him into a pit within an old chapel hard by. Whose head four days after
Captain Piers (the Seneschal of Clandeboy) cut off, and met therewith
the Deputy, who sent it before him staked on a pole to the Castle of
Dublin, where it now standeth."

Leaving garrisons in Glenarm, Belfast and Carrickfergus, Sir
Henry received the submission of all the chiefs who had fought
under Shan, and especially of Tirlough Lenagh, the Tanist
of Tyrone, who had been chosen O'Neill in his stead. He also
insisted on the immediate departure of the Scots, and returned
to Dublin leaving Ulster in such quiet as it had not known
for many years.

[1] For *An Epitaph made for Mistress Elizabeth Sidney, the daughter of the
Right Honourable Sir Henry Sidney*, etc., see Additional MSS. Eg. 2642,
fol. 214. There are twenty-four verses in English and also six in Latin—
Carmina in laudem et mortem ejusdem Eliz.

Sir Henry now proceeded to make sure the holding of what he had won. He fortified Carrickfergus and likewise Athenry —the chief town in Connaught. At Athlone he built a stone bridge over the swift-flowing Shannon, and built it so well that for the future certain and easy access to Connaught was assured. He began the re-edification of Dublin Castle, which was literally falling into ruin. The records of the kingdom he found

" in an open place subject to wind, rain and all weather, and so neglected that they were taken for common uses. Whereupon with great care and diligence he caused them to be perused and sorted and placed within the Castle of Dublin in a room well boarded with a chimney for a fire so that neither by the moisture of the walls nor any other means they could receive prejudice. And several divisions were made for laying them separate, and one of discretion and skill appointed to look after them with an assignment for his labour. He also caused the statutes and ordinances of the realm which lay hid and hardly known (but kept in safety) to be searched, surveyed and viewed by men of the best learning, skill and discretion he could select, giving them express charge to peruse all and collect so many thereof as they should think necessary and expedient to be made public. Which being perused he caused them to be printed[1]."

But whether engaged in the works of war or peace Sir Henry in the eyes of his sovereign was an unprofitable servant. Almost weekly he received sharp and bitter letters from her. Referring merely incidentally to the suppression of Shan, she complained that Sir Henry had not disbanded his forces, that he was spending money uselessly on forts and bridges, that none of the Butlers could have any justice in Ulster because of Sir John of Desmond, the Earl's brother. Disgusted with a service in which he had sacrificed his health and £3000 of his own money, Sir Henry was comforted only by Cecil's private assurances of sympathy and friendship. At length he managed on July 5th to procure license to return, but although he was expected from week to week throughout the summer, it was October before he arrived in England. On reaching Chester he was compelled by illness to wait several days before proceeding to London. " The Viceroy of Ireland is expected every

[1] Collins' *Memoirs*, p. 90.

day," de Silva wrote Philip on October 18th; "he has been delayed longer than was thought. His wife sends to tell me to-day that she looks for him hourly." He arrived accompanied by a large number of Irish chiefs and their followers, who came at their own suit " chiefly to behold the high majesty of our sacred sovereign." When Elizabeth beheld the cavalcade approaching Hampton Court she inquired with surprise who it was that came with such a brave show. On being informed, she replied : " It is well enough, for he hath two of the best offices in the kingdom."

"When I came to the Court," Sir Henry himself declared, "it was told me that it was no war that I had made nor worthy to be called a war, for that Shan O'Neill was but a beggar, an outlaw, and one of no force, and that the Scots stumbled on him by chance....And within few days after I was charged for not redressing the damages done to Ormond and his followers by Sir John of Desmond."

As if to complete Sir Henry's disgrace, Elizabeth, without consulting him, ordered Desmond and his brother to be sent over from Ireland and thrown into the Tower, where they were detained for seven years—a piece of impolicy which was directly responsible for the succeeding rebellion in Munster.

It was a dreary home-coming for Sir Henry. His health, as a result of the privations and hardships to which he had subjected himself, was wretched, the news of his little daughter's death in Dublin soon reached him, and the Queen's utter failure to appreciate his services wounded him deeply.

"Sidney, the Viceroy of Ireland, came to supper with me the night before last," wrote de Silva on November 15th...."Sidney is much dissatisfied with the way in which the Queen has treated him as both he and others have told me. They say his treatment is in consequence of his not having managed the Earl of Ormond's affairs well. He thinks that considering his services and the success of his administration in Ireland he ought to be rewarded."

Six weeks later he wrote : " I am told that the Viceroy has resigned, displeased with their treatment of him after his services there, and that the Queen has appointed the Vice-Chamberlain as his successor." An elaborate diagnosis of his disease—*The State of Sir H. Sidney's Body*—which was drawn up in February, 1568, reads in parts as though it had been made for the special purpose of keeping him at home, for in it he is warned against "all places full of bogs, fens and marshes"; moreover, " riding post long journeys or upon a stirring horse galloping the field clad in heavy armour and such-like are very hurtful for the stone." There was indeed some talk of sending Knowles, but from month to month it became more evident that the best available man would not be too good. Large numbers of Scots had landed on the Antrim coast, and Tirlough Lenagh's actions were causing suspicion : continually the Queen received letters from Ireland begging that Sir Henry might be sent back. " The people gape for the Lord Deputy's return," Captain Malby reported from Carrickfergus. On February 16th de Silva learned that after much entreaty the Viceroy had consented to return to his government.

Six months were to pass before Sir Henry actually set out, during which time he was constantly sent for to the Court to discuss Irish problems. No doubt he spent part of the time in his Presidency, where he was busy in June, as we have already seen, in securing to Philip quiet possession of Whitford parson-age. In July he became reconciled to his brother-in-law, Sussex, who was now at length consoled by the Presidency of York for Sir Henry's continued holding of the Welsh Presi-dency. Whether he was consulted before the forfeiture of all the Desmond holdings in Munster on July 12th there is no record. On August 2nd he paid a visit to Oxford, where Philip was now a student. He lodged in the Dean's House at Christ Church, and there the degree of M.A. was conferred on him. When a day or two later he left Oxford he took Philip with him. Just one month remained before Sir Henry was to return to Ireland and its insoluble problems, and he had determined to enjoy a few weeks of his boy's society before setting out. On their way to Wales they stopped to pay a visit to Kenil-worth, and it is pleasant to see the much-suffering Lord Deputy free from care for once.

" My dearest Lord," he wrote Leicester a few days later, " I could not come so near your fair and ancient Castle of Kenilworth as my way led me to do and leave it unseen, but thither I went where the entertainment that

my cousin Thomas Blount and other your servants gave me showed
their civility, and that they knew me to be your Lordship's well-beloved
brother.   There met me my Lord Berkeley, Sir Fulke Greville and John
Stanhope.   Sir Giles Poole and Thomas Throgmorton of Gloucestershire
came thither with me.   I would not hunt, but fish I did, and took an
hundred good breames at a draught, which I appointed to be kept for you
till your Lordship's coming.   I was never more in love with an old house,
nor never new work could better be bestowed than that which you have
done.   I have appointed *salvo meliori judicio* where your chapel shall
stand—in the void room by Caesar's tower or, agreeably with the stately
buildings of the house, to fill up a part of the room between John of Gaunt's
building and the porter's lodge.   Which chapel, if you will get me home
this next spring, I and Cox at our own proper cost and charges will be
bound to begin and finish within one year in fair, decent and durable
manner."

This letter was written from Shrewsbury on August 8th, when
for three days Sir Henry had been sore troubled with his disease.   On the same day he wrote to Cecil commending to his
care his wife and boy, and sending his regards to Lady Cecil,
Lady Bacon and Sir Nicholas.   Sir Henry spent the month
in Wales with Lady Mary and Philip, *lumen familiae suae* ;
to all of them it must have seemed a blessed interval.

By September 6th the Deputy had landed in Carrickfergus.
Separated from his family, he could at least know that they
were left under the protection of warm friends—of whom the
warmest was Her Majesty's Principal Secretary.   All Cecil's
letters at this time bear testimony to his enthusiasm and high
regard for the Sidneys.   In a letter of August 10th he begs
Sir Henry

" to keep an assured account of my inner hearty good will to you and
yours, and to measure me by deeds and not by words, for surely, sir, I
have neither many times such leisure, nor indeed pleasure to use many
words as I may have commodity in friendly offices to show myself your
assured bounden friend, and as you have gently and courteously remembered in your commendations my wife, and your little maid, my daughter
[Anne Cecil], so I wish health to my good Lady, your wife, and increase
of all goodness to your son, my darling master Philip[1]."

Three weeks later, and just before Sir Henry sailed, Cecil
wrote him :

[1] *State Papers—Ireland—Eliz.*, vol. xxv, Aug. 10, 1568.

"Now I have not many things of weight saving one, and that is heavy for you to bear, considering you have therein offended many, and not to detain you in longer expectation this it is ; you carried away your son and my scholar from Oxford, not only from his book but from the commodity to have been seen of my lords his uncles, and to have been opposed by me, and to have pleasured both me and my wife.   I think indeed either you forgot the Queen's progress to be so near, or else you have some matter of merit to allege both for your taking him from Oxford and for detaining of him so long in wild Wales.   I think my Lord of Leicester will challenge you earnestly, and therefore I will say *Dixi*[1]."

We have here another proof of Leicester's early devotion to his nephew and of Sir William's and Lady Cecil's enthusiastic liking for him.   Beneath the words of playful reproof there is an undertone of genuine disappointment.   Though dwelling constantly in a "tubful of business," Cecil found time to write Sir Henry frequent brief notes[2]—quite apart from the formal, Secretary's letters—in which he gave unwonted expression to his friendly sentiments.   Here is one written from Hampton Court on Nov. 19th.

"MY GOOD LORD :

    I find myself inwardly touched with some care for lack of understanding how and what you do, for since your departure out of England I never heard of your proceeding in Ireland, which to one that hath inwardly conceived and printed in his mind characters of true friendship towards you cannot but breed grief of mind, and in this sort have I of late time written sundry letters but to them I have no answer.   And yet if I may once hear that you do well I will take that only for a full satisfaction....My Lady, your wife, shall, I trust be here on Monday, and so I end."

Sir Henry, in acknowledging these "most kind and loving letters," could only protest that they gave him more comfort than ever he looked to enjoy in that government.   The constant knowledge of Cecil's approval and friendship was indeed Sir Henry's chief solace and support.

    From Carrickfergus the Deputy made a short progress through Ulster and, thanks to the exertions of Captains Piers and Malby, whom he had left in charge, found the country in

---

[1] *Ibid.*, Sept. 3, 1568.
[2] *Ibid.*, Oct. 24th, Nov. 5th, Nov. 19th, Nov. 29th.

W. L. S.

an unwonted state of order. He had satisfactory conferences
both with Tirlough Lenagh and the Antrim Scots. Of the
prosperity of the district about Carrickfergus Sir Henry himself
has left quite an idyllic picture—provisions were cheap and
abundant and trade was carried on with Scotland, the Isle of
Man and the English Pale; "out of France in one summer
three barks of forty tons apiece discharged their loading of
excellent good Gascoigne wine, the which they sold for nineteen
cow skins the hogshead."

But if Ulster was at peace Munster promised to keep
Sir Henry more than occupied. There the situation had changed
radically within the year. To pleasure Ormond Elizabeth had
not only imprisoned Desmond, but had meted out similar
treatment to his brother Sir John, whose government of
Desmond's country had called forth Sir Henry's commendation.
The imprisonment of the Geraldine chiefs was followed by the
forfeiting of their lands, and Sir Henry was ordered to proceed
with the work of sequestration. This would have been sufficient in itself to precipitate a rebellion, but two other courses
had been decided on, either one of which was almost equally
potent in the same direction. For the first time a serious
attempt was to be made to introduce Protestantism in a country
where all the natives were Catholics. Moreover, England
was about to attempt in the south and west of the island
the first of her fatal colonization schemes. In its inception
Sir Peter Carew made the mistake of beginning by seizing certain
lands belonging to the Earl of Ormond. The immediate effect of
this act was to drive the latter's brothers, Piers and Edmund
and "that blessed babe Edward Butler," who had been brought
up in Sir Henry Sidney's household, to raise troops for their
own defence, and James Fitzmaurice, a brother of the Earl
of Desmond, deemed the time opportune to make a supreme
effort to prevent the annihilation of the power of the Geraldines.
He was joined by the Earl of Clancarty and all the chieftains
of the south-west, he despatched the Archbishop of Cashel to
Spain to beseech Philip to aid him with an army, and he
had no difficulty in persuading the Earls of Thomond and
Clanricarde to rouse all Connaught and Tirlough Lenagh to take

the field in Ulster. Absurd stories to the effect that Leicester
was to be King of England and Sir Henry Sidney King of
Ireland fanned the flame, and by the summer of 1569 the whole
country was in a blaze.

Into the minute details and ramifications of this first
Desmond rebellion it is impossible for us to go now. Sir Henry
with such forces as he could muster marched through Munster,
through Connaught, and finally through Ulster to the very
north of the island, beating down all opposition. Had the
Butlers joined with the Geraldines, or had a Spanish army
actually landed, it is impossible to believe that the Deputy's
slender resources would have been equal to the occasion.
After returning from Ulster Sir Henry made a progress through
the whole south and west, holding sessions for the punishment
of the rebels. In Kilkenny alone he had above sixty persons
condemned and executed. " In this journey," he himself
says, " I did as good service as ever I did in any peaceable
progress."

It would be a mistake to assume that Sir Henry Sidney is
not to be held responsible for his full share of this wild work
of ruthless injustice and bloodshed. He was an enthusiastic
advocate of the solution of the Irish problem by means of
colonists, and no part of his work in Ireland was more gratify-
ing to him than the success of a colony of forty families of the
reformed churches of the Low Countries, which he planted in
the ruinous town of Swords near Dublin. We do not know
that he was apprised of the scheme of the Munster adventurers
from the beginning, but on June 30, 1569, he gave it his
definite approval. Three of the adventurers, St Leger, Carew
and Gilbert, were among his best friends and most trusted
lieutenants. Of his warm approval of St Leger we have already
heard. At the funeral of Sir Peter Carew a few years later
(he died on Nov. 27, 1575) Sir Henry said :

" Here lieth now in his last rest a most worthy and a noble gentle
knight, whose faith to his prince was never yet stained, his truth to his
country never spotted, and his valiantness in service never daunted.
A better subject the prince never had[1]."

Archæologia, vol. xxviii, p. 96.

Humphrey Gilbert he considered one of the best English captains in Ireland; his letters to Cecil frequently refer to Gilbert's abilities and worth, and Sir Henry knighted him for his services in helping to suppress this very rebellion. Sir Nicholas Malby—"the valiant Malby"—and Sir Edward Fitton, the President of the Connaught Council, of whom Sir Henry declared that he had "ministered nothing but justice and that too mildly," were men of the same stamp. They were all capable soldiers and administrators, not given to examining too closely the right or wrong of the enterprise in which they were engaged, and prepared ruthlessly to stamp out all opposition to the Queen's authority. The trouble was that Englishmen, one and all, had come to look on Ireland as a land given over to rebellion and barbarism; its inhabitants they considered as irreclaimable savages, and they contemplated a "killing" of them—men, women and children—much as they would have contemplated the work of freeing the land from a pack of wolves. Judged by the standard of his own day— the only fair criterion for judging any man—Sir Henry was conspicuous for his love of justice to every man of whatever condition, but even his humanity, for which he was known everywhere, did not extend to the wretched people whom he was sent to govern, when they were in rebellion against his sovereign. In saying this we are only recognizing that he shared a sentiment which was universal among Englishmen of his day.

Peace was once more temporarily established, but the Ormond barb remained fastened in Sir Henry's side. It was the same story. Ormond complained that he could get no justice of Sidney, the Queen wrote him "bitter" letters, and Ormond's exaction of coin and livery and his freedom from all charges on his lands, even those within the Pale, spread discontent and mutiny among his neighbours. "If you joy anything in my life," Sir Henry wrote Cecil at the beginning of 1570, "get me home this next April for I feel I shall not live here till midsummer." But Elizabeth had no wish to recall a servant whose ability she had never doubted. On May 4th he wrote to the Council beseeching them that Lady Sidney might have license to come to Dublin, and on June 21st he wrote to Tremayne, urging him to hasten her coming. A month later Tremayne was in Ireland, and he wrote to Cecil that unless the Lord Deputy were relieved of his griefs he could be of no long continuance in this world.

Poor Lady Mary's troubles at home had hardly been less grievous than those of her husband in Ireland, and they were not markedly different in kind. Her health was wretched, she was never able to satisfy her creditors, and she was made miserable by her sense of the Queen's ingratitude. Cecil had remained her steadfast friend. Sir Henry had frequently to thank him for his " courteous visitation " of his wife, and when her last son was born (March 25, 1569) Cecil and Sussex were the god-fathers. Probably to emphasize the newly established friendliness between the Sidneys and Sussex, the boy was named after him—Thomas—not much it would seem to Sir Henry's liking.

"I most heartily thank you," he wrote to Cecil, " for the great honour you did me in helping to make a Christian of my little son, rejoicing not a little in any kind of alliance that may be between us, and the straighter the more joyfuller to me. But indeed I have not my will for I left order that if it were a boy it should have been a William, if a wench Cycell[1]."

In many ways Cecil befriended Lady Sidney, and she did not hesitate constantly to avail herself of his friendship. In the following letter which she wrote to him on June 1st, 1570, regarding a suit to the Queen, we have a sadly realistic picture of her life at the time :

"Sir, these occasions force me to continue my troubling of you beseech-ing you to regard the greatness of the cause thereof unto me. First, sir, whereas it pleaseth you to send me word you think if I did move the matter myself it were likely I might obtain my suit, truly, to that, neither can I be there in any time before the progress so to benefit myself, for that I am entered upon great cause into the diet already. Neither if I were there could I have the face to speak so effectually as I am sure I should thereby profit myself in that I speak. I once again most humbly crave your goodness herein unto me as once more to continue earnestly to speak in it. And since there is no flat denial made I hope there may

---

[1] *State Papers—Ireland—Eliz.*, June 30, 1569.

be grace obtained....The term ends on Wednesday, the progress begins shortly after. I shall be left in miserable state any way if it please not your honour to take care of me, for after the term once ends I shall want my friends' assistance in all my causes."

She goes on to say that if it is granted later it will be of little " commodity " to her,

" where now if it were finished I am offered present money. Truly I have moved divers my friends in court....How then can she [the Queen] stick at so small a trifle as poor £22 a year for 12 years' service ? Well, God knows to what end I only desire it...."

To the long letter was added a postscript :

" Yet once more pardon me I beseech your Lordship that I crave again your speedy, earnest care of me even for God's sake that my poor creditors may be imprested their due. I know if you knew the miserable state I live in w'th my health for it, your virtue would move you to pity[1]."

It is a distressing picture—that of the high-born lady broken in health and cumbered with debt, and so eager to gain possession of even a small sum of money that she is willing to make some sacrifice of her dignity in the effort. There is no reason to suppose that she was able to go to Ireland as Sir Henry wished, and toward the end of the year he secured his recall.

To one important task Sir Henry had still to give his attention, the holding of a session of the Irish Parliament. Although about to leave Ireland, as he believed for the last time, he never exerted himself more strenuously for the well-being of the country. He was gratified by the passing of many laws which would put the permanent revenue on a more stable basis, and would make for the extension of law and justice. One of his schemes for the planting of grammar schools throughout the land had been allowed, but the Parliament, to Sir Henry's great sorrow, had negatived his desire to establish a University in Dublin.

On March 18, 1571, Sir Henry saw his children embarked for England, and one week later he followed them. At his departure he was given a remarkable proof of the high estimation

[1] *State Papers—Ireland—Eliz.,* June 1, 1570.

in which his services to the country were held. To quote
Campion :

"He was honoured at the point of his going with such recourse, pomp,
music, shows and interludes as no man remembereth the like. He took
ship towards England at the key of Divelin [Dublin] in Lent following,
accompanied to sea with the Estates and Worshipful of Ireland with
innumerable hearty prayers, and with that wish of his return whereof
but few Governors in these last sixty years have held possession. The
man was surely much loved of them from his first office of Treasurer
in the second year of Queen Mary, stately without disdain, familiar without contempt, very continent and chaste of body, no more than enough
liberal, learned in many languages and a great lover of learning, perfect
in blazoning of arms, skilful of antiquities, of wit fresh and lively, in
consultations very temperate, in utterance happy, which his experience
and wisdom have made artificial, a preferrer of many, a father of his
servants, both in war and peace of commendable courage."

With these words Campion concludes his *History*, and we
cannot but feel that in the contemporary character-sketch
we have a portrait of Sir Henry, which is fairly discriminating
and genuinely suggestive of the man.

CHAPTER VI

UNIVERSITY EDUCATION

THE only fact which we are able to record in the life of Philip Sidney between Michaelmas, 1566—the date of Marshall's last entry in his book of accounts—and August 2, 1568, when his father visited Oxford to receive the degree of M.A., is that at some time before the latter date Philip had become a student of Christ Church[1]. The matriculation and subscription books of the University are available, unfortunately, only from about 1570. There is no real evidence for assuming that 1568 was the year in which Philip began his college life rather than 1567, nor does his age make the one date more probable than the other. Richard Carew had entered Christ Church in 1566 at the age of eleven, and a University statute of 1581 recognizes matriculants under twelve and over sixteen years of age[2].

We have little detailed knowledge of the three or four years which Philip spent at the University, and the greater part of what we do know has to do not with his studies, but with his relation to his father's friend, Sir William Cecil. The intimacy between the two families had never been greater than it was during this summer of 1568, when we first hear of the boy's having attracted the great statesman's attention. In a letter to Sir Henry on August 10th, Cecil wrote :

"As you have gently and courteously remembered in your commendations my wife, and your little maid, my daughter, so I wish health to my good Lady, your wife, and increase of all goodness to your son, my darling master Philip[3]."

[1] Mr Fox-Bourne's claim to have fixed the date within a month or two cannot be allowed. See his Preface, IX.

[2] *Register of the University of Oxford* (Ox. Hist. Soc.), vol. II, p. 167.

[3] *State Papers—Ireland—Eliz.*, vol. XXV.

We have already heard him a few weeks later upbraiding Sir Henry for carrying off from Oxford " your son and my scholar." Some three months later Sir Henry wrote Cecil from Ireland :

"I most heartily thank you for your courteous visitation of my wife. I pray you sometime harken of our boy and be working how to get home the father. I have no more, but with my most hearty commendations to yourself, my lady and my sweet jewel, your daughter, I wish you all as well as I would myself[1]."

On January 29th Cecil wrote Sir Henry: " Your Philip is here, in whom I take more comfort than I do openly utter for avoiding of wrong interpretation. He is worthy to be loved, and so I do love him as he were my son[2]."

Cecil felt unwonted enthusiasm for his friend's handsome boy, and the expression with which his last letter concludes may have been drawn out by some tentative suggestion of Sir Henry regarding an alliance between the families. This at length took the form of a definite proposal that Philip and Anne Cecil, the sweet jewel of Sir Henry's letters, be betrothed. In the circumstances the proposal was a most natural one. Marriages in the sixteenth century were almost invariably arranged by the parents, and Cecil believed heartily in the practice ; " marry thy daughters in time lest they marry themselves," was the advice which he himself afterwards gave to his own son, Robert. The date of Anne Cecil's birth is not known, but she was probably about one year younger than Philip[3]. Cecil's reply to Sir Henry's proposal was highly characteristic :

"My good Lord: If my power for doing or my leisure for writing were as some portion of my desire is to testify to you my good will you should have as good proof thereof as I see you have in hope an assurance. I

---

[1] Collins' *Letters*, etc., p. 40, Nov. 30, 1568.

[2] *State Papers, ut supra*, vol. XXVII.

[3] On Nov. 30, 1557, Sir Philip Hoby wrote Cecil upbraiding him for not planning to visit Byssham, Sir Philip's seat, at Christmas, " all of which," he says, " I know doth come of my Lady because she cannot leave little Tannikin, her daughter....I pray you desire my Lady to come and to bring Tannikin with her, and I hope so to provide for her and her nurse as all the house shall be merry and that, notwithstanding, at her own ease and quiet." (*State Papers—Domestic—Mary*, vol. XI.) See Burghley's letter to Rutland (p. 93), from which it might be inferred that at the end of the year 1571, Anne was about sixteen years of age.

thank you for your free offer made to me by your letters by Cocker concerning your son, whom truly I do so like for his own conditions and singular towardness in all good things as I think you a happy father for so joyful a son. And as for the interest that it pleaseth you to offer me in him I must confess if the child alone were valued without the natural good that dependeth of you his father, I could not but think him worthy the love I bear him, which certainly is more than I do express outwardly for avoiding of sinister interpretation. For as for the account to have him my son I see so many incidenties as it sufficeth me to love the child for himself without regard therein of my daughter, whom surely I love so well as, so it be within my degree or not much above, I shall think none too good for her. Thus you see a father's fondness which to a father I dare discover, and so for this time it sufficeth[1]."

Cecil was essentially cold and calculating, and given to scanning sharply the " incidenties " of a situation. His letter to Sir Henry meant that the determining consideration in the choice of Anne Cecil's husband would be his rank and his wealth. Accordingly Sir Henry drew up a statement of his assets and liabilities and sent Edward Waterhouse, the Clerk of the Council, to negotiate with Cecil.

"Let me know what you would have me do," wrote Sir Henry, "and you shall find me ready. For before God in these matters I am utterly ignorant as one that never made a marriage in his life. But I mean truly and sincerely loving your daughter as one of my own, regarding her virtue above any other *dot*, and your friendship more than all the money you will give. And for my boy I confess that if I might have every week a boy I should never have none like him, and accordingly I have dealt with him, for I do not know above a hundred a year of mine that I have not already assured to him[2]."

The negotiating went on for nearly a year. In June Sir Henry sent commendations

" to my dear jewel and our daughter I trust, of whose recovery I rejoice not a little. In truth afore God I assure you that I joy in no child I have so much as in her, that child only except who, I trust shall enjoy her."

[1] *State Papers—Ireland—Eliz.*, vol. XXVII, Feb. 2, 1569.
[2] *Hist. Man. Com. Reports*—Salisbury MSS., Apr. 7, 1569. Perhaps Sir Henry had this matter in his mind when sometime in 1568 he caused a detailed statement to be drawn up of the yearly value of his lands and other possessions in the counties of Lincoln, Rutland, Kent and Surrey. The total amounted to £1140. 4s. 2d. per annum. (*Lansdowne MSS.*, vol. x, fol. 107 +. a Latin document of eleven pages.)

By August tentative marriage settlements were drawn up[1], and when the Earl of Leicester interested himself in the affair he and Cecil were able to agree on the amounts which should be settled on Philip and Anne respectively by their parents. Throughout the greater part of his life Philip was regarded as Leicester's heir, and no doubt this fact was of primary importance in the mind of the worldly Cecil. The terms were submitted to Sir Henry, who was not disposed to cavil. John Thomas, his treasurer, reported to Cecil that the Lord Deputy

" doth very well like every of them [the articles] and is ready to perform it in such sort as by yourself shall be thought meet. I moved him also touching the marriage money to know whether he would receive it himself or else bestow the same upon the two children, for so I promised your honour I would do. He is very well contented the money shall be employed to their commodity, and that he will receive no part of it himself, which he promised me he would affirm in his next letter unto your honour, etc.[2]"

Sir Henry evidently regarded the arrangement as settled. Two days later he wrote congratulations to Lady Cecil on the engagement between their children, and to Anne he sent his " loving and father's kiss." He begged Lady Cecil to have regard that her son [Philip] should not study too much " for I fear he will be too much given to his book, and yet I have heard of few wise fathers doubt that in their children[3]." Cecil, however, had by no means made up his mind. On Sept. 7th he wrote to Nicholas White, an agent of his in Ireland, asking him to look into the terms of the agreement as carefully as he could, and on Oct. 27th White replied :

"I have a doubt of the articles accorded between H. S. and your honour. I thought the land had been of greater value and I do not find what A. C. shall have if P. S. at the years of consent refuse to marry. But considering it is wisely provided that A. C. shall have free liberty of consenting at those years, the interim is well bestowed in mutual friendship which is plentifully perceived from your honour to him."

The marriage contract reached Sir Henry in Ireland when the Munster rebellion was at its height; he failed to return it at once and eventually it was mislaid. This served Cecil as a

---

[1] *Ibid.*, Aug. 6, 1569.
[2] *Ibid.*, vol. xxix, Oct. 24, 1569.
[3] *Hist. Man. Com. Reports*—Salisbury MSS., Oct. 26, 1569.

pretext to complain of Sir Henry's coldness in the matter—
the preliminary to his breaking off negotiations.

" I am sorry," Sir Henry answered, " that you find coldness anywhere
in proceeding where such good liking appeared in the beginning, but for
my part I never was more ready to perfect that matter than presently
I am, assuring you for my part if I might have the greatest Prince's
daughter in Christendom for him, the match spoken of between us on
my part should not be broken."

This letter was dated Feb. 24, 1570, and in it Sir Henry still
refers to " our daughter Anne," but we may feel sure that
before this time Cecil had decided against the match. It is not
difficult to guess at his reasons. Sir Henry grew less and less in
favour with Elizabeth, his patrimony was decreasing and he was
always in money difficulties. Philip's chances of some day being
Leicester's heir were very uncertain. Perhaps Lady Sidney's
constant applications for assistance may have had a share in
determining Cecil's attitude : " Be sure to keep some great man
thy friend but trouble him not for trifles," was another of his
maxims, the latter part of which Lady Sidney was wont to
violate. Perhaps his own elevation to be Baron of Burghley,
coinciding almost exactly as it does in time with the date of
Sir Henry's last letter, may have had something to do with his
resolving to look higher. At any rate within the next eighteen
months Cecil—or Burghley, as we must now call him—definitely
rejected Philip as a suitor for his daughter's hand, seriously considered another possible husband, and finally about Midsummer,
1571, decided on the young Earl of Oxford, who was already
reputed one of the most dissolute and wrong-headed of the
younger courtiers. As a ward he had lived for some years at Cecil
House, where in a fit of passion he had killed one of the servants
on July 23, 1567[1]. On August 3, 1571, Burghley notes : " The
Earl of Oxford declared to the Queen's Majesty at Hampton
Court his desire to match with my daughter Anne, whereto the
Queen assented[2]." Dazzled by the brilliance of the match
Burghley was able to perceive fine qualities in his prospective
son-in-law. A very interesting letter which he wrote to the

[1] Notes of Queen Elizabeth's reign by the Lord Treasurer Burghley (Murdin, *Burghley State Papers*).   [2] *Ibid.*

Duke of Rutland is illustrative both of his character and of his point of view in the matter of the marriage :

" I think it doth seem strange to your Lordship," he wrote on Aug. 15th, "to hear of a purposed determination in my Lord of Oxford to marry with my daughter, and so before his Lordship moved it to me might I have thought it. For at his own motion I could not well imagine what to think, considering I never meant to seek it nor hoped of it. And yet reason moved me to think well of my Lord, and to knowledge myself greatly beholding to him, as indeed I do. Truly, my Lord, after I was acquainted of the former intention of a marriage with Mr. Philip Sidney, whom always I loved and esteemed, I was fully determined to have of myself moved no marriage for my daughter until she should have been near sixteen years, that with moving I might also conclude. And yet I thought it not inconvenient in the meantime, being free, to harken to any motion made by such others as I should have cause to like. Truly, my Lord, my good will served me to have moved such a matter as this in another [direction than this] is, but having some occasion to doubt of the issue of the matter I did forbear, and in mine own concept I could have as well liked there as in any other place in England. Percase your Lordship may guess where I mean, and so shall I, for I will name nobody.

Now that the matter is determined betwixt my Lord of Oxford and me, I confess to your Lordship I do honour him as much as I can any subject, and I love him so dearly from my heart as I do mine own son, and in any case that may touch him for his honour and weal I shall think mine own interest therein. And surely, my Lord, by dealing with him I find that which I often heard of your Lordship that there is much more in him of understanding than any stranger to him would think. And for mine own part I find that whereof I take comfort in his wit and knowledge graven by good observation[1]."

By this time the match had been publicly announced, for Sir William FitzWilliam, on August 19th, wrote Burghley congratulations from Ireland, although he confessed to a wish that Philip were to be the bridegroom. The marriage took place in December, 1571, and for the rest of her short life Anne Cecil was to be the chief object upon which the almost insane brutality of her husband exercised itself.

To what extent Philip Sidney was personally interested in the plan for marrying him to Burghley's daughter we do not know. From the time of his entering the University he kept up a regular correspondence with the great statesman who had

---

[1] *Hist. Man. Com. Reports*—MSS. of the Duke of Rutland.

distinguished him with such especial marks of favour, but of this correspondence there have survived only three letters, all of them written by Philip, two in Latin and one in English. We first hear Philip talk *in propria persona* in the Latin letter of March 12, 1569; the English letter, the last of the three, is dated February 27, 1570—approximately the date when the marriage negotiations were broken off. Philip may have known little or nothing regarding the progress of the negotiations, but he now probably found himself on less free and intimate terms with Burghley and his household than he had hitherto been. The Latin letters, Philip's earliest extant writings, are as follows[1]:

"Your marvellous kindnesses, quite undeserved by me, lead me, most excellent Sir, though I cannot do it fitly and as becomes me, to write this letter to you; but this certainly I do not that you may see what favourable progress I have made in my studies. For on this point, to speak truthfully and not without heavy grief, I must confess that I can in no way satisfy either your expectation or my own desire. But I write this on purpose that I may not seem guilty of neglect towards one who has done me so many favours, and so show myself altogether unable to emulate his goodness. This is my reason then for troubling you, who are so busied about such weighty and extensive work, with my poor talk, that you may understand, as far as I can explain it, with what grateful memory I recall your kindnesses towards me; and I know that I shall never have any other thought than this. And I beseech you that what I am doing with the best intention you will receive in good part, and not condemn me for boldness and imprudence because I trouble you with a letter in order that you may know the mind which I have concerning you. The duties and the respect which I owe to you, and which I wish most heartily to perform, will bind me closely to you all life long, and always I shall set before myself, ever more and more eagerly, to find my happiness in deserving well of you. Farewell.

Your most devoted,

PHILIP SIDNEY."

The second Latin letter is dated some four months later (July 8th) and reads as follows:

"I am very well aware, honoured Sir, that I may have incurred your just censure in that I have not written to you for so long a time, since I knew that you expected me to write more frequently, and that you were pleased not only to accept in good part my letters, however crude they

[1] *State Papers—Dom.—Eliz.*, March 12, 1569. The translation is from Mr Fox-Bourne's *Memoir*, p. 34.

were, but to answer them most generously. This may have given rise in you to some natural suspicion of ingratitude on my part, than which I have always thought there is no vice more detestable, no offence more unworthy, and no crime more heinous ; in a youth it betrays rudeness of manners, in a mature man it is worthy of the deepest censure, in old age it is positively wicked. Therefore I beseech your honour to believe that nothing is farther from me, that there is nothing I would more carefully avoid. I might perhaps offer some just excuse both with regard to the place and time, but if I freely confess myself guilty of some negligence I hope you will not be too harsh in your judgment upon me. I would write to you at greater length and thank you for the many singular benefits and kindnesses which you have shown both to my father and me if I knew whether you wished me to write longer letters or whether I could do so creditably with my small ability. But why should I write more since I have speaking letters [a messenger ?] who can inform you more fully both concerning my father's affairs and my own. Farewell, and as you have begun I beseech you to continue to love me.

Yours in most humble sort,

PHILIP SIDNEY[1].

OXFORD, *July* 8, 1569."

Naturally these compositions are self-conscious and reveal little enough of the writer's personality; their elaborate apologies and moral generalizations remind one of the tone of the Queen's Latin orations before the Universities. The third letter—Philip's earliest extant piece of English composition— is much more satisfactory. It is dated February 26, 1570, and if its logic is not convincing it leaves no doubt of the aggressiveness of the young collegian, who was now little more than fifteen years of age. Some time before, Philip's enthusiasm for his tutor had led him to secure from Leicester and Burghley a promise that the next vacant canonry in Christ Church should be given to Thomas Thornton. Such a vacancy had now occurred, but, to Philip's great disgust, a rival candidate had appeared in Mr Toby Matthew. Philip's anxiety and indignation could not confine themselves within the bounds of the Latin in which he ordinarily wrote to Cecil. His letter reads :

"Right Honourable : I am forced for better expedition to use an unaccustomed manner of writing to you, the cause proceeding from a

---

[1] *Lansdowne MSS.*, vol. XI, fol. 169. The letter has been printed in the original Latin by Zouch, pp. 378–9.

report of some whom neither can I judge friendly to myself nor yet indifferent towards him from whom they seek by malice to prevent and detain
his worthy preferment, sued for and obtained by his honourable benefactors,
I mean my singular good Lord, my Lord of Leicester, and especially
yourself, by whose favour (attained by the request of my friends and his
desert towards me, assisted by the worthiness of his life and learning)
Mr Thornton, my reader, hath unto him granted the next preferment of
a canonry in this College of Christ Church. And sithence it hath pleased
God (as I gave you humbly to understand in my last letter) to call unto
his mercy one Thomas Day, by mean whereof it resteth in your honourable
favour to present (according to your former pretence) him, as well for whose
cause as divers others I do account myself no less bound than I ought.
For that it is very constantly reported that Mr Toby Matthew's friends
should use in his behalf some earnest suit unworthy their callings, because
it was moved before the death of the incumbent, by the which should
seem they sought rather by spite to prevent the one than honestly to prefer
the other, these are therefore most humbly to request such your wonted
favour as neither your honourable benefit may be revoked, my humble
and earnest suit prevented, neither the person himself so discredited,
but that he may with your favour enjoy his advowson by your means
obtained and yourself promised. Thus humbly commending my duty
unto your good opinion, myself prest at your commandment I humbly
end. From Oxford this 26th of February, *anno* 1569[1].

> Yours in as humble sort as your own,
>
> PHILIP SIDNEY."

It is not strange to find the youthful incumbent of Whitford
assuming the legitimacy of using high influence to secure a
benefice, and enthusiastic devotion to his friends was not more
characteristic of Philip Sidney as a boy than as a man. Toby
Matthew was the handsome youth whom, a few years earlier,
Philip had heard bid the Queen an eloquent farewell when she
left Christ Church, and who, a few months before the date of
Philip's letter, had been unanimously elected Public Orator of
the University at the age of twenty-three. Philip's intercession
on the present occasion was successful, and Thornton succeeded
to Thomas Day's stall[2], but in some unexplained way the

[1] Old Style. *Lansdowne MSS.*, vol. XII, fol. 111.

[2] Anthony à Wood is obviously wrong when he says that Thomas Thornton
succeeded Thomas Day as canon in 1567 (*Athenæ*, III, 922). For a contemporary scandalous ballad regarding the relations of this Thomas Day (who
had been canon of Christ Church since 1546) with the profligate wife of
Dr Cooper, the dean of Christ Church, see *Athenæ*, I, 610.

friends of Toby Matthew also had their desire when a few months later in the same year he too became a canon of Christ Church.

It is a difficult matter to gain a very clear idea of the kind of training which an undergraduate received at Oxford in the second half of the sixteenth century. A decade before the death of Henry VIII the fine enthusiasm which had marked the earlier years of the century had begun to decline, and during the troubled mid-century period learning in the Universities reached a low ebb. Nor was there any but very gradual improvement during the reign of Elizabeth. The number of students, indeed, had increased from about 1000 during the reign of Mary to between 1700 and 1800 at the time when Philip Sidney was an undergraduate ; by the end of the century there were probably about 2500[1]. The unsettled political conditions of the age and the engrossing interest in controversial theology were unfavourable to learning, and yet it is probable that the usual condemnation of the Universities at this time is too sweeping. It was a great transition period with regard to ideals of education. The old scholastic ideal was discredited, but in the home of lost causes it still stubbornly strove to hold its ground against the rising tide of humanistic and practical ideals. It is hardly possible to agree with Mr Pollard that the laments over the decay of University education at this time " refer only to scholastic learning which had been the speciality of a professional class[2]." What men like Roger Ascham lamented was rather a falling-off from the days when Smith and Cheke had made Cambridge famous throughout Europe for her Greek scholarship, or from the earlier days of the great Humanistic movement at Oxford. Ascham, though in this case he must be considered a special pleader, was able to rejoice in the " many goodly plants " which were once more springing up in the academic grove of Cambridge, and there were not wanting other contemporary panegyrists of the Universities. We have already noted Fitzherbert's rather dithyrambic account of the excellence of the discipline and of

---

[1] Huber, *Die Englische Universitäten*, trans. Newman, vol. i, p. 311.
[2] *The Political History of England*, 1547–1603, p. 322.

the zeal for learning.   Harrison[1] also emphasizes the strict discipline, the effectiveness of the colleges in training their own students, and the excellence of the instruction in the faculties of law and medicine, though he condemns strongly the favouritism which made it difficult for a poor man's son to hold a fellowship, and the appointment of those who by their conduct brought reproach upon the University.   On the other hand, Anthony à Wood is very harsh in his estimate.   The academic heads, he finds, concerned chiefly in political intrigues, the tutors slothful, the students given over to luxury and loose living and indifferent to study.   Wood's fervour of condemnation hardly suggests a judicial judgment, and one cannot but feel that it needs modification if, turning aside from the opinions of individual writers, he considers the character of the men who passed through the academic halls.   We shall look more closely into Philip's contemporaries at Oxford a little later, but we may here hazard the opinion that the ancient University has rarely counted within her walls at one time a group of men more distinguished in their after lives for scholarship, literary gifts, native ability and high character. To be sure none of these qualities may have been the direct product of the University in any given case, but it is difficult to believe that the society was hopelessly degenerate, from which went forth scholars like Sir Henry Savile, Camden and Hooker, or the band of devotees with Campion at their head, who were to become the Catholic martyrs.   Laurence Humphrey, the President of Magdalen, who was Regius Professor of Greek and Divinity, was a man no less eminent for scholarship than for high character ; even Wood admits this generously while condemning Humphrey's strong Puritanical tendencies.   Or again, if we consider the remarkable output of academic plays, chiefly in Latin, it is difficult to believe in the stagnation of all intellectual interests in the University.

"We do it" (i.e. give these plays), says William Gager, one of the dramatists, "to recreate ourselves, our house, and the better part of the University, with some learned Poem or other ; to practise our own style

---

[1] *The Description of England* (Holinshed's *Chronicles*, vol. I, pp. 251–2, ed. 1807).

either in prose or verse ; to be well acquainted with Seneca or Plautus...
to try their voices and confirm their memories, to frame their speech ;
to conform them to convenient action, to try what metal is in every one
and of what disposition they are[1]."

However defective the instruction, and however far from high
scholarly ideals the spirit of the University may have been,
there can be little doubt that it offered to the serious-minded
undergraduate much that was calculated to develop his
faculties and to quicken his interest in the things of the spirit.

As we have already said, it was a transition period in which
the old Trivium and Quadrivium were slowly yielding place
to more modern conceptions of education.

"For the other lectures," says Harrison, "as of philosophy, logic,
rhetoric and the quadrivials, although the latter (I mean arithmetic,
music, geometry and astronomy, and with them all skill in the perspectives)
are now smally regarded in either of them, the Universities themselves
do allow competent stipends to such as read the same[2]."

It was on Grammar, Rhetoric and Logic that the chief
emphasis was placed. Grammar had already ceased to be a
subject of instruction at Cambridge, where it was considered
a preparatory school subject, but at Oxford it still held an
important place in the curriculum of the first year. Indeed
the degree of " Bachelor of Grammar " was still given—a kind
of license to teach in secondary schools. Under " Grammar "
was comprised the chief part of the formally linguistic training
—the study of Latin authors, for Greek had sunk to a low place
and lectures in this subject were given only very irregularly.
Under " Rhetoric " was included not only what we understand
by formal Rhetoric, but also the literary and historical study
of classical authors, and the effective use of Latin in the
" disputations " or public debates. Logic consisted wholly in
the study of Aristotle, in Latin translations ; the system of
Ramus, which had gained a foothold at Cambridge, and in
which Philip Sidney was in later years to become especially
interested, was not tolerated at Oxford. After finishing
the work in these three subjects the student proceeded to
Mathematics (including Music), Philosophy, moral and natural,

[1] *Cambridge History of English Literature*, vol. VI, p. 303.   [2] *Op. cit.*, p. 252.

and Metaphysics. In Grammar and in Rhetoric the University provided two lecturers, and three in each of the other subjects —Logic, Arithmetic, Music, Geometry, Astronomy, Natural Philosophy, Moral Philosophy, and Metaphysics. The subjects of the " quadrivium," however, as we have already seen, were held in low esteem. The lecturers in Music for instance were frequently dispensed from giving the course, on the ground that no students presented themselves for instruction. Besides the lecturers just mentioned there were University professors of Greek and Hebrew[1].

Already, however, the instruction offered by the University was coming to assume a distinctly secondary place as compared to the work of the college tutors and lecturers. The colleges had also gained the right to elect the proctors, and accordingly both the discipline and the work of instruction were no longer primarily vested in the University proper, which concerned itself chiefly, through Congregation, with examining candidates for degrees. Not that formal examinations in our sense of the word were held : that system had been introduced at Cambridge, but for many years yet Oxford continued to exact no other test than that of " disputations."

Disputations served the purpose not only of examinations, but of training in Latin expression and in addressing an audience as well. Accordingly, all undergraduates from the time of their entering the University were required to " frequent the schools," that is to constitute the audience before whom the disputations took place. They were held on each Monday, Wednesday and Friday of the term, and on each occasion three students took part—one as a " respondent " and two as " opponents." Each candidate for the B.A. was required to " oppose " once before being " generalis creatus " (about the end of his third year), and to be " generalis creatus " in each of the four terms before his graduation. These disputations were very formal exercises. The disputants were conducted from St Mary's by the yeoman bedell of Arts to the Schools where four regent masters or lecturers known as

---

[1] Much of my material regarding the curriculum I have derived from the *Register of the University of Oxford*, vol. II, ed. A. Clark (Ox. Hist. Soc.).

" Moderators " presided. The subjects of debate were often fantastic enough, e.g. :

" Gloria beatorum erit inæqualis.

An virtus principis plus possit in curanda struma quam medicina.

An ob mundi senectam homines sint minus heroici nunc quam olim."

Although the undergraduate's only duty with regard to University disputations during the first two or three years of his course was that of attendance, he was required to take an active part from the first in the college disputations, which were much more searching and which constituted the " term examinations " of the course. It was on one of these occasions at Christ Church some time during 1569 that we hear of Philip Sidney's taking part.

"Being a scholar in Oxford," says Richard Carew, "of fourteen years age and three years standing, upon a wrong conceived opinion touching my sufficiency, I was there called to dispute extempore (*impar congressus Achilli*) with the matchless Sir Philip Sidney in presence of the Earls Leicester, Warwick and divers other great personages."

His biographer adds :

" Si quæritis hujus
Fortunam pugnæ, non est superatus ab illo[1]."

Of Philip's tutors at Oxford the first was Thomas Thornton, in whose behalf we have already seen him so zealous. Thornton was at this time a young man about twenty-eight years of age. He afterwards became Vice-Chancellor of the University, and in later life Master of Ledbury Hospital in Herefordshire, where he died and was buried in 1629. The inscription on the monument over his tomb bears witness to the purity of his Latinity and also " that he was a common refuge for young poor scholars of great hopes and parts, and tutor to Sir Philip Sidney when he was of Christ Church[2]." The fact that he took Camden,

[1] Carew's *Survey of Cornwall*, Book II, p. 103 (London, 1723).

[2] Wood's *Fasti*, Part I, col. 225. Thornton was a contributor to the *Exequiæ Illustrissimi Equitis D. Philippi Sidnaei*, etc., the memorial volume published by the University of Oxford in 1587. Some of his verses rise above mere frigid eulogy and almost amount to real characterization, e.g. :

" In plus quam Martis, pacis alumnus eras.
Relligio, pietas, doctrina, modestia, candor,
Consilium prudens, non temerata fides,
Hae te virtutes ornarunt: haec tua vera
Gloria: non durus, non truculentus eras."

then a poor scholar, from Broadgates Hall and transferred him
to Christ Church, where he kept his *protégé* at his own expense
and in his own lodgings, would seem to justify one part of the
eulogy. Whether Thornton's appointment was in any way
responsible for his ceasing to be Philip's tutor does not appear,
but, at any rate, less than one week after the date of Philip's
letter to Burghley we hear that he has a new tutor. Incidentally too, we learn that his health was not good. On March
3, 1570, the Earl of Leicester wrote to Parker, Archbishop
of Canterbury, praying " for license to be granted to my boy
Philip Sidney, who is somewhat subject to sickness, for eating
flesh this Lent." He asks that the said license be granted unto
him " in whatsoever form may seem best unto you so as he
may have with him Mr Doctor Cooper, who is his tutor[1]."
Doctor Thomas Cooper had been Dean of Christ Church since
1566, and Vice-Chancellor of the University from 1567 to 1570,
when he became Bishop of Lincoln. He was already famous
for the Dictionary which bore his name[2], and he afterwards
engaged in the Martin Marprelate controversy when as Bishop
of Winchester he published *An Admonition to the People of
England*, 1589. He died at Winchester in 1594. He was held
in universal respect both for " his learning and sanctity of
life[3]." He was probably the most distinguished man of his
day at Oxford, not even excepting Laurence Humphrey, the
Regius Professor of Greek, who succeeded him as Vice-
Chancellor.

Philip's third tutor was Nathaniel Baxter, who was to
become known as a minor poet and vigorous Puritan contro-
versialist. After holding an appointment in Ireland for some
years he became vicar of Troy in Monmouthshire, where he
composed his remarkable " philosophic " poem—*Sir Philip
Sidney's Ourania*[4], which he dedicated to Philip's sister, the
Countess of Pembroke, and which contains metrical epistles
to various ladies of the Sidney and Dudley families. As late

[1] Zouch, *Memoirs*, p. 29, where the letter is quoted *in extenso* from a MS.
in the library of Bene't College, Cambridge.
[2] *Thesaurus Linguæ Romanæ et Britannicæ*, etc., London, 1565.
[3] Wood's *Athenæ*, I, 608.
[4] Printed at London, 4to, 1606.

as 1635 Baxter was engaged in theological controversy with a Mr John Downes. In the *Ourania* the shade of Sir Philip approaches and inquires of Baxter who he is :

> "I was reader (quoth he) in former days
> Unto great Astrophill, but now am one,
> Stripped, and naked, destitute, alone.
> Naught but my Greekish pipe and staff have I
> To keep my Lambs and me in misery.
>
> Art thou (quoth he) my tutor Tergaster ?
> He answered, yea : such was my happy chance.
> I grieve (quoth Astrophill) at thy disaster ;
> But fate denies me learning to advance.
> Yet Cynthia shall afford thee maintenance.
> My dearest sister, keep my Tutor well,
> For in his element he doth excel."

" My tutor Tergaster," it has been pointed out, was evidently Philip's playful name for Back-ster or Baxter. " Cynthia " is Philip's sister Mary, the Countess of Pembroke[1].

What was the effect of Philip Sidney's training and what was his own estimate of it ? These are questions which we can answer only approximately. The Puritanic spirit was strong in the University at the time—a fact that is illustrated in men like Philip's tutors or in Laurence Humphrey, and we may assume that this made a lasting impression upon him. That he was a hard student we have the testimony, if it were needed, of his father, of two of his tutors, and of Fulke Greville. At least we have no reason to believe that he considered the Oxford fields mere barren pastures ; when we remember the character of some of his instructors and of his friends we would rather conclude that the University was in a real sense

---

[1] Mr Fox-Bourne, following Zouch, assumes that Robert Dorset was also a tutor of Philip. Dorset was a canon of Christ Church, who afterward became rector of Ewelme in Oxfordshire, a doctor of divinity, and dean of Chester. He died at Ewelme on May 29, 1580. Zouch evidently assumes that he was Philip's tutor on the strength of a letter written by Dorset to Philip in June, 1576. At this time Dorset was acting as tutor to Robert Sidney, and in writing to urge Philip to be his guest at Ewelme, Dorset refers to the warm interest which he had taken in Philip when the latter was a student at Oxford. But he does not say that he had been Philip's tutor. See Appendix to Zouch's *Memoirs*.

responsible for the genuine scholarship, the eager thirst for learning and for deeds of high emprise which distinguished his short life. Dr Humphrey in a Latin poem written after Philip's death makes him apostrophize his Alma Mater thus:

"Oxoniæ matri quid dicam? quidve rependam,
Quæ puri lactis flumina larga dedit[1]?"

Perhaps had he been speaking *in propria persona* Philip would have used more qualified language. Writing to his brother Robert ten years later, he recommends the study of Tacitus, Livy and Plutarch, emphasizes the value of Arithmetic and Geometry, belittles that of Astronomy, and regrets his own lack of Music. "So you can speak and write Latin, not barbarously," he adds, "I never require great study in Ciceronianism, the chief abuse of Oxford, *qui dum verba sectantur res ipsas negligunt[2].*" This sounds like an impatient reminiscence of disputations. In attempting to advise his brother he lays chief stress on more practical studies—of the topography, fortifications, manners, laws, commerce and polity of the countries of Europe. These were the things which seemed to him of first importance, and doubtless Oxford seemed to him too much occupied with splitting words. He was inclined in later days, too, to regret his small Greek—his being compelled to read Aristotle and Plutarch in translation. But we must not forget that a tendency, which was to be much stronger at the end of the century, had already set in, in favour of emphasizing the practical use of studies. This tendency may be recognized in the ideals of Sir Thomas Gresham in founding Gresham College, or in those which Sir Humphrey Gilbert propounded in his *Queen Elizabeth's Academy*, 1570. In 1560 Dr Humphrey himself, in a work on the education of nobles, had emphasized the importance of a knowledge of antiquities and the statutes of our realm, of geography and of religion. Indeed most books of the period which deal either directly or indirectly with education are witnesses to the silent change that was slowly proceeding, and the growing practice on the

---

[1] *Exequiæ*, opening poem.
[2] Pears, *The Correspondence of Sir Philip Sidney and Hubert Languet*, p. 201.

part of young men of noble birth to leave the University before graduating was only another indication of it.

Some such consideration may have decided Philip Sidney against completing his formal course. The period of undergraduate study was fixed at sixteen terms, that is four years, but an express exception was made for the sons of the nobility, and as the son of a knight, Philip might have taken his degree in three years. He might have done it in even less time, for " dispensations," which made this possible, were common enough, and were granted for a great variety of reasons. Possibly the pestilence, which in April, 1571, caused the suspension of University activity in Oxford, and which was so virulent that almost a year elapsed before the University resumed its work in the city, may have been responsible for his departure. We do not know, however, just when his connection with the University ceased.

There has been a persistent tradition that Philip was at one time a student at Cambridge. Fulke Greville passes over the story of their University days in silence, remarking only that Philip's " teachers found something in him to observe and learn above that which they had usually read or taught." The anonymous editor of Sidney's works who styles himself Philophilippos, assumes that he did not study at Cambridge, and Collins makes the same assumption. Of later writers the more uncritical, like Zouch, accept the tradition ; the more cautious, like Mr Fox-Bourne, Mr J. A. Symonds and Mr Flügel, reject it[1].

There is contemporary evidence, however, that leaves no reasonable doubt on the question. Among the great number of laudatory poems which were called forth by the death of Sidney in 1586, was one by George Whetstone, which appeared in 1587. Whetstone was present at Zutphen when Sidney fell, and he apologizes for the months that elapsed between the

---

[1] Hunter assumes that Philip studied at Cambridge but without any examination of the evidence. (*Chorus Vatum*, Bk. IV, p. 34.) Of the Cambridge historians Joseph Wilson is the only one to claim Philip, whom he declares to have been a student of Christ's College. (*Memorabilia Cantabrigiæ*, 1803.) James Smith, in *Wilton and its Associations*, says that Philip " was afterwards transferred to Cambridge."

time of that event and the publication of his biographical poem by declaring his desire " to be heedful that I publish nothing but truth of so true a Knight." In a gloss regarding Sidney's learning he says : " He was in his time and for his continuance reputed the best scholar in Cambridge[1]." Such evidence is not lightly to be set aside, but we have even more unimpeachable testimony to the fact that Philip spent some time at Cambridge in a more or less formal relation to the University. In the memorial volume published by the University of Oxford, the first poem is by Laurence Humphrey, the Vice-Chancellor, and is entitled " Ad Utramque Academiam Philippi Sidnaei Umbra." In it occur the following lines :

> " Cantabriæ grates ex toto pectore fundo.
> Hospes eram, gratum præbuit hospitium.
> . . . .
> Oxoniæ matri quid dicam ? quidve rependam,
> Quæ puri lactis flumina larga dedit ? "

These lines can only be interpreted as meaning that Philip studied at both Universities, though his sojourn at Cambridge was relatively unimportant. It is surely not permissible to interpret them as referring to some occasion when Philip was the " guest " of Cambridge and to the kindly welcome which she extended to him at that time. Such a reading would convict the Vice-Chancellor of incoherence in his composition.

The fact that within four months of Sidney's death (and several months before the appearance of either of the Oxford volumes) Cambridge had produced a memorial volume of many poems is not lacking in significance. It was published by Alexander Nevile, the scholarly secretary of Parker, Grindal and Whitgift, and an esteemed friend of Philip. The introductory poem of the volume is " Ad Academiam carmen consolatorium Al. Nevilli " :

> " Dic mater sobolis doctæ, laniata capellos
> Manibus ah, quorsum libas lamenta sepultis ?
> Nec risu gaudent superi, nec fletibus umbræ.
> Occidit heu nostræ lux, spes et gloria gentis,

---

[1] " *Sir Philip Sidney, his honourable life, his valiant death and true virtues etc. by G. W. Gent.*" London, Thomas Cadman [1586-7].

Unica lux aulæ, spes pacis, gloria belli.
Sidneius Tumulo clausus jacet hoc, jacet eheu[1]."

Of course it is possible that " the mother of the learned race "
is in such distress merely because a great and good man is
dead.   It is even more possible that " aulae " refers to the
court rather than to a college hall.   The natural interpretation,
however, would seem to be that Cambridge is bewailing the
loss of a son.

When Philip left Oxford we do not know.   Perhaps the
superior reputation of Cambridge as an institution of learning
attracted him ; perhaps the outbreak of the plague was the
occasion of his leaving.   The language of Humphrey's poem
suggests a comparatively short stay, and the phrase " for his
continuance," used by Whetstone, may possibly refer to the
same fact.   That he became acquainted there with Spenser and
Gabriel Harvey, is at least highly probable.   Spenser, on leaving Cambridge, spent some time with his relations in the north
of England, yet it was within a few months of his graduation
that he seems to have been employed in Ireland either under
Sir Henry Sidney or in an embassy to him[2].   This fact, and
his establishment a little later at Leicester House become
easily explicable if we may assume that his friendship with
Philip dated from their Cambridge days.

At Oxford Philip made the acquaintance of many of the
men with whom he was to be thrown into intimate contact
during the rest of his life.   Fulke Greville, his Shrewsbury
friend, was at Broadgates Hall, just across the street from
Christ Church.   There was a close relationship between the
wealthiest of the colleges and the most flourishing of the Halls;
many students were entered as of either the one or the other,
and many Broadgates students went over to Christ Church.
In the Hall Philip made several friends who were to become
famous.   Among these was William Camden (1551–1623), who

---

[1] *Academiæ Cantabrigiensis Lachrymæ Tumulo Nobilissimi Equitis D.
Philippi Sidneii Sacratæ* (London, 1587).   Nevile was cousin of Barnabe
Googe.

[2] In *A view of the present state of Ireland*, Irenæus (Spenser) speaks of his
having been present " at the execution of a notable traitor at Limerick called
Murrogh O'Brein."   This event took place in July, 1577.

as the greatest antiquary of his time acknowledged his deep obligations to Philip, both during their Oxford days and later. He had entered Magdalen as a sizar in 1566, but on the invitation of Mr Thornton had removed first to Broadgates and eventually to Christ Church, where Mr Thornton maintained him. Richard Carew (1555–1620) and his kinsman George Carew, both students of Broadgates, also encouraged the antiquarian bent of Camden. Richard we have already seen pitted against Philip in disputations : he is remembered chiefly for his *Survey of Cornwall*, but he also assisted Camden in writing his *Britannia*, and had a high reputation for scholarship. George Carew (1554–1629) also was known for his learning. In 1575 we find him serving under Sir Henry Sidney in Ireland, where he spent much of the next twenty-five years of his life. Charles I created him Earl of Totnes. His elder brother Peter, whose Latin oration had delighted Elizabeth in 1566, and who took his B.A. from Exeter in 1572, also went to Ireland, where after achieving knighthood, he died in battle on November 27, 1575. Another Broadgates man whom Philip perhaps did not meet was George Peele (1558?–1597?), the dramatist, who entered the Hall in March, 1571, and who, some three years later went over to Christ Church[1].

In his own college Philip's most famous contemporary was Richard Hakluyt (1553?–1616), who was admitted a student of Christ Church in 1570. In later life he and Philip were drawn together by their common interest in scholarship and " plantation," and in 1582 Hakluyt dedicated to Philip his first book, the *Divers Voyages*. Walter Raleigh entered Oriel College probably in 1567, and seems to have remained at the University at least two years. Fuller says that he was also of Christ Church, and there can be little doubt that his

---

[1] Most of Sidney's biographers, including Fox-Bourne, make the mistake of assuming that his friendship with Dyer dated from this time. But Dyer, who was probably ten years older than Philip, had left the University without a degree, had travelled on the Continent and was at Court by 1566. In 1573, Gilbert Talbot speaks of him as having been in Elizabeth's displeasure "these eleven years." In 1574, he was one of the most intimate of the friends of Sir Henry and Lady Mary Sidney at the Court. (*V*. letter from Lady Mary to Molyneux dated September 1, 1574, in Collins, *Letters*, etc., I, 67.)

acquaintance with Philip dated from this period. In after years
we find them thrown into occasional contact by the fact that
both were interested in schemes of colonization and discovery
in America, but we know little of their actual relations to each
other[1]. The most learned Englishman of the period was Henry
Savile (1549–1622), for whom Philip had the highest regard,
and with whom he afterwards corresponded familiarly[2]. He
became fellow of Merton in 1565, took his B.A. in 1566 and
his M.A. in 1570, and was afterwards to become Warden of
Merton and Provost of Eton. One of his closest friends both
now and throughout his life was Thomas Bodley, who had also
been a fellow of Merton since 1564. He took his M.A. in 1566
and in 1569 was elected junior proctor of the University. Like
Raleigh he claimed Exeter as his birthplace, and both he and
Savile had begun their life-long friendship with another Exeter
youth, who at this time was " still increasing in learning and
prudence...in humility and piety," Richard Hooker (1553?–
1600). Hooker entered Corpus Christi in 1567 ; in 1573 he
became a scholar of the foundation. There is no record of
Philip's personal relation to either Bodley or Hooker, but that
he knew them can hardly be doubted when we remember the
warm friendship that subsisted between them and Savile. We
are likewise ignorant of his relations to Fulke Greville's kinsman, John Lyly, who entered Magdalen College about 1569.
The fact that Lyly, soon after leaving the University, became
a *protégé* of the Earl of Oxford would lead us to infer that he
and Sidney were never on terms of intimacy, and indeed their
characters were so diverse that it is hardly credible they should
ever have been much attracted to each other.

Two others of Philip's contemporaries at Oxford demand a
word of notice—Edmund Campion (1540–1581) and Robert
Parsons (1546–1610). It is probable that his acquaintance with

---

[1] Raleigh wrote an epitaph on Sir Philip. (*V.* Collier's *Poetical Decameron,*
II. 143.) In *Sidneiana* (Roxburghe Club) is a letter from J. P. Collier in which
he seeks to prove that Raleigh was the author of the epitaph on "Sir Philip
Sidney, Knight, Lord Governor of Flushing," which was published in 1595 at
the end of Spenser's *Colin Clout*, and which finds a place in most modern
editions of Spenser.

[2] See letter from Philip to his brother Robert in Pears, *ut supra.*

Campion dated from 1566, when the young orator's eloquence called forth the enthusiastic praise and good will of both Elizabeth and Leicester. Since then Leicester and Sir Henry Sidney had patronized him ; he was now fellow of St John's College, and in 1568 was elected junior proctor. Parsons was a fellow of Balliol, and he too was an admirer of Sir Henry, whom he considered " a very honourable, calm and civil gentleman, nothing hot in the new religion, but rather a great friend to Catholics." Campion's theological disputes with Mr Thornton and Toby Matthew had already brought him under suspicion, and in 1570 he left the University and went to Dublin, where for nearly a year he was safe under the protection of Sir Henry Sidney and of James Stanihurst, the Speaker of the Irish House of Commons, and where he busied himself in writing his *History of Ireland*, and in entering warmly into Sir Henry's schemes for an Irish University. It was soon obvious, however, that he could not be safe in Ireland. One of Sir Henry's last acts before leaving the country in March, 1571, was to save Campion from arrest by sending him a private warning, and not long afterward the young enthusiast was on the Continent, where a few years later, as we shall see, he was once more to meet Philip Sidney.

It would be easily possible still further to expand the list of those who were Philip's contemporaries at Oxford, and who afterward achieved a certain degree of fame. For instance, there was Arthur Atey of Merton College, who took his M.A. in 1564 and became senior proctor in 1570. Two years later he succeeded Toby Matthew as Public Orator of the University, which position he held for ten years. Philip Sidney and Thomas Bodley were among his intimate friends, and for many years he was the secretary of the Earl of Leicester. Philip must also have known Richard Stanihurst, the son of the Irish Speaker, and a pupil of Campion. He was of University College and took his B.A. in 1568. He afterwards contributed a description of Ireland to Holinshed's *Chronicles*, but was best known for his remarkable translation of the first four books of the *Aeneid* in what Nash called " a foul, lumbering, boisterous, wallowing measure."

One cannot read this list of names without being struck by the number of famous men whose acquaintance Philip made at Oxford during his undergraduate days, and by the fact that they were almost without exception famous, at least in part, for their scholarship. If we remember that a University education consists of something more than the hearing of lectures we shall see how absurd is the assumption that Philip Sidney's Oxford years were barren of results. We shall assuredly be much nearer the truth if we assume that they were years spent in a stimulating, intellectual atmosphere, and that they were responsible in no small measure for the absorbing interest in history and literature which distinguished Philip's later life. During the three years of foreign travel which succeeded his University days his devotion to study, instead of yielding to the novel interest of seeing new men and cities, increased from year to year, as did also his desire to translate the knowledge which he had gained into worthy action. It is not to be thought of that such tastes and ideals had developed independently of the influence exerted by several years of familiar intercourse with men like Savile and Raleigh, Bodley and Spenser.

CHAPTER VII

SAINT BARTHOLOMEW

THE departure of Sir Henry Sidney from Ireland in the spring
of 1571 was the signal for a re-establishment of the anarchy
from which his firmness and untiring devotion had partially
redeemed the country. His brother-in-law, the Treasurer,
Sir William FitzWilliam, was left in command, but he was
given even less assistance from England than had been doled
out to his predecessor. Not a strong administrator under
any conditions, FitzWilliam could only write home fiercely
that he would not be responsible for holding the country
should any serious attack be made upon it, and he was helpless
as he saw his garrisons diminish, his soldiers grow mutinous
and the native chiefs flout whatever semblance of English
authority remained. Sir John Perrott, a capable soldier, was
sent over as President of Munster. For about a year, until
the supply of money which he had brought with him was
exhausted, he did terrible execution among the rebellious
natives ; then he too was left to his fate, and we have the old
story of mutinous soldiers reduced by necessity to live like
bands of brigands. Once more the fatuous lack of continuity
in the English policy in Ireland was illustrated by Elizabeth's
determination to try conciliation again in Munster. The Earl
of Desmond, who had been kept a prisoner in London for some
years, was allowed to return to Ireland, and the policy of
planting English colonies was renewed when a son of Sir Thomas
Smith was given a grant of lands near Knockfergus. This
latter enterprise soon added another to the list of English
failures in Ireland, but, not yet convinced of the impossibility

of success in this direction, Elizabeth determined on one more similar effort in Ulster on a grand scale under the Earl of Essex.

Meanwhile, Sir Henry Sidney, broken in health, was living in the less troubled atmosphere of London and his Welsh Presidency. In May, 1571, he sat on several parliamentary committees and in August one of his servants writing to him from Dublin, has heard that he has gone to Flanders to the Spae for the sake of his health[1]. In December, FitzWilliam heard a report that Sir Henry would return to Ireland as Lord Deputy, but the memory of his Irish experiences was still too fresh to permit of his again accepting the hopeless task. Throughout the year, however, he was constantly consulted by the Council on Irish matters, and in May, 1572, he again sat on a parliamentary committee " to consult and deliberate upon matters concerning the Queen of Scots." They were days of great national peril, and the northern rebellion and the Ridolphi conspiracy had been only the most conspicuous examples of the dangers which centred in Mary Stuart. Still Elizabeth refused to agree to her execution, even when a deputation from both houses of Parliament strongly urged her to this course. Norfolk, however, was executed on June 2nd and Northumberland on August 22nd, and the hopes of the Marian party were further dashed by the final consummation of the much-discussed treaty with France, by the terms of which each country bound itself to assist the other in case of invasion for any cause whatsoever. Once more England had succeeded in playing off one of the great continental powers against the other, and to gain so great a point Elizabeth was quite willing to discuss a project of marriage between herself and the French King's young brother, the Duc d'Alençon, who was nineteen years her junior, and who was now substituted for the older brother, Anjou.

It is difficult to understand the slight appreciation which Elizabeth showed of the work of those who did her the best service in these days of national stress. That Sir Henry Sidney should be given some signal reward for what he had

---

[1] *Salisbury MSS.*, August, 1571.

W. L. S.

accomplished in Ireland was generally assumed: Elizabeth offered him a peerage unaccompanied by any grant of land or money to support the greater dignity. The dismay which this offer caused Sir Henry and Lady Sidney is reflected in a letter written by the latter to Burghley. She refers to Sir Henry's " hard choice "

"as either to be a Baron, now called in the number of many far more able than himself to maintain it withal, either else in refusing it to incur her Highness' displeasure. . . . Titles of greater calling cannot be well wielded but with some amendment at the Prince's hand of a ruinated state or else to his discredit greatly that must take them upon him."

She acknowledges Burghley's goodness in trying to serve them, and, "a poor perplexed woman," she begs him "to stay the motion of this new title to be any further offered him[1]." Her request was probably granted, for Sir Henry received neither peerage nor money reward either at this time or later. For the next three years he was occupied almost exclusively in Wales, while Lady Sidney spent the greater part of the time in attendance on her majesty at Court.

Sir Henry and the Earl of Leicester had decided that Philip's education was to be continued by foreign travel, and throughout the month of May, 1572, his father and mother were busy making preparations for his departure. On May 25th the Queen granted her license

"to her trusty and well-beloved Philip Sidney, Esq., to go out of England into parts beyond the seas, with three servants and four horses, etc., to remain the space of two years immediately following his departure out of the realm, for his attaining the knowledge of foreign languages[2]."

The plan was that he should proceed to Paris where Sir Francis Walsingham, an old friend of his father, was resident ambassador, and that he should remain there several months. Toward autumn, if the times seemed propitious, he would proceed to Germany and from there to Austria and Italy.

Philip was now in his eighteenth year, a handsome, studious, eager-hearted boy, yearning for the large excitement that the coming years would yield. He could hardly have set out upon

[1] *State Papers—Ireland—Eliz.*, May 2, 1572.
[2] Collins' *Memoirs*, vol. I, p. 98. Quoted from the Penshurst original.

his travels under more favourable auspices. He had already made many friends and won some fame as a student, and he was now leaving England solely for the purpose of adding to his acquirements and of fitting himself to translate them into some form of service for his Queen and country. Both Burghley and Leicester commanded him to correspond with them during his stay on the Continent. His father supplied him most generously with money and provided for his being supplied regularly by means of a letter of credit drawn by the Italian banker and merchant, Acerbo Vellutelli, who resided in England. Indeed the expense of his travels must have been a serious drain on Sir Henry's resources. A Penshurst manuscript of date August 20, 1575, which is entitled " A brief note of sundry payments for Mr. Philip Sidney," enumerates sums amounting to £1576. 9s. 8d. during the preceding three years, and this account is obviously incomplete[1]. A letter in which the Earl of Leicester commended his nephew to Walsingham gives us an interesting glimpse of the young man besides showing us the Earl's almost paternal interest in him :

"Mr Walsingham : Forasmuch as my nephew, Philip Sidney, is licensed to travel, and doth presently repair to those parts with my Lord Admiral, I have thought good to commend him by these my letters friendly unto you as to one I am well assured will have a special care of him during his abode there. He is young and raw, and no doubt shall find those countries and the demeanours of the people somewhat strange unto him ; and therefore your good advice and counsel shall greatly behove him for his better direction, which I do most heartily pray you to vouchsafe him, with any friendly assurance you shall think needful for him. His father and I do intend his further travel if the world be quiet and you shall think it convenient for him ; otherwise we pray you we may be advertised thereof to the end the same his travel may be thereupon directed accordingly[2]."

Philip was to find the world strangely unquiet before he left France, and his experience of English religious troubles, of which the execution of the premier peer of the realm on the

---

[1] Other Penshurst MSS. are a receipt for £400 given by Philip Sidney to an agent of Vellutelli on November 6, 1573, and a similar receipt for £80 on February 2, 1576. There is also a receipt dated June 28, 1574, for £135 paid by Sir Henry to Vellutelli.

[2] *Add. MSS.* 34591, fol. 503. Leicester to Walsingham, May 26, 1572.

eve of his setting forth must have been a forcible reminder, was to pale before the experiences awaiting him in Paris. He left England in the train of the Lord High Admiral Edward Fiennes de Clinton, who was a warm friend of Sir Henry Sidney, and who on May 4th had been created Earl of Lincoln at the same time that the Queen had proposed to raise Sir Henry to the peerage. Lincoln was sent to the Court of Charles IX to ratify the French treaty and also to further the negotiations regarding the marriage of the English Queen and the Duc d'Alençon. He was accompanied by

"Lords Talbot, Clinton, Dacre, Sand, Rich, Sir Edward Hastings, Sir Henry Borough, Giles Brydges, Sir Arthur Champernowne, Philip Sidney, Sir Jerome Bowes, Messrs Charles Arundel, Middlemore, Scudamore, Ralph Bowes, Luke Paston and Captain Shule,"

according to an undated manuscript preserved in the Salisbury collection[1]. The Earl of Lincoln was all the more interesting, we may assume, in the eyes of Philip Sidney because of the fact that he was the husband of the fair Geraldine, whose praises had been sung by the Earl of Surrey, and who some twenty years before the time of which we write had become the third wife of the Lord High Admiral. The embassy reached Paris on June 8th, and was honoured with a series of magnificent entertainments. The joy of the King and the Court over the new league with England was unbounded, and shortly after the arrival of the Englishmen the King and his two brothers Anjou and Alençon dined alone with Lincoln, Walsingham and Sir Thomas Smith[2]. The general entertainment consisted of comedies, music and grand dinners, and all went merry as a marriage bell. Indeed the approaching marriage of Margaret, the King's youngest sister, and Henry, the young King of Navarre, which had been arranged by the King almost at the same time that he signed the English treaty, was a pledge of the sincerity of the English alliance, for, taken together, they meant the subordination of Spanish and Catholic influences at the French Court. To be sure there

[1] Conjecturally assigned to the year 1557 !
[2] Sir Thos. Smith to Burghley, June 18, 1572 (Ellis, *Original Letters*, Series 2, vol. III, p. 12).

were rumours that Elizabeth did not intend to support the
French King loyally in the war which they had agreed to wage
in support of the rebellious Netherlanders, that Margaret of
Valois really loved Henry of Guise not Henry of Navarre, and
that Charles IX, weak and vacillating as always, would soon
fall again under the dominion of his mother, Catherine de'
Medici. But these were only rumours. Coligny was obviously
the one trusted adviser of the King, and he was most anxious
to bring about the marriage of Alençon and the English Queen.
Charles loaded the English ambassadors with magnificent
presents[1], and when the Earl of Lincoln took his departure the
King expressed to him the hope that his sister's would not
be the only marriage on which those who wished well to Europe
would have cause to congratulate themselves[2].

Sidney remained in Paris about three months and during
that time we catch only infrequent glimpses of him. It was
now that he began his devoted friendship for Walsingham
with whom, we may infer from Leicester's letter, he had not
previously been acquainted. With the members of the Court
circle his relations seem to have been unusually intimate.

"He was so admired," we are told, "among the graver sort of courtiers
that when they could at any time have him in their company and conversation they would be very joyful, and no less delighted with his ready and
witty answers than astonished to hear him speak the French language
so well and aptly having been so short a while in the country[3]."

The young King of Navarre honoured him with his friendship, for Fulke Greville tells us that Henry "having measured and
mastered all the spirits in his own nation found out this master-
spirit among us and used him like an equal in nature, and so
fit for friendship with a King[4]." But the most striking mark
of favour came from the King himself when on August 9th

---

[1] Michelet, *Histoire de France*, Tome II, p. 339.

[2] Froude, *History of England*, x, p. 105.

[3] Lodovic Bryskett : *A Discourse of Civill Life Containing the Ethike Part
of Morall Philosophie* (Lond., 1606), p. 160. Bryskett made this statement on
the occasion of the famous meeting at his "little cottage which I had newly
built near unto Dublin" when Spenser told the party that he was engaged on
his *Faerie Queene*.

[4] *Life* (Oxford, 1907), p. 31.

Charles created the young Englishman a Gentleman Ordinary
of the Bedchamber and Baron de Sidenay. The patent—
a badly stained parchment—is preserved at Penshurst, where
we may still read the reasons which moved the King to bestow
this singular honour—the greatness of the house of Sidney,
their nearness to the English sovereigns, and then the young
man's own virtues—" pour les bonnes et louables vertus qui
sont en luy," " pour ces causes et autres." In later years
Sidney's German friends sometimes addressed their letters to the
Baron de Sidenay, and this form of address was used on at
least one occasion by the Burgomaster and Council of Flushing
in referring to him[1] : further than this, however, his new title
does not seem to have been used.

To what extent Sidney became acquainted with the remarkable company of famous men who were congregated in Paris
during these months we do not know. Coligny, his son-in-law,
Teligny, and Condé, the Huguenot leaders, he would surely
meet. Among the famous scholars who were in the city at
the time were Languet, Du Plessis Mornay, the reputed author
of the *Vindiciae contra Tyrannos*, Hotman, author of the
Franco Gallia, and Ramus, the great mathematician and philosopher, whose attacks on the Aristotelian logic had made his
name famous throughout Europe, and who was to be numbered
among the victims of the massacre[2]. Sidney knew Ramus
intimately. " You not only entertained the tenderest love for
the writer [Ramus] when alive," wrote one of Sidney's friends
a few years later, " but now that he is dead, esteem and reverence him[3]." There can be little doubt that it was at this
time also that he first met Languet, his most intimate guide
and friend during the succeeding two and a half years which
he spent on the Continent. Languet had lived in Paris on

---

[1] *Holland Correspondence*, vol. XI, fol. 7.

[2] For an account of his death *v.* Michelet, *op. cit.*, Tome II, pp. 388–393.

[3] Theophilus Banosius in his dedication to Sidney of his *Petri Rami Com-
mentariorum de Religione Christiana Libri Quatuor...Francofurti Apud Andream
Wechelum*, 1577. Banosius was one of Sidney's enthusiastic admirers : " I
remember well when I first saw you," he continues, " when I first contemplated
with wonder your uncommon endowments of mind and body ; I remember
well, I say, the words of Gregory who declared the Angli or English who were
at Rome to be really Angels." Quoted in Zouch's *Memoirs*, pp. 316–317.

behalf of the Elector of Saxony for some nine years, and now his life was in great danger[1]. One of his most intimate friends in the French capital was Walsingham. In a letter to Languet some eighteen months after this time Sidney refers to " your friend Walsingham[2]," and Languet in reply refers to his admiration of the English ambassador and to the kindnesses which he has experienced at his hands. Still later Languet's letters contain references to his correspondence with Walsingham. These considerations make it highly probable that Sidney would meet Languet for they must both have been constantly at the English embassy. He may also have met Michel de l'Hôpital (1505–1573), the Chancellor of France, regarding whom he afterwards expressed the opinion that France had " never brought forth a more accomplished judgment more firmly builded upon virtue." In later years Du Plessis Mornay became one of his most intimate friends.

Sidney would enjoy the series of pageants and celebrations in honour of the approaching marriage—the first *mariage mixte* between Catholics and Huguenots, which, it was fondly hoped, was to usher in the days of universal peace in France. Paris, even when not *en fête*, was the gayest and most beautiful city in Europe, famous for its fashions and its restaurants, and the centre of French intellectual life. The scene in Notre Dame on August 18th, when Margaret of Valois became the wife of Henry of Navarre, was one of very unusual interest. During the ceremony Margaret's willingness to accept Henry as her husband was indicated only when her royal brother put his hand on the back of her head and forced her to bow. While mass was being said the bridegroom and Coligny withdrew from the church[3]. The marriage had taken place in spite of the Pope's failure to send a dispensation, and the event was regarded as the climax of the success which the Huguenots under Coligny's leadership had achieved. There were those who declared that Coligny was mad to remain in the city with only a small

---

[1] *V*. his own statement: *Huberti Langueti Epistolæ Ad Philippum Sydnœium*, ed. Lord Hailes, Edinb., 1776, p. 19.

[2] Pears, *The Correspondence of Sir Philip Sidney and Hubert Languet*, p. 36.

[3] Michelet, *op. cit.*, Tome II, p. 352.

body-guard, and who pointed out the daily increasing strength of the Guises : on the other hand Henry of Guise had shaken Coligny's hand a few days before in the presence of the King, and the Huguenot leader relied for safety on the honour of Charles IX.

The immediate causes of the great massacre are still a matter of dispute, and this is not the place to discuss them. There can be little doubt that Charles IX was sincere, so far as such a weakling can be sincere about anything, when he pledged his word to Coligny, whom he treated as his bosom friend. When on August 22nd the Admiral was shot by an assassin concealed in a house belonging to Guise, it is incredible that the King's anger and indignation were simulated. He hastened to the bedside of the wounded man and, after excluding his mother and Anjou, had an interview with him in private. He swore that he would take such vengeance on the would-be murderers that the day should be remembered. Two days later he had consented to the great massacre. A weakling morally and intellectually, he was as clay in the hands of Catherine de' Medici and her minions. They told him that the Huguenots were arming everywhere in the belief that the King had sanctioned the attempt on the Admiral's life, and they worked upon his imagination and his fears to the point of persuading him that his own life depended on a successful counterstroke by the gentlemen of the house of Guise. The considerations which had prompted the Queen mother to throw in her lot with the Guises, whom she loved as little as the Huguenots, are more difficult to unravel, but there is small doubt that chief among them was her perception of Queen Elizabeth's insincerity both in the matter of the marriage with Alençon and of prosecuting the war in the Low Countries. If the Huguenots were not to have the support of a cordial and active alliance with England, then, Catherine concluded, the Valois dynasty had better rely on the Catholics who could count on the support of Spain.

The massacre of Saint Bartholomew is one of the blackest pages in French history. The actual killing began in the early hours of Sunday, August 24th, and continued for nearly

a week.   The royal palace itself was drenched in blood when the
victims were chased from room to room and after being despatched were thrown from the windows to the court below.
So infectious was the spirit of killing that Charles IX himself
joined in the sport.   The heart turns sick at the mere recital
of the events of those days and nights of carnage.   Men,
women, children—none were spared.   The cry "Voilà un
Huguenot!" was a sufficient warrant to the mob.   The number killed within the city has been variously estimated from
1000 to 10,000 ; outside Paris at least 10,000 were massacred[1].
But mere numbers give little idea of the real significance of
the crime.   The Huguenots never recovered from the blow,
never again found a leader like the great Admiral.   Condé and
Navarre were forced to become Catholics, and their example
was imitated by thousands of their followers, in whose hearts
reigned fear and distrust.   The seeds of selfishness, of cruelty
and insincerity which are sown by a Saint Bartholomew
produce their evil harvests through the centuries.   Hence
the bitter reflection of the great French historian, " C'est, je
crois, de ce temps qu'en français *sans doute* a voulu dire
peut-être[2]."

The scenes of perfidy and horror which Sidney witnessed
from the house of Walsingham, where he seems to have been
in no great personal danger, made a deep and lasting impression on his mind.   There can be no doubt that his attitude
to the French as a nation and to Catholicism was radically
modified for all future time by his awful experience.   An echo
from these days is heard in the letter written some eight years
later in which Sidney attempts to persuade Elizabeth to
reject Alençon as a husband—

"a Frenchman and a Papist, in whom (howsoever fine wits may find
further dealings or painted excuses) the very common people well know
this, that he is the son of a Jezabel of our age, and that his brother made
oblation of his own sister's marriage the easier to make massacres of our
brethren in belief[3]."

1 Armstrong, *The French Wars of Religion*, p. 33.
2 Michelet, XII, p. 7.
3 Collins, vol. I, p. 288.

The horror which the news of the massacre inspired in England may easily be imagined, and the anxiety which must have tortured Sir Henry and Lady Sidney until they were assured of their son's safety, is suggested by a letter written by Sir Thomas Smith to Walsingham[1]. After referring to "these new treasons and cruelties more barbarous than ever the Scythians used," he proceeds :

"I am glad yet in these tumults that you did escape, and the young gentlemen that be there with you ; and that the King had so great pity and care of our nation, so lately with strait amity confederate unto him. ....How fearful and careful the mothers and parents that be here be of such young gentlemen as be there you may easily guess by my Lady Lane, who prayeth very earnestly that her son might be safely sent home with as much speed as may be."

Two days earlier (September 9th) the Council had already addressed to Walsingham the following letter[2] :

"Where we understand that the English gentlemen that were in Paris at the time of the execution of the murder, were forced to retire to your house, where they did wisely ; for your care of them we and their friends are beholding to you, and now we think good that they be advised to return home ; and namely we desire you to procure for the Lord Wharton and Mr Philip Sidney the King's license and safe-conduct to come thence, and so we do require you to give them true knowledge of our minds herein."

Whether we are to credit Charles IX with so great pity and care of our nation as Sir Thomas Smith ascribes to him, or whether we are to consider the report as one invented by the *politiques* of the time to allay popular feeling, we cannot now determine. As to the strength of the popular feeling in England there can be no question. " Sith these late and execrable murders of the true servants of God there," wrote Smith to Walsingham on December 11th[3], "the minds of the most number are much alienated from that nation, even of the very Papists, much more of the Protestants here," and the reception of the French ambassador by Elizabeth and her Council strained diplomatic relations between the two countries to the

---

[1] Ellis, *Original Letters*, Series 3, vol. III, p. 377.
[2] Digges' *Compleat Ambassador*, p. 250.
[3] Ellis, *op. cit.*, Series 3, vol. IV, p. 5.

breaking-point. Nevertheless politic considerations prevailed over sentimental. England could not afford to further an alliance between the two great Catholic powers of Europe ; Walsingham remained at Paris, Elizabeth continued to discuss the Alençon marriage, and when in October a daughter was born to the French Queen the Queen of England consented to be the godmother and sent the Earl of Worcester in state to represent her at the ceremony.

CHAPTER VIII

CONTINENTAL TRAVEL

BEFORE Walsingham received the letter from the English Council in which Sidney was ordered to return home, he had already sent his young charge forward into Germany. A favourable opportunity for doing so had presented itself in the fact that a party including Dr John Watson, the dean of Winchester, was travelling in that direction. On October 17th Walsingham wrote to Leicester:

"It may please your Lordship to understand that by certain that return from Frankfort I understand that one of the gentlemen that departed hence with intention to accompany your nephew Mr Philip Sidney to Heidelberg died by the way at a place called Bladin in Lorraine, who by diverse conjectures I took to be the Dean of Winchester, who, as I advertised your Lordship by Mr Argall, I employed to encounter the evil practices of your said nephew's servant. If, then, your Lordship, now he being void, may not speedily take order in that behalf, if already it be not done, the young gentleman your nephew shall be in danger of a very lewd practice, which were great pity in respect of the rare gifts that are in him[1]."

What the practices were to which Walsingham refers we have no means of determining, but at least he was mistaken in his conjecture that the dean of Winchester had died by the way[2]. Sidney reached Frankfort safely and took up his residence in the house of Andrew Wechel, the famous printer. Wechel was one of the best representatives of the scholar-printer in Europe, and in this respect was only carrying on the tradition

---

[1] *Harley MSS.*, vol. 260, p. 348 *b*.
[2] John Watson (1520–1584). Appointed dean of Winchester in 1570. In 1580 he became bishop of Winchester. Sir Francis Walsingham was one of the "chief overseers" of his will.

established by his father, Christian Wechel. He too had escaped
with difficulty from Paris during the massacre, and it is quite
possible that Sidney had known him there.

It is probable that Sidney found himself domiciled in
Wechel's house primarily because Hubert Languet, one of the
best known of contemporary Protestant scholars and diplo-
mats, was also living there. There is good reason to believe
that Sidney had made his acquaintance in Paris, and had there
begun what was to prove the most notable friendship of his
life. Born at Vitteaux in Burgundy, in 1518, Languet had
pursued scholarly ideals from his very childhood, and after
studying at different French and Italian Universities, had
received the doctorate from the University of Padua. When
he was about thirty years of age he came under the influence
of Melanchthon, embraced the reformed religion, and for several
years spent much time at Wittenberg. His interest in contemporary politics was as great as his devotion to learning and
religion, and between 1551 and 1560 he visited Denmark,
Sweden, Norway and Lapland, besides twice revisiting Italy.
For some years he resided in his native France, where he was
esteemed one of the wisest and most enlightened counsellors
of the Huguenots. During this period he was the official representative at the French Court of the Elector of Saxony, and
numbered among his friends all the famous Protestant scholars
of the period. It was in this capacity that he was residing in
Paris at the time of the massacre, and he owed his life to the
good offices of the bishop of Orleans, who protected him in
his house and found means to enable him to leave the country.
It is one of the remarkable incidents in Sidney's career that
before he had completed his eighteenth year he should have
attracted in so notable a way the interest and devotion of this
elderly man of the world. Throughout the remaining years of
his life Languet devoted himself to his youthful friend with a
truly fatherly devotion, and to his wisdom and high ideals of
living Sidney owed more than he owed to the influence of any
other of his large number of noteworthy friends.

We have no detailed information of Sidney's occupation
during the first winter which he spent on the Continent, but

we can easily imagine how seriously he pursued his studies under Languet's guidance, and how much he enjoyed the opportunity of meeting the many famous or learned men with whom he was thrown into contact. On March 23rd he wrote to his uncle, the Earl of Leicester, that he had spent the preceding Thursday with Count Lodowick (Louis of Nassau), the Prince of Orange's second brother, with whom was one Shambourg, an Almain whom Sidney had known at the French Court. He asks Leicester to thank Culverwell, the bearer of the letter, for courtesy shown Sidney when the latter was in some extremity for money[1]. This is the first record of the money difficulties in which Sidney was almost continuously involved during the rest of his life, for he always used his means lavishly, and he seems never to have learned the art of adjusting his expenditure to his income. Three days before the date of this letter he had drawn a bill of exchange for £120 sterling on William Blunt, Master of the Counter in Wood Street, for merchandise which he had received from Christian Rolgin in Frankfort[2].

Languet's duties as ambassador of the Elector of Saxony had taken him to the Imperial Court at Vienna, and thither Sidney followed him some time during the early summer. He proceeded by way of Heidelberg and Strassburg and seems even to have visited Basle[3]. In Heidelberg he met, for the first time, the famous printer, Henry Stephens, and a warm friendship at once sprang up between them. Stephens made a visit to Strassburg for the express purpose of again seeing his young friend, and on this occasion he presented Sidney with a small manuscript volume containing Greek maxims, copied by his own hand[4]. Some time later Stephens again met Sidney at Vienna, where they saw much of each other, and Stephens has himself recorded his increase of affection for the young Englishman as he had greater opportunities of

---

[1] Appendix to the *Third Report of the Historical Manuscripts Commission*. The Marquis of Bath's MSS. at Longleat, page 200, item 213, chest F. 10.

[2] Quoted *in extenso* in Zouch's *Memoirs*, p. 81.

[3] *V.* Flügel's *Einleitung* to his edition of *Astrophel and Stella* and *Defence of Poesie*, s. xvi.

[4] Hunter's *Chorus Vatum*, vol. iv, p. 12.

knowing him[1]. In Strassburg Sidney also made the acquaintance
of another famous scholar, who showed him much courtesy,
John Sturm. Lord Burghley, writing to Sturm on July 18th,
acknowledges the receipt of a letter from him which had
been brought by a servant of Sidney. Burghley sends his
reply by the same messenger and says : " I thank you very
much for your kind reception of Philip Sidney, and I know that
his most honoured parents will thank you a great deal
more[2]."

On arriving at Vienna Sidney was eagerly welcomed by
Languet, whose solicitude for his welfare could not have been
greater had the young Englishman been his own son. Sidney
now made the acquaintance of many well-known men at the
Imperial Court, and Languet's friends became his. His eagerness to acquaint himself with the European situation as widely
as possible, however, urged him to continue his travels. Toward
the end of August he set out for a three days' trip in Hungary,
but several weeks elapsed before he returned to Vienna. During
these weeks, as also during the remainder of his travels, he
found Languet's friends willing and eager to show him courtesy.
He had carried with him a letter of introduction to a Doctor
Purkircher, whose kindnesses to him he acknowledged in a
letter to Languet. In his reply Languet complains of his
young friend's protracted stay : while commending Sidney's
eagerness to become acquainted with foreign cities and the
manners of men, he fears the dangers of the journey, and he
wishes that Sidney might be accompanied by some one who
could act as a guide and wise interpreter. Such an one
Languet could easily have provided had he known Sidney's plans.
This is the first of Languet's extant letters to his *protégé*, and
it is similar in tone to the great majority of those which he was
to write. They are filled with superlative expressions of his
friendship and of his solicitude, and, mingled with these,

---

[1] In the Latin dedication (seven pages) to Sidney of the *Novum Testa-
mentum* (Greek)—Excudebat Henricus Stephanus, anno MDLXXVI. In 1578
he sent to Sidney a copy of his edition of Plato in three volumes, and in 1581
dedicated to him his edition of Herodian.

[2] *Zurich Letters*, Second Series, p. 217.

complaints regarding Sidney's failure to write letters regularly or to conform his plans to Languet's ideas.

Sidney spent October with his friend in Vienna and made the acquaintance of many learned men, among whom Vulcobius, Abondius, and Bouchetell continued their friendship with him by means of letters for several years. Languet in turn became warmly attached to two of Sidney's English friends who were with him in Vienna—Lodowick Bryskett[1] and Thomas Coningsby[2], and he was much relieved to learn that they were to accompany Sidney when, about the beginning of November[3], he set out for Italy. Languet was most reluctant to see him go, and attempted to persuade him to travel in Germany until the inauguration of the King of Poland—an event which Languet was most anxious that Sidney should witness, if for no other reason than that he considered Englishmen culpably indifferent to Polish affairs[4]. Italy was the land of the sorceress who corrupted men's morals and undermined their religious convictions, and Languet must remember that Sidney was only nineteen years of age. He extorted from him a promise that he would not visit Rome at any rate—a promise which Sidney kept, though he often afterwards reproached Languet for having prevented him from seeing the eternal city.

Languet's fears regarding the corrupting influence of Rome upon young men were shared by many Englishmen of the time. The Italianated Englishman of the proverb had obtained a wide notoriety. Ascham's strictures on Italian travel are

[1] He had been clerk of the Irish Council under Sir Henry Sidney, and later held several minor offices in Ireland especially under Lord Grey de Wilton. He is best known, of course, because of his friendship with Spenser, and for his account of the party of friends who had met at his house near Dublin on one occasion when Spenser announced to them that he was engaged on the *Faerie Queene* He contributed two poems to the collection of elegies published by Spenser after Sidney's death under the title of *Astrophel.*

[2] Knighted in 1591 for his bravery in the French war of which he has left a valuable account (ed. J. G. Nicholls—*Miscellanies*, Camden Society). He married Philippa, second daughter of Sir William FitzWilliam, and therefore a first cousin of Philip Sidney.

[3] A receipt signed by Sidney in Venice for money which he received from Thomaso Balbani on his letter of credit from Vetturelli is dated November 6, 1573. The receipt is among the Penshurst MSS.

[4] *Epistolæ*, p. 13.

too well known to need repetition, but many other references to the subject are found among Elizabethan writers. In the precepts which Lord Burghley gave to his son we find the following : " Suffer not thy sons to pass the Alps. For they shall learn nothing there but pride, blasphemy and atheism." In popular estimation Italy was responsible for much of the corruption of morals and manners in contemporary England. While her achievements in letters and the arts attracted the young Englishman of the time irresistibly, those who were most solicitous for the preservation of the soundest traits in the national character, when they saw their sons depart upon their travels, could not but remember that in the home of the Renaissance decadence had set in. Especially to the Puritanic, Italy was synonymous with irreligiousness, insincerity, indolence and gross immorality. Paris shared the same bad reputation only in a lesser degree. " Englishmen who come hither are soon corrupted," wrote Lord Cobham, the English ambassador at Paris, to Sir Henry Sidney, " and by many enticements drawn to leave their religion[1]."

Accompanied by Bryskett, Coningsby and Griffin Madox, a faithful Welsh servant, Sidney left Vienna. Languet had given him many letters of introduction, and when Sidney parted from his old friend his tears scarcely permitted him to say farewell. He had promised to write regularly, to avoid all unnecessary dangers, and to take special care of his health, and Languet was comforted by the assurance that they would soon meet each other again at Cracow, where they both expected to be present at the inauguration of the King of Poland, to which dignity the Duke of Anjou had been elected in the preceding May. The journey to Venice was uneventful and Bryskett has left us a pleasant picture of their travels written many years later :

"Through many a hill and dale,
Through pleasant woods, and many an unknowne way,
Along the bankes of many silver streames,
Thou with him yodest ; and with him didst scale

---

[1] *State Papers—Foreign—Eliz.*, Feb. 21, 1580.

W. L. S.

The craggie rocks of th' Alpes and Appenine !
Still with the Muses sporting, while those beames
Of vertue kindled in his noble brest,
Which after did so gloriously forth shine[1] ! "

Only one definite event of the journey is recorded, and it throws some rather unpleasant light on one side of Sidney's character. We have not the details of the story, but it would appear that when a dishonest host overcharged Sidney for his lodgings, the latter accused Coningsby of having in some way purloined the money. When he discovered that he was mistaken he does not seem to have been especially concerned regarding his own conduct. We shall find that this was not the only occasion when his fiery, emotional temper bore down his instincts of generosity and even of common justice.

On his arrival in Venice Sidney was warmly received by several of Languet's friends, chief among whom were the Count of Hanau, who was to become one of Sidney's warmest friends on the Continent, and Arnaud du Ferrier, the French ambassador at Venice and a friend of Fra Paolo Sarpi. They were both untiring in their efforts to be of service to him, and through them he had an opportunity of seeing what he himself calls the magnificent magnificences of the magnificoes of Venice. He was just too late to meet the famous French scholar, Francis Perrot, another of Fra Paolo's friends, nor is there any reason to believe that he met the great Servite friar who at this time was living at Mantua. How he must have delighted in the picturesque beauty of the city we can imagine, and its romantic history would make a very special appeal to him.

The greatness of Venice had begun to decline before the time of Sidney's visit ; both her political and commercial prestige was being questioned. It was now almost half a century since the Peace of Cambrai had shorn her of much of her power, but the consciousness of the fact that she had fallen from her high estate came slowly. Both in her own eyes and in those of Europe she still held the gorgeous East in fee, and if she was no longer regarded as the sole safeguard of the

---

[1] *A Pastoral Aeglogue*, etc. Spenser's Works, Globe ed., p. 567.

West, she was at least a powerful buffer State against the
Turk, and likely to be one of the most important members
of any coalition that might be formed against that dreaded
enemy. For a quarter of a century she had been less slow to
resent the insolence of the Ottoman power in the Levant than
she would have been when her greatness was at its zenith.
Her long enjoyment of commercial prosperity and her employment of mercenary troops had both tended to unfit her for
strenuous warfare. But when, in 1570, the Turk attacked
Cyprus, the Venetians had risen to the occasion in a manner
not unbefitting their former greatness. The defence of Fama-
gosta (1571) was one of the brightest pages in their history,
and when within a few months the allied Venetian, Spanish
and Papal forces won the battle of Lepanto, Europe knew that
one of the greatest battles in defence of civilization had been
fought, and that the Venetian admiral had been the chief
instrument in checking the Ottoman ambition of overrunning
the whole Continent.

But the Pope and Philip of Spain were too busy suppressing
heresy to continue their assistance against the invader, and
only a few months before Sidney visited Venice she had been
compelled to cede Cyprus to the Turk and to pay him a huge
indemnity. The blow was a fatal one as far as her political
status and her commercial pre-eminence were concerned, but
her love of liberty and independence was still to be evidenced
in the work of Fra Paolo and in his country's loyal appreciation of his services, and at the very moment Tintoretto and
Paolo Veronese were producing their masterpieces within the
city. The glories of the republic, both past and present, must
have made his visit a wonderful experience for the young
Englishman, and it is pleasant to think of his delight as he
made the acquaintance of the churches and palaces rich with
the productions of Giovanni Bellini and Carpaccio.

It was the diminution in the glory of the city-republic,
however, of which Sidney seems to have been most conscious,
and he confessed his disappointment to Languet, who interpreted it as a vindication of his own lack of enthusiasm for
Italian travel.

"I judge from your letter," he wrote on December 21st, "that the splendour of Venice does not equal your expectation; nevertheless Italy has nothing fit to be compared to it, so that if this does not please you, the rest will disgust you. You will admire the wit and sagacity of the people. They are in truth witty and keen, and yet most of them carry more on the surface than they have within, and they very generally spoil their attainments by display and make themselves offensive[1]."

Sidney's mature opinion of Italy and of Venice in particular he recorded some years later in a letter to his brother :

"Also for Italy, we know not what we have, or can have to do with them but to buy their silks and wines, and as for the other point, except Venice, whose good laws and customs we can hardly proportion to ourselves because they are quite of a contrary government ; there is little there but tyrannous oppression, and servile yielding to them that have little or no right over them. And for the men you shall have there, although indeed some be excellently learned, yet are they all given to counterfeit learning, as a man shall learn among them more false grounds of things than in any place else that I know ; for from a tapster upwards they are all discoursers. In fine, certain matters and qualities, as horsemanship, weapons, painting and such, are better there than in other countries ; but for other matters, as well, if not better, you shall have them in nearer places[2]."

Sidney was always too good an Englishman to appreciate the virtues of other countries at more than their true worth.

To what he counted true learning Sidney devoted himself most assiduously under Languet's guidance. To write easily in Latin Languet considered the principal object of his studies, the indispensable means whereby he would be able in future to continue the friendships which he was now contracting. Accordingly they agreed to write once each week. Languet was better than his word ; Sidney seems to have fallen somewhat short of it, but at least he wrote regularly enough to earn the elder man's enthusiastic praise for the improvement in his Latinity. In some respects Languet's are curious letters. They deal chiefly with contemporary politics, but in the majority of them are elaborate protestations of affection mingled with upbraidings for Sidney's failure to write regularly— surely a sign of the cooling of his friendship. He addresses

---

[1] Pears, p. 12.
[2] Letter to Robert Sidney, 1579. Quoted by Pears, p. 198.

the young man as his son, but often the letters read like those of a jealous lover to his mistress. Languet excuses his tone on the ground of his devotion, and nowhere is that devotion more evident than in his detailed advice regarding Sidney's studies. He urges him to read Cicero's letters, both for the matter contained in them and for the purpose of " double translation," in order to improve his style, though he warns him against mere Ciceronianism or such devotion to imitative graces in his style that he should give a secondary place to the matter. Latin pronunciation Languet also considered of the greatest importance[1]. In December Sidney writes that he is learning the sphere and a little music, asks Languet if he can procure Plutarch's works for him in French, and offers to send any of a number of Italian historical works which he has been reading. Sidney's extreme devotion to study indeed aroused Languet's fears when in response to several inquiries Sidney confessed that his health was indifferent and that he was in rather low spirits. Languet suspected that lack of money might be partly responsible for the young man's troubles and authorized him to draw upon him for whatever amount he needed. He also urged him to go to Padua, whither the Count of Hanau had already gone, and where Sidney would find more quiet, better friends and an atmosphere more to his liking[2].

Sidney had already taken a house in the old University town, and immediately after taking up his abode in it he wrote to Languet, on January 15th, in much better spirits.

"Behold at last my letter from Padua ! not that you are to expect any greater eloquence than is usually to be found in my epistles, but that you may know I have arrived here as I purposed and in safety....I have already visited his Excellency, the Count, and the Baron Slavata, your worthy young friends, and while I enjoy their acquaintance with the greatest pleasure to myself I am perpetually reminded of your surpassing love of me[3]."

The University atmosphere only increased his thirst for learning, and Languet begs him to be careful of his health while he advises him regarding his studies. " I call those things essential to you," he wrote, " which it is discreditable for a

Epistolæ, p. 22.   [2] *Ibid.*   [3] Pears, p. 22.

man of high birth not to know, and which may, one day, be
an ornament and a resource to you[1]." Accordingly he approves
of the elements of astronomy and geometry because of their
practical use in war, though he fears that close application to
mathematics may depress both Sidney's spirits and his health,
" and," he adds, " you know you have no health to spare."
He is afraid that Sidney will not be able to devote sufficient
time to Greek to justify the effort he must expend on acquiring
it ; some superficial knowledge of German in addition to the
four languages with which Sidney is already acquainted would
probably be of more practical use. But it was on philosophy,
history and contemporary politics that Languet laid most stress :

"Next to the knowledge of the way of salvation, which is the most
essential thing of all, and which we learn from the sacred Scriptures, next to
this, I believe that nothing will be of greater use to you than to study that
branch of moral philosophy which treats of justice and injustice. I
need not speak to you of reading history, by which more than anything
else men's judgments are shaped, because your own inclination carries
you to it and you have made great progress in it[2]."

And, lastly, Languet never tired of emphasizing the importance of the education which is derived from intercourse with
good and great men. We shall be in little danger of over-
estimating the influence which he exercised on the character
of Sidney's mind. He gives long accounts of contemporary
political happenings, primarily, one feels, for the sake of
shaping the young man's mind and of relating events to the
great movements they illustrate. Languet was not only a
good man but a statesman of no mean calibre, and his whole
interest in his *protégé's* education was that it should be a
training in character and statesmanship. The melancholy
which was becoming habitual to him was banished by nothing
so effectively as by a letter from Ferrier or Count Lewis of
Hanau reciting the praises of the young Englishman, for these
letters he prized as pledges of a happy issue for the great
hopes which he had founded on the boy.

Meantime Languet was growing impatient over Sidney's
protracted stay. In every letter he refers to the approaching

[1] Pears, p. 25. [2] *Ibid.*, p. 26.

inauguration of the King of Poland as to an event of supreme importance. In one letter he tells of having made the acquaintance of a young Pole of Cracow, a noble youth of scholarly attainments, who is to entertain Sidney at the great celebration. In another he tells of the multitude of minstrels, players, jugglers and clowns who are all making their way to Cracow[1]. Nevertheless he hardly makes us appreciate the reasons for his laying so much stress upon the event, and Sidney seems to have been in no hurry to leave Italy. He alleges "business" at first which prevents his immediate return, and then his desire to travel to Poland in the company of the Count of Hanau, whose journeyings about Italy will delay his setting out for some time. Accordingly it was midsummer before he again crossed the Alps.

We know only a few details of his further stay in Italy. There is no reason to believe that he was formally enrolled as a student in the University of Padua, attracted to it as he must have been by the long tradition of English scholars who had studied or lectured there. Languet constantly fears for his health and discourages his interest in pure scholarship. He never tires of urging what Sidney himself so eloquently declared in later years, that the highest end of knowledge consists " in the knowledge of a man's self, in the ethic and politic consideration with the end of well doing and not of well knowing only,"—" the ending end of all earthly learning being virtuous action[2]." He also warns Sidney constantly against his over-seriousness, and Sidney confesses :

"I readily allow that I am often more serious than either my age or my pursuits demand ; yet this I have learned by experience that I am never less a prey to melancholy than when I am earnestly applying the feeble powers of my mind to some high and difficult object[3]."

Languet rejoices in Sidney's friendship with the Count of Hanau and Baron Slavata, and reminds him of Cicero's dictum that friendship is the salt and condiment of life[4]. He fears, however, lest new friends rob him of the place he holds in Sidney's affection.

[1] *Epistolæ*, p. 22.   [2] *Apologie for Poetrie*, ed. Collins p. 13.
[3] Pears, p. 29.   [4] *Epistolæ*, p. 31.

By February 26th Sidney was once more in Venice, where he had his portrait painted. Before he left Venice Abondius had drawn a sketch of him for his own amusement, and Languet wrote that he had consoled himself for his young friend's absence by visiting his likeness at the house of Abondius. Accordingly Sidney in his reply presented this sketch to Languet, who, not yet content, insisted that Sidney have his portrait painted in Venice, where the services of the greatest painters in the world might be had. Titian was still living there, an old man, but we do not know that Sidney ever met him. He hesitated in his choice between the great master's two greatest pupils—Tintoretto and Veronese, but on February 26th he wrote to Languet : " This day one Paul of Verona has begun my portrait for which I must stay here two or three days longer[1]." Some six weeks later the portrait was forwarded to Languet. Two of Sidney's English friends, Robert Corbett and Richard Shelley, were travelling from Venice to Vienna, and to them Sidney entrusted it. His sense of humour was sufficient, however, to prevent his complying with one of Languet's requests. Inspired by Abondius' portrait Languet for the first time in his life became a poet, and he had forwarded his verses to Sidney with the request that they be written under the portrait—" if there shall be room for them."

"As to your lines," Sidney wrote in reply, "although it is truly a thing to boast of, 'to be praised by one so full of praise,' and though they are most welcome to me as testifying your undying affection for me, yet I cannot think of sinning so grievously against modesty as to have such a proclamation of my praises, especially as I do not deserve them, inscribed on my portrait."

Languet received it safely and at once wrote his first impressions :

"Master Corbett showed me your portrait, which I kept with me some hours to feast my eyes on it, but my appetite was rather increased than diminished by the sight. It seems to me to represent some one like you rather than yourself, and, at first, I thought it was your brother. Most of your features are well drawn, but it is far more juvenile than it ought to be. I should think you were not unlike it in your 12th or 13th year[2]."

---

[1] Pears, p. 42.   [2] Pears, p. 77—Letter of June 11, 1574.

A year later he wrote :

"As long as I enjoyed the sight of you I made no great account of the portrait which you gave me, and scarcely thanked you for so beautiful a present. I was led by regret for you, on my return from Frankfort, to place it in a frame and fix it in a conspicuous place. When I had done this it appeared to me to be so beautiful, and so strongly to resemble you, that I possess nothing which I value more. Master Vulcobius is so struck with its elegance that he is looking for an artist to copy it. The painter has represented you sad and thoughtful. I should have been better pleased if your face had worn a more cheerful look when you sat for the painting[1]."

I have discovered no reference to the portrait after this time. Should it even yet some day come to light few unearthings of sixteenth century treasures would be of such surpassing interest.

From Venice Sidney made a short excursion to Florence and Genoa, much to the distress of Languet, who wrote him a long letter reciting the innate wickedness of the Etruscans and Savoyards and supporting his contentions with much historical evidence. He feared both for Sidney's personal safety and for his morals, and he was much relieved to learn that the traveller was once more in Padua, whither he had returned about the middle of April after spending a few more days in Venice. In these two cities he passed the spring and early summer, now in the one, now in the other. Of his occupation during these months we know but little. He wrote very often but rather irregularly to Languet, thus calling down voluminous reproaches upon himself. He had not taken his counsellor's advice as to making the excursion to Florence from Venice, nor did he write to him until his return. Languet was much hurt by such conduct. All he wanted, he declared, was a letter in which Sidney should have said, " I am alive and well—at Florence, or Genoa[2]." But a letter from Sidney full of affection and tender solicitude dispelled all Languet's fears and irritation at the same time, and he breaks forth into a pæan of praise in honour of the day when he had the good fortune first to meet so noble a youth. He has lost nearly all the friends of his earlier days—many of them at St Bartholomew,

---

[1] Pears, p. 94—Letter of June 6, 1575.
[2] *Epistolæ*, p. 64.

many in the civil commotions of the rest of Europe, and as Sidney was always the dearest of these friends so is he now almost the only surviving one[1].

None of Sidney's letters to his parents or friends in England at this period has been preserved. In writing to Languet he occasionally refers to his having received a letter from his father, or of having sent one to the Earl of Leicester, but these have all disappeared. One interesting reference to his life at this time is preserved in Venice, where, after his return from Florence and Genoa, he took out a license to carry arms. On April 19th a motion was made in the Council of Ten

"that license be given to Sir (!) Philip Sidney, an Englishman, son of the most illustrious Sir Henry Sidney, Governor of the province of Calais (!), who is staying here on his way to Padua, where he designs to take up his abode for the purpose of studying, to carry arms in this city of Venice and all cities, towns, and other places of our dominion, with a gentleman attending him (*appresso di lui*) named Lodovico Bruschetto, and with three servants, whose names are to be noted in the office of the Chiefs of this Council, and in the Chanceries of the places where he shall sojourn he taking oath that they shall remain in his house and at his charges.

Ayes 13.   Noes 0.   Neutral 1[2]."

It had been finally arranged between Sidney and Languet that Sidney should return to the north in the company of the Count of Hanau.

"It will be far more convenient for you to travel through Germany with the Count," Languet had written, "especially as none of your people speak German, and therefore it is better you should wait for his coming, so that he comes away before Midsummer : for I fear the heat for you, spare-framed as you are, and knowing as I do your voracious appetite for fruit ; and therefore I forewarn you of fever and dysentery if you stay there during the summer[3]."

Sidney was loath, however, definitely to turn his back on the more remote parts of the civilized world, which he might never visit again. From Corbett Languet learned that Sidney was waiting for a letter from his father before determining on his

---

[1] *Epistolæ*, p. 69.

[2] *Calendar of State Papers—Venetian*, No. 583, April 19, 1574, Consiglio Comune, No. 31.

[3] Pears, p. 64.

immediate future, and Languet concluded that his wilful
protégé was meditating not only a visit to Rome but also to
Constantinople.   The dangers of the latter journey—from the
pirates by sea and brigands by land—had become proverbial,
but fearful to contemplate as were these hazards they were not
equal in Languet's opinion to those moral dangers which were
involved in a visit to the city of the Popes.   It is probable that
lack of money prevented Sidney's embarking on either expedition.   In the beginning of June he learned of the death of the
French King, and Languet soon wrote him that the King of
Poland would visit Venice before returning to France to claim
his new dignity.

"I would gladly give all that is dearest and most precious to me in the
world," Languet wrote on June 25th, "to have you here with us now,
that you might be made known to the King of France and form an acquaintance with some of his suite.   It would be useful to you if ever you return
to the French court[1]."

Under the circumstances the worldly-wise diplomat busied
himself with making friends for Sidney, among those who
might secure him the opportunity in Venice which was impossible
in Vienna.

"I advise you to do what you can to become known to the King," he
wrote.   "You will be able to do so through Du Ferrier or Montmorino
or Pibrac or Bellievre.   Du Ferrier you know well, Montmorino too
knows you and loves you.   I have mentioned you in fitting terms to
Bellievre and Pibrac from each of whom I have received the strongest
expressions of good will.   You will remember, however, that in the midst
of hurry and tumult you must watch for your opportunity and not be too
bashful[2]."

Whether Sidney actually met the King we do not know.   He
met Pibrac and wrote to Languet some rather harsh strictures
on that statesman's conduct in connection with the Massacre
of St Bartholomew.   It is interesting to read Languet's reply
and to see how uniformly he attempts to translate all sorts of
events into educational material.   Very gently he condemns
the practice of assuming that a man is a villain because he has

---

[1] Pears, p. 78.   [2] *Ibid.*, p. 83.

erred in some slight point. All sins are not equal. Pibrac's learning, genius and eloquence are eulogized, and Languet does not believe that he ever advised an unprincipled course of conduct.

Languet's last letter to Sidney is dated July 24th, and some time during the next month, we may assume, Sidney returned to the north in the company of the Count of Hanau. During July he had been far from well, and he had written Languet of having severe pains in his head and of having barely escaped a pleurisy. To his ill-health Languet ascribed the young man's rather petty complaints of the ungracious behaviour of certain of his friends who had gone away without bidding him farewell. The older man's reply is in his wisest, paternal tone. Sidney had digested his wrath and Languet reminds him : " You will have to adopt this plan many times before you reach my age unless you wish to pass your whole life in quarrelling." He saw Sidney's tendency to take himself too seriously, and probably rightly ascribed it to a certain haughtiness and lack of a sense of humour ; he never wearies of urging him to moderate his pretensions in his relations to other men and to curb his impulse to harsh and unconsidered criticism.

On August 4th Sidney drew the last of the money which was to his credit in Venice[1], and he probably left Italy soon afterward. On arriving in Vienna, he became seriously ill, with the result that he was detained there for some time[2], and we can imagine with what solicitude and tender care Languet attended him. On recovering sufficiently he made a visit of some duration in Poland, " which time," he wrote to Lord Burghley, " I might perchance have employed in more profitable, at least more pleasant voyages[3]." He was in Vienna again on November 27th, when he wrote the Earl of Leicester, giving him an account of the political situation in Poland and at the Emperor's Court[4]. Once more he found himself " not

---

[1] Accerbo Vetturelli to Sir Henry Sidney, October 21, 1574 (*Add. MSS.* 17520, 2). Sir Henry had deposited £135 with Vetturelli on June 28th according to a receipt given by John Lugerini, an agent of Vetturelli, which is preserved at Penshurst.

[2] Sidney to Burghley December 17, 1574 (*State Papers—Foreign—Eliz.*).

[3] *Ibid.*

[4] *Cotton MSS. Galba*, B, XI, p. 370.

in very good estate of body." References of this kind recur so frequently throughout Sidney's later life that in spite of his reputation for horsemanship and prowess in the tournament, we must conclude that he had inherited something of his mother's physical weakness.

The winter of 1574–5 Sidney spent with Languet at the Imperial Court. Of these months we know little except that the delight of the two friends in each other's society knew no diminution, and that they both contracted a warm friendship for Edward Wotton, who was also residing in Vienna, and who was afterwards one of Sidney's warmest friends. From the opening sentence of the *Apologie for Poetrie* we know that they both gave themselves to the study of horsemanship under the tuition of John Pietro Pugliano, an equerry at the Emperor's Court. Sidney corresponded with certain of his Venetian friends, especially Don Cæsar Caraffa, who wrote to him on February 3rd of the death of Edward, the young Earl of Windsor, and asked Sidney, on returning to England, to convey his love and condolences to each of Windsor's relatives[1]. Sidney's intimacy with his Venetian friends had been so pronounced that it had caused rumours to reach his friends in England that he was succumbing to the attractions of Catholicism. Walsingham mentioned the rumours in a letter to Languet.

"I will write to Master Walsingham on this subject," Languet reported to Sidney, "and if he has entertained such a thought about you, I will do what I can to remove it; and I hope my letter will have sufficient weight with him not only to make him believe what I shall say of you, but also endeavour to convince others of the same[2]."

Of the new friends whom Sidney made during this winter at Vienna two stand out prominently—Banosius, the future biographer of Ramus and editor of his Commentaries, and Charles de l'Ecluse. They were both friends of Languet, and

---

[1] *Add. MSS.* 15914, 15.

[2] Pears, p. 92. Simpson in his life of Campion (p. 114) says that these suspicions were aroused by Sidney's intimacy with his cousin Shelley, the English prior of Malta. The explanation, however, is not very plausible, especially if we remember that Shelley was travelling with Robert Corbett, a staunch Protestant, whom Sidney called "my very greatest friend."

Sidney was especially attracted to them because of their interest
in literature. For many years they were among his most regular correspondents. The Count of Hanau was compelled to
leave Vienna before Sidney had returned from Poland—much
to the regret of both young men. Their intimacy is evidenced
by a letter which the Count wrote to him on January 30th :

"Sir : I hoped very much before I left Vienna that you would return from
Poland that I might again have the pleasure of your society which I prize
so highly and of which your long stay has deprived me to my great regret.
Nevertheless I trust, by the help of Providence, to see you again at the
next Frankfort fair, together with Monsieur Languet, who has assured
me that you will come. I beg you also to do me the great favour of coming
to spend some time at Hanau in order that we may revive and continue
the friendship with which you have honoured me from the very beginning of
our acquaintance, which I hope to preserve in its entirety, and of which
I hope to give you proof in deeds whenever an opportunity presents
itself. I have not written you sooner partly because of the tedium of
my travels and partly because I have not been able to find any assured
means of having my letters conveyed to you. I arrived at my house of
Steinaw with all my suite safe and sound, thanks to God, on the first day
of January, and was warmly welcomed by my subjects. I have come here
to my house at Ortenburgh in order to attend to some business, and I hope
within two or three days to be on the way to Dillenburgh. From there
I go to Heidelberg to visit the Elector Palatine, and then to Busweiler,
from whence, when I have finished some business, I hope to return to
Hanau as soon as possible in order to await your coming with Monsieur
Languet. I shall welcome you both as heartily as I now send you my
affectionate greetings. I pray God that he may keep you in perfect health
and give you a long and happy life with the complete fulfilment of your
noble and virtuous aspirations. From the Chateau of Ortenburgh this
30th of January, 1575. Your affectionate friend at your service.

PHILIP LOUIS, Count of Hanau, etc.[1]"

In his letter to Leicester, written at the end of November,
Sidney had informed him that in the near future the Emperor
would probably visit Prague where for two years he had been
much wished for, in order that he might determine the question
of the Bohemian succession. He left Vienna toward the end
of February, and Languet found it necessary in his official

---

[1] *Add. MSS.* 21522, fol. 138 [French].

capacity to accompany him. The time was now drawing near when Sidney must return to England for he had already long overstayed the period of absence mentioned in his license[1], but in order to postpone as long as possible the separation from his friend he too determined on another visit of a few days to Prague. It was only for a few days, however. Languet busied himself in planning each detail of Sidney's journey ; he wrote letters of introduction for him—to Doctor Ursinus at Heidelberg, to Count Louis of Witgenstein at the Court of the Elector Palatine, and having done all that paternal solicitude could do he took leave of the young man who had come to occupy so warm a place in his heart. Sidney was ill supplied with money as usual : Languet lent him what he needed, and wrote to Wechel, the Frankfort printer, and a Doctor Glauburg, asking them to furnish him, should he need more money before leaving the Continent. Sidney gave to Languet a bond for what he had received and asked Wotton also to sign it—much to Languet's displeasure. "You wrong me," he wrote, "if you imagine I trust anyone more than yourself[2]."

On March 5th Sidney reached Dresden[3] where Wotton was to join him. From here he proceeded to Heidelberg, and then to Strassburg[4], where he met Lobetius and Sturm, with both of whom he was already acquainted. Of his further travels we have no clear account. Languet speaks of his plans for visiting Basle and of proceeding through Burgundy to Paris, but we have no record of his having actually undertaken the journey. Overcome by his desire to see Sidney once more, Languet journeyed from Prague to Frankfort where they spent some time together. Whether they were able to accept the Count of Hanau's invitation to visit him or not we do not know. About the middle of May Languet was compelled to return to Prague after which time Sidney wrote to him from

---

[1] No doubt the period had been formally extended. On February 16th Thos. Wilkes was sent secretly to the Count Palatine, and in his instructions the Queen "would have the occasion of his journey known to be as for the meeting with Philip Sidney." (*State Papers—Foreign—Eliz.*, February 16, 1575.)

[2] Pears, p. 93.   [3] *Epistolæ*, p. 105.

[4] *Harl. MSS.* 6992, 18 (quoted by Flügel, s. xxii). *V.* also Pears, p. 92.

Heidelberg[1]. On May 31st he took ship at Antwerp for England[2] accompanied by Edward Wotton and the faithful Griffin Madox.

Sidney had been absent from England almost exactly three years, and wonderfully fruitful years they had been for him. He was no longer the boy—"young and somewhat raw" as his uncle had described him when he set out on his travels—but a man of the world, whose dearest interests were those of the mature and talented men of his day. The most sanguine hopes of Sir Henry Sidney and the Earl of Leicester when they "designed him to travel" had been more than realized. He had spent several months at the French Court and a much longer period at that of the Emperor. He had been an eyewitness of the greatest tragedy in the history of his time, he had seen something of the splendours of Italy and had familiarized himself with her relation to the Great Turk in other than a vague, hearsay fashion. He had gained a grasp of the complicated European political situation, not only as far as France, Spain and the Netherlands were concerned, but in the German States, in Poland, Bohemia and the Empire. He had gained this knowledge not only from books, though his historical reading had been very wide, but by meeting personally and discussing affairs with the nobility, the statesmen and the most famous literary men of Europe.

The supreme influence exerted on Sidney's character during these decisive years was, of course, that of Languet. He it was who taught him to interpret the significance of contemporary events, and who communicated to him his own philosophy of history. They had been drawn together inevitably by their common high-mindedness, their common interest in history, literature and politics, and perhaps also by their having shared a common danger. A more intimate acquaintance only increased their friendship, and it was an incalculable piece of good fortune for Sidney that he should have excited the interest and affection of so wise and devoted a diplomatist as Hubert Languet. Their friendship constitutes an almost

---

[1] *Epistolæ*, p. 115.
[2] Sidney to Count of Hanau, London, June 12, 1575 (Pears, p. 224).

unique example of highly paternal devotion on the one hand repaid by deep, affectionate respect on the other. Languet saw to it that his friends became Sidney's, and he also took care that Sidney's studies should be directed in such a way that the young Englishman might be able to keep in touch with continental politics, not only by reason of his intelligent comprehension of the situation but by means of his facility in the use of Latin. No education, in Languet's judgment, was comparable in importance to that which was derived from intercourse with the men who were chiefly responsible for the making of the history of the time.

Our eulogy of Languet's influence must be modified, perhaps, by the recognition of a certain worldly wisdom in his ideas, which was hardly consistent with the proud integrity of the man, and in which we may recognize the defect of the quality last mentioned. The point is illustrated in some sentences from one of the last of his letters before Sidney sailed for home.

"When you reach England," he wrote, "see to it that you cultivate the good-will of Cecil, who is friendly to you and who can smooth your path in every way. In no way will you be able to secure his favour more certainly than by your affection for his children, or at least by pretending that you love them. But remember that an astute old man who has been made wise by his long experience in affairs of state will easily see through the pretences of youth. It will also be to your advantage to cultivate the friendship of Mr. Walsingham. . . . Men are wont to feel warmly towards youths who, they see, are seeking out the society of the wise. . . . To sum up, it is necessary that he who wishes to live above contempt in the courts of powerful Kings should moderate his pretensions, digest many injuries, avoid with the utmost care every occasion for quarrelling, and cultivate the good-will of those in whose hands rests his fortune. But I shall cease to weary you further, for you understand all these things better than I[1]."

Sidney was to understand some of these things very well in the years that followed, as we shall see. He was to remain in essentials the noble-minded youth, devoted whole-heartedly to whatever things were of good report, in whom his contemporaries delighted to recognize the president of noblesse and of chivalry, but he was also a child of his age. Perhaps the

[1] *Epistolæ*, p. 104 (March 10, 1575).

W. L. S.

scorn of consequence was illustrated in his actions more than in those of any Englishman of his day, but he was by no means a stranger to the faith in politic considerations, in indirection of method, and in the effectiveness of the personal influence of the great. It was a faith that was almost inseparable from the conditions of Court life at the time and not inconsistent with essential nobility of character. We have already seen it exemplified in the character of a man of such downright honesty as Sidney's father, and it must be taken into account in any estimate of Burghley or Walsingham, of Bacon or Henry of Navarre or even of Hubert Languet.

CHAPTER IX

AT COURT

A FEW days after arriving in England Sidney wrote to his friend the Count of Hanau :

"On the last day of May a fair wind wafted me to this our island nest, where I found all my family well ; the Queen, though somewhat advanced in years, yet hitherto vigorous in her health, which as it is God's will that our safety should hang on so frail a thread is with good reason earnestly commended to the care of Almighty God in the prayers of our people. She is to us a Meleager's brand ; when it perishes farewell to all our quietness[1]."

Sidney had at once taken his place at the Court of the Queen, where he was to experience all the vicissitudes of the courtier's lot. It must not be imagined that he was too young to expect employment. Men matured early in the days of Elizabeth, and the young man in his twenty-first year who could speak of his sovereign as "somewhat advanced in years" before she was forty-two, might legitimately hope that she would entrust to him some not insignificant rôle in the administration of his country's affairs.

From the letter quoted above it would seem certain that before leaving the Continent Sidney had learned of the death of his sister Ambrosia[2], which had taken place at Ludlow Castle

[1] June 12, 1575 (Pears, p. 96).

[2] The inscription on her tomb states that she was the fourth daughter of Sir Henry and Lady Mary, and I conjecture that she was born in the autumn of 1565 shortly before her parents set out for Ireland. It is possible that her birth is referred to in a letter written by Cecil to Sir Henry on November 4, 1565, in which he wishes health and strength to Lady Sidney "that she may when you both shall think meet follow your Lordship." (*State Papers—Irish—*

on February 22nd. She was probably about nine or ten years
of age, and as her short life coincided with the period spent by
Philip at Shrewsbury, Oxford and Cambridge and on the Continent, it is probable that he had only rarely seen her. She was
buried in the Collegiate Parish Church at Ludlow, where Sir
Henry raised a sumptuous monument to her memory[1].

During the three years of Philip's absence from England
Sir Henry had been occupied chiefly in administering the affairs
of his Welsh presidency, though he was frequently summoned
to spend weeks and even months at the Court to consult on
Irish affairs. To Sir Henry they were years of comparative
peace and quiet, and he steadily resisted the pressure which
was put upon him to take charge once more of English affairs
in Ireland. There matters could hardly have been worse.
The characteristic vacillation of the English policy had never
been more pronounced. Essex's enterprise in Ulster had failed
utterly ; Desmond was again an independent chief in Munster ;
the wild chiefs of Connaught were vowing that they would
capture Dublin itself. The year 1573 ended with what Froude
defines as "the universal destruction of the English power in
Ireland." FitzWilliam, the Deputy, and Essex quarrelled continually regarding the limits of their respective jurisdictions,
and were agreed in nothing but their bitter indignation
against the Queen and Council for their lack of adequate
support. Essex retrieved his reputation in a very dubious
way by the treacherous massacre of the O'Neills in 1574, and
by perpetrating the horror of the Rathlin massacre in the
following year.

Eliz.)   The dates of birth of the different children of Sir Henry and Lady Mary,
as nearly as I have been able to determine them, are as follows :
> Philip, November 30, 1554.
> Margaret, 1556. She died in 1558, aged one year and three-quarters accord-
>   ing to the inscription on her tomb in Penshurst Church.
> Elizabeth, October, 1560. She died in 1567. *V.* p. 22.
> Mary, October 27, 1561.
> Robert, November 19, 1563.
> Ambrosia, 1565 ?.
> Thomas, March 25, 1569.

[1] Churchyard, in *The Worthiness of Wales* (Spenser Soc.), gives an elaborate
description of the tomb. *V.* p. 67.

FitzWilliam had long been demanding his recall, now with threats, now with tears, but the Queen found no one to whom she was willing to entrust the office who was also willing to take it. That she must again turn to Sir Henry had been felt by all those most conversant with Irish affairs from the time he left the country in 1571. It is little wonder, however, that he was not eager to assume again what he himself called his "thankless charge." His duties as Lord President of Wales were a source of the greatest satisfaction to him. "A happy place of government it is," he once declared, "for a better people to govern, or better subjects to their Sovereign, Europe holdeth not[1]." He took an honest pride in the effectiveness of his government, and he delighted in the work of restoring the royal castles and collecting and preserving the antiquities of the country. As a zealous and learned antiquarian he was known throughout England. Matthew Parker, Archbishop of Canterbury, and founder in 1572 of the Elizabethan Society of Antiquaries, was one of his intimate friends, and we have a glimpse of their relation to each other during this year in an extant letter of the Archbishop. In sending to Sir Henry a copy of his edition of Thomas of Walsingham he recognizes his friend's love of antiquities, and begs for the loan of some rare volumes from Sir Henry's library[2]. Queen Elizabeth, too, was much more gracious to the man who had served her well, when he was not "putting her to charge." Obeying a rare impulse of human sympathy, she wrote to Sir Henry, on the death of his daughter Ambrosia, the kindliest of her letters to him. It is written in Elizabeth's involved, characteristic style but is sufficiently unusual to be worth quoting[3].

"Good Sidney[4]:
    Although we are well assured that by your wisdom and great experience of worldly chances and necessities, nothing can happen unto you so heavy but you can and will bear them as they ought to be rightly taken, and, namely, such as happen by the special appointment and work

[1] Letter to Walsingham, March 1, 1583.
[2] Collins, vol. I, p. 67.
[3] *State Papers—Dom.—Eliz. Warrant Book*, vol. I, p. 83, February. 1575.
[4] This address is substituted for the formal 'Right trusty and well beloved' which has been struck out.

of Almighty God which he hath lately showed by taking unto Him from your company a daughter of yours, yet, forasmuch as we conceive the grief you yet feel thereby, as in such cases natural parents are accustomed, we would not have you ignorant (to ease your sorrow as much as may be) how we take part of your grief upon us, whereof these our letters unto you are witness, and will use no further persuasions to confirm you respecting the good counsel yourself can take of yourself but to consider that God doth nothing evil, to whose holy will all is subject and must yield at times to us uncertain. He hath yet left unto you the comfort of one daughter of very good hope, whom, if you shall think good to remove from those parts of unpleasant air (if it be so) into better in these parts, and will send her unto us before Easter, or when you shall think good, assure yourself that we will have a special care of her, not doubting but as you are well persuaded of our favour toward yourself, so will we make further demonstration thereof in her, if you will send her unto us. And so comforting you for the one, and leaving this our offer of our good will to your own consideration for the other, we commit you to Almighty God."

Mary Sidney, who was thus early summoned to the life of a court, was not yet fourteen years of age. During the next two years which she spent in attendance on the Queen she became known as one of the most beautiful and attractive of the young ladies of the Court.

Of Lady Sidney's life during this period we know little that is not depressing. Utterly broken in health and harassed by money difficulties, she had become embittered and her letters are usually querulous in tone. The Earl of Leicester evidently showed little disposition to assist her, and it was to Burghley that she turned for help in her difficulties. We are only very imperfectly acquainted with her, but it is difficult to put aside entirely the suspicion that the poor lady was herself the cause of some of her troubles. In a letter of February 1, 1573, addressed to Sussex, the Lord Chamberlain, she begs him

"to lend me three or four linen pieces of hangings, for that it may please you understand her Majesty hath commanded me to come to the Court, and my chamber is very cold, and my own hangings very scant and nothing warm : myself rather a little recovered of great extremity of sickness than that I can either boast of hope of perfect health or dare adventure to lie in so cold a lodging without some further health [1]."

---

[1] *Cottonian MSS. Vespasian,* F. xii, fol. 179.

She goes on to exonerate herself from the charge of having been negligent about returning similar "wardrobe stuff" on a previous occasion. In another very long undated letter to Sussex she pours out her complaints bitterly about having been deprived of her wonted lodgings at the Court :

"The chamber the Gentleman Usher saith your Lordship hath appointed me, truly, my Lord, was never yet but the place for my servants : neither is it fit for the coldness and wideness of it for one of my weakness and sickliness, having, besides, no way out of it for me but through the open cloister either to her Majesty or otherwise, which it hath always this many years pleased her Highness to give me favourable respect of, and for that occasion and my health did herself will my brother, the Earl of Leicester, 5 years past to let me have his good-will to have those two chambers whereof one now is taken from me, and never before since that time, and the best of both, and the most convenient as well for my repair to her Majesty as for the way into the garden[1]."

Sussex was constantly at enmity with his brother-in-law, Sir Henry, and he detested Leicester ; it is just possible that he subjected Lady Sidney to petty indignities which go far to excusing her unrestrained, voluble outpouring of her woes. In a letter to Burghley[2] acknowledging his kindnesses she refers to her long friendship with Lady Hoby "whom of long time I have been very greatly beholding and bound unto for her Ladyship's good-will towards me." She also speaks of having been "not able to stir abroad by extreme sickness." She apologizes for having troubled Burghley so much with "letters for a man of mine" and promises not to sin again in this respect. In almost all of her letters there is a depressing recurrence of the same themes,—her illness, her lack of money, her prosecution of suits at Court, the various forms of injustice that are meted out to her. To her servant John Cokram she writes "from her Majesty's manor of Greenwich this Tuesday after Saint Barthelmew's day, 1573," begging him to send her £10. She enumerates the various sums she has had to expend since her husband's departure—for medical attention, for hats and gloves, and adds in a postscript :

[1] *Cottonian MSS. Titus*, B. ii, fol. 304.
[2] *State Papers—Dom.—Eliz.* vol. xci, April, 1573.

"I have written you this long discourse that you may if need so require send it to my lord to satisfy him why I send to you his warrant so soon, but if you list to use me otherwise it shall not be the worse for you. £11 hath the heartening of my first suit cost me since my lord went, for which I am promised £300 at all aventure to the party that hath bought it.... And so helping me presently with my money you shall be troubled no more with me this year. But under £10 at this present will not serve my turn. And once again as you esteem of my good will and quiet with you, deal this honestly with me as to send it this night though you strain your uttermost credit[1]."

A month later she wrote to Burghley asking for a lease of lands belonging to "Nicholas Halswell her Highness' ward." Only the signature and the following postscript are written in her own hand :

"I beseech your Lordship pardon me I write no larger nor with my own hand for I am so very sick as I cannot endure to write although I must confess it were my part not to trouble your good Lordship in this or any other suit without further respect of your great courtesies and noble dealings with me[2]."

Lady Sidney was to write many similar letters[3] in the immediately succeeding years—letters which illustrate the widespread ramifications of the woes of the courtier's lot. That she had many devoted friends we know, among whom "the wise, noble Mr Dyer," as she calls him in one of her letters, was among the most eager to serve her, but the conclusion is inevitable that she was wretched both in body and mind, and there was nothing ennobling in her unhappiness. When not in attendance on the Queen she lived in a house near Paul's Wharf[4] in the neighbourhood of the residence of her sister, the

---

[1] *Add. MSS.* 15914, f. 12.

[2] *Lansdowne MSS.* vol. xvii, fol. 41 (September 12, 1573).

[3] On August 7, 1576, she wrote to Burghley on hearing that the Queen had denied her suit : "my present estate being such by reason of my debts as I cannot go forward with any honourable course of my living....Her Majesty's unkindness brings me no small disgrace amongst such as are not determined to wish me well." (*State Papers—Dom.—Eliz.*) In another long letter to Burghley she rails against her "monstrous vile and wicked" detractors, and says she has not been able to hold up her head to write. (*Lansdowne MSS.* vol. xxiii, fol. 184, October 29, 1576.)

[4] Perhaps to be identified with "my house at Saint Anthony's," from which she wrote the first of the letters to Sussex which has been quoted.

Countess of Huntingdon, and of Baynard's Castle, the town residence of her daughter Mary after her marriage in 1577 to the Earl of Pembroke. Some of her letters are written from Durham House, the residence in the Strand of the Earl of Essex. When Sidney returned to England[1] the joy of home-coming must have been forgotten by him in the sight of his mother's unhappiness.

A few days after his arrival in London Sidney wrote to Languet a letter in which he conveyed to his old friend the good wishes of Sir Henry and Lady Sidney. He was able to report himself almost restored in health ; he announced that he would be absent from London for some time and that in consequence he would not be able to send letters to the Continent until his return. Instinctively Languet felt that there was a danger of the young man's giving himself up to the frivolities of Court life, and in his reply he besought him "amid the turmoil of a court and so many temptations to waste time" not to give up the practice of the Latin language ; if so, he would have to charge him with indolence and love of ease. Probably neither of the friends guessed that almost six months would elapse before Sidney should write his next letter to Languet.

Queen Elizabeth was about to set out on the most extended and most magnificent of all her progresses, and the whole Court was in a pleasurable state of excitement in anticipation of the gaieties incidental to these provincial tours. Moreover, it was rumoured that the entertainment which the Earl of Leicester was providing for her Majesty at Kenilworth would far outshine that which had ever before been offered by a noble-man to his sovereign. Kenilworth—and everything else which the Earl possessed—had been given to him by the Queen, and he was determined not only to express his gratitude in a form which made a singular appeal to the heart of Elizabeth, but to

---

[1] Just at this time Lady Sidney had a less distressing problem on her hands. Mary Wynibanke, who was in her service, refused to perform her contract of marriage with Sebastian D'Auvalx, gentleman of France, who sought redress through the French ambassador. Sir Henry was no further helpful than "to will him to take his remedy by law."

make a supreme demonstration of his devotion to her, in the
hope that even at this late day she might consider him as a
prospective husband.   It is obvious that Sidney's natural
interest in the progress would be much heightened by the fact
that his uncle was to play the most conspicuous rôle among the
noblemen who surrounded the Queen.   Besides, it had been
definitely understood for some time that Sir Henry Sidney had
at length agreed once more to accept the Irish Deputyship,
the Queen having been persuaded by the urgency of the situation
to agree to the conditions laid down by Sir Henry[1].   Wearied
out by the recriminations and ill-success of FitzWilliam and the
Earl of Essex, Elizabeth was once more dispatching Sir Henry
to Ireland, but there were many preliminaries to arrange, and
Sir Henry, together with his wife and daughter, who were in
attendance on the Queen, was to accompany the Court in its
progress.   Philip was thus able to look forward to the rare
opportunity of spending two or three months in the company
of his father, mother and sister ; moreover, the majority of
the noblemen and ladies who accompanied the Court were
either relatives or intimate friends of his family.

The Earl of Leicester's entertainment of the Queen at
Kenilworth is so well known and was of such an elaborate and
detailed character that only the briefest sketch of it can be
given here[2].   After dinner at Long Ichington and "pleasant
pastime in hunting by the way after," her Majesty reached Kenilworth at eight o'clock on the ninth of July.   She was welcomed
by a Sybil who "pronounced a proper poesie in English rhyme
and meter."   Then six trumpeters, "every one an eight foot
high" proved themselves "harmonious blasters," and their music
was followed by the appearance of the Lady of the Lake who
recited to Her Majesty the history of the Castle from the time
of King Arthur, and concluded her speech by declaring

"The Lake, the Lodge, the Lord, are yours for to command."

---

[1] In a letter to Sir Henry dated May 15th Walsingham assumes that the
matter is settled.   (Collins, p. 70.)

[2] The sources of our information regarding the Kenilworth entertainment
are, of course, Laneham's letter and Gascoigne's *Princely Pleasures,* both of
which are printed in the first volume of Nichols' *Progresses.*   Laneham's letter
is most easily accessible in Dr Furnivall's edition in *The Shakespeare Library.*

At length the Queen reached her chamber, "when after did follow so great a peal of guns and such lightning by fire work a long space together, as Jupiter would show himself to be no further behind with his welcome than the rest of his Gods." The next day was Sunday, and the forenoon was spent in hearing divine service ; in the afternoon there was pleasant music and dancing, and in the evening there were fireworks of such magnificent and realistic sort that honest Laneham, a dependent of Leicester, to whose account of the proceedings we are indebted for our most vivid picture of them, would have been "vengeably afeard" had he not known that Jupiter did all in amity. The next day the Queen hunted the "hart of force" and had delectable sport: Laneham describes for us "the earning of the hounds in continuance of their cry, the swiftness of the deer, the running of footmen, the galloping of horses, the blasting of horns, the hallowing and hueing of the huntsmen, with the excellent echoes between whiles from the woods and waters in valleys resounding." At every turn the Queen was met by allegorical personages who reminded her of "the rare and singular qualities of both body and mind in her Majesty conjoined, and so apparent at eye." As Her Majesty was crossing a bridge, Proteus appeared in the character of Arion sitting on a dolphin's back, and, after a consort of music had sounded from within the dolphin, Proteus sang to the Queen a song of congratulation.

And so with great variety of sports the days passed. There was much of hunting and bear-baiting ; there was tumbling and a rustic bride-ale, morris-dancing and running at the quintain, masques, an old historical show by the men of Coventry in which the chief rôle was taken by Captain Cox— "the foremost figure in English story-book and ballad history[1]," and the singing of a ballad of "King Arthur at Camelot" by a minstrel to the accompaniment of his harp. Knighthood was conferred on certain gentlemen of worship, and at last on July 27th the Queen departed. Laneham's unqualified delight in everything from the abundant food and drink to the magnificence and liberality of his master and his own proximity to the great of the land is very infectious, and few spectacular

[1] Furnivall's *Forewords* to his edition, p. ix.

events have had a more worthy chronicler. We may assume that Sidney knew him well, and we may hope that he delighted in the rare fellow who was "sometime at my good Lady Sidney's chamber, a noblewoman that I am as much bound unto as any poor man may be unto so gracious a lady[1]."

From Kenilworth the Court removed to Lichfield, where for eight days the Queen enjoyed the Cathedral music and made excursions into the neighbourhood. From here she proceeded to Chartley, the seat of the Earl of Essex. Lady Essex was no favourite of Elizabeth, who did her the honour of this visit probably to please the absent Earl. From Chartley, Elizabeth wrote to him in her most friendly vein. There is every reason to suppose that Sidney, too, visited Chartley at this time, though we have no definite record of the fact. If so, he would make the acquaintance of Penelope Devereux, the eldest daughter of the Earl and Countess, who was some years later to inspire his chief poetical work. She was now about twelve years of age—a mere child from our point of view—but probably much less of a child in the eyes of her contemporaries. Mary Sidney was only two years her senior, but she was already installed as a member of the Court circle of ladies, and a month later when the Queen was at Woodstock a Court poet could address Mistress Mary in the lines,

> "Though young in years, yet old in wit, a gest due to your race,
> If you hold on as you begin, who is't you'll not deface[2]?"

Whether Sidney was especially attracted to Penelope at this time we cannot say; the whole question of their relation to each other will be discussed elsewhere.

After leaving Chartley the Queen visited Stafford Castle, Dudley Castle, Hartlebury Castle and the City of Worcester, where she remained from August 13th to August 20th. On September 11th she was at Woodstock, where she remained for some days, and after a visit to Reading she returned to Windsor Castle.

---

[1] Laneham's *Letter* (ed. Furnivall), p. 59.
[2] The *Queenes Majesties Entertainment at Woodstock*. *V.* article by J. W. Cunliffe in *Pub. Mod. Lang. Ass.*, March, 1911, p. 100.

On July 31st Sir Henry Sidney was sworn one of Her Majesty's Privy Council[1], and two days later by letters patent was appointed Lord Deputy of Ireland[2]. His 'Instructions' were dated at Lichfield on the same day[3], and on August 3rd he was present at a meeting of the Privy Council[4]. On August 12th he took leave of her Majesty, "kissing her sacred hands, with most gracious and comfortable words," at Dudley Castle, from whence she wrote to Essex announcing that Sir Henry would embark within eight days ; in the same letter she wrote her unqualified, matter-of-fact approval of the Rathlin slaughter[5]. On August 20th Sir Henry made his will, which was signed by Philip Sidney, Edward Montague, W. Blunt and five other persons[6]. The father and son paid a visit to Shrewsbury together, of which we know nothing more than is told us by the following entry in the corporation accounts :

"Spent and given to Mr Philip Sidney at his coming to this town with my Lord President, his father, in wine and cakes and other things—7s. 2d."

At the same time the corporation entertained Mr Robert Corbet "at his return home from beyond the seas[7]." It was September 8th before Sir Henry landed in Ireland and proceeded to Drogheda.

We may be sure that Philip did not take leave of his father until immediately before the latter set sail. In a letter to Languet apologizing for his long silence he pleads in excuse that he had to accompany the Queen in her progress and to see his father off[8]. That the magnificence of his apparel during the Kenilworth festivities was comparable with that of his visit to Oxford during the Queen's visit some nine years earlier may

[1] *Acts of the Privy Council.*

[2] Burghley's *Notes of Queen Elizabeth's Reign* (Murdin).

[3] *Calendar of State Papers, Carew.*

[4] *Acts of the Privy Council.*

[5] *Calendar of State Papers, Carew.*

[6] Marquis of Bath's MSS. (*Appendix to third Report of Hist. Man. Com.* p. 199).

[7] Owen and Blakeway, *op. cit.* p. 360. The date given in the accounts is 1574,—a palpable error. The reference to Corbet shows that 1575 is the correct date.

[8] *Praetexes tuae cessationi vestros progressus et deductionem illustris tui parentis.* (*Epistolæ*, p. 139.)

be deduced from the following note of hand which is still preserved among the Penshurst MSS. :

"Be it known to all men by these presents that I Philip Sidney, Esquire, do owe unto Richard Rodway, citizen and merchant tailor of London, the sum of forty-two pounds six shillings of lawful money of England, to be paid to the said Richard Rodway, his executors, administrators or assigns, or to one of them, the nine and twentieth day of September next coming after the date hereof. To the whole payment well and truly to be made I bind me, my heirs, executors and administrators by these presents. Sealed with my seal given the 8th day of August in the 17th year of the reign of our sovereign lady Elizabeth, by the grace of God Queen of England, France and Ireland, Defender of the Faith, etc. By me Philippe Sidney.

Sealed and delivered in the presence of us

HENRY WHITE.   GRIFFITH MADDOX."

The indebtedness was well and truly paid, for a stroke has been drawn through the words 'By me Philippe Sidney.'

In October Sidney took part in London in another elaborate ceremony when the eldest daughter of Lord and Lady Russell was baptized in Westminster Abbey. Lady Russell was Elizabeth, the fourth daughter of Sir Anthony Cooke ; she had been the wife of Sir Thomas Hoby, who died in 1566, and, it will be remembered that she had long been one of Lady Sidney's warmest friends. In 1574 she had married Lord Russell, second son of the Duke of Bedford, and the Queen had consented to be godmother when their first child was baptized, for she had long admired and liked Lady Russell. As the Court was at Windsor, however, the Queen appointed the Countess of Warwick to act as her deputy : the Countess of Sussex was also godmother and the Earl of Leicester godfather. The baptismal ceremony on October 27th was unusually splendid, and there was assembled a great company of lords and ladies, knights, barons and earls. The Countess of Warwick's train was borne by Lady Burghley and Lady Bacon, sisters of Lady Russell. The child was baptized by the dean and given the name of Elizabeth.

"In the meantime Mr. Philip Sidney came out of the chapel called St. Edward's Shrine, having a towel on his left shoulder, and with him came Mr. Delves, bearing the basin and ewer, and took the say Then the deputy came forth, her train borne, and they two kneeling she washed,—

then other gentlemen with two basins and ewers, came to the Countess of Sussex and the Earl of Leicester ; and they having washed, immediately came from the aforesaid place of St. Edward's shrine gentlemen with cups of hippocras and wafers ; that done, they all departed out of the church."

The ceremony was followed by "a stately and costly delicate banquet[1]."

Absorbing as Sidney's interest in the varied pageantry of the summer must naturally have been, it is difficult to forgive his utter neglect of the man to whom he had been under the greatest of obligations during the preceding three years. On December 2nd Languet received the first letter which Sidney had written since reaching England six months before except that which he wrote immediately after his arrival in early June. The old man was in no mood to accept conventional excuses. His letters to Sidney had never been more frequent nor longer than during these months, and moreover he knew that Sidney had found time to write to other friends on the Continent. The letter which Sidney at length sent is lost and we know of its contents only by Languet's references in his reply. The young man's light-hearted explanations of his silence were especially irritating : he had been much occupied—but Cæsar had been even more so, and had found time to write his commentaries in camp.

"Just consider, I beg you," Languet continued, "what it means that for such a long period you did not choose to devote a single hour to those who love you dearly as you know, and who are more concerned for your welfare than for their own. Had you sacrificed one dance per month you could have satisfied us abundantly. Last year you were here with us for three or four months together. Recall to mind how many excellent authors you read, and how much good you derived from reading them ; if in such a short time you were able to learn so much that was of value in the right ordering of your life, surely the memory of it should have withheld you from burying yourself in mere empty pleasures[2]."

After further reproaching Sidney for his surrender of himself to frivolity, Languet adopts a milder tone. His sternness, he declares, is a poor return for the kindliness of Sidney's letter.

---

[1] *Hargreave MSS.* Quoted in Wiffen's *House of Russell*, vol. I, pp. 502–505.
[2] *Epistolæ*, p. 139.

He is deeply grieved to learn that Sidney's health is indifferent, though he is inclined to ascribe his ill-health to his unrestrained devotion to pleasure. Sidney had written something in jest about taking a wife ; Languet insists on discussing the subject seriously. He rejoices to hear of the favours lavished on the young man by his relatives and friends, and he sends greetings to Wotton, Corbet and his other English acquaintances. "Farewell," he concludes, "and remember that you have to do with a man who does not easily endure being put off with mere words."

There is no reason for supposing that Sidney's jesting reference to marriage had any relation to a particular young lady, though we may be sure that there was much speculation as to the future wife of the young man who was looked on as the heir not only of his father but also of the great Earls of Leicester and Warwick. We may notice here one project of marriage for Sidney with a daughter of Lord Berkeley which had been discussed during his absence on the Continent. A great lawsuit had been pending between the Berkeleys and the Lords Lisle ever since the death in 1418 of Thomas, Lord Berkeley, who had married Margaret the sole heiress of Warine, Lord Lisle, and at Penshurst there are still extant in two large folio volumes papers relating to this suit, which lasted for almost two centuries. Sir Henry Sidney was on friendly terms with the Lord Berkeley of his day[1] and the proposal of marriage seems to have originated with Leicester, probably with a view to compounding the quarrel. At any rate, on October 26, 1573, four friends of Lord Berkeley wrote to him the following frank expression of their opinion in the matter :

" Because you are over resolutely determined to leave your daughter to inherit your land, and not to give the same to any heir male of your house, which is great pity, we think it necessary for you upon reasonable conditions to accept the offer of Mr. Philip Sidney if the same be again made ; if also a further offer be made by Mr. Robert Sidney for one of your younger daughters we likewise hold the same nothing necessary for you to refuse.

[1] See Sir Henry's letter to Leicester on August 8, 1568 (Collins, vol. I, p. 34), in which he tells of meeting Lord Berkeley and Thomas Throkmorton at Kenilworth. Throkmorton is one of the subscribers of the letter which follows.

Your Lordship cannot bestow your daughter more honourably in this land, as we think ; for these possibilities are very deed certain, or to be made very certain, the Earl of Leicester greatly tendering the younger son for that he is his godson and beareth his name[1]."

There is no record of the negotiations having proceeded further.

A curious story to the effect that Sidney was at one time a candidate for the Kingship of Poland may be dealt with here, as it was at this time that Stephen Bathori, the Prince of Transylvania, was raised to that dignity by the Electors, and as his death did not occur until a short time after that of Sidney. Bathori's great competitor for the vacant Polish throne was no less a personage than the Emperor, and Languet's letters to Sidney contain long accounts of the varied progress of their respective candidacies. Needless to say they contain no hint that the young Englishman was personally interested in the outcome. The story was first related, it would seem, by Naunton in his *Fragmenta Regalia*, which was probably written about 1630, where it is stated that Queen Elizabeth "refused to further his [Sidney's] advancement, not out of emulation, but out of fear to lose the jewel of her times." The story has been repeated by Fuller, Anthony à Wood, Collins, Nichols, Zouch, Gray and Fox-Bourne, but it may be dismissed as an absurdity. It probably originated in Sidney's well-known interest in Polish politics in general, and in Stephen Bathori's rule in particular, to which Fulke Greville makes reference in his *Life*.

In London Sidney probably lived part of the time with his mother in the house opposite Paul's Wharf but generally at Leicester House, to which address his numerous letters from his continental friends were always directed. From Venice Don Cæsar Caraffa continued to send him news and warm

---

[1] MSS. of Lord Fitzhardinge at Berkeley Castle (*Appendix to Third Report of Hist. Man. Com.*, 1872). Sidney has a passing reference to the great lawsuit in his 'Defence' of Leicester (Collins, *Mem.* p. 65). In his will, the Earl of Leicester bequeathed lands recovered from Lord Berkeley and refers to them as having come by descent. (*Ibid.* p. 72.) The quarrel was finally settled by arbitration in 1604, when Robert Sidney was the Dudley claimant. (*Ibid.* 116.) A reference to the great sum which the suit had cost is made in the Memorial of Thomas Nevitt to the Earl of Leicester (*Sidneiana*).

regards to the members of his family[1]. From Vienna Charles
de l'Ecluse wrote frequently. In December he sent a long
friendly letter to 'Baron Sidney' in which we learn of the latter's
anxiety to procure a certain portrait which Abondius feels
certain he can buy—probably the same portrait which, six
months later, Languet has to confess his inability to secure
because the rogue who owned it would not part with it[2]. In
the following May de l'Ecluse expresses his pleasure that Sidney
liked his book which he had sent him, and in June he sends an
account of a dinner at which Dr Purkircher was present when
they drank Sidney's health in very good Austrian wine and
promised themselves to drink it in still better Hungarian when
they met again[3]. Sidney's most indefatigable correspondent,
however, was Banosius, the translator of the *Commentaries* of
Ramus and his biographer. No less than eight of his letters
to Sidney, all written within the space of a few months, have
been preserved[4]; they deal largely with his dedication of his
works on Ramus to Sidney but contain much information on
the affairs of Poland and Casimir's military movements, as well
as personal news of many of Sidney's friends, and an account
of the festivities at the Count of Hanau's marriage. From
these letters one comes to feel how deep an impression Sidney
had made on these men, all of whom were devoted friends of
Languet.

During the winter of 1575–1576 Sidney's practical interest
in English politics began. He was especially interested in
Ireland on his father's account, but he was at least equally
interested in the foreign policy of the Queen with which the
fortunes of the Netherlands were so intimately bound up. In
the autumn of 1575 William of Orange had dispatched St
Aldegonde and two other commissioners to England to implore
Elizabeth to accept the sovereignty of their country. The
Queen was not at all anxious to do anything of the sort. She

---

[1] *V.* his letters of October 22, 1575, and December 2, 1575 (*Add. MSS.*
17520, 4, and 15914, 25).

[2] *Add. MSS.* 17520, 6. Languet, *Epistolæ*, p. 151.

[3] *Add. MSS.* 15914, folios 29 and 31.

[4] *Add. MSS.* 15914, 21, 27 and 28 ; 17520, 8 ; 18675, 4, 6, 7, and 8.

would consider the proposal only when she became convinced
that the alternative was to see the provinces fall into the
hands of France. Just at the moment the danger from that
source was promising to dissolve. The Duc d'Alençon, the
King's younger brother, had fled from the Court and had
placed himself at the head of a Huguenot army. Under
leaders like La Noue, Condé, Duke Casimir, and, a few months
later, Henry of Navarre, the Huguenots swept everything
before them. On the outcome of the struggle would depend
Elizabeth's answer to the envoys of Orange. She was delighted
to find the power of the Guises checked, for they were the sworn
friends of Spain: on the other hand, she did not wish the
Huguenots to become all-powerful in France, for in that event
they would almost certainly be willing to do for the Netherlands what the Queen preferred not to do. Any such increase
in the power of France she could not consider. "France and
Spain," declared Camden in his *Annals*, "are, as it were, the
scales in the balance of Europe, and England the tongue or
holder of the balance." When the French King brought about
a suspension of hostilities by renewing the toleration edicts
Elizabeth was well pleased. She was once more able to hold
the balance without undue alarm, and accordingly she dismissed St Aldegonde with scant ceremony.

What Sidney thought of such a policy it is not difficult to
guess. Even before the Huguenots had risen, Alençon had
succeeded his brother in the rôle of suitor for the hand of
Elizabeth, and the French ambassador urged the match by
every means in his power. As usual, Elizabeth was non-
committal. She lent Alençon money, but she insisted that
she must see him before making a decisive reply to his proposal.
Many of her Council approved of the match, and it is quite
possible that Sidney at this time may also have regarded
Alençon as the head of the French Protestants and eligible as
a husband for the Queen. At any rate it is a very interesting
fact that Alençon wrote to him urging him to visit France[1].
Sidney seems to have seriously meditated taking a part in the

[1] Languet, *Epistolæ*, p. 151.

Huguenot war[1], and Languet was inclined to think that he might welcome the opportunity of spending several months in France and becoming acquainted with that country as he already knew Germany and Italy, thus carrying out the plans which had been interrupted by the St Bartholomew massacre. The Renaissance spirit was still strong at the French Court and was exercising a powerful influence on England. Even Alençon himself was a poet and encouraged sculptors and painters; in Catherine de' Medici the traditions of her race still lived and gave colour to the life of her Court. Why Sidney gave up his project we do not know. Perhaps the sudden conclusion of peace and the breaking off of the marriage project are a sufficient explanation.

During the same winter Sidney contracted a warm friendship with the Earl of Essex, who was spending his sojourn in England at Durham House in the Strand. We have already seen an instance of the interest which Essex took in Sidney when the latter was but a small boy[2]; their respective ages were now thirty-six and twenty-one, and they were attracted to each other by common interest in the Irish question and by similarity of temperament. Essex found himself hopelessly compromised financially as a result of his Irish enterprise, and he was now engaged in a long-drawn-out attempt to persuade the Queen "to shape some gracious resolution" for him. She had insisted on his mortgaging to her the greater portion of his estates for the repayment of the sums expended in his former expedition, and now he found that "my land being entangled to her, no man will give me credit for any money[3]." The Queen's first offers were rejected by Essex, and some details relating to his future employment in Ireland were

---

[1] On February 2nd he received £80 from the banker Vellutelli, and on February 21 £350 from Walter Alderford, an agent of his father. The receipts which he gave are now among the Penshurst MSS. On February 22nd he addressed a letter to "Servant Walker" asking him to pay £20 to his sister's old governess, Mrs Anne Mantell, as that sum was owing her for wages. This letter is also preserved at Penshurst, and is endorsed "Received £10 in part of payment. Robert Mantell."

[2] See pp. 52–53.

[3] Devereux, *Lives of the Earls of Essex*, I, p. 130.

referred to Sir Henry Sidney. The latter's reply was most favourable to the Earl, to whom personally it was quite satisfactory ; Sir Henry's secretary, Waterhouse, reported to him that the only criticism of its contents had come from the Earl of Leicester, who thought that Sir Henry "had not made it apparent enough to her Majesty, or the Lords, that you earnestly wished the Earl's return[1]." The passage has been cited to prove that Leicester had already begun his intrigue with Lady Essex, who, after her lord's death, eventually became Lady Leicester, but we can only say that it is one of those pieces of very inconclusive evidence which in the eyes of his contemporary detractors were sufficient to convict him of treasons capital and proved, if not confessed. Waterhouse's letter tells us that it was Philip Sidney who accompanied Sir Henry's messenger to deliver his letters to Essex, and further gives us the interesting information that the Earl called him his son by adoption. Of their intimacy we have many proofs, and it is probable that the Earl already hoped that he might some day call the young man his son by marriage, but we have no evidence that Sidney felt any special interest at this time in the Earl's eldest daughter whom, no doubt, he had opportunities of meeting daily.

Some time during the year 1576 Sidney was appointed "Cup-bearer" to the Queen with an annual fee of £30[2]. On June 16th Robert Dorset, his old Oxford tutor, sent him an urgent invitation to be his guest[3]. Dorset was living at Ewelm, near Oxford, where he was acting as tutor to Robert Sidney, now a lad in his thirteenth year, and on hearing that his old pupil was about to visit the University he hastened to extend his invitation. Whether the visit actually took place we do not know.

On May 9th Essex was appointed by letters patent Earl Marshal of Ireland after having sold a considerable portion of his estates in order to satisfy his creditors. He went to Chartley to put his affairs in order, deposited his will in the safe keeping of Sir Francis Walsingham, and, on July 22nd,

[1] Collins, i, 168.   [2] Hunter, *Chorus Vatum*, p. 8.
[3] Zouch, p. 376.

set sail from Holyhead. He reached Dublin next day. Sir Henry was absent from the capital, but on August 10th they met some 28 miles from Dublin and "there was great shew of friendly salutations of permanent friendships[1]."

It is highly probable that Philip Sidney accompanied his friend to Ireland.

"I am convinced," Languet wrote him on August 13th, "from the letter which you wrote to me from London on the 21st of June that you had intended to tell me nothing of your journey to Ireland unless my letter had reached you just before your departure ; for you had written word of your intention to other friends some time before, who had informed me of it, and you were equipped for your expedition when you wrote to me[2]."

He probably joined his father in Connaught immediately after landing, for on August 15th Sir Henry wrote to Walsingham as though Philip had been with him some time. "This journey finished," he wrote, "I intend to return Philip Sidney by whom you shall understand as much as I can write or report[3]."

Since leaving England Sir Henry had spent a strenuous year, during which, in his own words, "I have passed through each province and have been almost in each county thereof[4]." His problem seemed to him less hopeless than it had ever seemed before, and he began to dream of yet seeing Ireland obedient and prosperous. "If I might once see it," he wrote to Burghley, "it should be more joy to me than to get an earldom of lands in England[5]." Whatever we may think of Sir Henry's enthusiasm for forcing on the Irish people a religion which they did not want, we must respect the high-minded unselfishness and the zeal for reform which characterized all his efforts. The financial problem remained, as always, insoluble. The £20,000 per annum which he was granted for the Irish establishment was not sufficient to allow him to relax the 'cess' which was levied on landowners, and there were ominous mutterings against the tax among the gentlemen of the Pale.

Of Philip Sidney's visit to his father we know only a few

---

[1] Devereux, *op. cit.* p. 136.

[2] *Epistolæ*, p. 154. Froude is mistaken in supposing that Philip accompanied his father to Ireland in 1575. *V. History*, vol. x, p. 531.

[3] *State Papers—Ireland—Eliz.*, vol. LVI, fol. 40.

[4] *Ibid.* Sir Henry to Elizabeth, April 29, 1576. [5] *Ibid.* May 3, 1576.

details. We have already seen that on August 10th Sir Henry was approaching Dublin. His stay there was to be a short one, for he learned almost immediately after his arrival that the young Burkes had broken their parole, had crossed the Shannon after cutting their English garments in pieces to manifest their contempt for English authority, and were attempting to raise the whole west country[1]. Two thousand Scots had already landed in Connaught to assist them, and on August 15th Sir Henry wrote to the Privy Council : "I intend, God willing, to be amongst them myself within these ten days," as he was "now almost in a readiness to advance towards Connaught to repress the stirs there[2]." During the next six weeks Philip had an opportunity to learn at first hand the terribly effective methods which his father employed against Irish rebels. Here is Sir Henry's account of their expedition :

"I passed the river Shannon, I went to the Earl of Clanrickard's chief house before named, I broke it and took him, he protesting ignorance and innocence, but God knoweth untruly, and so hath since most manifestly been proved. I proclaimed the sons rebels and traitors, and committed, led away and still detained the father ; I planted there two worthy and sufficient gentlemen, namely Thomas Le Strange and Captain Collier with a garrison of 250 men, who valiantly did their devoir as well in offending the rebels as in defending the subjects. I sent for the Earl's followers to come to Galway, as well English as Irish, whose names I have forgotten saving only MacKenzie and Mackremmon[3]."

Sir Henry and Philip were at Athlone on September 4th[4] and had reached Galway some time before September 16th[5]. Of their stay in Galway Sir Henry has left us one picturesque detail :

"There came to me also a most famous feminine sea-captain, called Granny O'Malley, and offered her services unto me wheresoever I would command her, with three galleys and two hundred fighting men, either in Ireland or Scotland. She brought with her her husband, for she was as well by sea as by land more than master's mate with him. He was of the nether Burkes, and now as I hear Mack William Euter, and called by

---

[1] Sir Henry to Walsingham, March 1, 1583.
[2] *State Papers—Irish—Eliz.*, Aug. 15, 1576
[3] Letter to Walsingham, March 1, 1583.   [4] Collins, i, p. 128.
[5] The letter written to Philip by Charles de l'Ecluse from Vienna on June 8, 1576, is endorsed (not in Philip's hand) "Reçu a Galway le 16 Septemb. 1576."

nickname Richard in Iron. This was a notorious woman in all the coast of Ireland : this woman did Sir Philip Sidney see and speak with ; he can more at large inform you of her[1]."

On September 20th Sir Henry wrote to the Council an account of his operations.

"I have been still occupied as presently I am," he wrote, "in a kind of an actual war and continual search for the rebels, sometimes dispersing one part of my forces into one part of the country, and sometimes into another, as I was directed by the best intelligence where their haunt was. But the hollow hearts of the inhabitants and the secret lurking of the rebels is such, and hath been yet hitherto as I have had no great hand upon them, though I have at sundry times slain of their men, taken their prey, and some of their best and strongest holds from them."

It had been strenuous work, and Sir Henry as he was about to set out for Sligo confesses that he is "not a little wearied with the toilsome travel of this wearisome journey in tracing and searching the rebels from place to place and the ill-success I have to light upon them[2]."

What share Philip took in these strenuous operations is not recorded. Whetstone refers to "his service in Ireland[3]" in a fashion which suggests that he had taken his full share of the attendant hardships. The reference in the *Apologie for Poetrie* to the bareness of learning in Ireland and to the devout reverence of the Irish for their poets was probably based on his personal experiences at this time. Whatever these experiences were they were to be brought to a sudden termination.

"Here heard we first," Sir Henry writes, "of the extreme and hopeless sickness of the Earl of Essex, by whom Sir Philip being often most lovingly and earnestly wished and written for, he with all the speed he could make went to him, but found him dead before his coming, in the castle at Dublin[4]."

Philip probably set out from Galway on September 20th or very shortly afterwards, for in a letter to Sussex dated September 19th

---

[1] Letter to Walsingham, March 1, 1583. Froude's statement that "a close acquaintance sprang up as was natural between herself and young Philip" (*Hist.* x, 532) must be set down as a mere embellishment of the story. He also errs in placing the scene of their meeting at Cork.

[2] Collins, I, p. 130.

[3] *Sir Philip Sidney, his honourable life, etc.*

[4] Letter to Walsingham, March 1, 1583.

Sir Henry refers him " to the report of this bringer, my son[1]," and in a letter to Burghley dated the following day he writes: " I pray your Lordship in the rest of [the affairs of] Ireland for this time give credit to Ph. Sidney[2]."

The unfortunate Essex had been taken ill with an attack of dysentery on August 20th from which it became gradually evident that he was not to recover. On his death-bed his chief thought was for his children, and in the hope that he might secure their future he busied himself in writing letters to the Queen and Burghley, and in arranging the details of his will. On September 22nd he passed away.

How deep Sidney's grief must have been when he reached Dublin only to find that he was too late we may easily imagine. During the course of his illness Essex had dispatched messengers into the west country in the hope that he might see his young friend once more, but when he knew that his wish was not to be gratified he left him a message on the subject that was nearest his heart.

" Tell him," said the dying man, "I send him nothing, but I wish him well, and so well that if God do move both their hearts I wish that he might match with my daughter. I call him son; he is so wise, so virtuous and godly; and if he go on in the course he hath begun, he will be as famous and worthy a gentleman as ever England bred[3]."

The Earl's body was conveyed to England, and on November 26th was interred at Carmarthen. Edward Waterhouse had charge of the arrangements, and it is probable that Sidney was closely associated with him in the task, for Waterhouse, writing to Sir Henry Sidney from Chartley on November 14th to give an account of his proceedings since leaving Ireland, says that he will "stand to the report of Sir [sic!] Philip Sidney above any other[4]."

It was not until October 13th that Sir Henry Sidney was able to reach Dublin[5], where he heard rumours to the effect

---

[1] *Cottonian MSS. Vespasian,* F. XII.   [2] *State Papers—Irish—Eliz.*
[3] Devereux, *op. cit.* I, p. 139.   [4] Collins, I, p. 147.

[5] Flügel, in his usually accurate study of Sidney's life, is in error in supposing that Philip too returned to Dublin only on October 13th, and that Sir Henry went over to Carmarthen to attend the funeral of Essex. (*Einleitung,* S. xxvi.)

that Essex had died of poison. He at once instituted a careful inquiry into all the circumstances, and was able to report to Walsingham that "there was no appearance or cause of suspicion that could be gathered that he died of poison[1]." The rumours were revived some three years later when the marriage of Lady Essex to the Earl of Leicester became known, and they have been preserved in various vindictive accounts of Leicester's life. There was no evidence, however, which gave to these suspicions a shadow of probability.

While occupying himself in attempting to reduce to order the tangled affairs of the deceased Earl, Sidney must have looked with unusual interest on Penelope Devereux, the eldest daughter. Not only had Essex's last wish been communicated to him, but the subject had become one of general interest and was being much discussed.

"All these Lords," wrote Waterhouse to Sir Henry, "that wish well to the children [of Essex] and, I suppose, all the best sort of the English lords besides, do expect what will become of the treaty between Mr. Philip and my Lady Penelope. Truly, my Lord, I must say to your Lordship, as I have said to my Lord of Leicester and Mr. Philip, the breaking-off from this match if the default be on your parts will turn to more dishonour than can be repaired with any other marriage in England[2]."

We shall see later that there is no reason to suppose that Sidney at this time felt any special interest in Penelope, whom he probably regarded as a mere child. The question of his attitude toward their possible marriage was one on which at least it was not necessary to make up his mind at present. We catch only a glimpse of him during the remaining months of this year. On reaching London he found letters awaiting him from his continental friends—one from Andreas Paulus and two from Languet, who not only continued to send detailed reports on current events in the Empire and in Poland, but enclosed special papers which he thought might interest Sidney on Persian and Spanish affairs.

"I hope my letters will find you in London," he wrote, "after a safe passage from Ireland, and that you are enjoying the delightful ease of your court, which after the perils and hardships of your wearisome journey will seem even more pleasant to you now than formerly."

[1] Collins, I, p. 140.   [2] Collins, I, p. 147.

The delightfulness of his return to Court must have been modified once more by his mother's troubles. The longest of her letters to Burghley is dated October 29, 1576, and the theme is only a variation on those we have heard in her earlier letters. Medley, the alchemist, who had a few years earlier been held in high estimation by such men as Burghley himself, Leicester, Sir Thomas Smith and Sir Humphrey Gilbert, was now discredited and imprisoned in the Counter. Just what Lady Mary's relation to him was we cannot well determine, but a few extracts from her letter will suggest her unhappiness and bitterness of spirit. She writes "as soon as I have been able to hold up my head to write since the receipt of your most honourable and most dear welcome letter." She does not dare "to renew my suit to your Lordship for any more liberty for the unhappy prisoner because I see you have no liking thereto," though she insists that there is "the less likelihood of so great ill in him for that his accusers be so monstrous vile and wicked themselves." She pours forth complaints in general and in detail for her own "discredit by such mates," and leaves on our minds an impression that her life was one of constant vexation.

From Greenwich Sidney wrote on November 4th to Robert Walker, his father's steward at Oxford, asking him to make "provision of a stable and hay and provender for half a score of horses which are coming out of Ireland. Within this ten days I look for them[1]." We may assume that he was at Carmarthen on November 26th at the funeral of Essex, and soon afterward we find him engrossed in preparations for undertaking his first public employment.

[1] *Penshurst MS.*

CHAPTER X

AN AMBASSADOR OF THE QUEEN

THE year 1577 opened auspiciously for the younger members of the Sidney family. Mary Sidney had just completed her fifteenth year, but she was already reputed one of the most beautiful and interesting young women of the Court circle, and gossip was busy regarding her future husband. In December a correspondent of the Earl of Rutland wrote from the Court that some people thought that Mrs Sidney would be the Lady of Wilton but that he was not of that mind[1]. The rumour was well founded, however. The Earl of Pembroke, whose first wife, Catherine Talbot, a daughter of the Earl of Shrewsbury, had been dead a little more than a year, was now about forty years of age. He was an especial friend of Leicester, who communicated to Sir Henry the likelihood of the match provided he could find a sufficient dowry. Sir Henry was delighted with the news ; the disparity between the ages of his daughter and her prospective husband does not seem to have given him any concern, and although he was deeply troubled as to how he was to find the dowry, he wrote to Leicester "protesting before the Almighty God that if he and all the powers on earth would give me my choice for a husband for her I would choose the Earl of Pembroke[2]."

In the same letter Sir Henry wrote : "Good my Lord, send Philip to me ; there was never father had more need of his son than I have of him. Once again, good my Lord, let

---

[1] R. Brackinbury to Earl of Rutland, December 12, 1576. Belvoir MSS. *Hist. Man. Com.*)

[2] February 4, 1577 (Collins, I, p. 89).

me have him." No doubt Sir Henry, besides craving for his
son's companionship, had learned during Philip's brief visit
to prize his judgment. Ireland was for the moment unusually
quiet, but the Lord Deputy's perplexities were hardly lessened
by the fact. Ormond, whom he heartily detested, was losing
no opportunity of thwarting his plans, the Queen was insisting
that the quarterly allowance to the Lord Deputy should be
reduced in amount, and the mutterings against the cess on
the part of the gentlemen of the Pale were threatening to develop
into an open refusal to pay.

Sir Henry had evidently heard no rumour that Philip was
to be sent on a mission for the Queen, for even in the following
month he addressed to his son a letter asking him to show all
possible courtesies to Sir Cormack MacTeige MacCartye, an
Irish chief who was about to visit London[1]. For some time,
however, Philip had been busily occupied in preparing for a
visit to the Continent. Perhaps it was in order to learn
whether he would set out under good auspices that he paid a
visit on January 16th to Dr John Dee, the famous astrologer,
at Mortlake[2]. Philip was accompanied on this occasion by
the Earl of Leicester, Dyer, and other friends ; we may notice
here that Dr Dee numbered amongst his clients not only all
the famous navigators of the day, but Burghley, Walsingham
and the Queen herself. Philip's 'Instructions[3]' were drawn on
February 7th. As ambassador for the Queen he was sent to
the Emperor Rudolf and his mother to "condole the death" of
the late Emperor, and on his way he was to visit the Count
Palatines Lewis and Casimir to "condole the death" of their
father. The document makes it clear, however, that the chief
duty of the young envoy was to inform himself as thoroughly
as possible regarding contemporary political and religious
affairs in the Empire and among the Princes of Germany.
Leicester provided him with a letter of introduction to Count
Casimir[4], and he set out accompanied by his friends Fulke

[1] March, 1577 (Collins, I, p. 163).
[2] *Dr Dee's Diary* (Camden Soc.) p. 2.
[3] *Harley MSS.* vol. XXXVI, p. 295.
[4] *Cotton MSS. Galba*, B. XI, f. 412, February 20, 1577.

Greville[1] and Edward Dyer[2] and a distinguished company of attendants[3]. He was evidently not forgetful of the dignity that attaches to the Queen's representative, for in all places where he lodged he caused a tablet to be hung upon which were inscribed the following lines beneath the Sidney coat of arms:

Illustrissimi & Generosissimi Viri
Philippi Sidnaei Angli
Pro-regis Hiberniae filii, Comitum Warwici
Et Leicestriae Nepotis, Serenissimi
Reginae Angliae ad Caesarem Legati[4].

On March 1st Dr Thomas Wilson, the English ambassador at Brussels, wrote to Walsingham that he had provided lodgings for Philip Sidney and was making ready to wait upon him and give him the best advice he could[5]. Four days later Sidney had arrived, and Wilson announced that they were about to ride over to Louvain to pay their respects to Don John of Austria, the hero of Lepanto, and now Governor of the Netherlands for his half-brother, Philip of Spain. The interview took place the next day, and notwithstanding Sidney's plain speech they had fair and sweet answers. Fulke Greville gives the following quaint account of Don John's attitude:

"Though at the first in his Spanish haughture, he gave him access as by descent to a youth, of grace as to a stranger, and in particular competition (as he conceived) to an enemy; yet after a while that he had taken his just altitude, he found himself so stricken with this extraordinary Planet, that the beholders wondered to see what ingenuous tribute that brave and high-minded Prince paid to his worth; giving more honour and respect to this hopeful young gentleman than to the embassadors of mighty Princes[6]."

[1] Languet, p. 162.

[2] *V. State Papers—Foreign—Eliz.*, July 20, 1577.   Daniel Rogers to Walsingham.

[3] "On Monday next Mr. Sidney goes toward the Emperor accompanied by Sir H. Lea, Sir Jerome Bowes, Mr. Basset, Mr. Cressie, Mr. Brouker (if he be well) Mr. M. Stanhope and others." Thos. Screvan to Earl of Rutland, February 16, 1577. (Belvoir MSS.—*Hist. Man. Com. Report*.)

[4] Collins, *Memoirs*, p. 100. Sir Henry Wotton was accustomed to set up a similar tablet wherever he travelled on the Continent (*v.* Pearsall Smith's *Life and Letters of Sir Henry Wotton*, I, 93).

[5] *State Papers—Foreign—Eliz.* Brussels, March 1, March 5, and March 10, 1577.

[6] Greville, *op. cit.* p. 32.

From Brussels and Louvain Sidney proceeded to Heidelberg to visit the Elector Palatine and his brother Prince Casimir. On March 22nd he wrote Burghley a short letter[1] in which he was able to assure him of his good health and referred him for details of his journey to the report which he had written on the same day to Walsingham[2]. It is an admirable letter— serious and formal in tone, lucid and succinct. The Elector was at present at Amberg, a town in the Upper Palatinate, and Sidney proposed to visit him there while on his way to Prague; meanwhile he had spent some time with Casimir and had carried out Her Majesty's instructions as far as that Prince was concerned. We may conjecture that the absence of the Elector caused the young ambassador no serious disappoint- ment, for Fulke Greville tells us that the mere conveying of compliments "sorted better with his youth than his spirit," and that his real interest centred in that article of his instruc- tions "which gave him scope (as he passed) to salute such German Princes as were interested in the cause of our Religion or their own native liberty[3]." Casimir, like his father, was an earnest Calvinist, and was eager to see the establishment of a Protestant League or *Foedus Evangelicum* not only throughout Germany but in the whole of Europe. This was a project dear to Sidney's heart, and he found in Casimir "great mis- contentment that his brother begins to make alteration in Religion," having already established Lutheranism in the Upper Palatinate. The Elector, Sidney declared, was

"of a soft nature, led to these things only through conscience, and Prince Casimir wise that can temper well with the other's weakness. The other Princes of Germany have no care but how to grow rich and to please their senses, the Duke of Saxony so carried away with the ubiquity that he grows bitter to the true Lutherians. The rest are of the same mould, thinking they should be safe though all the world were on fire about them, except it be the Landgrave William and his bretheren and this Prince Casimir."

On the whole the prospects for a League were far from bright. Casimir hoped soon to lead an army to the support of the

---

[1] *State Papers—Foreign—Eliz.*   Heidelberg, March 22, 1577.
[2] *Cotton MSS. Galba*, B. XI, f. 387.   [3] *Op. cit.* p. 41.

Huguenots, and then he "saith that I shall hear that he is dead or that he hath left a miserable France of the Popish side." Casimir had also told him of a rumour that Don John was to marry the Queen of Scots "and so to stir troubles in England."

On the day on which this dispatch was written Sidney left Heidelberg[1]. Failing to find the Elector Palatine at Amberg as he had hoped to do, he proceeded toward Prague and reached the city on Maundy Thursday. On Easter Monday he had audience and expressed to the Emperor "how greatly her Majesty was grieved with the loss of so worthy a [friend as] the Emperor his father was." He went on to relate "her Majesty's good hope of him that he would second his father in his virtues and the manner of his government." Lastly he gave him to understand "how nobly her Majesty had proceeded in the Low Country matters and up[on what] good grounds[2]."

"He answered me in Latin with very few words," Sidney reported, but those words were gracious and friendly if somewhat indefinite, and when the young ambassador took his leave the Emperor presented him with a great chain[3]. The next day Sidney delivered the Queen's letters to the Empress, a sister of Philip of Spain, and to her daughter, the widow of Charles IX of France. His own brief account of the interview suggests the sympathetic tact with which he performed his duty.

"Of the Emperor deceased I used but few words because in truth I saw it bred some trouble unto her [the Empress] to hear him mentioned in that kind. She answered me with many courteous speeches and great acknowledging of her own beholdingness to her Majesty. And for her son she said she hoped he would do well, but that for her own part she said

[1] The account of his visit to the Imperial Court is derived from the second of his formal reports to Walsingham written on May 3rd after his return to Heidelberg. The document is among the Cottonian MSS. (Galba, B. xi, f. 363); one edge was seriously injured by the fire which wrought havoc among the MSS. of that collection.

[2] Sidney has been credited by several of his biographers with having made a bitterly anti-Catholic speech on this occasion and of having exhorted the Emperor to beware of Rome and Spain. The story, which does little credit to his judgment, arose from a confusion of the accounts of what he said to the Emperor and of what Fulke Greville reports that he said to the Princes of Germany in general.

[3] Waterhouse to Sir Henry Sidney, June 10, 1577 (Collins, i, 193).

she had given herself from the world, and would not greatly stir from
thenceforward in it.   Then did I deliver the Queen of France's letter, she
standing by the Empress, using such speeches as I thought were fit for her
double sorrow, and her Majesty's good will unto her, confirmed by her
wise and noble governing of herself in the time of her being in France.
Her answer was full of humbleness, but she spake so low that I could not
understand many of her words."

Sidney then visited the young princes and informed himself
regarding their characters and the probable trend of events
at the Imperial Court.   He discovered that the Emperor was
"wholly by his inclination given to the wars, few of words,
sullen of disposition, very secret and resolute, nothing the
manner his father had in winning men in his behaviour, but
yet constant in keeping them."   His brother Ernest was
similar to him and both were "extremely Spaniolated."   Then
follow brief notes on Mathias, Maximilian, Albertus and Wen-
ceslaus, younger princes of the house.   Much detailed information
which he had collected he would report to Walsingham on his
arrival in England.

One other interesting event of Sidney's visit to Prague was
his meeting with Campion, whom he had known at Oxford and
who had been a *protégé* of Sir Henry Sidney.   Campion had
left England in April, 1571, and entered the Seminary at
Douai.   In the autumn of 1572 he had proceeded to Rome and
a few months later had become a member of the Jesuit order.
He had spent the year of his novitiate at Prague and Brünn,
and since September, 1574, he had been Professor of Rhetoric
in the Jesuit College at Prague.   Of this meeting with Sidney
his biographer, Simpson, gives the following account :

"When Sidney reached Prague he wished much to see Campion, whom
he had known at Oxford, and whom his father had protected in Ireland.
Their meeting, says Parsons, was difficult, for Sir Philip was afraid of so
many spies set and sent about him by the English Council ; but he managed
to have divers large and secret conferences with his old friend.   After
much argument he professed himself convinced, but said that it was necessary for him to hold on the course which he had hitherto followed ; yet
he promised never to hurt or injure any Catholic, which for the most part
he performed ; and for Father Campion himself he assured him that
whereinsoever he could stand him in stead he should find him a trusty
friend, which he performed not, for afterwards, Campion being condemned

W. L. S.

to death, and the other in most high favour, when he might have done him favour he denied to do it, for fear not to offend.... According to a letter of Father Thomas Fitzherbert of February 1, 1628, Sidney had the courage to confess in England that one of the most memorable things he had witnessed abroad was a sermon by Campion at which he had assisted with the Emperor in Prague[1]."

Campion's own account is contained in a letter which he wrote a few months later to his old tutor, John Bavand :

"Now listen to my news. The Emperor Rudolf, a prudent, brave and good youth, and a sincere son of the Church, has fixed upon himself the eyes and the hearts of the Germans and Bohemians. If he lives great things are expected of him. The Empress Dowager, Maximilian's widow, and sister of Philip of Spain, is living at Prague. A few months ago Philip Sidney came from England to Prague as ambassador, magnificently provided. He had much conversation with me,—I hope not in vain, for to all appearance he was most eager. I commend him to your sacrifices, for he asked the prayers of all good men, and at the same time put into my hands some alms to be distributed to the poor for him, which I have done. Tell this to Dr. Nicholas Sanders, because if any one of the labourers sent into the vineyard from the Douai seminary has an opportunity of watering this plant, he may watch the occasion for helping a poor wavering soul. If this young man, so wonderfully beloved and admired by his countrymen, chances to be converted, he will astonish his noble father, the Deputy of Ireland, his uncles the Dudleys, and all the young courtiers, and Cecil himself. Let it be kept secret[1]."

Campion's assumption that Sidney was almost ready to embrace Catholicism is absurd enough, as everything else that we know about him at this time bears witness, and Parsons' statement that Sidney professed himself convinced is negatived by Campion's own letter. That Sidney was attracted to the brilliant young Englishman who in his devotion to an ideal had turned his back on all worldly ambitions, that he asked the prayers of all good men and gave Campion alms to distribute—this is probable enough. It is just possible that in his desire to appreciate the point of view of a high-minded English Catholic he allowed Campion to suppose that he was more friendly to Catholicism than he really was. The story may serve at least to dispose of the foolish statement which has

---

[1] *Edmund Campion, A Biography*, 1896 edition, pp. 115–116.
[2] *Ibid.* p. 123.

sometimes been made that Sidney was distinguished by his bigotry toward Catholics. The truth is that both he and his father always deprecated harsh measures toward them when the political importance of such an attitude was not obvious. Simpson describes him accurately enough as "hating the Spanish faction," but "not at all disposed to force all Catholics into it by an indiscriminate persecution[1]." Sir Henry might refer to "the poison of Papistry" in his reports to the Council, but on many occasions we find him using his good offices in favour of recusants—to such an extent indeed that he sometimes laid himself open to sharp criticism[2]. Philip's sympathy for individual recusants who were persecuted is well illustrated in a kindly letter which he wrote to Lady Kitson on March 28, 1581[3], in response to her request that he would intercede with Walsingham for Sir Thomas Cornwallis. His desire to contribute something toward bringing about "a speedy easing of the greatness of her burden" is very evident. We shall find him in later years approving of harsh measures and even profiting from recusants' fines, but his condemnation was reserved for their treason, not for their religion. For almost ten years of his short life he was closely associated in the popular mind with the struggle in the Netherlands, a fact which sufficiently explains the dedication to him of violently anti-Catholic pamphlets and the growth of the erroneous idea that he was especially bitter in his feeling toward recusants.

His mission to the Imperial Court concluded, Sidney left Prague and returned to Heidelberg, arriving there on April 30th. The next day he had a friendly audience with the weak Elector Palatine at Neustadt[4]. After conveying to him

---

[1] *Op. cit.* p. 334.

[2] Cf. Walsingham's letter to Sir Henry, August 9, 1580 (Lucy Aikin, *Memoirs of the Court of Queen Elizabeth,* II, p. 163). Cf., too, a petition dated October, 1582, to the Corporation of Hereford praying for the removal of two recusants from the Council with whom Sir Henry "has most painfully, charitably and learnedly used all godly means to reconcile them, but all in vain." The Corporation of Hereford MSS. (*Hist. Man. Com. Reports*).

[3] Nichols, *Progresses of Queen Elizabeth,* vol. II, p. 250.

[4] Ludwig, Count Palatine to Queen, Neustadt, May 1, 1577 (*State Papers— Foreign—Eliz.*).

the Queen's condolences, Sidney urged him in Her Majesty's name

"to have merciful consideration of the Church of the Religion so notably established by his father as in all Germany there is not such a number of excellent, learned men, and truly would rue any man to see the desolation of them."

Much more he added in the same vein, but the Elector merely replied that for her Majesty's sake he would do much, and that he misliked not of the men but must be constrained to do as the other Princes of the Empire. Naturally Sidney was not hopeful as to the prospects of the *Foedus Evangelicum.* He was about to leave Heidelberg to visit the Landgrave and reserved his final judgment until he had once more discussed the situation with Casimir, but he confessed to Walsingham, "My hope doth every day grow less and less[1]."

On May 4th, Sidney set out for Kaiserslautern intending to proceed to visit the Landgrave[2], but a few days later he was compelled to send the Queen's letter by a messenger who was to explain that the Queen for weighty reasons had recalled him[3]. At Cologne he parted from Languet, who had probably been with him during the greater part of his visit except during the time that he spent in Prague.

"I felt incredible satisfaction from our intercourse during so many days," Languet wrote him[4], but he adds, "My pleasure, great as it was, produced a greater sorrow than I ever before felt and it has scarcely yet subsided."

He refers to his jesting at their separation "with a view to drive away your low spirits and my own." Languet had especially enjoyed making the acquaintance of Fulke Greville and the other members of the party, and Sidney had been able to exact from him a definite promise that he would visit them in England[5]. Of a very important subject which they discussed in detail we shall hear presently.

When Sidney left Cologne Languet saw that he was

---

[1] *Cotton MSS. Galba*, B. xi, f. 363.   [2] *Ibid.*
[3] William Landgrave of Hesse to Elizabeth, May 20, 1577. Cassel (*State Papers—Foreign—Eliz.*).
[4] *Epistolæ*, p. 163 (June 14, 1577).
[5] Sidney to Languet, October 1, 1577 (Pears, *op. cit.* p. 116).

"burning to be presented to Orange and form an acquaintance with him," but Languet urged him not to depart from the letter of his instructions and to return to England forthwith. By great good fortune, however, another messenger arrived with a letter from the Queen directing him to visit the Prince. He proceeded to Antwerp, and, after failing to meet the Prince at Brussels, he left Antwerp on May 27th and went by way of Breda to Gertruidenberg, where the Prince and Princess were staying[1]. The days that followed his arrival must have been among the happiest that Sidney ever spent. We can imagine his delight in this opportunity of spending some time in the society of William of Orange and his noble accomplished wife, Charlotte of Bourbon. St Aldegonde, too, was visiting the Prince and they both expressed to Sidney their high admiration for his friend Languet. Sidney stood godfather to the Prince's daughter[2]—the second of six that Charlotte of Bourbon was to bear to him ; she was named Elizabeth, no doubt in honour of the English Queen. At Sidney's departure the Princess gave him a chain of gold and a fair jewel[3]. Of his conversations with Orange during these days we have no detailed record, but of their importance we may judge by the fact that Sidney was commissioned in the name of Orange to offer to Her Majesty the union of the two provinces of Holland and Zealand with the Crown of England[4]. This was a proposal which Elizabeth was by no means eager to accept ; accordingly she sent another envoy to discuss the matter, who reported to her among other things that the Prince had conceived a great opinion of Mr Sidney[5]. A more remarkable testimony to the impression which Sidney made on Orange at this time is given us by Fulke Greville, who relates a conversation which he had with the Prince some two years later. On that occasion Orange requested Greville to say to the Queen that, although he had been either an actor or at least acquainted with the greatest

---

[1] Wilson to Burghley, Antwerp, May 28, 1577 (*State Papers—Foreign—Eliz.*).

[2] Collins, I, p. 192.   [3] *Ibid.* p. 193.

[4] Daniel Rogers to Walsingham, Horn in North Holland, July 20, 1577 (*State Papers—Foreign—Eliz.*).

[5] *Ibid.*

actions and affairs of Europe during the last twenty years, he protested that, if he could judge

"her Majesty had one of the ripest and greatest Counsellors of Estate in Sir Philip Sidney that at this day lived in Europe : to the trial of which he was pleased to leave his own credit engaged, until her Majesty might please to employ this gentleman either amongst her friends or enemies[1]."

As we shall see presently, Orange gave the young Englishman an even more striking evidence of his regard.

Sidney's visit to the Prince came to an end on one of the early days of June. On June 2nd both the Prince and Princess wrote letters to Elizabeth acknowledging those which they had received from her, and referring to Sidney's visit. We may assume that he conveyed these letters to the Queen in person and that he left Gertruidenberg shortly after they were written[2]. He was at Bruges on June 5th[3], and probably sailed within a day or two. Both Walsingham and Waterhouse wrote to Sir Henry on June 10th announcing Philip's arrival.

"Mr. Sidney is returned safe into England," Waterhouse reported, "with great good acceptation of his service at her Majesty's hands, allowed of by all the Lords to have been handled with great judgment and discretion, and hath been honoured abroad in all the Princes' courts with much extraordinary favour....God blessed him so," he adds, "that neither man, boy or horse failed him, or was sick in this journey ; only Fulke Greville had an ague in his return at Rochester[4]."

Walsingham's letter might well have caused the father's heart to swell with pride. Already on April 9th he had written Sir Henry that Philip was winning golden opinions, and Sir Henry in his reply modestly expressed his great joy[5]. Walsingham's second letter concludes as follows[6] :

"Now touching your Lordship's particular, I am to impart unto you the return of the young gentleman, Mr. Sidney, your son, whose message very sufficiently performed, and the relating thereof, is no less gratefully received and well liked of her Majesty, than the honourable opinion he hath left

---

[1] Greville's *Life*, pp. 26–27.
[2] Waterhouse wrote Sir Henry Sidney on June 1st, that Philip was expected within ten days (Collins, i, 192).
[3] *Epistolæ*, p. 163.   [4] Collins, i, p. 193.
[5] *Cotton MSS. Titus*, B. x, f. 1–172, May 15, 1577.
[6] Collins, i, p. 193.

behind him with all the Princes with whom he had to negotiate hath left a most sweet savour and grateful remembrance of his name in those parts. The gentleman hath given no small arguments of great hope, the fruits whereof I doubt not but your Lordship shall reap, as the benefit of the good parts which are in him, and whereof he hath given some taste in this voyage, is to redound to more than your Lordship and himself. There hath not been any gentleman I am sure these many years that hath gone through so honourable a charge with as great commendations as he. In consideration whereof I could not but communicate this part of my joy with your Lordship, being no less a refreshing unto me in these my troublesome business than the soil is to the chafed stag. And so wishing the increase of his good parts to your Lordship's comfort and the service of her Majesty and his country I humbly take my leave."

From the time of his return to England in 1577 Sidney's one absorbing interest during the remainder of his life was in the cause of continental Protestantism, with which he believed the welfare of England to be bound up. Primarily he devoted himself to rendering assistance, in whatever way seemed possible, to the oppressed Netherlanders in their struggle to throw off the intolerable yoke of Spain, not only because of his natural sympathy for a brave people who were fighting for their religious and political liberty, but because he saw that the outcome of the struggle would, in all probability, be decisive of the fate of all Europe. In William of Orange he found a hero after his own heart, a man inspired by the pure love of liberty, and in no sense of the word a merely bigoted leader of a religious party. Sidney was now personally acquainted with all the more prominent Protestant leaders of the Continent, in the Netherlands, in Germany, and in France, and we hear much of his voluminous correspondence with them. One of the most notable of the Huguenot thinkers, Philip du Plessis Mornay, had come to England some two months before Sidney's return, on a mission from the King of Navarre, and, as Languet prophesied, the similarity of their characters made them friends. Mme de Mornay says that her husband's most intimate friends during the eighteen months which he spent in London were Walsingham and Sidney, the latter of whom she describes as "the most accomplished gentleman in England[1]."

---

[1] *Mémoires de Mme du Plessis Mornay*, p. 117.

Sidney's interest in the Low Countries at this time was of a much more personal kind than has ordinarily been supposed. Languet's letters abound in references, intentionally enigmatic, to a proposal which he had been commissioned to make to Sidney, and to which Sidney was unable to give a decisive answer. In the first letter which Languet wrote him after his departure he says : "See that you do not forget what I said to you at the mouth of the Maine, and write about it as soon as you can, as you have more than once promised me. (June 14, 1577)." In his next letter Languet returns to the subject :

"You remember how often I have begged you to let me know as soon as possible the opinion of your friends concerning that matter of which I spoke to you at the mouth of the Maine, and you promised that you would do so. And now, forsooth, you have written me from Bruges that there are reasons which almost make you despair of the possibility of a successful issue, and you have asked me as far as I can to discourage the hopes of the other parties. But you should not on that account grow cold; you should have found out the desire of your own people and communicated it to us forthwith as you promised to do. I know what has come into your mind to make you consider the matter a difficult one to arrange, for when the other parties discussed the project with me it instantly occurred to me that you were the son of a family; I did not, however, wish to diminish the expectations of these people lest they should cancel the commission which they had given to me to approach you and sound your feelings. I did not wish to elaborate even to you the difficulties which I thought might easily arise. You will say, What is the point of all this? Was it that you might deceive both parties? On the contrary I did it out of affection for you. I simply made a proposal to you which others had ordered me to make, nor, if you remember rightly, did I use any persuasion; I simply referred the whole matter to your consideration. You answered that what I proposed was not displeasing to you but that you were not absolutely your own master, that you would return to your own people, discover their wishes, and report the result to me without delay. How this has shown my affection for you, you do not yet see, but now I shall explain. I thought that the opinion which those friends of ours had conceived of you would redound to your honour wherever it was known, and assuredly you were bound by your promise to point out this fact to those without whose consent the affair cannot go forward. If at the very beginning you had cast aside all hope of carrying the matter through, you would not have promised me what you did promise, and such is your modesty that you would have kept silent to avoid the imputation of vanity. Now, as it is, you have considered it necessary to take some persons into your confidence in order to keep your promise to me, and no one could suspect that you were doing anything from personal motives. However, there was no need for you to be so anxious as to how you could justify yourself to others in the event of failure. I myself would have had your justification ready if you had written in reply, and I would still have it ready now had I your letter. And I implore you by our friendship to send it, lest those friends of ours think they are being slighted by you, or that I have not acted in good faith in this matter. On my return from Cologne I wrote to our common friend and said that I had made the proposal to you, as we had agreed, and that you liked it well, and were grateful to them for having such an opinion of you, but that you could not come to any determination on the subject until you had consulted those who had a control over you ; that you promised to learn their will as soon as you returned to your country, and to acquaint us with it. I have now received a letter from that friend of ours, in which he says : 'L'affaire que sçavez est enseveli. Nous attendons la resolution de vostre part, c'est a dire de celuy que sçavez. Car de nostre costé nous sommes asseurez ayans le consentement de la principale personne. Monsieur Ley en a parlé. Tout est resolu moyennant qu'ayez response ou resolution de l'autre costé.' You see in what a strait I am placed. I really have been afraid on this account to go to them, although they have invited me more than once, and I have devised various excuses for not going, for I did not wish to deprive them of all hopes of concluding the business, until I should hear from you that no hope remained. For though I think that the thing is very difficult I do not believe it is quite impossible. What if your fortune or some good genius should infuse into your friends or even your Zenobia a spirit of liberality towards you ? I am now sent for by our friends on matters of such importance that I must needs obey the call. When they ask me what news I bring on this matter of ours I shall have nothing to say except that I have not yet heard from you. If, as I said before, you had written anything of any kind I might have made up some tale to satisfy them without any loss of their regard for you." (July 15.)

The subject recurs continually in the correspondence of the two friends, as will be seen from the subjoined extracts:

Languet to Sidney (September 23).

"I beseech you to pardon me if, much less gently than I should, I have importuned you to send me an answer regarding that matter which was agreed upon between us. I have done so, I assure you, for this reason, that both your reputation and my own have begun to suffer with our friends here. They are persuaded that you changed your mind in Holland, and that you preferred another proposal to that which was agreed upon between us. Moreover, they believe that I am aware of all these things, but that

I conceal my knowledge from them. I called God to witness that I was utterly ignorant of those things which they were saying about you, that I did not believe they were true, and that I had not up to that time received a letter from you, for, indeed, I have not received that which you say you wrote to me on July 23. After I have learned your wish in the matter I shall bring it about, as I hope, that they will accept in good part whatever you have decided upon, and that without any diminution of their affection for you."

Sidney to Languet (October 1).

"The leaning of our minds is such at this present time that (should the wars be continued in Flanders) I am in some hope that the prediction which you formerly uttered respecting me at Vienna will have a happy fulfilment....I have written to you three times on that important affair of mine, so that I think you are satisfied on that score."

Languet to Sidney (October 9).

"You remember of whom we spoke as we were walking at the mouth of the Maine. The Elector of Brandenburg is said to be looking eagerly in that direction, but the other's constancy has not yet yielded to his rank and greatness, so strong are the hopes which she has conceived. So now she will sigh when she discovers the uselessness of her constancy and the frustration of her hopes. I beseech you to pardon me if I have, perchance, been too insistent in importuning an answer to the matters we agreed upon."

Languet to Sidney (November 28).

"The Elector of Brandenburg was a suitor for the hand of the Princess of whom we spoke as we walked at the mouth of the Maine. But she considered that her word was given to one whom you know of, and so as she had promised her brother, seeing that no answer had arrived from him, she would not transfer her affections to another object; and therefore he has married a daughter of the Prince of Anhalt. I do not know whether you laugh at the prophecy I uttered at Vienna. But I begin to hope I shall not be a false prophet, for things seem to tend to the quarter which I pointed out. It is your business to drive them on, and if you do so you will do well for the peace and quietness of your country."

There are other similar references in the correspondence. Sidney wrote no letters between October 1st and March 1st, and in a letter of the latter date he rails against his own "indolent ease" and "a corrupt age," and declares that he will be a cynic unless Languet reclaim him. "Regarding her of whom I readily acknowledge how unworthy I am," he adds, "I have written you my reasons long since, briefly indeed, but yet as well as I was able." Ten days later he writes: "I seem to myself to see our cause withering away, and am now meditating with myself some Indian project." Languet in his letters frequently urges the advantages of matrimony.

I have given these long extracts from the letters in order that it may be seen how seriously the project was discussed. Evidently marriage with a princess was under discussion, and it was intimately connected with a prophecy which Languet had made regarding Sidney's future. The clue to both of these allusions is to be found in a report sent by Mendoza, the Spanish ambassador, to the King of Spain, on April 12, 1578 :

"There is much talk here," he writes, "of a marriage between Sidney, Leicester's nephew, the heir of Henry Sidney, of the Earl of Warwick, and of Leicester's property, and a sister of Orange, who enters very willingly into the suggestion, and promises as a dowry to make him lord of Holland and Zealand, by this means and other gifts gaining over Leicester, who has now turned his back upon France, to which he was formerly so much attached[1]."

The story furnishes us with one more remarkable instance of the impression which Sidney made upon the ablest men of his day. It is not difficult to understand why the project failed, and indeed Sidney seems to have been convinced that it was impracticable as soon as he was able to reflect upon it. So definitely did he feel this that Languet says he had some difficulty in persuading Orange that Sidney was not acting an insincere part. But Orange did not know Elizabeth as her own subjects knew her. Her objection to any Englishman's accepting foreign honours was notorious ; moreover, had she openly countenanced the proposal of Orange her consent would have been bitterly resented by Spain, and Elizabeth was not yet ready for an open breach. It is clear, however, that she did not at once refuse her assent, and, a year after negotiations had been begun, the subject was being openly discussed in the Court. During this period, and for some months longer, Elizabeth blew hot and cold alternately, but at length Sidney understood that what he wished was impossible.

[1] *State Papers—Spanish—Eliz.*, p 575.

His admiration of the Prince of Orange only increased as the years went by and was warmly reciprocated ; the freedom of the Netherlands was the dearest interest of the remainder of his days, and in seeking to further it he was to give his life.

On April 21st, while Sidney was absent on his continental embassy, his sister Mary became the wife of the Earl of Pembroke[1]. She had not yet half completed her sixteenth year. "She was a beautiful lady and had an excellent wit," Aubrey tells us, "and had the best breeding that that age could afford. She had a pretty, sharp oval face. Her hair was of a reddish yellow." Her portrait, attributed to Gheerardt, which now hangs in the National Portrait Gallery, is remarkably life-like, and suggests the sprightliness, the charm of manner, and the intellectual powers for which she was famed among her contemporaries.

The match had been arranged entirely through the good offices of the Earl of Leicester, and, although Sir Henry was sorely troubled as to where he was to find his daughter's dowry, his delight was as unbounded as was his gratitude to his brother-in-law.

"I pray you let me know," he wrote to him, "what sum of money and at what days you have ordered me to pay my Lord of Pembroke. I am made very happy by the match. If God should take me away it would be more charge to your nephew or yourself than if it be done in my time[2]."

The marriage portion had been fixed at £3000, and Sir Henry was sorely perplexed as to where he could raise such a sum.

"I beseech you, sir," he wrote to Walsingham, "favour me in getting my payment for my warrant of £3000 and the £1600 which I laid out for debt due before my entering into charge....I have no other means to satisfy my Lord of Pembroke for my daughter's marriage money but this way[3]."

The warrant, however, remained unpaid. Sir Henry had already paid Pembroke £1500, and on December 18th he gave him £1000 more[4], which he had borrowed three days earlier

---

[1] *Sidney Psalter.*
[2] *State Papers, Carew,* May 19, 1577.
[3] *State Papers—Ireland—Eliz.,* September 16, 1577.
[4] *Add. MSS.* 15552, fol. I.   Pembroke's receipt.

from his brother-in-law, Sir James Harrington[1] ; on February 3, 1578, he made the final payment of £500[2].

Sidney was warmly attached to his sister, and henceforth he was to spend much time in her company either at Wilton, or at Baynard's Castle, the Earl's town house. Almost immediately after his return home he seems to have determined to visit his father in Ireland again[3], but he changed his plans,—probably, as we shall see, because he found that he could be of more help to Sir Henry at the Court. He may possibly have been at Kenilworth in the last days of June when Leicester, Warwick and Lord and Lady Pembroke visited the old castle[4] ; together with his brother Robert he was at Wilton on August 21st on a visit to the Earl and Countess, and on September 5th he had not yet returned to the Court[5]. He was again at Wilton on December 16th, when he wrote to Leicester to ask if he might venture to "remain absent from the Court this Christmas time[6]."

Other interests and duties, however, kept him very busily employed throughout the year. Of these the most absorbing was his desire to do something to promote the League, and to persuade Elizabeth to intervene actively in the affairs of the Low Countries. To this end he wrote many long letters to Casimir and the Prince of Orange, to both of whom Elizabeth had sent her thanks for their courtesies shown to Mr Sidney,

---

[1] *Add. MS.* 17520, fol. 12. "A Book of all my receipts of money, payments and allowances out of the same since November, 1577. At which time your L. sent me over into England to receive such sums as hereafter followeth, and to make payment thereof accordingly. Ed. Pakenham." Pakenham was employed by Sir Henry as his treasurer for some years. He was related to his master, as Sir Henry's mother was a Pakenham. He was among the mourners at Sir Philip's funeral.

[2] *Ibid.* "Paid unto Philip Williams to the use of the Earl of Pembroke in clear and full payment of £3000 promised unto the same Earl for the dower of your L. daughter, now wife to the aforesaid Earl, the sum of five hundred pounds as by his L. acquittance confessing the receipt thereof bearing date the 3rd of February may appear."

[3] Waterhouse to Sir Henry, June 26, 1577 (Collins, p. 199).

[4] *Belvoir MSS.* (*Hist. Man. Com. Reports*). George Savile to the Earl Rutland, June 26, 1577.

[5] Waterhouse to Sir Henry (Collins, pp. 209, 211).

[6] *Harleian MS.* 6992, fol. 42.

and vague assurances of good will. For negotiating the proposed League for the advancement of the common cause she
sent over to them Daniel Rogers and, afterwards, Robert
Beale, both friends of Sidney, and for many months, as we have
seen, it seemed not improbable that she would countenance
some of the projects that were nearest Sidney's heart. Languet,
however, was never really deceived either as to the feasibility
or the desirability of the League.

"Those who are only moderately versed in the affairs of Germany," he
wrote, "know that it is not an easy task to bring about that which Master
Rogers attempted in the first instance with a few princes and Beale afterwards with more."

The chief value of their embassies, he believed, consisted in
the fact that they "added not a little to the reputation of your
most gracious queen in Germany," but he knew that with the
exception of Casimir, the Duke of Brandenburg, and the Duke
of Brunswick, there was none of the German princes inclined
to sacrifice his personal interests for the sake of a cause. In the
autumn Sidney expected to start on a visit to the Prince of
Orange almost immediately. Orange was urgent that Elizabeth
should appoint Leicester to a command of English troops in
Flanders and send Sidney as his deputy[1]. These hopes were
fed by moderate encouragement from the Queen but she had
no real intention of taking a decided step. Accordingly
Sidney was alternately hopeful and despondent.

As the defender at the Court of his father's reputation and
actions, he found much to occupy him during these months.
We have already seen that certain gentlemen of the Pale had
begun to complain bitterly against the cess which Sir Henry
found it necessary to impose if his administration was to be
kept really effective ; they declared that this ancient tax in
kind on every plough-land amounted to an enormous sum, but
they were no better pleased when Sir Henry proposed to convert
the cess into a modest annual rental. His waiving the Lord
Deputy's right to purchase supplies for his own household at
arbitrary rates, and his proving by old records that the cess

---

[1] *State Papers—Foreign—Eliz.* [Davison] to Leicester, October 3, 1577.

had been a legitimate imposition since the times of Edward III, availed no more, and at length Sir Henry had some of those who refused payment locked up in Dublin Castle. The members of a deputation sent over to England on behalf of the discontented landowners were imprisoned in the Fleet.

One of the chief difficulties in administering the law in Ireland consisted in the fact that Elizabeth wished her favourite, the Earl of Ormond, to be free from all such impositions as the cess,—an exception which did much to embitter the opposition of lesser landowners. Sir Henry insisted on levying the tax on all impartially even though Walsingham warned him that the man who governed Ireland successfully must count Ormond among his friends, and accordingly he drew upon himself the Queen's reproaches, not only because of his treatment of Ormond, but also because of the necessity of furnishing ships and treasure to meet the rumoured invasion of Ireland by James Fitzmaurice. "Her Majesty angry at the first, when money was demanded, said that Henry Sidney did always seek to put her to charge," Waterhouse reported. However, he was able to add that the supplies were granted, and that in Leicester, Walsingham, and other members of the Council, Sir Henry had staunch friends.

In all his activity as Sir Henry's agent in England Waterhouse refers to the fact that his conduct is being directed by Philip Sidney. The latter was well aware that Ormond had been at enmity with his father for many years, and that now, as he had done in the past, he was spreading reports to the effect that Sir Henry was to be recalled as he was enriching himself and stirring up discontent in Ireland. It was difficult to do much in the face of a situation of this sort : something of Sidney's attitude is revealed in a letter sent by Waterhouse to Sir Henry on September 16th from the Court at Oatlands :

"Some little occasions of discourtesies have passed between the Earl of Ormond and Mr. Philip Sidney, because the Earl lately spake unto him and he answered not, but was in dead silence of purpose, because he imputeth to the Earl such practices as have been made to alienate her Majesty's mind from your Lordship.... The Earl of Ormond saith he will accept no quarrels from a gentleman that is bound by nature to defend his father's causes, and who is otherwise furnished with so many virtues as he knows

Mr. Philip to be ; and on the other side Mr. Philip hath gone as far, and showed as much magnanimity as is convenient, unless he could charge him with any particularities, which I perceive he yet cannot[1]."

The letter suggests something of the anger and indignation which must have possessed Sidney's soul. He had already, however, taken steps to do something in a more constructive way to further his father's interests. Writing from Windsor Castle on the last of September, Waterhouse reported to Sir Henry that

"Mr. Philip had gathered a collection of all the articles which have been enviously objected to your government, whereunto he hath framed an answer in way of discourse, the most excellently (if I have any judgment) that ever I read in my life ; the substance whereof is now approved in your letters and notes by Mr. Whitten. But let no man compare with Mr. Philip's pen. I know he will send it to your Lordship, and when you read it you shall have more cause to pray God for him than to impute affection to me in this my opinion of him[2]."

Sidney's *Discourse on Irish Affairs*[3] is divided into seven parts, of which the first three are lost. It deals almost entirely with the cess troubles, and is a clear, manly defence of his father's record. He maintains that the levy of a tax on the gentlemen of the Pale for the defence of the country is a most reasonable proceeding, and he approves with especial warmth his father's attempts to make it apply to all landowners impartially. He refers to his father as "an honest servant, full of zeal in his prince's service, and not without well-grounded hopes of good success." Regarding England's general policy in Ireland he held the same views as his father, and as all other English statesmen of the time :

"For until by time they find the sweetness of due subjection it is impossible that any gentle means should put out the remembrance of their lost liberty, and the Irishman is that way as obstinate as any nation, with whom no other passion can prevail but fear.... For under the sun there is not a nation which live more tyrannously than they do one over the other.... For little is lenity to prevail in minds so possessed with a natural inconstancy ever to go to a new fortune, with a revengeful heart to all English as to their only conquerors, and that which is most of all with so ignorant obstinacy in papistry that they do in their souls detest the present government."

[1] Collins, I, p. 227.   [2] *Ibid.* p. 228.
[3] *Cotton MSS. Titus*, B. XII, fol. 557.

These extracts show sufficiently how difficult was the conception of real toleration in Elizabeth's day, even for one who was formed by nature to love justice, to respect the rights of other men, and to prefer kindly dealings to harsh measures. It is strange to reflect that Sidney's mind was untroubled by the idea that there was anything in the Irish obstinacy in papistry which was akin to the Dutch obstinacy in Protestantism. That his *Discourse* had any effect upon the Queen there is no reason to suppose ; her attitude was determined by less academic considerations. The rumours that Sir Henry was to be recalled continued to spread, and early in January Walsingham wrote to his friend that although the Queen was somewhat appeased she seemed disposed to recall him under colour of a conference regarding a plan to diminish charges in Ireland. Walsingham could only add by way of comfort that they were urging upon her the desirability of her bestowing on Sir Henry some mark of favour, either nobilitation, or granting his suit for certain lands, or both. In February he was ordered to repair to Her Majesty's presence. In April Mendoza heard, first, that Sir Henry was to come over to take charge of the Queen of Scots, and then that he was to lead ten thousand men into Flanders. Both of these reports we may set down as 'colours.' He could not come at once, as he was anxious to leave the country 'in universal quiet,' and to compose certain cess difficulties. It was September 18th before he reached Chester bringing with him the Earl of Clanrickard, 'that arch traitor,' and his son. He was so ill that he could not proceed to London for some ten days.

"When I came to the Court to know how I was entertained," he says, "I confess well, but not so well as I thought and in conscience felt I had deserved....Notwithstanding all these my painful services I was accounted *servus inutilis* for that I had exceeded a supposed commission...and although somewhat I had exceeded in spending her Majesty's treasure, I had too far exceeded in spoiling my own patrimony[1]."

To none of her servants did the Queen show less gratitude than to Sir Henry Sidney. He was the most capable administrator sent by England to Ireland in Elizabeth's reign, and

---

[1] Sir Henry Sidney to Walsingham, March 1, 1583.

W. L. S.

he left behind him a reputation for honesty and a love of justice that is unique. In the years that followed his withdrawal the Irish State Papers abound in expressions of the hope that he may return. "If Sir Henry Sidney can but sit in his chair he will do more good than others with all their limbs." "Sir Henry Sidney is cried for by the children in the street." "The public desire Sir Henry Sidney above all others to be Lord Deputy." These are a few of the opinions expressed by various correspondents of Burghley and Walsingham, and after Sir Henry had passed from all earthly cares Auditor Jenyson, in reporting to Burghley the joy of the Irish multitude in the news that Lord Deputy Perrott was to be recalled, adds :

"Sir Henry Sidney was of great credit and also famous in this government as by divers his erections appeareth, and most chiefly by the bridge at Athlone, which is one of the best acts done for the commonwealth[1]."

[1] *State Papers—Irish—Eliz.*, January 26, 1587.

CHAPTER XI

1577—1579

FOR a year or more there is little to record in Sidney's life but thwarted plans and disappointed hopes. His eager enthusiasm for taking an active part in the affairs of the Low Countries had been chilled by Elizabeth's failure to take any decided stand, and accordingly we find him vacillating between the plan of joining Orange or Casimir in a private capacity and that of launching on some Indian project. In each of Frobisher's voyages of 1576, 1577 and 1578 he was an adventurer to the amount of £25, £50 and £67. 10s. respectively[1], and in the spring of 1577 Languet noticed in him a certain wish to accompany that great navigator. When Frobisher returned in September and it was learned that he had brought much 'ore' with him Sidney was greatly excited by the marvellous tales that were current in London. In a letter to Languet he says : "I wrote to you a year ago about a certain Frobisher who, in rivalry of Magellan, has explored that sea which he supposes to wash the north part of America. It is a marvellous history." He goes on to relate how a young man who had accompanied Frobisher on this first voyage had brought back a piece of earth which the London assayers pronounced "the purest gold and without any intermixture of other metal !" Frobisher had now returned a second time with two hundred tons of the same ore. It was his opinion that the island from which it had been dug "is so productive in metals as to seem very far to surpass the country of Peru. There are also six other islands near to this which seem very little inferior." Sidney wishes Languet to send him at once any information he may possess regarding the working of mines and the reduction of ores, and he is much concerned as to the best means of

[1] *Calendar of State Papers, Colonial,* vol. I.

protecting the new Eldorado against possible incursions of Spaniards or Danes[1].

Languet was by no means sceptical regarding his young friend's wonderful narrative but he was inclined to play the rôle of the moralist rather than to rejoice.

"If what you say of your Frobisher is true," he wrote, "he will doubtless eclipse the reputation not only of Magellan, but even of Christopher Columbus himself. Who could have expected that the extreme north would at last supply us with so great incitement to evil. You may now well despise the voyage to the Indies since you have stumbled on that gift of nature, of all others the most fatal and hurtful to mankind, which nevertheless nearly all men desire with so insane a longing that it is the most powerful of all motives to them to incur the risk."

He fears that the undermining of England's prosperity which was begun by the converting of much of her arable lands into pasture will be completed by the rush of Englishmen to the new world, and by the spilling of English blood which will be necessary to keep possession. He fears, too, the effect on Sidney himself of

"these islands all of gold, which I dare say stand before your mind's eye day and night. Beware, I entreat you, and do not let the cursed hunger after gold which the Poet speaks of, creep over that spirit of yours, into which nothing has hitherto been admitted but the love of goodness, and the desire of earning the good-will of all men[2]."

Sidney's illusions and, with them, Languet's fears, were soon dispelled when the assayers pronounced the ore worthless. Sidney's interest in American and Indian projects, however, was to continue to be one of the great interests of the remaining years of his life. No doubt he took a less active part in these enterprises than he would otherwise have done had his means been greater. His name figures prominently in the list of those who as late as April, 1579, had not completed the payment of their subscriptions to Frobisher's ventures, and we constantly hear of his borrowing money[3].

[1] Pears, p. 118.   [2] Pears, p. 124.

[3] On September 28, 1577, he gave to Anthony Gamage, citizen and alderman of London, an acknowledgment of indebtedness to the extent of £300 for which sum Robert Walker and Wm. Blount were equally bound with him. The document was witnessed by Edward Dyer and Arthur Atye, and the condition of the obligation was such that if £210 were paid Gamage on

His relation to his uncle, the Earl of Leicester, seems to
have been of the closest, and we frequently find their names associated. Together with Warwick they spent part of December
at Wilton, and in the letter which Sidney wrote Leicester
after his departure we hear of a 'poor stranger musician' to
whom the Earl had shown favour at his nephew's suit. The
letter concludes with words which form a more striking proof
of their intimacy. "I will no further trouble your Lordship,"
Sidney writes, "but with remembrance of my duty to your
Lordship and my Lady and aunt. And so I humbly leave you
both to the Eternal who always prosper you[1]." These words
can only mean that Leicester was already married to the
recently widowed Countess of Essex. and that Sidney was
aware of the fact. There were probably very few persons in the
secret at this time[2], and it was not until September 20th of the
following year that Sir Francis Knowles, the Countess' father,
insisted upon a repetition of the marriage ceremony at Wanstead. It is significant that Sidney was one of the Earl's few
confidants, though we cannot but wonder at his indiscretion
in committing to paper such momentous information.

Sidney was at Court again before New Year's Day, when he
presented 'a smock of camerick' as a gift to the Queen. During
the winter he saw much of Du Plessis, to whose daughter he
became godfather a few months later[3], and of one or two
continental friends, notably Butrech, who were sojourning in
London. From Languet and the Frankfurt booksellers he
received various books on continental affairs. But he could
not shake off his sense of disappointment in the Queen's
vacillating, indefinite policy. Always inclined to melancholy,
he now felt utterly depressed by Elizabeth's failure to show
any adequate appreciation of his father's services or to be

April 5th ensuing, the obligation was to be void and of none effect (Latin
parchment at Penshurst). On February 7, 1578, Sidney borrowed £100 of
Mr Williby of Bore Place (*Add. MSS.* 17520, 12).

[1] *Harleian MS.* 6992, f. 42. Sidney to Leicester, December 16, 1577.
Collins prints the letter with an incorrect date—1582.

[2] The author of *Leicester's Commonwealth* says that the first ceremony took
place at Kenilworth (1st edition, 1584, p. 49).

[3] *Mémoires de Mme du Plessis Mornay*, p. 119.

really interested in his own plans. In no very admirable mood he wrote to Languet on March 1st :

"The use of the pen, as you may perceive, has plainly fallen from me, and my mind itself, if it was ever active in anything, is now beginning, by reason of my indolent ease, imperceptibly to lose its strength, and to relax without any reluctance. For to what purpose should our thoughts be directed to various kinds of knowledge unless room be afforded for putting it into practice so that public advantage may be the result which in a corrupt age we cannot hope for....Do you not see that I am cleverly playing the stoic ?   Yea and I shall be a cynic too unless you reclaim me[1]."

He had evidently in mind the principle which he had often formulated that the end of all education was virtuous action, and he was now drawing the deduction that if a corrupt age afforded no room for such action why should one not allow his mind to relax in indolent ease ?   Sidney was never capable of indulging such a mood for a very long period, and at least we must admit that he was sorely tried.   In October Orange had been urgent that Leicester should come over and bring Sidney as his deputy[2], and now Casimir was begging the Queen that Sidney be sent as a kind of joint commander with himself[3]. The Court was eagerly discussing the prospect of his marriage with Orange's sister, but in spite of all these things Sidney saw little prospect of anything definite being done.   For some time indeed it appeared that he would actually proceed to the Low Countries[4].   Languet heard that the Queen had decided to send troops under the command of Leicester, and Mendoza reported that

"the Queen has appointed Lord Howard to be Admiral of the six ships which are being fitted out with Henry [sic] Sidney, a nephew of Leicester's to be Vice-Admiral, the other captains being selected men.   It is under-stood that these ships will take three standards of infantry raised by the Guilds or trained bands of this city, although some suspect that they will go over to Flanders.   Walsingham is going there, and he is such a devilish heretic that he constantly favours those like himself and persecutes the Catholics in order to pledge the Queen more deeply to his way of thinking[5]."

---

[1] Pears, p. 143.

[2] *State Papers—Foreign—Eliz.* Davison to Leicester, October 3, 1577.

[3] *Ibid.* Casimir to Sidney, April 25, 1578.

[4] A correspondent of Walsingham in April assumes that Sidney's departure is imminent (*Calender of Scottish Papers*).

[5] *State Papers—Spanish—Eliz.* Mendoza to Zayas, June 13, 1578.

Butrech reported the rumour to Languet, whom it filled with rejoicing, but nothing seems to have come of it. Perhaps Mendoza, who had been in England only a few months, did not yet know how difficult Walsingham or any one else would find such a task. Elizabeth finally decided that Leicester should not go, and that Sidney might do so only as a private person.

"I have sent you a letter," Leicester wrote to Hatton in July, "which I received yesterday from Casimir; it is of no new date. You may see what he writes and how earnestly. Since my hap is not to be in so honourable a voyage nor charge, I would be most glad that my nephew might go to Casimir; and if he may not as from her Majesty, yet after the other sort you say her Majesty could like of, I beseech you further it, and I shall be most glad it may be obtained[1]."

The leave was granted, but as Sidney was on the point of setting out the Queen added the last straw to the burden of disappointed hopes which he carried, by insisting that he should be the bearer of a message calculated to dash any expectations which Casimir might entertain of her assistance. Leicester reports the incident to Walsingham thus :

"When my nephew Philip was to take his leave and receive his dispatch, among other small comforts he should have brought to the Prince, he was specially commanded by her Majesty to tell Duke Casimir that she marvelled not a little, and was offended with him for giving out that his coming was by her means, and that she misliked any such speeches, and prayed her name might not be so abused, since she did not command him to come, but the States had entertained him and they should maintain his coming ; with such other small encouragement to that prince, whose cause of coming you and I and almost all men know. Yet this earnestly has she commanded Philip to say to him, writing such a letter besides of cold comfort that when I heard of both I did all I could to stay him at home, and with much ado I think I shall, seeing I know not what he should do there but bring discouragement to all her best friends. For my part I had rather he perished in the sea than that he should be the instrument of it[2]."

Leicester was certainly right in dissuading his nephew. Elizabeth was not to be ready for several years to interest herself actively

[1] July 9, 1578 (*Add. MSS.* 15891). "A Book of Letters received by Sir Christopher Hatton, Vice-Chamberlain to Queen's Majesty from sundry persons and procured by him to be written in this same book." The great majority of these letters have been printed *in extenso* in Nicolas' *Life of Hatton* (1848).

[2] *State Papers—Foreign—Eliz.*, August 1, 1578.

in the affairs of the Netherlands, and Sidney could have served only as an instrument of discouragement to his friends.

No doubt he was also influenced by the fact that his father was about to return and needed his help. Sir Henry had already written earnestly to Leicester on the subject[1] :

"I understand by Philip that he hath put on a determination to go into the Low Countries to serve the States in company and under the conduct of Casimir, which if it be so, what lack his presence shall be unto me at my coming over, having to answer so many complaints and informations as the malice of my enemies here devised against me, I leave to your Lordship to consider. But if the matter be not of that weight as his stay shall be requisite to assist me I would not then hinder his determination in a matter wherein he is to purchase himself so much honour and credit to stay him."

Sir Henry wrote in a similar tone to his son on the same day[2], and his earnestness is a proof of the extent to which he now relied on that son's judgment.

The difficulties which beset his father weighed no less heavily on Sidney's mind than did his own problems. We have already seen something of his activity on behalf of Sir Henry ; in the summer of 1577 he had been on the point of visiting him in Ireland[3], and he probably remained in England only because he felt that he could there the better counter the attacks of Ormond. After Sir Henry's recall in February, 1578, Sidney was in constant communication with him, and urged him to postpone his actual return for some months in order that his enemies might not interpret his home-coming in a derogatory manner. Walsingham was labouring to secure nobilitation for him or some other notable recognition of his services, and Sidney was anxious that Sir Henry's friends should make his path as pleasant as possible before his arrival. "Among which friends," he tells his father, "before God there is none proceeds either so thoroughly or so wisely as my Lady, my mother. For mine own part I have had only light from her[4]." Sidney's recorded references to his mother are very

[1] *Cotton MS. Titus*, B. XIII, fol. 257, August 1, 1578.
[2] *Sidney Papers*, I, p. 392.
[3] *Ibid.* I, p. 199. Waterhouse to Sir Henry, June 26, 1577.
[4] *Ibid.* I, p. 247, April 25, 1578.

few in number, but it is pleasant to be able to believe from such
as we have that his society did much to lighten the burden of
her days. Something of the exasperation which possessed him
while engaged in these devious businesses is shown in a letter
which he wrote at this time. He had been irritated and filled
with suspiciousness by the fact that whatever he himself wrote
to his father or learned from him was as promptly known by
the Ormond faction. Evidently without a tittle of evidence he
decided that Molyneux, Sir Henry's faithful secretary, was the
culprit, and he wrote him as follows :

"MR. MOLLINEUX :
    Few words are best. My letters to my father have come to the
eyes of some. Neither can I condemn any but you for it. If it be so,
you have played the very knave with me ; and so I will make you know
if I have good proof of it. But that for so much as is past. For that is
to come, I assure you before God that if ever I know you do so much as
read any letter I write to my father, without his commandment, or my
consent, I will thrust my dagger into you. And trust to it for I speak it
in earnest. In the meantime, farewell. From Court, this last of May,
1578.
By me,
PHILIP SIDNEY[1]."

The letter was as little creditable to Sidney's heart as it evidently was to his head, and we may hope that Molyneux' dignified
reply caused his young master to be ashamed of himself.
Angry, and baffled in his hopes, he allowed his impulsiveness
and the dash of arrogance and self-righteousness in his temperament to override his sense of courtesy and justice. In extenu-
ation we can only plead that the morbid anger that possessed
him had been stirred by the sight of what he believed to be the
unforgivable wrongs suffered by his father. No doubt, too,
his mother's wretched condition both in health and spirits
tended to depress him. Poor Lady Mary's bitterness of heart
found little to assuage it, and the petty yet intolerable character of her griefs is illustrated in an incident connected with
her husband's return to Court. She had requested Molyneux
to make arrangements with the Lord Chamberlain Sussex to

---

[1] *Sidney Papers*, I, p. 256.

assign a room in Hampton Court to Sir Henry where he might meet people on Irish and Welsh business. The application was unsuccessful : no room could be spared. Lady Mary then urged Molyneux to try to procure a room on condition that it be used in the daytime only and for the dispatch of business only.

"When the worst is known," she concludes rather bitterly, "old Lord Harry and his old Moll will do as well as they can in parting like good friends the small portion allotted our long service in Court, which as little as it is seems something too much[1]."

It is not strange that Sidney at this time wrote Languet that he was weary of the life of the Court and would fain fly from its light to betake himself to the privacy of secluded places.

During this year, when the Queen's attitude was making Orange despair of ever receiving real assistance from her, when Burghley, Walsingham, Leicester and Davison were indignant and apologetic by turns, as their mistress tended by turns to assist in crushing the Dutch by demanding instant repayment of the money she had lent them or gave them fair words, Elizabeth was pursuing the same policy which had actuated her throughout her reign. She had no interest, it must be repeated, in the efforts of the Dutch to achieve either religious or political liberty. Her interest was in balancing the power of France against Spain. To the Regent Morton in Scotland she refused all assistance until he was driven from the Regency and the spectre of a Gallic invasion of the northern kingdom in favour of the Queen of Scots once more rose before her eyes. When Orange in despair of English aid accepted the offer of Alençon to come to his aid as a volunteer Elizabeth was once more frightened by the possibility of the States becoming a French dependency. Her tactics at this juncture were a repetition of those she had employed very often in the past. The marriage project with Alençon which had been dropped for some two years was now revived and with a sufficient promise of success to persuade Alençon to withdraw from his project of aiding Orange. There were the usual long pre-liminaries—she must first meet her proposed husband ; if

[1] *Sidney Papers*, I, p. 272.

their hearts were inclined to each other, then, etc., etc. But, she stipulated, she must be entirely free to accept or reject. Alençon was invited to come over privately and without ostentation ; he preferred to come publicly and to have his coming celebrated in a fashion befitting its importance. He finally insisted that he should send M. Simier as his ambassador to arrange preliminaries, and to this the Queen at length reluctantly agreed. The French Court was delighted with the prospect of the marriage though somewhat suspicious from past experience : the whole English nation hated the prospect, for the very name of Alençon was inseparably associated in their minds with St Bartholomew and Catherine de' Medici.

In the initial negotiations Sidney took a small part, and, as we shall soon see, he was to take a more serious share in the proceedings somewhat later. The English ambassador at Paris wrote in December that a bastard brother of Morton had arrived at the French Court and had been warmly welcomed and entertained. The ambassador urged that until the reason of his visit was discovered it would be desirable that the Queen send someone to the King of France to make an excuse for delaying the coming of M. Simier.

"She has therefore sent Philip Sidney," Mendoza reported to his master, "which has had the effect of stopping Simier, who is understood to have arrived at Calais. The ambassador has also written several times and now confirms it that the King of France is one of the sovereigns who have entered into the League formed by your Majesty and the Pope, and this news greatly disturbs the Queen[1]."

The news was not sufficiently disturbing, however, to prevent Simier's arrival on January 5th—an event that was to prove of moment in the lives of several of the men in whom we are interested.

In the meantime an event took place which gave very great pleasure to Sidney and helped to revive his drooping spirits. This was the unexpected visit to the English Court of Casimir and Languet. The news of their coming was brought from Ghent by a servant of Sidney who chanced to be there on

---

[1] *Calendar of State Papers—Spanish—Eliz.*, December 31, 1578.

business for the Earl of Leicester, and the messenger had
hardly reached London before those whom he announced also
arrived. Casimir had suddenly resolved "to make a voyage
into England to see her Majesty before he return home being
so near the sea as he is." The object of his visit according to
the Spanish ambassador was "to reconcile him with the French."
Nothing so definite, however, is needed to explain it. Casimir
had experienced within the last few months a full measure
of the Queen's waywardness, and no doubt hoped by a personal
interview to place himself on a less equivocal footing. He had
been encouraged by Elizabeth to take an active part on behalf
of Orange, and she had to a considerable extent directed his
movements ; on the other hand she had expressly forbidden
him to assert that his coming into the Low Countries had been
instigated by her, and had disclaimed all responsibility for his
acts. In other words, she wished him to serve her as her own
piratical men of Devon did : he should act according to her
directions, and if he were successful, or if it proved convenient
for the Queen to acknowledge his successes, the glory should
be hers ; if it proved otherwise he must be prepared to assume
the odium and to declare solemnly that he alone was the author
of his own acts. Casimir did not yet understand the theory
of service on these conditions, and he came to England to
persuade the Queen to give him substantial and open assistance.

Two days before Casimir left Ghent (January 13th) Languet
wrote to Sidney from that city evidently without a thought of
coming to England. He had been very ill for some two months
but he had been cheered by more frequent letters from his
young friend and especially by a long letter full of kindness
from Sir Henry Sidney. Languet's heart overflowed in
gratitude, and he speaks of his great desire once more to
see Sidney. The opportunity suddenly presented itself, and
Languet, conscious of rapidly failing health, obeyed an imperious impulse to visit England and the young man who had
come to occupy the chief place in his heart, before it should
be too late. On January 20th both Sidney and his father were
commissioned by the Queen to meet Casimir when he landed

and to accompany him to London[1]. The visitors reached the
Tower on the evening of January 22nd, and Casimir "was
there by divers noblemen and others honourably received and
conveyed by cresset light and torch light to Sir Thomas Gresham's house in Bishopsgate Street, where he was received
with sounding of trumpets, drums, fifes, and other instruments
of music, and there both lodged and feasted till Sunday next;
that he was by the nobility fetched to the Court at Westminster, where he talked with her Majesty, and after lodged
in Somerset House. In the week following he hunted at Hampton Court. On Sunday, the first of February, he beheld a
valiant justing and running at the tilt at Westminster; on
the next morrow he saw them fight at barriers with swords
on horseback. On Tuesday he dined with the Lord Mayor of
London; on Wednesday with the Duchess of Suffolk at her
house called the Burgokening, or Barbican, by Red-cross
Street; on Thursday at the Stilyard, etc. On the 8th of
February the Queen made him Knight of the Garter, by deliver-
ing to him the collar and putting the Garter on his leg at Whitehall. On the 14th of February he departed from London
homewards, with great rewards given by the Queen's Majesty,
the nobility, men of honour, the Mayor of London, and citizens
of that city[2]."

Casimir had made a good impression on the Queen and she
had shown him unusual courtesies. The good-will of the
Londoners toward the Low Countries was reflected in their
banqueting of Casimir and presenting to him a chain and
plate to the value of 2000 crowns. Leicester was in constant
attendance on him and took him to visit Wanstead.

Languet's pleasure in the opportunity which he now had
of meeting Sidney's friends and the members of his family
was unbounded. The friendship of Edward Dyer he called
"a precious gem added to my store"; regarding Fulke Greville
he was no less enthusiastic. Sir Henry Sidney, whose generous
soul never forgot an obligation, devoted himself to showing

[1] *Spanish State Papers.* Mendoza to Zayas, January 19, 1579. *Add.*
MSS. 17520. 12.
[2] Nichols' *Progresses*, II, p. 277.

honour to the man to whom his son owed more than to any other single person, and a warm friendship and mutual regard sprang up between the two men. One of the most popular forms of entertainment of the time was to take one's guests to see the bear-baiting and bull-baiting[1]. Paris Garden, the headquarters of the sport, was directly across the river from Sir Henry's house at Paul's Wharf, and on at least one occasion he accompanied Casimir to the famous resort. On the day when the visitors left London Sir Henry presented to Languet a gold chain for which he paid £45[2] and then accompanied him to Dover. From here Languet wrote to the Elector of Saxony on February 17th. Casimir's party hastened their departure to such an extent that Languet had no opportunity of bidding Sidney and Dyer farewell.

"I cannot think," he wrote to Sidney from Flushing, "by what ill-luck it fell out that I had no opportunity of taking leave of yourself and Master

[1] Machyn in his *Diary* gives us several instances of its popularity : "The same day at afternoon was a bear-baiting on the Bankside, and there the great blind bear broke loose, and in running away he caught a serving man by the calf of the leg and bit a great piece away, and after that by the hockle-bone, that within three days after he died." (December 9, 1554, p. 78.) "Afore the Queen one of the bears was baited, and after the morris-dancers went into the court, dancing in many offices." (March 21, 1559, p. 191.) "The 25th day (of May, 1559) they (the French ambassadors) were brought to the Court with music to dinner, for there was great cheer ; and after dinner the bear and bull-baiting, and the Queen's grace and the ambassadors stood in the gallery looking of the pastime until six at night...the 26th day of May they went from the Bishop's House to Paul's Wharf and took barge and so to Paris Garden, for there was both bear and bull-baiting, and the captain with a hundred of the guard to keep room for them to see the baiting" (p. 198). "The 28th day of October (1561), the which was Saint Simon and Jude's day, was at Whitehall great baiting of the bull and bear for the ambassadors of France that came out of Scotland, the which the Queen's grace was there, and her Council and many noblemen" (p. 270). Laneham's description of the bear-baiting at Kenilworth in 1575 is well known.

[2] The following items are taken from a manuscript book of accounts kept by Edward Pakenham, Sir Henry's treasurer (*Add. MSS.* 17520, 12): "For my boat-hire from the Court to follow your L. when you went in haste to meet Duke Casimir the 20th of January. For my boat-hire when your L. went to the Parrish Garden with Casimir, going and coming...3s. For money given unto your L. to give unto Dethick, the goldsmith, for colouring my chain which your L. gave unto Mr. Languet, and for his pains in going and coming to your L. the 14th of February...15s. For the price of my chain which your L. gave to Mr. Languet the same day...£45.

Allowed by me—H. SIDNEY."

Dyer, though in truth I had nothing for you but tears and sighs. Yet I am sorry that I could not let you see even tears and sighs as pledges of my great regard for you; but it was not my fault, for our party was hastening away as if they were taking leave of enemies, not of friends, and I should have given great offence if I alone had behaved with common sense instead of being mad with the rest. As it was I did not make such speed but that before I crossed the river which flows by Sandwich, all the horses which were to have conveyed us, were gone, and had not Sir Hales had compassion on me, and lent me his servant's horse, I must have returned to the town. When we reached the Foreland of Kent, though the wind was not quite favourable, I persisted in urging my friends to embark, until they consented, that we might not any longer trespass on the politeness of your noble father[1]."

Fulke Greville accompanied Languet on the voyage, and their friendship increased with further acquaintance.

Since the preceding summer Sidney's brother Robert had been in Germany to perfect himself in languages and to see the world. After passing from the care of Robert Dorset at Ewelme he had matriculated at Christ Church in 1574[2]; his attendance at the University had been irregular, however, and he was a rather desultory student. "I am sure you cannot but find what lack in learning you have by your often departing from Oxford[3]," his father wrote him, and Languet declared to Philip that he had not taken such care as he ought of his brother's education[4]. Nevertheless Languet considered his natural disposition excellent, and Sir Henry could write to him of the happiness he derived from "the universal testimony that is made of you, of the virtuous course you hold in this your juvenile age, and how much you profit in the same, and what excellent parts God hath already planted in you." Another letter of Sir Henry's written a few months earlier concludes, "God bless you my sweet child, in this world and forever, as I in this world find myself happy by my children[5]." In the midst of harassing cares of many kinds Sir Henry and Lady Sidney knew little but happiness in their relation to their children.

---

[1] Pears, p. 157.
[2] *Register of Univ. of Oxford (Ox. Hist. Soc.)*, Part ii, p. 57
[3] *Sidney Papers*, i, p. 247, March 25, 1579.
[4] *Epistolæ*, p. 215.
[5] *Sidney Papers*, i, p. 272, October 28, 1578.

Robert was now living with a servant of Sir Henry's—Harry White—and was finding great difficulty in making the £100 per year which his father allowed him meet his needs. When Languet was asked to superintend his education he feared lest the young man had enjoyed so much of liberty that it might be difficult to hold him in check.

Sir Henry Sidney's reliance on the judgment of his elder son as well as his pride in that son's character appears everywhere in his letters to Robert,—kindly paternal letters filled with expressions of affection, good advice, and reproof of Robert's failure to keep his expenditure within the sum allowed him. "I hear well of you and the company you keep which is of great comfort to me. To be of noble parentage usually raises an emulation to follow their great examples." "Pray daily ; speak no thing but truly. Do no dishonest thing for any respect." "Write to me monthly, and either in Latin or French." In similar fashion Sir Henry had written to Philip some twelve years before. But the one piece of advice which Sir Henry reiterates until Robert must have become somewhat restive under it, is that he should imitate in all things his elder brother. To Philip was committed the direction of his studies, of his travels and of his conduct.

"Follow the direction of your most loving brother who in loving you is comparable with me or exceedeth me. Imitate his virtues, exercises, studies and actions; he is a rare ornament of this age, the very formular that all well-disposed young gentlemen of our Court do form also their manners and life by. In truth I speak it without flattery of him or of myself: he hath the most rare virtues that ever I found in any man.... In your travels these documents I will give you, not as mine, but his practices. Seek the knowledge of the estate of every prince, court and city that you pass through. Address yourself to the company to learn this of the elder sort, and yet neglect not the younger....These he effectually observed with great gain of understanding. Once again I say, imitate him[1]."

Sidney justified his father's estimate of him as far as his relation to his brother was concerned by the warm, half fraternal, half paternal interest which he took in him. Perhaps with something of a fellow-feeling for Robert's tendency to spend

[1] *Sidney Papers*, I, p. 246.

his money freely, he supplemented his allowance generously
and at infrequent intervals wrote him long, kindly letters in
which expressions of brotherly affection were mingled with
very solemn and very wise advice.

"I am sure, he writes, "you have imprinted in your mind the scope and
mark you mean by your pains to shoot at, for if you should travel but to
travel, or to say you had travelled, certainly you should prove a pilgrim—
no more.   But I presume so well of you that though a great number of
us never thought in ourselves why we went, but a certain tickling humour
to do as other men had done, you purpose, being a gentleman born, to
furnish yourself with the knowledge of such things as may be serviceable
for your country and calling ; which certainly stands not in the change
of air, for the warmest sun makes not a wise man,—no, nor in learning
languages, although they be of serviceable use, for words are but words
in what language soever they be,—and much less in that all of us come home
full of disguisements not only of apparel, but of our countenances as though
the credit of a traveller stood all upon his outside, but in the right informing
your mind with those things which are most notable in those places which
you come into.   Of which as the one kind is so vain as I think, ere it be
long, like the mountebanks in Italy, we travellers shall be made sport of in
comedies, so may I justly say who rightly travels with the eye of Ulysses
doth take one of the most excellent ways of worldly wisdom.   For hard sure
it is to know England without you know it by comparing it with some
other country[1]."

Sidney goes on to specify worthy subjects that may engage
the traveller's attention—political situations, national resources, topography, fortification, manners and morals, religion,
policies and laws.   Here we have a protest against the
affected Euphuistic Court, the character of which depressed
Languet during his brief visit.

"The habits of your Court," Languet wrote a few months after his return
to the Continent, "seemed to me somewhat less manly than I could have
wished, and most of your noblemen appeared to me to seek for a reputation more by a kind of affected courtesy than by those virtues which are
wholesome to the State and which are most becoming to generous spirits
and to men of high birth.   I was sorry, therefore, and so were other friends
of yours, to see you wasting the flower of your life on such things, and I
feared lest that noble nature of yours should be dulled, and lest from
habit you should be brought to take pleasure in pursuits which only
enervate the mind[2]."

[1] Printed in *Instructions for Travellers* (1633).
[2] Pears, p. 167, November 14, 1579.

W. L. S.

The old Huguenot was not likely to be imposed on by the accomplishments of the Hattons and Oxfords by whom Elizabeth was surrounded.

When Languet returned to the Continent Robert Sidney met him at Flushing, and henceforth Languet lavished on him something of the devoted care which a few years earlier he had shown to Philip. He at once put himself into communication with Dr Lobetius and John Sturm, the famous educational reformer, regarding the course of study most profitable for the young man, and they travelled together by way of Antwerp, Cologne and Frankfort to Strassburg. To Orange and La Noue, the greatest of Huguenot soldiers, who was now in command of the Dutch troops, Languet carried letters from Sidney, and both were exceedingly kind to Sidney's young brother. Orange seated him at dinner between his wife and daughter, and La Noue was most gracious[1].

"I have taken care," Languet wrote, "that he should make the acquaintance and prepare a way to the friendship of such persons here as I consider eminent for their character. The Prince of Orange and La Noue especially welcomed him, and La Noue, who is full of courtesy showed him every attention yesterday as long as we were in the citadel. Your letters gave great pleasure to La Noue and the Prince ; both of them thanked me warmly for what I had done towards gaining them your good will. I have no doubt they will show you in their letters how well pleased they are."

At Arnheim, Languet presented Robert to Prince John of Nassau, and from Frankfort they turned aside to Neustadt to pay their respects once more to the Prince " for he had made your brother promise him this when he was in Zealand." After a hard journey in which Languet, Robert and Henry White, his servant, all suffered from fever or colds they reached Strassburg on April 28th, and Languet, after arranging with some difficulty for a supply of money for his *protégé*, set to work to find him a suitable tutor—a difficult task, for Languet insisted on his being not only learned but of polished manners. He finally chose a certain Peter Hubner, a Silesian who had studied under Ursinus at Heidelberg, and he was fortunate in finding lodgings for young Sidney in Sturm's household.

[1] *Epistolæ*, p. 219, March 11, 1579.

Languet watched over the boy, whose disposition pleased him
"more and more," as if he had been his father[1], and he never
seems to have felt that his responsibility for the rather wayward
youth was a burden, though his own health was wretched from
this time onward and he was rarely free from bodily discomfort
or pain[2].

Sidney, meanwhile, was sharing in the apprehension, not
to say disgust, which was almost universal in England as a
consequence of the arrival of Simier to negotiate a marriage
between his master and the English Queen. Of the Council
Sussex alone was favourable; Burghley alone hesitated.
The Queen seemed really inclined to the match, and Burghley
weighed the advantages of a secured French alliance and the
possibility of a child's being born who would be undisputed
heir of the throne, against the very obvious disadvantages
of a marriage between a woman of forty-six and a youth of
twenty-three, especially when that youth was a Papist, a Frenchman, a son of Catherine de' Medici, and an object of aversion
to the whole English nation. There was no pretence of con-
cealing this national dislike of the marriage project. In March
the preacher at the Royal Chapel declared in the Queen's
presence that England did not need a second foreign marriage;
Queen Mary's experience was sufficient[3]. In April the Bishop
of Ely wrote a letter to the Queen in which he attempted
earnestly to dissuade her from the marriage[4]. The Queen
seemed now hot, now cold, but as evidences increased of the
universal opposition of both courtiers and people, the spirit of
perversity or some other equally incalculable cause led her to
grow more and more favourable. Simier was fêted and at
once became a favourite with her Majesty—her *petit singe*.
In August Alençon himself arrived—a man unprepossessing
both in appearance and character in the eyes of everyone

---

[1] See a letter of Languet to Hubner, June 4, 1579, admonishing him to
see to it that Robert learns to speak German (*Zurich Letters*, ii, p. 310).

[2] On May 24th he wrote to Sidney a very long letter wholly on the subject
of Robert's temperament, his needs, and the plans which Languet was making
for his education (*Epistolæ*, p. 231).

[3] Froude, vol. x, p. 487.

[4] *Lansdowne MSS.* vol. xxviii, No. 70.

except the Queen. "She, who was accustomed to the stately presence of the Dudleys and the Sidneys, declared she had never seen a man who pleased her so well, never one whom she could so willingly make her husband[1]." When Alençon after a few days returned to France the belief was general that he would soon be King of England.

Perhaps the Queen was inclined to look more favourably on her foreign suitor at this juncture for the very reason that one of the Dudleys had ceased for the time being to be fair in her eyes. At the beginning of July Simier had made the momentous discovery of Leicester's marriage, and had lost no time in imparting his information to the Queen. Her anger was unbounded and was not lessened by the fact that Hatton—her *mouton*—had contracted a similar secret marriage. "Leicester and Hatton are married secretly," wrote the Queen of Scots to the Archbishop of Glasgow, "which hath so offended this queen, it is thought she has been led upon such miscontentment to agree to the sight of the Duke of Alençon[2]." Mendoza, who had evidently not heard the reason for Leicester's disgrace, reported that he

"has retired to a house of his five miles away where the Queen has been to see him, and where she remained two days because he feigned illness. She afterwards returned secretly to London. A sister of Leicester's of whom the Queen was very fond, and to whom she had given apartments at Court, retired at the same time as her brother[3]."

This refers doubtless to Lady Sidney. Fulke Greville says that Leicester "like a wise man under colour of taking physic voluntarily became prisoner in his chamber[4]." According to Camden he was ordered not to stir from Greenwich Castle, and Elizabeth was dissuaded from her purpose of sending him to the Tower only on the advice of Sussex.

Sussex, however, was at bitter enmity with Leicester now as always, for he was the chief of the pro-French faction[5].

---

[1] Froude, x, p. 494.   [2] Quoted by Froude, x, p. 493, July 4, 1579.
[3] *Spanish State Papers—Eliz.*, July 6, 1579.   [4] *Life*, p. 60.
[5] The author of *Leicester's Commonwealth* accuses Leicester of attempting to poison Simier and Sussex, but Leicester attempted to murder most of the prominent characters of the time according to his detractor. *V.* pp. 28 and 37.

Oxford, a mere time-server, was also of the party, though only a year before Mendoza had described him as "a very gallant lad" who did not wish to entertain Frenchmen, while Leicester, Walsingham, Pembroke and Hatton were the leaders of the bitter opposition to the project.

"The whole Council," declared Mendoza, "except Sussex and Burghley disapprove of the Alençon marriage and have told the Queen so....Many documents have been sent to her lately dissuading her from the business. This has been managed through Leicester and Hatton through whose hands most of the papers have reached her[1]."

With one of these documents we are especially concerned, for it was written by Sidney, and its origin is probably indicated in another of Mendoza's letters. Leicester was allowed to return to London about the middle of August and after an interview with the Queen "his emotion was remarked."

"A meeting was held on the same night at the Earl of Pembroke's house, there being present Lord Sidney [sic] and other friends and relatives. They no doubt discussed the matter, and some of them afterwards remarked that Parliament would have something to say as to whether the Queen married or not. The people in general seem to threaten revolution about it[2]."

It was probably at this meeting at Baynard's Castle that Sidney undertook to write a letter to the Queen in which he should point out to her the inconveniences attendant upon the match. He told Languet afterward that he was ordered to write by those whom he was bound to obey, and with this clue we may conjecture that besides the Earl of Pembroke and Sir Henry Sidney there were present that night the Earl of Leicester, Walsingham and possibly Sir Christopher Hatton, with whom Leicester and his nephew were both on terms of especial intimacy at this time. Before considering the letter itself, however, we must turn our attention to an unpleasant incident which had given Sidney much notoriety a few days earlier.

We have seen that no one had been more ostentatiously in favour of the French match than the Earl of Oxford, Burghley's

---

[1] *State Papers—Spanish—Eliz.*, October 16, 1579.
[2] *Ibid.*, August 25, 1579.

scapegrace son-in-law. Unhampered by any principles except that of self-advancement, this brutal debauchee[1] was anxious only to say what was pleasing to the Queen, and so successful was he that he had become one of her favourites. He was much in the company of Alençon's suite during the few days of that Prince's visit to London. Sidney, on the other hand, was recognized as one of the chief of the younger men who were most opposed to the marriage, although he maintained "a liberal conversation with the French, reverenced amongst the worthiest of them for himself[2]." Of the encounter between these two strangely diverse courtiers our only version is that given by Fulke Greville. Speaking of Sidney he says :

"Being one day at tennis, a peer of this realm, born great, greater by alliance, and superlative in the prince's favour, abruptly came into the tennis-court, and speaking out of these three paramount authorities, he forgot to entreat that which he could not legally command...at last with rage (which is ever ill-disciplined) he commands them to depart the Court. To this Sir Philip temperately answers that if his Lordship had been pleased to express desire in milder characters, perchance he might have led out those that he should now find would not be driven out with any scourge of fury. This answer (like a bellows) blowing up the sparks of excess already kindled, made my Lord scornfully call Sir Philip by the name of puppy....The French Commissioners unfortunately had that day audience in those private galleries whose windows looked into the tennis-court. They instantly drew all to this tumult, every sort of quarrels sorting well with their humours, especially this. Which Sir Philip perceiving, and rising with inward strength by the prospect of a mighty faction against him, asked my Lord with a loud voice that which he heard clearly enough before. Who (like an echo that still multiplies by reflexions) repeated this epithet of puppy the second time. Sir Philip, resolving in one answer to conclude both the attentive hearers and passionate actor, gave my Lord a lie, impossible (as he averred to be retorted) in respect all the world knows puppies are gotten by dogs and children by men.

Hereupon these glorious inequalities of fortune in his Lordship were put to a kind of pause by a precious inequality of nature in this gentleman. So that they both stood silent a while like a dumb show in a tragedy, till Sir Philip, sensible of his own wrong, the foreign and factious spirits that attended, and yet even in this question between him and his superior,

---

[1] Some two years later Lord Henry Howard declared that Oxford had attempted to murder Leicester on his way to Wanstead, and Philip Sidney in his bed (*State Papers—Dom.—Eliz.*, vol. CLI).

[2] Greville, *Life*, p. 63.

tender to his country's honour, with some words of sharp accent led the way abruptly out of the tennis-court, as if so unexpected an accident were not fit to be decided any farther in that place. Whereof the great Lord making another sense continues his play without any advantage of reputation as by the standard of humours in those times it was conceived.

A day Sir Philip remains in suspense when hearing nothing of or from the Lord he sends a gentleman of worth to awake him out of his trance, wherein the French would assuredly think any pause, if not death, yet a lethargy of true honour in both. This stirred a resolution in his Lordship to send Sir Philip a challenge[1]. Notwithstanding, these thoughts in the great Lord wandered so long between glory, anger and inequality of state as the Lords of her Majesty's Council took notice of the differences, commanded peace, and laboured a reconciliation between them[2]."

Finding neither Oxford nor Sidney amenable to their wishes, the Council referred the quarrel to the Queen. Characteristically she pointed out to Sidney the difference in degree between earls and gentlemen and the respect inferiors owed to their superiors. He replied with spirit that place was never intended for privilege to wrong, and that the difference of degrees between free men could not challenge any other homage than precedency. Nevertheless the Queen's command was sufficient to prevent the duel actually taking place.

For us the chief interest of the incident consists in the fact that Sidney seems to have had no misgivings whatever regarding what it was necessary for him to do to preserve his honour. Writing to Sir Christopher Hatton a few days later he said :

"As for the matter depending between the Earl of Oxford and me certainly, Sir, however I might have forgiven him, I should never have forgiven myself if I had lain under so proud an injury as he would have laid upon me ; neither can anything under the sun make me repent it, nor any misery make me go one half-word back from it. Let him, therefore, as he will, digest it. For my part I think tying up makes some things seem fiercer than they would be[3]."

Even Languet, when he received Sidney's letter giving an account of the quarrel, was far from unequivocal condemnation

---

[1] The challenge is said to have been carried by Sir Walter Raleigh, who was a friend of both Sidney and Oxford.

[2] *Life*, pp. 63–67.

[3] August 28, 1579. *Add. MS.* 15891, fol. 31. Printed in Nicolas' *Life of Sir Christopher Hatton* (1847), p. 128.

"I am aware," he wrote, "that by a habit inveterate in all Christendom, a nobleman is disgraced if he does not resent such an insult ; still I think you were unfortunate to be drawn into this contention although I see that no blame is to be attached to you for it. You can derive no true honour from it, even if it gave you occasion to display to the world your constancy and courage."

He goes on to observe that several writers learned in the law have in our own time discussed duelling, and that an English writer, William Newburgh, has cited the decrees of a certain synod in which duelling is absolutely condemned and forbidden to Christians. On this point Languet expresses no opinion ; he is more concerned for Sidney's personal safety.

"Since your adversary has attached himself to Anjou's party," he adds, "if your wooer shall return to you with a crowd of French noblemen about him, you must be on your guard, for you know the fiery nature of my countrymen[1]."

Sidney himself was simply conscious of his own rectitude and had no impulse to fly in the face of the accepted traditions of the society in which he lived. It was a greater and more original genius almost contemporary with Sidney who was the first to lend the weight of his authority to a condemnation of the practice.

Almost immediately after the quarrel with Oxford Sidney submitted a letter to the Queen in which he summed up the arguments which counted chiefly in his own mind against the marriage project. He had already by words delivered to her most gracious ear the general sum of his travelling thoughts on the subject, as he phrased it : now in more formal fashion, and after consultation with his friends and relatives[2], he essays the task in writing. The letter[3] is amazingly frank and direct, and it is a question whether all Sidney's elaborated arguments had any object except to show the Queen how intense and bitter was the popular aversion. He deals little in flattery, though he does not altogether neglect it. With little of apology or

[1] *Epistolæ*, pp. 238–240.

[2] Sir Henry Sidney in a Council meeting declared "The marriage cannot be made good by all the counsel between England and Rome. A mass may not be suffered in the Court." He affirmed all of Sir Walter Mildmay's anti-Papist speech. Murdin, *Burghley Papers*, October 6, 1579.

[3] Printed by Collins, p. 287.

introduction he opens his argument. The Queen's chief strength consists in the Protestant section of her own people whose hearts will "be galled if not aliened when they shall see you take a husband, a Frenchman and a Papist, in whom (howsoever fine wits may find further dealings or painted excuses) the very common people well know this, that he is the son of a Jezabel of our age ; that his brother made oblation of his own sister's marriage, the easier to make massacres of our brethren in belief ; that he himself, contrary to his promise and all gratefulness, having his liberty and principal estate by the Huguenots' means, did sack Lacharists, and utterly spoil them with fire and sword. This I say even at first sight gives occasion to all, truly religious, to abhor such a master, and consequently to diminish much of the hopeful love they have long held to you." The English Catholics, whom he describes, perhaps thinking of his own father's impoverished state, as "men...of great riches because the affairs of state have not lain on them," he charges with essential disloyalty ; he cites the Northern rebellion and declares that at this present they want nothing so much as a head.

Against Alençon (he was now Duke of Anjou also, but was generally referred to in England as 'Monsieur') he urges his light ambition, the French disposition, his own education, his inconstant temper against his brother, his thrusting himself into the Low Country matters, his sometimes seeking the King of Spain's daughter, sometimes your Majesty, his being sometimes hot and sometimes cold, the race's unfaithfulness.

"He of the Romish religion and if he be a man, must needs have that manlike property to desire that all men be of his mind : you the erector and defender of the contrary and the only sun that dazzleth their eyes. He French, and desiring to make France great ; your Majesty English and desiring nothing less than that France should not grow great."

The idea that an alliance with Monsieur can strengthen England in her foreign relations, he scouts. England's strength is in the loyalty of her own people, who are devoted to the Queen and who live in so rare a government "where neighbours' fires give us light to see our quietness." "In the behalf of your subjects I durst with my blood answer it that there was

never monarch held in more precious reckoning of her people."
He glances at the fact that Queen Mary made "an odious
marriage with a stranger which is now in question whether
your Majesty shall do or no." Reverting to his own cherished
project of the Protestant League he says :

"I do with most humble heart say unto your Majesty (having assayed
this dangerous help) for your standing alone you must take it for a singular
honour God hath done you to be indeed the only Protector of his Church,
and yet in worldly respects your Kingdom very sufficient so to do, if you
make that religion upon which you stand, to carry the only strength,
and have abroad those that still maintain the same course, who as long
as they may be kept from utter falling your Majesty is sure enough from
your mightiest enemies." He concludes with a final contemptuous thrust
at Monsieur : "As for this man, as long as he is but Monsieur in might,
and a Papist in profession, he neither can nor will greatly shield you ; and
if he get once to be King his defence will be like Ajax's shield, which rather
weighed them down than defended those that bare it."

Elizabeth had probably never in the whole course of her
reign received a letter comparable with this for boldness and
frankness of speech. The correspondence of her better advisers
is characterized by indirectness and elaborateness—perhaps a
reflection of her own epistolary style ; that of the worser sort
abounds in insincere servility and adulation. No doubt those
for whom Sidney was spokesman chose him because he
would speak plainly. The sentiments are those of Walsingham
and Burghley ; the style is Sidney's own. In a remarkable
sense of the word Sidney exemplified what was best in the
popular ideals of his day, and in this letter his intense anti-
French, anti-Catholic prejudices are essentially English. " I
wonder," Languet wrote him a few months later, "why the Duke
of Anjou has conceived this dislike of you. If he hates you
only because you opposed him in England, he will soon be
reconciled to you." If Anjou had ever seen this letter we
should need no laboured explanation of his dislike. Fulke
Greville answers the question, Whether it were not an error,
and a dangerous one, for Sir Philip, being neither magistrate
nor councillor, to oppose himself against his sovereign's pleasure
in things indifferent ? by saying that his worth, truth, favour

and sincerity of heart, together with his real manner of proceeding in it, were his privileges. He goes on to say that
although Sidney found a sweet stream of sovereign humours
in that well-tempered Lady to run against him, yet found he
safety in herself ; her princely heart was a sanctuary unto him
and he kept his access to Her Majesty as before. Elizabeth
was no doubt amused by the *naïveté* of such a letter, at the
same time that she approved of the honest loyalty which it
evinced. Nevertheless Sidney had boldly opposed her will
and was the spokesman of the Leicestrian faction : it was
not Elizabeth's wont to let such an act pass without punishment,
and for some months Sidney tasted to a mild degree of the
disfavour which Dudleys and Sidneys alike were experiencing.
Over his fortunes in the ensuing months there hung what Languet
called " a sort of cloud," and it was just a year later that he was
able to congratulate Sidney on having " again come forth from
the shadows into the open light of the Court."   It was to be
a happy and a fruitful year in his life, at least in comparison
with those which had immediately preceded it.

CHAPTER XII

SIDNEY A MAN OF LETTERS—THE *ARCADIA* AND THE *APOLOGIE FOR POETRIE*

AFTER discharging his duty to Queen and country by writing this letter Sidney seems to have ceased from further active opposition to the French match. To this course Languet had urged him strongly :

"I admire your courage in freely admonishing the Queen and your countrymen of that which is to the State's advantage. But you must take care not to go so far that the unpopularity of your conduct be more than you can bear....I advise you to persevere as long as you can do anything that may benefit your country, but when you find that your opposition only draws on you dislike and aversion, and that neither your country, your friends, nor yourself derive any advantage from it, I advise you to give way to necessity and reserve yourself for better times ; for time itself will bring you occasions and means of serving your country[1]."

There was indeed little reason to believe that continued opposition could be of service. The Puritan, John Stubbs, who had written a bitter and injudicious pamphlet against the French marriage, and Page, the bookseller who had sold it, were made example of in November when in front of the Palace at Westminster "their right hands were struck off with a cleaver driven through the wrist with a beetle." It was one of Elizabeth's most unworthy acts. The bravery and dignity of both men as they underwent punishment made a deep impression on the people[2].

Sidney's first impulse was to join Orange. Languet urged him to do so, and emphasized the value of military experience

---

[1] Pears, p. 170.

[2] "Mr. Stubbs, his words upon the scaffold, etc." Harington, *Nugæ Antiquæ* (ed. 1779), III, p. 179.

under two such pre-eminent leaders as Orange and La Noue, both of whom were warmly attached to the young Englishman. He advised him, however, to make up his mind definitely before discussing the plan in public.

"You know that last year you gave some persons a hope that you were coming into this country, and though it was no fault of yours that you did not come, still if the same thing should happen again, many persons will feel that there is a want of constancy in you."

Du Plessis thought Sidney would be unwise to leave his own country. Sidney hesitated when he heard that Alençon would probably return to the Low Countries. Languet was able to assure him that at least many months would elapse before Alençon's return—months which might be used to wonderful advantage under La Noue's tuition. When the States decided in May, 1580, to send an ambassador to Alençon, offering him the sovereignty of their country, Languet accompanied the party on private business for the Prince and Princess of Orange, and before he set out he wrote to Sidney regarding plans he had made for his reception[1]. So certain did Languet feel about it that he reminded Sidney once more of the prophecy he had once made in Vienna[2].

But Sidney did not leave England. As we shall see, his interest in various literary matters had developed strongly even before the time of his submitting his letter to the Queen, and it was to develop strongly for some time. Hitherto his reputation had been great as a favourer of learning and a patron of men of letters[3].

"The Universities abroad and at home accounted him a general Maecenas of learning," Fulke Greville tells us, "dedicated their books to him, and communicated every invention or improvement of knowledge with him... there was not a cunning painter, a skilful engineer, an excellent musician or any other artificer of extraordinary fame that made not himself known to this famous spirit and found him his true friend without hire."

[1] *Epistolæ*, p. 271, May 6, 1580.
[2] *Ibid.* p. 262, March 12, 1580.
[3] In November, 1579, Lambertus Danaeus, the Genevan theologian, sent to Sidney through Languet a copy of his *Geographiam Poeticam* which he had dedicated to Sidney. *Epistolæ*, p. 248.

He "did not only encourage learning and honour in the schools," Greville continues, "but brought the affection and true use thereof into the Court and Camp." For a year or more after the partial withdrawal of the Queen's favour literature was to be his chief interest and writing his chief occupation. He spent the time partly at Leicester House[1] but principally at Wilton in the society of his sister, Mary, the Countess of Pembroke, to whom he was warmly attached, and whose tastes coincided in a remarkable degree with his own. He was by no means free from melancholy—partly because he was temperamentally inclined to it, partly because he did not regard his literary work in a serious way. It was merely a diversion to fill in months of enforced inaction when he would have wished to be performing some work that would be of advantage to his country or to the Protestant cause. He was able to see much of the various members of his family, however, and from his relations to his family his most unalloyed happiness was always derived.

Early in February Sir Henry Sidney proceeded to Wales to assume the duties of his Presidency, and about the same time Philip went down to Wilton[2]. Lady Pembroke's eldest son William (who was to become Shakespeare's patron) was born on April 8th. The Countess of Warwick represented the Queen as godmother, and the godfathers were the Earls of Warwick and Leicester—the latter represented by his deputy Philip Sidney[3]. Sir Henry was accustomed to take advantage of his

---

[1] During the autumn months he was in London, as is shown by Spenser's letters, and also by a letter written to him on October 16th by the Earl of Clanrickard asking him "to be a mean to my very good Lord, your father, on my behalf" (*State Papers—Ireland—Eliz.*, vol. LXIX). On New Year's Day he presented to the Queen a cup of cristall with a cover (Nichols, II, 289), and he was evidently still in London on January 16th when Fabianus Niphus wrote to Dannewitz, the secretary of Archduke Matthias, that "Philip Sidney, a young man of eminent wit and virtue, is wholly with us, and displays great affection for our prince" (*State Papers—Foreign—Eliz.*).

[2] From there he wrote to Arthur Atye, Leicester's secretary, on March 25th (*State Papers—Dom.—Eliz.*, vol. CXXXVI). No doubt he occasionally visited London. Spenser's letter to Harvey of April, 1580, reports Sidney in good health. Haslewood, p. 259.

[3] *Sidney Psalter.*

proximity to Wilton to visit his children, but in June Walsingham informed him of Her Majesty's pleasure

"for your continual residence within your charge without any kind of
removing from thence these dangerous times...and this care she hath
commanded me to recommend unto your Lordship the more earnestly
for that she is given to understand that your Lordship doth sometime
resort to Wilton[1]."

There seemed to be something almost of personal spitefulness
in Elizabeth's attitude to Sir Henry. Irish affairs were going
badly. James Fitzmaurice and Sanders had landed in the
preceding autumn and the Desmond rebellion was blazing
throughout the southern half of the island. Ormond had
been dispatched as military governor of Munster, but he too
was complaining bitterly of inadequate supplies, and capable
soldiers like Malbie and Drury were declaring that Sir Henry
Sidney was the only man who could handle the situation.
Meanwhile the Queen had found no one willing to be his successor, and although Sir Henry was at this very time giving
every assistance which he could possibly render to Arthur,
Lord Grey[2], who had been designated Lord Deputy, the Queen
in her fatuousness seemed to visit on his head all her troubles
in Ireland.   In August Walsingham was compelled to communicate to his friend a second rebuke consequent on his failure to
proceed vigorously against "recusants and obstinate persons
in religion," and to this letter he added a friendly foot-note :
"Your Lordship had need to walk warily for your doings are
narrowly observed, and her Majesty is apt to give ear to any
that shall ill you[3]."   It is little wonder that Sir Henry, so
broken in health that he could no longer use a pen, when he
reflected on the character of his service to the Queen during
the past twenty years, was filled with bitterness of heart.

---

[1] *Sidney Papers*, i, p. 274.

[2] See a long detailed letter of advice written by Sir Henry to Lord Grey
(*Sidney Papers*, i, 279).   "You shall have the best advice that I shall be able
to give you, protesting that if Philip Sidney were in your place, who most
earnestly and often hath spoken and written to do this loving office, he, I say,
should have no more of me than I most willingly will write to you from time
to time."

[3] *Sidney Papers*, i, p. 276.

Sidney probably returned to Court in the early autumn. In a letter to his uncle written at Clarinton on August 2nd in which he tells of having brought his sister home, he says that he has a bad cold which keeps him from Court. He doubts not that Her Majesty will ask for him, "but," he adds cynically, "so long as she sees a silk doublet upon me Her Highness will think me in good case[1]." On November 29th he described himself as ill and melancholy in a letter to Sebastian Pardini, the Paris agent of Don Antonio of Portugal[2]. Possibly because of his literary preoccupation there are comparatively few facts to chronicle in Sidney's life during 1580. At some time during the year he was one of the defenders in a tournament when the Earl of Arundell with his assistant, Sir William Drury, challenged all comers[3], and it was also during this year that he received a grant from the Earl of Leicester of the Stewardship to the Bishop of Winchester[4]. His finances were now as always a source of trouble. On April 23rd he and his father had sold to Sir Stephen Twilbie a Lincolnshire manor[5], and on June 1st of the following year he gave to his father a release for the manor of Eppesbrook near Penshurst, which they had jointly purchased a short time before from Thomas Willoughby[6]. Obscure in significance as these facts may be, they suggest that Sidney was in need of money. This we know independently by references in Languet's letters to Robert's impecunious condition.

A long letter to this brother written from Leicester House in October of this year gives us one of the pleasanter pictures of Sidney's life at the time. Languet's reports of the young man had been on the whole very favourable and encouraging. Dr Lobetius had had direct oversight of him during his stay in Sturm's household at Strassburg, and when Lobetius left the city Robert had removed with the concurrence of Languet

---

[1] MS. of C. Cottrell Dormer, Esq. *Appendix to Third Report of Hist. MSS. Com.*

[2] *State Papers—Foreign—Eliz.* Pardini to Sidney, February 21, 1581. Italian.

[3] Nichols' *Progresses*, II, p. 334.

[4] Marquis of Bath's MSS. *Appendix to Third Report of Hist. MSS. Com.*

[5] *Penshurst Latin Parchment.*　　　　[6] *Ibid.*

and Sidney to Leipzig. Apart from his inability to make his means meet his necessities Languet's only criticism of the youth had been regarding a report he had heard that Robert was anxious to join Casimir when the latter led his forces into France, and in defence of himself Robert might have urged that his elder brother had advised him to see "any good wars" if he could hear of such. The following extracts will illustrate the tone of the letter referred to[1] :

"MY DEAR BROTHER :

For the money you have received assure yourself, for it is true, there is nothing I spend so pleaseth me as that which is for you. If ever I have ability you will find it ; if not, yet shall not any brother living be better beloved than you of me. I cannot write now to N. White ; do you excuse me. For his nephew, they are but passions in my father which we must bear with reverence, but I am sorry he should return till he had the circuit of his travel, for you shall never have such a servant as he would prove ; use your own discretion therein. For your counten- ance, I would for no cause have it diminished in Germany ; in Italy your greatest expense must be upon worthy men and not upon householding. Look to your diet, sweet Robin, and hold up your heart in courage and virtue ; truly great part of my comfort is in you."

After a long discourse on the manner of reading history, he proceeds :

"My time exceeding short will suffer me to write no more leisurely : Stephen can tell you who stands with me while I am writing. Now, dear brother, take delight likewise in the Mathematicals; Mr. Savile is excellent in them. I think you understand the sphere ; if you do I care little for any more astronomy in you. Arithmetic and geometry I would wish you well seen in, so as both in matter of number and measure you might have a feeling and active judgment. I would you did bear the mechanical instruments wherein the Dutch excel. I write this to you as one that for myself have given over the delight in the world, but wish to you as much, if not more, than to myself. So you can speak and write Latin, not bar- barously, I never require great study in Ciceronianism, the chief abuse of Oxford, *Qui dum verba sectantur, res ipsas negligunt.* My toyful books, I will send, with God's help, by February, at which time you shall have your money. And for £200 a year assure yourself if the estates of England remain you shall not fail of it ; use it to your best profit. My Lord Leicester sends you forty pounds, as I understand by Stephen, and promiseth he will continue that stipend yearly at the least ; then that is above Commons. In any case write largely and diligently unto him, for in truth I have good

[1] *Sidney Papers,* I, p. 283.

W. L. S.

proof that he means to be every way good unto you. The odd £30 shall come with the hundred or else my father and I will jarl. Now, sweet brother, take a delight to keep and increase your music ; you will not believe what a want I find of it in my melancholy times. At horsemanship when you exercise it read *Crison Claudio*, and a book that is called *La Gloria de l'Cavallo* withal, that you may join the thorough contemplation of it with the exercise, and so shall you profit more in a month than others in a year, and mark the bitting, saddling and curing of horses. I would by the way, your worship would learn a better hand : you write worse than I, and I write evil enough. Once again have a care of your diet and consequently of your complexion ; remember *Gratior est veniens in pulchro corpore Virtus*. Now, sir, for news I refer myself to this bearer ; he can tell you how idle we look on our neighbour's fires, and nothing is happened notable at home save only Drake's return, of which yet I know not the secret points, but about the world he hath been, and rich he is returned. Portugal, we say, is lost, and, to conclude, my eyes are almost closed up, overwatched with tedious business. God bless you, sweet boy, and accomplish the joyful hope I conceive of you....Lord, how I have babbled ! Once again farewell, dearest brother.

Your most loving and careful brother,
PHILIP SIDNEY.

At Leicester House this
18th of October, 1580."

In these latter months of 1580 Sidney's inaction and consequent gloom are reflected in all we hear of him. We have heard him describe himself as " ill and melancholy " to Pardini, and to Robert, as one who has given over the delight in the world. Languet, in his last extant letter, is deeply concerned lest Sidney sink into slothful ease, and urges him to seek Dyer's counsel in arriving at some definite resolution as to his future course[1]. He reminds him that however pleasant it may be to enjoy familiar intercourse with his family, and however useful he may be to his father, his first duty is to his country, and in the present circumstances he can do nothing better for her than acquire military training under La Noue and Orange which may one day prove of the highest value.

"If the advice which you offered, believing it to be good for England, was not received as it deserved," Languet had already written him, "you must not therefore be angry with your country, for good citizens ought to pardon her every wrong, and not for any such reason desist from working for her preservation."

---

[1] *Epistolæ*, pp. 287, 288, October 28, 1580.

Sidney's reference to his "toyful books" of which Robert has heard, shows how lightly he estimated such work : evidently he had never ventured even to confess to Languet that he had been engaged in such vain, amatorious occupations.

To these occupations we must now give our attention. It is in the spring of 1578 that we first hear of Sidney's especial interest in literature.   Early in May the Queen paid a visit to Leicester at Wanstead, and part of her entertainment consisted of a masque or pastoral farce—*The Lady of May*—written by Sidney.   It is a very slight, unpretentious production—some ten pages written in prose through which are interspersed several short poems.   The Lady of May has two suitors,—a forester of many deserts and many faults, and a shepherd of small deserts and no faults.   She likes them both but loves neither, and she appeals to the Queen "as to the beautifullest Lady these woods have ever received" to help her decide. Rhombus, a neighbouring schoolmaster, "that is to say, a Pedagogue, one not a little versed in the disciplinating of the juvenal frie," attempts to present the case to Her Majesty, but is repulsed by the May-lady for his tedious pompousness.   The suitors then present their own cases in verse; another shepherd and another forester revile each other in prose, and after Rhombus has again tried to "endoctrinate their plumbeous cere-brosities," the Queen finally delivers judgment for the shepherd. The piece is rather an extempore pastoral scene in which are elements of both the farce and the masque, than a regular masque as that form came to be understood somewhat later.   The graceful phrasing of the flattery of the Queen, the out-of-doors atmo-sphere, the picturesque contrasts in the costumes, and the really amusing pompousness of the schoolmaster unite to give the little play considerable merit, though it is chiefly notable in that Rhombus is without doubt the prototype of Holofernes.

Some two months after the Wanstead entertainment, on July 26th, the Queen visited Audley End at Saffron Walden, and there she was waited on by the Vice-Chancellor, heads of colleges, and scholars of the University of Cambridge.   Sidney was now on the point of setting out for Holland, and it was only when he had come to Audley End to take his leave that he

learned in full the conditions under which he was to go. As
we have seen, he declined the office of carrying discouragement
to his continental friends[1]. We may assume that he now
renewed Cambridge acquaintances. When Gabriel Harvey,
who was present at the Audley End celebrations, a few weeks
later published his *Gratulationes Valdinenses* he dedicated one
division of the book to Sidney—*mihi multis nominibus longe
charissimum*. When Harvey was presented to the Queen
she spoke of having previously heard of him from Leicester,
and we have already seen that a year before the time with which
we are now dealing, Spenser was with Sir Henry Sidney in
Ireland; these facts suggest that Sidney's relation to his
former Cambridge acquaintances had been much more intimate
in the years that had passed since he left the University than
has ordinarily been supposed. What is certain is that by the
latter part of 1579 Spenser had come to London and was
living at Leicester House, that he was on terms of familiarity
with Sidney and Dyer, and that they together discussed literary
questions. In the following winter Spenser published his
Shepherd's Calendar and dedicated it to Sidney—

> "To him that is the president
> Of Noblesse and of chevelree."

The prefatory letter written by Spenser's friend, Edward
Kirke, described Sidney as "a special favourer and maintainer
of all kind of learning." In after days Spenser was generous
in his expressions of indebtedness. He calls Sidney "the
patron of my young Muses," and refers to him as "that most
heroic spirit"

> "Who first my muse did lift out of the floor
> To sing his sweet delights in lowly lays."

The title of one of Spenser's lost works, *Stemmata Dudleiana*,
suggests that it was written to recognize the favours shown him
by Leicester and his nephew, and many years later, in dedicating
The Ruins of Time to the Countess of Pembroke, Spenser refers
to his "most entire love and humble affection unto that most
brave knight your brother deceased." The references to

---

[1] See pp. 199–200.

Sidney in Spenser's *Astrophel* and *Colin Clout* similarly express
the warmest enthusiasm and admiration. These references,
however, together with the Spenser-Harvey correspondence,
furnish us with the whole of our information as to the relations
of the two men whose tastes and character fitted them in an
unusual degree for friendship, and from these sources we learn
only very little that is not of a general character. Our scanty
stock of detailed information has been eked out by two statements, one or both of which have been very generally repeated
by writers on the subject[1]—statements which are calculated
to ·enable the imagination to conjure up a picture of more
intimate relations than we are warranted in affirming. The
first of these is that Spenser was for a time Sidney's guest at
Penshurst, the second that they were both members of a
literary club in London called the Areopagus which also numbered Harvey, Edward Dyer, Fulke Greville, and others of
Sidney's courtly friends among its members. For neither
statement have I been able to find any justification[2]. The
second is based on the following extract from a letter written
by Spenser to Harvey :

" As for the two worthy gentlemen, Master Sidney and Master Dyer, they
have me, I thank them, in some use of familiarity ; of whom and to whom,
what speech passeth for your credit and estimation, I leave yourself to
conceive, having always so well conceived of my unfeigned affection and
zeal towards you. And now they have proclaimed in their αρειωπαγώ a
general surceasing and silence of bald rhymers, and also of the very best,
too : instead whereof they have by authority of their whole Senate,
prescribed certain laws and rules of quantities of English syllables for
English verse, having had thereof already great practice, and drawn me
to their faction[3]."

Spenser obviously intends to give his friend a humorous
account of what he well knew was a Herculean task, and accordingly he refers to the partnership of Sidney and Dyer as an
Areopagus or whole Senate. Harvey evidently understands him
in this sense when he replies : " Your new-founded αρειωπαγον

[1] By Fox-Bourne, Flügel, Sidney Lee, etc.
[2] Harvey's reference to " a goodly Kentish garden of your old Lords" is an
altogether inadequate foundation for the first statement.
[3] Haslewood, *Ancient Critical Essays*, vol. ii, p. 288.

I honour more than you will or can suppose; and make greater
account of the two worthy gentlemen than of two hundred
Dionisy Areopagitae or the very notablest senators that ever
Athens did afford of that number." He several times refers to the
opinions of the "two gentlemen" but expressly forbids Spenser
even to show his poems to "any else, friend or foe"; the
letters contain no reference to Greville or any "others of Sidney's
courtly friends." It would be pleasant to know that there
was a warm personal friendship between Sidney and Spenser,
and that Sidney knew and appreciated at its true worth the
Faerie Queene, of which Harvey had such a poor opinion, but
these are subjects for pleasant speculation only. Sidney's
rather grudging appreciation of the *Shepherd's Calendar* in
his *Apologie* must give us pause when we are contemplating
any such imaginative flights. We simply know that Sidney
and Dyer had Spenser "in some use of familiarity." Though
living at Leicester House, Spenser can only promise Harvey to
show his Iambics to Sidney and Dyer "at my next going to
the Court." Within a few months Spenser went to Ireland as
secretary to Lord Grey, and he did not return to England
until some three years after Sidney's death.

From the extracts already quoted we learn that Sidney and
Dyer have become enthusiasts for English quantitative verse
and are scourging 'bald rhymers' as no true poets. Harvey
seems to suggest that he himself was the originator of the
movement :

"I cannot choose but thank and honour the good angel (whether it were
Gabriel or some other) that put so good a motion into the heads of those
two excellent gentlemen, Mr. Sidney and Mr. Dyer, the two very diamonds
of her Majesty's court for many special and rare qualities, as to help
forward our new famous enterprise for the exchanging of barbarous and
balductum rhymes with artificial verses."

Harvey's own prosody varied somewhat from that observed
by Sidney, Dyer and Spenser—a scheme which had been drawn
up by 'Master Drant' and revised by Sidney and Spenser.
They all laboured hard to hold each other's attempts "in great
good liking and estimation," but it was an uphill task. Harvey
confessed that he was "wont to have some prejudice of the

man"—Drant—and utterly rejected his authority. He and Spenser both confess their great difficulty with the accent, and though Harvey virtuously condemns all wrenching, and the devising of any 'counterfeit, fantastical accent of our own,' he feels that his own practice needs much explanation, and relieves himself by flings at " this ill-favoured orthography or rather pseudography," which hopelessly confuses the determination of the quantity. The result of Sidney's efforts remains in the poems of the *Arcadia* ; the majority of Spenser's have happily perished. When somewhat later Sidney wrote his *Apologie* he was much more tolerant of rhyme.

Harvey regards Sidney and Dyer as " our very Castor and Pollux" in the writing of " delicate and choice elegant Poesie," and he can hardly refer, except to a slight extent, to poems of the equivocal sort which we have been discussing. The chronology of Sidney's various works is still far from being accurately determined, but we can glean from various sources something definite on the subject. In the *Apologie* Sidney speaks of "in these my not old years and idlest times having slipt into the title of a poet," and he also gives us his reason for having practised in this "unelected vocation." "Overmastered by some thoughts," he says, "I yielded an inky tribute unto them." Of his own efforts he always spoke in disparaging tones. They were the product of his idlest times ; he allowed none of them to be printed during his lifetime ; probably many of his best friends, like Languet, were unaware of their existence. However Sidney might exalt the function of the poet and of poetry, he could not forget that in England poets "are almost in as good reputation as the mountebanks in Venice." Like several others of the noble youth of the Court, he paid tribute to the promptings of the Renaissance spirit by writing both prose and verse, but he is extremely anxious that it be understood that these are but 'toyful books' produced for the entertainment of indulgent friends. At no time did he set any serious estimate on the value of the books he wrote.

In 1579–1580 Sidney was known as a writer of poems, and as we shall see there is no reasonable doubt that these poems are included in the sonnet sequence of *Astrophel and Stella.*

It was almost certainly in 1580, during his residence with his sister at Wilton, that he wrote the *Arcadia*. It was written, he tells us, in the letter prefaced to the first printed edition, because she desired him to do it. He further says that it was written on loose sheets of paper, most of it in his sister's presence, the rest by sheets sent unto her as fast as they were done. It was done only for her, only to her. She is urged to keep it to herself, or to such friends as will weigh errors in the balance of good-will. His excuse for writing is that

"a young head, not so well stayed as I would it were, and shall be when God will, having many many fancies begotten in it, if it had not been in some way delivered, would have grown a monster, and more sorry would I be that they came in than that they got out. But his chief safety shall be the not walking abroad."

Aubrey tells a story on the authority of his great-uncle, who remembered Sidney, that "he was often wont, as he was hunting on our pleasant plains, to take his table-book out of his pocket and write down his notions as they came into his head when he was writing his *Arcadia*[1]"—and the context shows that he is referring to Salisbury Plain. At Wilton an avenue of trees is still pointed out as that in which, according to tradition, Sidney composed the *Arcadia*.

An important reference to the romance is contained in a letter[2] written by Greville to Sir Francis Walsingham in November, 1586,—immediately after Sidney's death.

"Sir," writes Greville, "this day one Ponsonby, a book-binder in Paul's Churchyard, came to me and told me that there was one in hand to print Sir Philip Sidney's old *Arcadia*, asking me if it were done with your honour's voice or any other of his friends. I told him to my knowledge, no, then he advised me to give warning of it, either to the archbishop or Doctor Cousin, who have, as he says, a copy to peruse to that end. Sir, I am loath to renew his memory unto you, but yet in this I must presume, for I have sent my lady, your daughter, at her request, a correction of that old one, done four or five years since, which he left in trust with me, whereof there is no more copies, and fitter to be printed than the first, which is so common : notwithstanding, even that to be amended by a direction set down under his own hand, how and why, so as in many respects, especially the care of printing of it, is to be done with more deliberation."

[1] Vol. II, p. 248.   [2] *State Papers—Dom.—Eliz.* vol. CXCV.

From this letter we learn that there were two versions of the novel—the old *Arcadia*—of which there were many manuscript copies, and a revised version, of which there was a single copy. If we are to take Greville's statement literally the old *Arcadia* was completed in 1581 or 1582 : this may have been the case, or, again, it is quite possible that the statement is not exact. The project referred to in the letter was thwarted, and on August 23, 1588, Ponsonby himself was licensed to print the work[1]. It appeared in 1590 in quarto form. It was divided into chapters each of which was preceded by a summary, and a preface informed the reader that "The division and summary of the chapters was not of Sir Philip Sidney's doing, but adventured by the overseer of the print for the more ease of the readers." It is almost beyond doubt that this edition was printed from the revised version of which we have just heard, and that Fulke Greville was the "overseer[2]." Its differences from the old *Arcadia* were at once remarked. In 1591, Sir John Harington, in his notes to his translation of the *Orlando Furioso,* printed a sonnet which he described as "that excellent verse of Sir Philip Sidney in his first Arcadia, (which I know not by what mishap is left out in the printed book[3])." The second edition appeared in 1593 in folio, and differed from the first chiefly in the fact that half of the third book and the whole of the fourth and fifth were additions. According to a prefatory address to the reader by H. S., this second edition was superintended by the Countess of Pembroke. H. S. speaks of the disfigured face wherewith the work had appeared in the first edition, and describes the work of the Countess as that of correcting the faults and also supplying the defects. As a matter of fact, however, the quarto varies only slightly from that portion of the first folio edition which corresponds to it[4].

---

[1] Arber's *Transcript of the Register of the Company of Stationers,* II, fol. 231*b*.

[2] W. W. Greg's *Pastoral Poetry and Pastoral Drama,* p. 148.

[3] Collier's *Poetical Decameron,* vol. I, p. 66.

[4] In the years 1907 and 1908 Mr Bertram Dobell became possessed of three manuscripts all of them copies, as he believes, of the old *Arcadia.* A detailed account of the differences between these texts and that of the first folio would lead us too far afield. The title of one of the manuscripts refers to the romance as having been made in the year 1580. *V.* Mr Dobell's article in the *Quarterly Review,* July, 1909.

The text of the first folio remained substantially that of the
many editions which succeeded it[1], although "a supplement
of a defect in the third part of this history" was added by
Sir W. Alexander in 1621 and a sixth book by R. Beling in 1624.
The identity of H. S. who writes the prefatory letter to the
reader, and who evidently speaks for the Countess, has hitherto
remained unknown. It is not a matter of any great importance,
but as it has caused more or less speculation on the part of
most students of Sidney, I am glad to be able to furnish the
solution of the riddle. Aubrey says that the letters are the
initials of Mr Henry Sandford, the Earl of Pembroke's secretary[2],
but his statement has been ignored by all later writers—perhaps
because of Aubrey's reputation for giving unreliable information.
In this case, however, he was telling the truth. The proof is
to be found in one of the Harleian manuscripts in the British
Museum[3]—John Hoskins' "Directions for Speech and Style
containing all the Figures of Rhetoric etc. etc. The Quotations
being taken out of Sir Philip Sidney's *Arcadia*, the first edition
in quarto without Samford's additions." Of Hoskins' information there can be no question. He had been a student at New
College and afterward of the Middle Temple. He knew Sidney
personally, as we shall see, and was on intimate terms with
Sir Walter Raleigh, John Donne and Sir Henry Wotton[4].
In the *Peplus*, the memorial volume published in 1587 in memory
of Sidney by alumni of New College, Oxford, eight of the
poems are by Hoskins. Across the top of the pictorial frontis-
piece of this little volume is a banner on which is inscribed
the word 'Arcadia.' Hoskins' admiration of Sidney's romance
and of its author is reiterated throughout his *Rhetoric*, and it
would be absurd to impeach his testimony as to the identity
of H. S. Sandford was "a good scholar and poet" according
to Aubrey, and we know that the Earl of Pembroke entrusted
weighty matters to him[5].

[1] In an account book at Belvoir Castle the following item occurs for the
year 1598–9 : "For Sir Ph. Sidney's *Arcadia. 9s.*" (*Hist. Man. Com. Reports.*)
[2] Vol. I, p. 311.
[3] MS. 4604. On the outside is written large in red pencil "Ban. Man-
waring's Booke MDCXXX." It contains 49 pages.
[4] *Reliquiæ Wottonianæ*, 1685, pp. 378, 432.
[5] V. *Sidney Papers*, vol. I, pp. 353, 370.

Any attempt to discuss adequately the many bibliographical and literary questions connected with the *Arcadia* would require at least many chapters. Its popularity was unbounded, and before the close of the seventeenth century it had gone through fifteen editions. It was translated into French in 1625 and into German in 1629. The names of the English writers whose work was influenced by it would make a long list. That Shakespeare made use in *King Lear* of an incident from the romance, and that Milton showed his remarkable familiarity with it in his *Eikonoklastes,* is known to everyone. Its sources have of course been made the subject of minute investigation. One of the early references to the question occurs in John Hoskins' unpublished *Rhetoric* to which we have just referred. After ascribing Sidney's eloquence and his powers of description to his familiarity with Aristotle's *Rhetoric,* Hoskins continues : "I think also that he had much help out of *Theophrasti Imagines.* For the web (as it were) of his story he followed three—Heliodorus in Greek, Sanazarus' Arcadia in Italian and Diana de Montemaior in Spanish." Later study of the question has confirmed and elaborated Hoskins' analysis.

From an early date, too, there has been an effort to discover what more is meant than meets the eye in *Arcadia.* Just one hundred years after Sidney's death a correspondent of Aubrey furnished him with a rough interpretation of the characters, derived, he says, from relatives of Sidney. According to this letter, Philoclea and Pamela in the novel are the ladies Penelope and Dorothy Devereux ; Pyrocles and Musidorus are their husbands. Gynecia is hesitatingly identified with the ladies' mother and both Amphialus and Philisides with Sidney himself. Some very incorrect historical information is added, and we may agree with the writer of the letter that his key "is not worth anything." There is general agreement that in the mouth of Philisides, the melancholy shepherd, Sidney put many of his own sentiments, and it would be strange, considering the date of composition of the *Arcadia,* had the heroine, Philoclea, not reflected to a greater or less degree the charms of Penelope Devereux. Further than this it would not be safe to go. There are, to be sure, occasional local references.

No one could fail to recognize in Sidney's description of Helen, Queen of Corinth, another Queen well known to readers of the romance, or rather it was the kind of conventional description of her which that Queen loved to hear.

"For, being brought, by right of birth, a woman, a young woman, a fair woman, to govern a people in nature mutinously proud, and always before so used to hard governors as they knew not how to obey without the sword were drawn, yet could she for some years so carry herself among them, that they found cause, in the delicacy of her sex, of admiration, not of contempt, and, which was notable, even in the time that many countries about her were full of wars, which, for old grudges to Corinth, were thought still would conclude there, yet so handled she the matter that the threatened ever smarted in the threateners, she using so strange, and yet so well-succeeeding a temper that she made her people, by peace, warlike, her courtiers, by sports, learned, her ladies, by love, chaste....So as it seemed that court to have been the marriage-place of Love and Virtue, and that herself was a Diana apparelled in garments of Venus."

The real biographical significance of the *Arcadia* consists in its style, which is of the man himself. In its combination of Arcadian and heroic elements, its vagueness as to time and place, in its very confusion of episode, the unreality of its portraiture and the dreaminess of its atmosphere is reflected Sidney's tendency to turn in spirit from the world of things as they were to the world of things as they might be. According to his own definition it is a poem in which is expressed the ideality of his own nature. In Arcadia there are men who are brave, high-minded, chivalric, and women who are beautiful and good, and if there are also others who are selfish or wicked they are subordinates who make the virtues of the heroes and heroines 'stick more fiery off.' In this world there is much of magnificent pageantry ; everywhere the æsthetic sense is charmed by beauty of landscape, beauty of architecture, beauty of dress. These beauties are elaborated in long, involved parenthetic sentences suggestive of the rich abundance of the material and of the author's unwillingness to pass from the enumeration of the details of beauty to the more prosaic business or relating a story. The test of narrative is no more applicable in the estimation of the *Arcadia* than it would be in the case of

the *Faerie Queene* or *The Eve of St Agnes*.   The Elizabethan
zest for experience and delight in deeds of adventure and high
emprise have overwhelmed considerations of exact coherence and
literary form.

Milton's stricture on the romance—that it was a vain
amatorious poem—cannot be brushed aside.   The god of
Arcadia is Love, and, like Musidorus, we are sometimes uncertain
whether he should be apostrophized as a celestial or as an
infernal spirit.   The preoccupation of the writer's mind with
the facts of sex is much in evidence ; even the father and mother
of Philoclea and Pamela are made to fill sufficiently unedifying
rôles.   In spite of his deep moral earnestness there was nothing
of the Puritan in Sidney.   He represents rather the more
complex Renaissance type in which moral earnestness was not
incompatible with an impatient rejection of all ascetic ideals.
His melancholy was a melancholy of his own, compounded of
many simples, but it was not akin to the Puritan's melancholy
which was a recrudescence of the ideals of the mediaeval Church,
and which condemned as evil in themselves the desires and
passions of the natural man.   Sidney had no enthusiasm for
special prohibitions and restraints, and he would probably
have allowed great latitude to the man whose aims in life were
on the whole upright.

The date of composition of Sidney's *Apologie for Poetrie*
has never been accurately determined.   Mr Fox-Bourne, for
instance, assigns it to the year 1583, Shuckburgh and Churton
Collins to 1580–1.   There has been general agreement, however,
that in writing it Sidney had in mind Gosson's *School of Abuse,*
which appeared in August, 1579, and, consequently, that his
own work is of later date.

Gosson had dedicated his book to Sidney evidently without
having sought permission.   On October 15th Spenser wrote to
Harvey :

" New books I hear of none, but only of one that writing a certain book
called *The School of Abuse* and dedicating it to Master Sidney was for his
labour scorned, if at least it be in the goodness of that nature to scorn.
Such folly is it not to regard aforehand the inclination and quality of him
to whom we dedicate our books."

Primarily *The School of Abuse* is an attack upon the abuses of the contemporary stage, but the author includes "poets and pipers and such peevish cattle" in his denunciation. With Gosson's strictures on the indecency of many comedies of the time Sidney was in perfect sympathy. In the *Apologie* he too condemns plays that stir laughter in sinful things ; he denounces their scurrility and declares that they are not without cause cried out against. Gosson's attack on the stage had not been in quite unmeasured terms ; he had even admitted that some players were sober, discreet, properly learned and honest, and that some of their plays were without rebuke. It was his more or less incidental attack on poets and poetry that stirred Sidney's scorn, for it exemplified all the narrowness and illiberalism which for some time had been revealing themselves as the characteristic defects of the qualities of puritanism. Gosson's name is nowhere mentioned in the *Apologie*; his book was probably present specifically to Sidney's mind only when he was composing one short section of the *Apologie*—that in which he enumerates "the most important imputations laid to the poor poets." That Gosson was in any sense responsible for Sidney's undertaking to write the essay there is no reason to believe. Though the *Apologie* remained in manuscript, it is at least improbable that Gosson would have dedicated to Sidney the second edition of *The School of Abuse* in 1586 had Sidney's work been generally recognized as a reply to Gosson.

In the absence of all definite evidence as to the date of composition of the *Apologie* we may hazard the opinion that the work as we have it to-day was not composed at one time. Mr Shuckburgh has pointed out the similarity between many of the ideas expressed by Sidney in the letter which he wrote to his brother Robert in October, 1580, and those elaborated in the earlier part of the *Apologie* where the various functions of the historian, orator, philosopher and poet are treated. Spenser's lost work *The English Poet* may have originated in conversations which also gave rise to the *Apologie*, in the months immediately preceding Spenser's departure for Ireland. On the other hand, the last division of the *Apologie*, which deals with the state of contemporary English literature, must surely

have been written several years later. The references to the
Shepherd's Calendar and to the tedious prattling of euphuism
" in certain printed discourses" suggest a period when Spenser's
poem and Lyly's novel had become well known. Moreover,
Sidney's antipathy to rhyme has disappeared ; he now finds
in it both the sweetness and majesty of quantitative verse.
A more convincing argument, perhaps, may be based on his
contemptuous reference to the artificial love-songs and sonnets
of the day. He condemns them not only because of their
insincerity but because he remembers how much better poetic
ability might be employed in singing the praises of the immortal
beauty, the immortal goodness of that God who giveth us
hands to write and wits to conceive. It is difficult to believe
that this passage was written before Sidney's own sonnet-
writing days had passed. He himself has been admitted to
the company of these paper blurrers, he tells us, and he offers
as an excuse that he had yielded an inky tribute to certain
thoughts by which he had been overmastered. The tone
recalls that of the last sonnet :

"Leave me, O Love, that reachest but to dust,"

and the air of detachment from all such trivialities and the
religious tone accord rather with the latter period when Sidney
was translating into English the religious works of Du Bartas
and Du Plessis Mornay. We may conjecture that the *Apologie*
was begun towards the end of 1579 or during 1580 and that
it was concluded in 1583 or 1584.

The little volume which appeared in two editions in 1595
(one by Henry Olney entitled *An Apologie for Poetrie,* the
other by William Ponsonby entitled *The Defence of Poesie*)
has been accounted by common consent the most unequivocally
successful of Sidney's literary works. While showing a perfect
familiarity with Aristotle and Scaliger, the author treats his
subject in a genuinely original way. Like most writers of
the time he overloads his pages with classical references, but
rather, one feels, because he has lived with classical authors
until they have become a part of himself than from any vain
desire to parade his learning. Indeed no quality is more

alien to the style of the essay than pedantry. In its mingling
of gravity and gaiety, of colloquialism and dignified, elevated
speech, it is a true reflection of Sidney's character. His mind
plays easily over the field which he is treating, and the enthusiasm
of his personality fuses the seemingly incongruous elements. More
than history or philosophy or any of the sciences, he maintains,
poetry tends to elevate the whole man. Its delightful teaching
leads us to virtuous action, the rational object of all learning.
Sidney's love of beauty includes the beauty of a well-ordered
life ; all other beauty reaches but to dust. It is because, like
Arnold, he believes that as time passes our race will find a
surer and surer stay in poetry that he urges its claims in such
unqualified terms, because he believes that its future is immense.
His criticisms of contemporary literature missed the mark in
some instances, but his book endures because in essence it is
profoundly true, and because it is a true reflex of the author's
versatile, high-minded, gracious personality.

CHAPTER XIII

ASTROPHEL AND STELLA

No episode in Sidney's life has been more widely discussed or more variously interpreted than that which constitutes the theme of his sonnet sequence, *Astrophel and Stella*. This has been due in part no doubt to the promise which the poems seem to contain of introducing us to the author's very self—of revealing to us the human side of a man regarding whom we have known only facts of comparatively slight significance as to his real character. On the other hand, much of the discussion of the subject has been little more than the love of spicy gossip which masquerades as love of literature. It has been held that

"the whole series form a regular design, the object being to exercise the imagination on a set theme, according to the traditional rules of a particular poetical convention," and that to suppose that Sidney "after having been seasoned in all the fashions of society, should suddenly have been carried away by an irresistible passion for a woman, with whom he had long been accustomed to associate without any feelings beyond those of simple friendship, and who had just become the wife of another, is as injurious to his intellect, as his readiness to blazon abroad his illicit relations with Stella, assuming that his passion was sincere, would be to his delicacy and sense of honour[1]."

Again, the sonnets have been read as an illustration of that theory of Platonic love which Castiglione's *Courtier* had made especially familiar to Elizabethans[2]. On the other hand, many scholars have considered the sonnets essentially autobiographical, in spite of their obviously conventional character in many respects[3]. Their high poetic quality, the "obviousness"

[1] Courthope, *A History of English Poetry*, II, p. 228.
[2] Fletcher, *Did Astrophel Love Stella?* *Modern Philology*, October, 1907.
[3] Jusserand, Pollard, Schelling, for example.

W. L. S.

of their sincerity, and Sidney's own statement that he writes 'in pure simplicity' have been cited on the one hand, while their "obvious" artificiality and the fact that they are imitative of early sonnets by Petrarch and the members of the *Pléiade* have appeared equally unanswerable arguments by those who hold the other view.

Before entering on controversial ground we may somewhat reduce the distance between the opposing points of view by recognizing certain facts that are indisputable. Sidney was an eager student of Italian and French literature, and there is no question whatever that the influence of Petrarch, Ronsard and Du Bellay is seen in many of his own poems. Man is an imitative creature, and when Sidney decided to write sonnets he went to those who were the recognized masters of the form in order to learn from them. These borrowings are in no sense furtive or concealed : they were patent to anyone who could read with understanding. Nor is there any question of the conventionality of the early sonnets in the sequence quite apart from all question of imitation. The beauty and hard-heartedness of the lady are ever recurring themes. There is much talk of the murdering boy, Cupid, and of his dart ; Stella's brows are his bows and Astrophel is shot by a glance of her eye. Moreover, the sonnets are saturated with the Neo-Platonic doctrine of Love. The poet recognizes that it is

"True, that true beauty virtue is indeed,
Whereof this beauty can be but a shade";

and the strife between Desire and Virtue or Reason is constantly before us. There was no book better known to the Court circle of Sidney's day than the *Courtier*. It had been translated by Sir Thomas Hoby, whose wife was the intimate friend of Lady Sidney. Sir Thomas died in 1566 ; Lady Hoby some years later married Lord Russell, a son of the Duke of Bedford, and in the elaborate christening festivities of the eldest child of this marriage we have already seen Sidney taking a part[1]. The intimacy of the Sidney family with that of the translator of Castiglione makes it doubly probable that Sidney was

[1] *V.* page 158.

intimately acquainted with a book which must have seemed
to him one of the most noteworthy products of the period, and
something of the noble idealism of which he managed to trans-
fuse into his own *Arcadia*. The Court of Urbino must often
have been in his mind if for no other reason than that the
Court of Elizabeth suggested it by contrast.

That *Astrophel and Stella* is imitative in some of its poems,
conventional in others, and illustrative of the theories of Neo-
Platonism throughout is beyond question, but these are considerations which have little or no bearing on the question of
Sidney's "sincerity." Arnold's *Thyrsis* is no less sincere
because it, too, is written in a conventional form, and Neo-
Platonism was in the Elizabethan atmosphere. The question
which we must ask ourselves is this : What kind of evidence
shall we seek in our endeavour to arrive at some determination
of the question ? Recognizing that Sidney's poems followed
in a measure the model which had been set by others, and remembering that they were the progenitors of a line of sonnet
sequences, many of them, like Watson's *Passionate Centurie of
Love*, purely conventional and literary in character, how are
we to sift out the fact from the fiction in Sidney's own poems?
The answer can hardly be doubtful. In the first place we
must look for whatever external evidence there may be,
quite outside of the poems, and in the second place we must
study the poems themselves ; we must ask whether they
present a coherent story and whether this story is in accord
with what we know of the facts of Sidney's life, and, more
especially, with our conception of Sidney's character. It will
not do to rely on purely general considerations relating to the
literary tendencies of the time. Our only hope lies in a first-
hand study of Sidney's life and character, and in that light
seeking for an interpretation. Such a method will hardly lead
us to an actual demonstration of the truth, but it will at least
bring us nearer to probability than we can otherwise attain[1].

---

[1] Mr Pollard's study of the question (*Sir Philip's Sidney's Astrophel and
Stella*, London, 1888) is by far the most thorough and most convincing with
which I am acquainted. My own indebtedness to him will be obvious to anyone
familiar with his book.

Apart from the sonnets, our information regarding Sidney's relations with Penelope Devereux is, unfortunately, scanty. She was probably some eight years younger than he, though there is no exact information as to the date of her birth. Sidney probably met her for the first time, as we have seen, at Chartley in the summer of 1575 ; at this time she was about thirteen years of age. During the next year Sidney saw much of her father, who was residing temporarily at Durham House, and in the summer of 1576 he accompanied Essex to Ireland. The Earl's affection for his young friend was evidenced in his dying wish that Sidney might some day marry Penelope. There had evidently been previous discussion of the plan, for something like a formal betrothal seems to be referred to by Waterhouse when he speaks of "the treaty between Mr. Philip and my Lady Penelope" and adds:

"Truly, my lord, I must say to your Lordship as I have said to my Lord of Leicester and Mr. Philip, the breaking off from the match, if the default be on your parts, will turn to more dishonour than can be repaired with any other marriage in England[1]."

Almost certainly, then, a formal agreement of marriage had been drawn up and accepted by Sir Henry Sidney and Leicester of the one part and the Earl of Essex of the other. Essex was accustomed to call Philip his 'son.'

Waterhouse's reference to "the breaking off from the match" was no doubt occasioned by the fact that when Essex died his estates were hopelessly encumbered, and hence his fatherless daughter would be no great match in the eyes of the worldly wise. Besides, Sir Henry Sidney did not share his son's enthusiasm for Essex : in a letter to Leicester he once took God to record that he could not brook him. To Penelope and also to her younger sister, Dorothy, the Earl had been able to leave only £100 yearly, and a further sum of £2000 each "for their advancement in marriage[2]." Philip Sidney, on the other hand, was heir presumptive to the vast estates of the Earl of

[1] Waterhouse to Sir Henry Sidney, November 14, 1576 (*Sidney Papers*, I, 147).
[2] *Lansdowne MSS.* vol. x, fol. 107. The Earl of Essex' will, September 22, 1576.

Leicester as well as to the properties of his father and the Earl of Warwick. Penelope's mother, a daughter of Sir Francis Knowles, was Elizabeth's cousin, but was more detested by the Queen than perhaps any other woman at the Court. Scandal declared that her relations with Leicester had not been innocent during the lifetime of Essex; within a few months of his death she and Leicester were married. Sidney, as we know, was aware of this marriage, and he must have recognized at once that he was now a much less eligible *parti* than he had recently been regarded. We may be quite sure that from some time in the year 1577, at the latest, the Earl of Leicester would have considered a marriage between his impecunious nephew and his step-daughter as mere midsummer madness, and there is no reason to suppose that Sidney would have dissented from this opinion. We know that he had put aside absolutely all thought of the marriage which had been contemplated, for we have seen him anxious during part of the years 1577 and 1578 to win the consent of the Queen to his union with a princess of the house of Orange. Nor is there the least reason to suppose that Sidney would of necessity object to the theory of a *mariage de convenance*. He probably rejoiced as much in the great match which his sister made at this time as did his father, and we have no reason to believe that the personal charms of Orange's sister had anything to do with Sidney's eagerness to marry her.

For nearly five years before Penelope's marriage in 1581 Sidney must have had very unusual opportunities of seeing her constantly, for during a great part of this period he was living at Leicester House, which was, of course, her home. During this time she grew from childhood to be a beautiful, clever and fascinating woman, and it would have been strange, indeed, had propinquity in this case failed to work in any degree the results for which it is proverbial. Sidney has himself confessed to his susceptibility to the charms of women[1], and we may be sure that he had not been adamant to those of Penelope. We may be equally sure, however, that he had not succumbed to them in any serious sense at any early period

[1] Sonnet XVI.

in their acquaintance, for during these years we find him absorbed in Irish and continental politics, and planning his own marriage with Orange's sister. As late as March, 1580, Languet still cherished the hope that this project might yet be feasible, and even though Sidney probably knew better, it will hardly be seriously contended that he allowed Languet to prosecute such hopes, especially if we remember their high political significance, while he himself was deeply in love with another woman. In his own words, he saw and liked; he liked but loved not.

Just one year after Languet's last reference to Sidney's high hopes in Holland, we hear of negotiations for the marriage of Penelope Devereux and the young Lord Rich. Burghley, Walsingham and the Earl of Huntingdon had been designated by the Earl of Essex guardians of his children, and the idea of the match was conceived by one of these guardians and by him communicated to the others. On March 10, 1581, the Earl of Huntingdon wrote Burghley as follows :

"May it please your Lordship: Hearing that God hath taken to his mercy my Lord Rich who hath left to his heir a proper gentleman and one in years very fit for my Lady Penelope Devereux if with the favour and liking of her Majesty the matter might be brought to pass. And because I know your Lordship's good affections to the father gone, and also your favour to his children, I am bold to pray your furtherance now in this matter, which may, I think, by your good means be brought to such pass as I desire. Her Majesty was pleased the last year to give me leave at times convenient to put her Highness in mind of these young ladies, and therefore I am by this occasion of my Lord's death the bolder to move your Lordship in this matter. I have also written to Mr. Secretary Walsingham herein. And so hoping of your Lordship's good favour, I do commit you to the tuition of the Almighty. At Newcastle, the 10th of March, 1580[1].

> Your Lordship's most assured,
> H. HUNTINGDON[2]."

Penelope's guardians were not concerned as to whether she wished to marry the young Lord Rich or not; they no doubt expected her, as a well-behaved young woman, to follow their

---

[1] Old style. Huntingdon was Lord President of the North.
[2] *Lansdowne MSS.* vol. XXXI, No. 40.

wishes in the matter implicitly. The marriage was arranged,
like a majority of the marriages in the Court circle of the time,
like the marriage of Anne Cecil or Mary Sidney for example,
on purely worldly considerations. Lord Rich was a proper
gentleman, that is, he was wealthy; moreover (a gratuitous
argument), he was very fit in years to be Penelope's husband.
The marriage took place, probably without delay. Our only
information as to what Penelope's sentiments were at the
time is contained in a letter written many years later by the
Earl of Devonshire, her second husband, to King James. In
this letter the Earl of Devonshire, defending his marriage,
writes the king that Lady Rich

"being in the power of her friends, was married against her will unto one
against whom she did protest at the very solemnity, and ever after;
between whom, from the first day, there ensued continual discord, although
the same fears that forced her to marry constrained her to live with him[1]."

This statement is our only evidence as to Penelope's attitude
toward her husband at the time of their marriage. On August
23rd of that year her young brother, now Earl of Essex,
announced in a letter to Burghley that he was leaving the
University for a short time with young Lord Rich, "*qui mihi
multis de causis, tuae sapientiae non obscuris, est charissimus*[2]."
On September 29th the Bishop of London had to complain to
Burghley of disorders in Lord Rich's house[3].

At the time of the marriage of Penelope Devereux there is
no reason to think that Sidney considered himself her lover
in any but a conventional, a literary sense. Those who were
responsible for arranging the match were among his warmest
well-wishers. Huntingdon was his uncle by marriage, Burghley
had admired and loved him from his earliest years. His
friendship with Walsingham was closer than with either of the
others[4]. It is hardly credible that these men would thwart
Sidney's wishes, nor is it any more credible that they arranged

---

[1] Devereux, *The Devereux Earls of Essex*, i, p. 155.

[2] *Lansdowne MSS.* vol. xxxiii, fol. 20.

[3] *Ibid.* fol. 24.

[4] On April 10th he wrote to Molyneux asking his assistance in securing an
office in Wales for Fulke Greville; the next day Walsingham wrote to Sir
Henry Sidney to the same effect. Collins, i, p. 293.

the marriage of Penelope Devereux, to whom he had once been betrothed, and to whom he had more recently been writing sonnets, without Sidney's hearing of the project, unless the marriage followed hard upon the opening of negotiations. That would be in accord with the custom of the times, and Penelope's mood may have been an additional argument against postponement. What that mood was Sidney must have known, we may be sure, when we remember that he was in daily contact with many persons closely related to Lady Rich— her mother and step-father and Lady Huntingdon, for example. A wave of honest indignation must have broken over him as he learned of the essentially brutal treatment which had been accorded her, and with Sidney to feel was to act where action was at all possible.

To proceed further with the story it is necessary to rely entirely on the sonnets. To this statement there is one exception. In all Sidney's other works and letters which are extant we have, as far as I am aware, only one reference to these poems, but, fortunately, for our purpose it is a highly significant reference. In the *Apologie* he tells us, in the depreciatory manner he was accustomed to assume when speaking of his own literary works, that he has slipped into the title of a poet "in these my not old years and idlest times." Toward the end of the work he says : "But I, as I never desired the title, so have I neglected the means to come by it. Only, *overmastered by some thoughts I yielded an inky tribute unto them.*" This statement is all the more significant because of the incidental character of its occurrence, and it is strange that it has not attracted the attention of those who have studied the subject. Surely the natural interpretation of these words is that Sidney sought in his sonnets, or in those of them which he has in mind, to give expression to an overmastering passion which possessed him.

None of the sonnets was published during Sidney's lifetime. Three editions appeared in the year 1591, two by Thomas Newman, the first of which contained an Epistle to the Reader by Thomas Nash and a considerable number of sonnets by other authors, and one by Matthew Lownes which was little more than a reprint of Newman's first edition. In the second edition of the *Arcadia* (1593) the 'overseer' of the work, Henry Sandford, the Countess of Pembroke's secretary, declares that the pains which the Countess has taken with the volume will not be the last which her love of her brother will make her consecrate to his memory. This promise was redeemed when the first collected edition of Sidney's works appeared under the direction of the Countess in 1598. In this volume the sonnets follow the order of the earlier editions, but they are now for the first time numbered, and they are printed from a better text. There are significant changes however. The 'Songs' which in the earlier editions had been printed together after the sonnets, are now distributed through them. There is one new sonnet—XXXVII; there are additions to Songs VIII and X, and Song XI is new. All these additions are of such a character as to make inevitable the deduction that they had been previously withheld from publication—or circulation—because they revealed too much. A last addition consisted of *Certain Sonnets Written by Sir Philip Sidney*—27 in number—19 of which were now printed for the first time, the remaining eight having appeared in Constable's *Diana* (1594). Why they were not incorporated in the larger sonnet sequence, of which at least some of them are assuredly an essential part, does not appear. The text, and the arrangement of sonnets and songs in the 1598 edition, supervised as it was by the person most competent to edit it intelligently, we must accept as definitive, and there is the less difficulty in doing so since it is not possible to change the order in such a way as to make any real gain in the coherence of the story.

The first 32 sonnets, with the single exception of number 24—the punning invective against Lord Rich[1]—were obviously written before Penelope's marriage, and they bear out the theory that up to this time both Sidney and Penelope were heart-whole. During this time he was

> "Studying inventions fine, her wits to entertain,
>   Oft turning others' leaves."

[1] Mr Pollard suggests that the sonnet was given its present position for the purpose of misleading the over-curious.

We learn that Stella is cold of heart, fair of skin, and black-eyed, but we hear nothing more specific about her than praise of her beauty and complaint of her hardness of heart. The poet condemns Euphuistic writing and conventional imitation of Petrarch, he discusses various phases of Neo-Platonic doctrine, he introduces mythological tales, and talks much of Cupid. He declares that he had wished to devote himself to literary work and to the study of Philosophy and Science (Sonnet X). Again he upbraids himself as a bankrupt of all those goods which heaven had lent to him ; his youth is wasting and his knowledge brings forth but toys (Sonnet XVIII) ; his own writings show his wits quick in vain thoughts, in virtue lame (Sonnet XXI).   Further he tells us that his pensive melancholy face is remarked by his friends (XXIII), that he is often in dark abstracted guise, " with dearth of words or answers quite awry" (XXXII), and he is conscious that the May of his years has much declined from the promise of his earlier youth (XXI). It would be an excess of scepticism that would fail to recognize in these references Sidney's just description of himself in the period following the destruction of his hopes of taking a worthy place in the Dutch struggle.   The " toys" which his knowledge brings forth, his vain writings, are the " toyful books" to which he had referred in his letter to Robert of October, 1580.   In that letter he had described himself as one who had given over the delight in the world ; he speaks of " my melancholy times," and in a letter written a month later we have heard him say that he is ill and melancholy.   We may assume that his sonnet-writing began in his "idlest times," perhaps after the Wanstead interview in the summer of 1578 when the Queen made it impossible for him to go abroad, more probably somewhat later when he, Dyer and Spenser were stimulating each other's literary interests.   His melancholy was due to his enforced inactivity ; he was conscious that his youth was passing, he saw no prospect of worthy employment and, as Molyneux has informed us, " he could endure at no time to be idle and void of action[1]."   It is little wonder that he was melancholy.   That

---

[1] Holinshed's *Chronicle*.

the " toyful books" which he wrote during this time would do
more than anything else to preserve his fame to posterity
never occurred to him.   The impression which one gains from
this first section of the sonnets is of a man, moody and angry
with fate, one who would fain have some man's work to do,
who is conscious of abilities that are rusting unused, and who
is voicing his mood of dissatisfaction with life in the form of
conventional love sonnets.

With the thirty-third sonnet the atmosphere has changed.
Stella is now the wife of another man and Sidney's first
thought is one of self-reproach for his own inertia :

> " I might—unhappy word—O, me, I might,
> And then would not, or could not, see my bliss,
> Till now wrapt in a most infernal night,
> I find how heavenly day, wretch ! I did miss.
> Heart, rent thyself, thou doest thyself but right ;
> No lovely Paris made thy Helen his,
> No force, no fraud robbed thee of thy delight,
> Nor Fortune of thy fortune author is ;
> But to myself myself did give the blow,
> While too much wit, forsooth, so troubled me,
> That I respects for both our sakes must show :
> And yet could not by rising morn foresee
> How fair a day was near : O punished eyes,
> That I had been more foolish, or more wise ! "

Now that Stella is definitely lost to him he upbraids himself
for the politic considerations which had made him willing to
give her up.   He evidently has not heard that Stella was forced
into marriage, and his first references to her new name—Rich
(Sonnets XXXV and XXXVII)—are unaccompanied by the
fierce invective against her husband which characterizes the
misplaced Sonnet XXIV.   The mood of self-reproach soon
yields, however, to a determination not to accept the situation.
He has probably learned more of the circumstances of Stella's
marriage, and he fiercely determines to ignore the existence of
the unholy arrangement.   This attitude is expressed in the
last stanza of *The Smokes of Melancholy*—one of the 'Certain
Sonnets.'

> " For me, alas, I am fully resolv'd
> Those bonds, alas, shall not be dissolv'd ;
> Nor break my word, though reward come late ;
> Nor fail my faith in my failing fate ;
> Nor change in change, though change change my state :
> But always one myself with eagle-eyed Truth to fly
> Up to the sun, although the sun my wings do fry ;
> For if those flames burn my desire
> Yet shall I die in Phoenix fire."

At first Stella's attitude to Sidney is unchanged even when she sees the very face of woe painted in his beclouded stormy face.   She discusses Court gossip with him, listens to his reading of his sonnets and herself sings them, affecting to believe that they are still the literary exercises which pleased and amused them both before her marriage.   At length she is persuaded, probably having been made more willing to learn by her own wretchedness, and she counsels him regarding the selflessness of true love.   She also confesses her own love for him—a love which will not let him decline from nobler courses : he is to anchor himself fast on Virtue's shore.   With Stella's confession the winter of his misery is gone ; his 'heavenly joy' bursts forth in sonnet after sonnet.   He finds her asleep and steals a kiss ; she is angry and threatens, but he makes his defence and sings his triumph in several sonnets more.   But when he urges that Love shall have its course Stella is firm in her refusal (Songs IV and VIII).

> " Astrophel, said she, my love,
> Cease in these effects, to prove ;
> Now be still, yet still believe me,
> Thy grief more than death would grieve me.
>
> If that any thought in me
> Can taste comfort but of thee,
> Let me, fed with hellish anguish,
> Joyless, hopeless, endless languish.
>
> Trust me, while I thee deny,
> In myself the smart I try :
> Tyrant Honour doth thus use thee,
> Stella's self might not refuse thee."

Hereafter the poet's song is 'broken.' He tries by absence to cure his passion but he lives in Sorrow's night. Like Cleopatra his imagination can exercise itself on one only subject :

> " I would know whether she did sit or walk,
> How cloth'd ; how waited on ; sighed she or smiled ?
> Whereof, with whom, how often she did talk ;
> With what pastime time's journey she beguiled.
> If her lips deigned to sweeten my poor name.
> Say all ; and all well said, still say the same."

The story now draws rapidly to a close. On one occasion the poet is guilty of an undefined *faux pas* which vexes Stella though his fault was due not to carelessness but rather to 'too much care.' She tries with choice delights and rarest company to drive the clouds from out his heavy cheer, but in vain. We hear of her being sick, of her sailing on the Thames when he sees her from a window (of Leicester House or Baynard's Castle ?) : he rides past the house where she lives and wears stars upon his armour, he curses his ill-luck in missing an opportunity of seeing her when her coachman drove past rapidly and the falling of a torch from her page's hand made him fail to recognize her until it was too late. He asks her for a while to give respite to his heart while he devotes his thought " to this great cause which needs both use and art"—a reference which it is not possible to explain satisfactorily. In the last sonnet of the sequence his sorrow is alleviated only by the joy which shines from Stella. The story is concluded by the last and most beautiful of the poems in the 'Certain Sonnets,'— a sonnet that is properly dissociated from the sequence to indicate an undetermined period during which the transition in the lover's attitude took place :

> " Leave me, O Love, that reachest but to dust :
> And thou, my mind, aspire to higher things ;
> Grow rich in that which never taketh rust ;
> Whatever fades, but fading pleasure brings.
> Draw in thy beams, and humble all thy might
> To that sweet yoke where lasting freedoms be ;
> Which breaks the clouds, and opens forth the light,
> That doth both shine, and give us sight to see.
> O take fast hold ; let that light be thy guide
> In this small course which birth draws out to death,

> And think how evil becometh him to slide,
> Who seeketh heaven, and comes of heavenly breath.
> Then farewell, world ; thy uttermost I see,
> Eternal Love, maintain thy life in me."

And so renunciation is exalted, and the strains of the hymn to earthly love are drowned in the fuller music of the heavenly love. It must be noted that there is here no reprobation of past conduct, no stigmatizing of the character of that love or desire which reaches but to dust. Throughout the story Sidney is true to himself. Stella's marriage to Lord Rich was an ugly, a wicked thing ; the poet's love for Stella—earthly love with its imperious desires, and which reaches but to dust—is a beautiful and ennobling thing. Why should the baser fact stand in the way of the nobler ? That Sidney should assume this attitude is in no sense of the word surprising or inconsistent with his own character. Essentially idealistic, to him right was right, wrong was wrong. He hated the politic, prudential considerations which modified the conduct of organized society and persuaded it to deviate from the more obvious duty of the moment. Hence his disgust with Elizabeth's continental policy. The nobleness and chivalry of his age acclaimed him its president : his transparent honesty and love of all things excellent were proverbial. But he was, withal, impulsive, somewhat imperious, not easily brooking the thwarting of his desires. At the time of Penelope Devereux's marriage he was chafing under the lack of worthy occupation, and his sense of personal grievance was deepened by what must have seemed to him the outrage of her union with Lord Rich. All his chivalrous and pugnacious instincts were aroused, and he decided to play the rôle of the knight-errant against the villain who had forcibly carried off the beautiful lady. An unquestioning consciousness of rectitude attends him throughout. Even Desire frames the manners and fears nought but shame. To those literal-minded critics who talk of the sin of violating the sanctities of marriage he would have retorted by asking them to point out wherein the sanctity of the marriage of Lord and Lady Rich consisted.

But with reflection Sidney came to know that this defence of his conduct was in essence unsound. His love for Stella

could not continue to contribute to the ennobling of their characters, and it is man's chief end in this world to be good rather
than to be happy. The fault may be in the constitution of
human society, but at any rate Sidney learned, what Stella
with instinctive wisdom seems to have known from the beginning, that their affection for each other in the world in which
they lived could not be ultimately good nor even bring to them
lasting happiness. When Sidney attained to self-mastery it
is impossible to say, but the later sonnets give the impression
of having been struck out at a heat, and they probably represent
the experiences of weeks rather than months. As we shall see,
it was only a few months after Penelope Devereux became
Lady Rich that Sidney began to plan his own marriage with
the daughter of his friend Walsingham, though she was now
a child of not more than fourteen years. Before this time we
may be sure that his passion had swept over him, and there is
no reason to believe that it had left him with a jaundiced eye.

It is necessary to add a word to refute two arguments
which have been put forward by those who object to the
sonnets being read as autobiography. One of these has to
do with Sidney's " readiness to blazon abroad his illicit relations
with Stella, assuming that his passion was sincere." Why his
action would have been less reprehensible had his passion
been feigned does not appear. The answer to this rather
irritating argument is that Sidney did not blazon abroad his
story, that some of his poems were written frankly as literary
exercises, and that the more intimate of them were probably
reserved for Stella's self and perhaps the Countess of Pembroke.
" A special dear friend he should be," says Molyneux regarding
the *Arcadia*[1], " that could have a sight, but much more dear
that could once obtain a copy of it." If this was true of the
Arcadia it was much truer of *Astrophel and Stella*. A number
of the more intimate poems, as we have seen, were not published
until that edition appeared which was supervised by Sidney's
sister some twelve years after his death. It was probably
only by some carelessness on the part of Sidney's closest friends
that Newman, the publisher, had managed to secure so many

---

[1] Holinshed's *Chronicle*.

of the sonnets in 1591 ; in the circumstances, however, the Countess of Pembroke seems to have felt that there was no good reason for withholding the remaining poems from publication in 1598—when Lady Rich had long been separated from her husband, and Sidney's widow had long been remarried to Lady Rich's brother. In support of this explanation it is significant that Fulke Greville, in a letter to Walsingham a month after Sidney's death, makes no mention of the sonnets among those works of his friend which should be edited for publication. The poems were never thought of as material for publication either by their author or his friends who knew them. The significance of Fulke Greville's omission, it must be admitted, is lessened by the fact that he also omits mention of the *Apologie*.

A second argument that has been urged against the "sincerity" of the sonnets is that "the dedication of Spenser's *Astrophel* to Sidney's wife deprives of serious autobiographical significance his description in the sonnets of his pursuit of Stella's affections[1]." The answer, of course, is that Spenser left England in July, 1580, and that it is most improbable that he was acquainted with any of the sonnets written after that time. Under these circumstances *Astrophel and Stella* to him meant the conventional poems written by Sidney in confessed imitation of Petrarch or the French sonneteers during the period when Spenser was living at Leicester House. Who Stella actually was may well have escaped his memory, as, indeed, it was a matter of no importance. We may be sure that he had never heard of the later sonnets, and we may be sure that his ignorance was shared during Sidney's life by the great majority of his more intimate friends[2].

Penelope Devereux should not be dismissed without a word regarding her later life. She lived with Lord Rich for many years and bore him three sons and three daughters. She was on terms of special intimacy with the Sidney family and

[1] Sidney Lee, *Eliz. Sonnets*, Introd.

[2] Spenser was probably similarly ignorant of the existence of the *Arcadia*. Molyneux' statement suggests it, and we may remember that in October, 1580, Sidney was able to promise Robert a copy of his "toyful books" only for the next February.

their connections, and Lord Rich was on friendly terms with
Robert Sidney. She was eventually divorced from Lord Rich
shortly after 1600, but for many years before this time she had
lived openly with Lord Mountjoy, to whom she bore three sons
and two daughters. Oddly enough from our point of view,
she suffered no ostracism either at the Court of Elizabeth or
James I, and her conduct does not seem to have alienated any
of her friends. When Robert Sidney's son, Robert, was
christened on New Year's Eve, 1596, Lady Rich was godmother
and Lord Mountjoy one of the godfathers. Lady Essex (Sir
Philip Sidney's widow), with two of her children, was also
present at the ceremony, which had been intended for a week
earlier. It was postponed at Lady Rich's request and a
correspondent of Robert Sidney's informed him that

> "I do rather think it to be a tetter that suddenly broke out in her fair
> white forehead, which will not be well in five or six days that keeps your
> son from being christened. But my Lady Rich's desires are obeyed as
> commandment by my Lady [Sidney][1]."

Her name appears frequently in accounts of Court festivities,
and she shared in the agonies of her brother's family during the
last weeks of his life. James I on his accession granted to
Lady Rich

> "the place and rank of the ancientest Earls of Essex, called Bourchier
> whose heir her father was, she having by her marriage, according to the
> customs of the laws of honour, ranked herself according to her husband's
> barony. By this gracious grant she took rank of all the baronesses
> of the kingdom, and of all Earls' daughters except Arundel, Oxford,
> Northumberland and Shrewsbury[2]."

She was an especial favourite of Queen Anne, and James I
created Mountjoy, Earl of Devonshire. They were married
on December 26, 1605[3], and this act—the re-marriage of a
divorced woman—called down upon them the wrath of the
King. Devonshire died a few months later, and when he was
buried in Westminster Abbey the heralds determined that his

---

[1] Rowland Whyte to Sir Robert Sidney, London, St Stephen's Day, 1595.
Collins, I, 385.

[2] Devereux, *op. cit.* I, p. 154.

[3] By William Laud, afterwards Archbishop.

W. L. S.

arms should be put up without those of his wife. She survived her husband only a year[1].

To attempt to pass judgment on the character of Penelope Devereux would be absurd. We know that she was possessed of unusual personal charm and cleverness, and she evidently had very many warm friends. Her irregular connection with Lord Mountjoy was not censured by her sovereign nor by her friends, and this constitutes a very good reason why those living under different social conventions should cast no stones at her. Without much fuller knowledge than we possess our eulogy and our condemnation are alike impertinent[2].

---

[1] Lady Dorothy Devereux had a similarly troubled marital story. In July, 1583, she was clandestinely married to Sir Thomas Perrot, and the ceremony was performed under most unseemly circumstances. (Devereux, I, 156.) In September she wrote to Burghley to thank him for "the releasing of Mr. Perrot out of the Fleet," where he had been confined by the Queen's order as a punishment for the escapade, and she begged Burghley to be "an earnest mean unto the Queen's Majesty to vouchsafe her gracious letter to Sir John Perrot as well for a release from his promise made to her Highness not to do us any good without her consent, as also for her Majesty's sake he will do like a father of his ability to his children of that sort and condition we are of." This will bring them "some Michaelmas rent," of which they are in great need, and she also begs that her marriage money may be paid, "for our infection is like a pleurisy that hath need of present remedy." (*Lansdowne MSS.* No. 39, f. 172.) Her second husband was Henry Percy, ninth Earl of Northumberland, to whom she was married in 1595. She died on August 3, 1619.

[2] The time indications in the sonnets themselves are not very definite. In Sonnet XXII the sun was 'Progressing then from fair Twins' golden place' —*i.e.* it was the end of May or beginning of June. Both the position of the sonnet in the sequence and its tone suggest a date before Stella's marriage— probably 1580. Sonnet XLI, which begins with the lines

> "Having this day my horse, my hand, my lance,
> Guided so well that I obtained the prize
> Both by the judgment of the English eyes
> And of some sent by that sweet enemy France,"

certainly refers to a tourney at which were present the French Commissioners appointed to re-open the negotiations for the Queen's marriage to Anjou. They reached England on April 17, 1581. Sonnet LIII records further successes in the tournament and may be ascribed to the same period. The eighth song was written when "May, then young" was showing its pied weeks, and as Stella's "fair neck a foul yoke bare" at the time, the date is almost certainly May of 1581. The only other sonnet which contains an indication of the time when it was written is the thirtieth, which reads as follows :

> "Whether the Turkish new-moon minded be
> To fill his horns this year on Christian coast ?
> How Poles' right King means without leave of host
> To warm with ill-made fire cold Muscovy ?

> If French can yet three parts in one agree?
> What now the Dutch in their full diets boast?
> How Holland hearts, now so good towns be lost,
> Trust in the shade of pleasing Orange-tree?
> How Ulster likes of that same golden bit
> Wherewith my father once made it half tame?
> If in the Scotch court be no weltring yet?
> These questions busy wits to me do frame."

Mr Pollard thinks that these allusions agree better with the first few weeks of 1581 than with any other date. No one of them is absolutely definite in its reference to a specific event, but I am inclined to assign the sonnet to the last months of 1580. The reference to the Turks and Poles would seem to have been suggested by the following extract from Languet's last letter to Sidney—that of October 28, 1580.

"The Archduke Matthias has heard from Vienna that peace is made between the Turks and Persians, and letters from Constantinople imply the same, but do not directly affirm it. They add that the Sultan has commanded Ochiali to have a number of new galleys built, so that it is expected he will make some attempt against the Spaniards next summer.......What we heard about the death of the King of Poland, is not true. They say he has penetrated with his victorious army into the heart of Muscovy, and that the Muscovite is sueing to him for peace."

Stephen Bathori's success against the Russians was not complete until the next year. On August 22, 1581, he besieged Pskov, until, on December 13th, Ivan the Terrible concluded peace with him at Zapoli by ceding the whole of Polotsk and Livonia. The three parties in France of course were the Huguenots, the Catholics, and the Politiques led by Catherine de' Medici and her sons. The boasting of the Dutch in their diets and elsewhere was proverbial in England. They had suffered during the past year from a kind of "epidemic treason"; De Bours, governor of Mechlin, had surrendered the city and fled to Parma, and a few months later Count Renneberg traitorously handed over Groningen to the enemy. These were probably the good towns to which Sidney referred. Ulster at this time was in comparative quiet. The Desmond rebellion which had raised the South and West had had little effect on the North where the work of suppression which had been carried out by Sir Henry Sidney was showing its effects. 'Weltring' was the normal condition of the Scottish Court, where Protestant and Catholic, French and English influences were in perpetual conflict, and where the country's fate depended largely on the boy-king's whims in choosing favourites. Morton, President of the Council, the friend of England and Protestantism, had failed to carry out a plot against the life of Lennox, the representative of French influences, the Guises and Catholicism. In the last months of 1580 Lennox had Morton at his mercy, and England was waiting to learn what special form the inevitable 'weltring' would take.

CHAPTER XIV

1581

DURING the months immediately before and after the marriage of Penelope Devereux we know little of Sidney's life, apart from what we are told in the sonnets, which gives any hint of the emotional crisis through which he was passing. On New Year's Day, 1581, he presented to the Queen " a jewel of gold, being a whip, garnished with small diamonds in four rows and cords of small seed pearl[1] "—in token of his submission to the will of Her Majesty. Fragmentary records of small offices of kindness are to be constantly found in a study of Sidney's life : his biography might be cumbered with a multitude of such references. In January he wrote to Arthur Atey, Leicester's secretary, in favour of some man, and his servant, Griffith Maddax, wrote Atye again on the same subject[2]. On February 6th he acknowledged in kindly words a letter from Hotman—a French Huguenot student at Oxford, whose father was one of Sidney's friends[3]. From a letter which he wrote to Lady Kitson on March 28th we learn something of the trouble he was willing to take to assist anyone in distress, even when the cause of distress was recusancy, with which particular sin he can have had but little sympathy[4]. In April he was active in attempting to secure for Fulke Greville some post in Wales, and together with Sir Thomas Leighton served as an arbitrator in the matter at the request of the Welsh Council[5].

[1] Nichols, II, p. 301.
[2] *State Papers—Dom.—Eliz.* vol. CXLVII.
[3] *Add. MSS.* 12102, f. 1.
[4] Nichols, II, 250.
[5] *Sidney Papers*, I, pp. 293 and 295.

No trait of Sidney's character is more in evidence than that of loyalty to his friends and kindliness toward all men.

In the meantime he was able to find some satisfaction of his desire to be engaged in the public service by securing a seat in the House of Commons. It was the third and last session of that Parliament which had met in 1572 and 1576, and Sidney had been elected probably in the stead of some member who had died. Fulke Greville had been returned as member for the town of Southampton in place of Sir Henry Wallop, who was absent on the Queen's service in Ireland, but his claim to the seat was finally disallowed by the House together with that of several other members similarly situated. In the session of 1576 the House of Commons had shown itself restive under the royal control. Referring to the rumours that were constantly current in the House that the Queen would like this or disapprove that, and to the royal messages which were calculated to stifle freedom of speech, Mr Peter Wentworth had been bold to declare, " I would to God, Mr. Speaker, that these two were buried in hell ; I mean rumours and messages[1]." On the motion of Burghley he was committed to the Tower, and although by the Queen's special favour he was soon set free and restored to his place in the House, the incident had had its effect. In 1581 the House received Her Majesty's rebukes or commendations in a properly humble spirit. Mr John Popham, the Solicitor-General, was chosen Speaker. They began badly by ordering a public fast and daily preaching—an act which the Queen found to be an infringement of her ecclesiastical prerogative. Through Hatton she expressed " her great admiration of the rashness of this House," and almost unanimously the House expressed regret and submission. One member who wished to make a motion " for the liberty of the House " was not recognized by Mr Speaker.

A long speech by Sir Walter Mildmay set the tone of the proceedings. He called attention to the fact that England's one great danger consisted in Catholic machinations both foreign and domestic. The dangerous Desmond rebellion with all that it implied of Spanish and Papal enmity was one form

[1] D'Ewes, *Journals*, p. 237.

which the danger assumed ; another consisted in " the swarming
hither of a number of Popish priests and monkish Jesuits." Two
steps were necessary. They must make a provision of laws more
strict and more severe to constrain recusants, and they must
strengthen both the naval and land forces.

"God hath placed this kingdom in an island," he declared, "environed
with the sea as with a natural and strong wall, whereby we are not subject
to those sudden invasions which other frontier countries be. One of our
greatest defences standing by sea, the number of good ships is of the most
importance for us."

He lauded the Queen as one who " still holdeth fast the profession of the gospel that hath so long upholden her, and made us
to live in peace twenty-two years and more under her most
gracious government," and he bid any man who was so dull as not
to appreciate the blessedness of this our golden peace, to " cast
his eyes over the seas into our neighbours' countries, and there
behold what trouble the Pope and his ministers have stirred
against such as profess the same religion of Jesus Christ as we
do[1]." A large committee was appointed to consult regarding
such bills as were convenient to be framed to meet the dangers
indicated, and of this committee Mr Philip Sidney was a
member[2]. To another committee to which was committed
the " Bill against slanderous words and rumours and other
seditious practices against the Queen's Majesty," he was appointed on February 1st, as was also Fulke Greville[3]. The
first of these committees recommended much more vigorous
penalties against recusants, in which action, presumably,
Sidney concurred. This is somewhat difficult to reconcile with
his letter to Lady Kitson on March 28th in which he comforts
her with the assurance that " there is a present intention
of a general mitigation to be used in respect of recusants,"
and that Sir Francis Walsingham tells him that there is meant
" a speedy easing of the greatness of your burden." A few
months later, on December 1st, Campion was executed, and
we can imagine how Sidney's mind must have been torn

[1] *Ibid.*, pp. 285–288.
[2] *Ibid.*, p. 288.
[3] *Journals of the House of Commons*, vol. I, p. 121.

with conflicting emotions as he remembered their long acquaintance and pondered England's new threatening perils.

What share Sidney took in the other proceedings of this
Parliament we do not know. Considerable time was devoted
to the case of a member, Arthur Hall, who had published an
anonymous book impugning the authority of the House and
defaming certain of its members. He was imprisoned in the
Tower, fined five hundred marks, and "severed and cut off from
being a member of this House any more during the continuance
of this present Parliament." Many bills were passed of many
kinds, from one providing for the paving the street without
Aldgate to one "for the punishment of heretics called the Family
of Love," and another against the false packing of hops. On
March 18th the Queen prorogued Parliament after giving her
assent to thirty bills and thanking both Houses for their work,
"not yet comprehending within those general thanks such
members of the House of Commons as have this session dealt
more rashly in some things than was fit for them to do."

For some time the tension between England and Spain
had been growing greater. England was alarmed at the great
increase in power and resources that had come to Spain through
her easy annexation of Portugal and the Portuguese colonies.
Spain was exasperated by the successful outcome of Drake's
voyage of plunder and the Queen's cynical indifference to
demands for restitution. These causes tended to draw closer
together once more the English and French Courts, and soon
the Alençon marriage project was being once more discussed.
Alençon on January 23rd had accepted the sovereignty of the
Netherlands, and the Queen now declared herself ready to marry
him. A magnificent embassy sent from Paris to revise the
marriage treaty reached Dover on April 17th; they were received
in London with much firing of guns and their entertainment
was of the most lavish sort[1]. Only with the greatest difficulty,
however, could they persuade the Queen to discuss the object
of their visit. But at length the treaty was drawn and accepted,

---

[1] A magnificent banqueting house was built for their reception whereon
375 workmen laboured for nearly four weeks. Among other remarkable
characteristics it had 292 lights of glass. (Nichols, II, 312.)

and was to be binding when the Duke and the Queen both declared themselves satisfied.

Those who had formerly opposed the match were at last convinced that further opposition was useless, although they were by no means certain as to what the Queen intended to do.   Among the festivities with which the French commissioners were entertained was a magnificent tournament in which Sidney took a prominent part.   The Queen had set the example of magnificence in the entertainment of the ambassadors by sumptuous feasts and banquetings, and her example was emulated in a most elaborate 'triumph' which was shown on Whitsun Monday and Tuesday.   The gallery at the end of the tilt-yard adjoining Whitehall was fitted up as 'the Castle or Fortress of Perfect Beauty' and the whole device consisted in an attack upon the fortress by four challengers—the Earl of Arundel, Lord Windsor, Philip Sidney and Fulke Greville, who called themselves the four Foster Children of Desire.   That Sidney was responsible for the conception of the triumph there can be little doubt; the speeches are written in the strained, highly wrought and elaborately decorated style of the *Arcadia*, and the whole device represented the combination of magnificent pageantry and chivalrous speech which is familiar to all readers of Sidney's romance.

The first defiance of the challengers was uttered on Sunday, the 16th of April, as her Majesty came from the Chapel. Their messenger was a boy apparelled in red and white—the colours of Desire—who addressed the Queen as follows :

"O Lady, that doth intitle the titles you possess with the honour of your worthiness, rather crowning the great crown you hold with the fame to have so excelling an owner, than you receiving to yourself any increase keeping that outward ornament."

He proceeds in true Arcadian speech to inform the Queen that the four Foster Children of Desire will her that she shall no longer exclude virtuous Desire from Perfect Beauty.   Should this request be not granted they announce that on April 24th they will besiege that fatal fortress, and will meet any knights of Her Majesty's Court first at the tilt in so many courses as she shall be pleased to appoint, and then with lance and sword.

After several postponements the device was at length performed on Whitsun Monday. The challengers entered the tilt-yard one after the other and in such magnificent fashion that the eyes of the spectators were dazzled. We cannot enter into all the details of the occasion but we may at least hear the contemporary chronicler's description of our hero :

"Then proceeded Master Philip Sidney in very sumptuous manner with armour part blue and the rest gilt and engraven, with four spare horses having caparisons and furniture very rich and costly, as some of cloth of gold embroidered with pearl, and some embroidered with gold and silver feathers very richly and cunningly wrought; he had four pages that rode on his four spare horses, who had cassock coats and Venetian hose of all cloth of silver laid with gold lace, and hats of the same with gold bands and white feathers, and each one a pair of white buskins. Then had he a thirty gentlemen and yeomen, and four Trumpeters who were all in cassock coats and Venetian hose of yellow velvet laid with silver lace, yellow velvet caps with silver bands and white feathers, and every one a pair of white buskins ; and they had upon their coats a scroll or band of silver which came scarf wise over the shoulder and so down under the arm, with this poesy or sentence written upon it both before and behind, *Sic nos non nobis.*"

When the challengers and their retinues had all entered the tilt-yard the boy messenger offered parley from the besiegers and then from a rolling trench or mount of earth which accompanied them the Queen was assailed with music. Two delectable songs were sung to the accompaniment of cornets—one summoning the fortress to yield, the other sounding the alarm to the besiegers when it was apparent that there would be no yielding. Then cannon were shot off, "one with sweet powder, and the other with sweet water, very odoriferous and pleasant," and the footmen threw flowers against the walls.

By this time the defendants, a large company, each of whom was elaborately attended, had arrived. Of these Sir Thomas Perrot and Master Anthony Cooke announced themselves as Adam and Eve, who had learned that the sun was besieged and had hastened to the defence. An angel vouches for their identity to the Queen, and, addressing the challengers, asks : " Will you subdue the sun ? Who shall rest in the shadow where the weary take breath, the disquiet rest and all comfort ? Will ye bereave all men of those glistering and gladsome beams ?" Then followed a speech by a page of Master Thomas Ratcliffe and by another on behalf of the four sons of Sir Francis Knolles. Each defendant then ran six courses against the challengers "who performed their parts so valiantly on both sides that their prowess hath demerited perpetual memory." The coming of night brought the day's sport to a close.

On the next day the Foster Children of Desire entered the lists in a brave chariot drawn by horses apparelled in white and carnation silk. From the chariot sounded very doleful music. After they had again bid defiance the defendants entered.

"Then went they to the tourney where they did very nobly as the shivering of the swords might very well testify; and after that to the barriers where they lashed it out lustily, and fought courageously as if the Greeks and Trojans had dealt their deadly dole."

Towards evening a boy, clothed in ash-coloured garments and bearing an olive branch, approached the Queen and elaborately made the submission of the Foster Children of Desire who acknowledged themselves to be overcome as to be slaves to this fortress for ever. When Her Majesty had given praise and great thanks to all they departed in the same order in which they had entered the lists[1].

Sidney was especially interested in these feats of arms, and his reputation as a swordsman is frequently mentioned. In the preceding year he was one of the defendants in a tournament in which the Earl of Arundel and his assistant, Sir William Drury, challenged all comers. On this occasion the prize was given to the Earl of Oxford. It was the last of chivalric usages to survive, and as such would appeal to Sidney, quite apart from the fact that horsemanship and the use of the sword stood first in the list of gentlemanly accomplishments in Elizabeth's day. One of Sidney's *protégés* was Christopher Clifford, the author of *The School of Horsemanship*[2], which was

---

[1] The contemporary account is written by Henry Goldwell, and is reprinted in Nichols, II, pp. 312–329.

[2] Printed by Thomas Cadman, London, 1585.

dedicated to Sidney "both because of your great knowledge and experience in horsemanship, and in all other virtues, whereby ye draw to you the hearts of everyone that knows you; and also for your special courtesy showed unto me." That Sidney's enthusiasm for the noble art equalled that of his first master, Pugliano, is evidenced by many passages in the *Arcadia*[1].

At some time during this year Sidney visited Oxford when Gager's Latin play *Meleager* was performed before the Earl of Pembroke, the Earl of Leicester, Sidney, and many other persons of importance. Gager was the most prominent of the dramatists who produced Latin plays after the Senecan style at the universities, and, according to Wood, Sidney had a very great respect for his learning and virtues[2]. It was possibly on this occasion that he became interested in the candidacy of Dr Toby Matthew for the Deanery of Durham. In a letter to Sir Thomas Heneage, on September 7th, Matthew, who was indignant at the rival claims of a certain Dr Bellamy for the appointment, writes:

"Have I, poor man, entreated my Lord, mine old Master, chiefly by yourself, by my Lord of York's grace, by my Lord of Sarum, by Mr. Captain Horsey, Mr. Philip Sidney etc.; hath my Lord of Warwick been contented to stay his own suit for Mr. Griffin in respect of me, that a third man, and such a man, and by such means, may prevent both us and all others[3]?"

Matthew secured the appointment only after some two years of strenuous canvassing.

The annexation of Portugal to Spain, with its ominous increase of Spanish power, had already engaged Sidney's attention and special interest. In the famous battle of Alcazar which was fought in the interior of Morocco on August 4th,

---

[1] *V*. for example p. 178 (Feuillerat's edition).

[2] *Athenæ Oxonienses*, ed. Bliss, 3rd ed., 1813 vol. ii, col. 88. Gager was a contributor to the *Exequiæ Illustrissimi Equitis D. Philippi Sidnæi, etc.*, and the dedication of the volume to Leicester is signed by him at Christ Church. He is perhaps best known for his defence of stage plays contained in a letter to John Rainolds (v. *Fortnightly Review*, August, 1907).

[3] *Add. MS.* 15891, f. 87. Printed in Nicolas' *Life of Hatton*, p. 192.

1578, Sebastian, the King of Portugal, was slain[1], and he was succeeded by his great-uncle, a priest, known as the Cardinal King, who survived him only until January 31, 1580. On his death Philip of Spain promptly assumed the sovereignty. He was the son of a sister of John III of Portugal, and his claim to the succession was opposed only by Don Antonio, the baseborn son of a younger brother of John III. In a battle at Oporto the Duke of Alva crushed all opposition and Don Antonio fled from the country.

Both England and France were deeply concerned over these events and both extended friendly words at least to the exile. Sidney's interest in his fortunes began early[2], and on May 13th Don Antonio wrote to him from Tunis an account of his preparations both of men and ships. "Though many more should go," he writes, "if I did not see you in the company, I shall say, *Numerum non habet illa suum*[3]." At the French Court he was received by the king, and in June he suddenly appeared in England—for the purpose of fitting out ships against Spain. Elizabeth was at first indignant and refused to see him; then it seemed possible to her that an open alliance with France against Spain might relieve her of the necessity of marrying Monsieur. To this open course Burghley and Walsingham urged her warmly, but it meant the spending of money, and the Queen could not face the prospect. She had bought the Braganza jewels from Don Antonio for £12,000, with which he had fitted out a fleet at Plymouth. Drake and Hawkins were ready to sail with him, but the Queen would not grant them permission to depart, vainly hoping that she might involve France with Spain while she herself stood aside. At length on September 10th Mendoza reported that Lord

---

[1] Sir Thomas Stukely and the Emperor of Morocco were also killed in the same battle, which made a great appeal to the imagination of the Englishmen of the time.

[2] The *Biographia Literaria* says that while Sidney was engaged in writing the *Arcadia* Don Antonio solicited his aid.

[3] Translated by Collins, I, p. 294. The original letter is among the Penshurst MSS. and is signed " 13 de Maio—Vostro major Amigo—Rey." There is no indication of the year. Collins evidently supplied the "1581." The letter is addressed *Al Illustre Filipe Cidnei mi amado Sobrino*.

Howard, Philip Sidney and the Earl of Oxford had been ordered to accompany Don Antonio, who was leaving England[1]; a few days later he announced the departure of Don Antonio, who was accompanied to Gravesend by the French ambassador, and was joined shortly afterward by Philip Sidney with a message from the Queen[2]. Still the Queen had not decided that the pretender was to be openly countenanced. On September 26th Sidney wrote to Hatton from Dover as follows :

"The delay of this Prince's departure is so long as truly I grow very weary of it, having divers businesses of mine own and my father's that something import me ; and, to deal plainly with you, being grown almost to the bottom of my purse. Therefore your Honour shall do me a singular favour if you can find means to send for me away ; the King himself being desirous I should be at the Court to remember him unto her Majesty, where I had been ere this time, but, being sent hither by her Highness, I durst not depart without her especial revocation and commandment. The Queen means, I think, that I should go over with him ; which at this present might hinder me greatly, and nothing avail the King for any service I should be able to do him. I find, by him, he will see all his ships out of the Thames before he will remove. They are all wind-bound, and the other that came hither, the wind being strainable at the east, hath driven them toward the Isle of Wight, being no safe harbour here to receive them ; so that he is constrained to make longer abode, if it were but to be wafted over. I beseech you, Sir, do me this favour, for which I can promise nothing, seeing all is yours already[3]."

The ships finally sailed only after they had been forbidden to do so, and a private letter from Walsingham had explained that the order might be ignored. Sidney's letter to Hatton was probably effective : at any rate he was in London again on October 10th.

He had grown to the bottom of his purse in a very special sense. During no period of his life are references lacking to his embarrassed financial condition, and there can be no doubt that his inability to limit his expenditure to the amount of his income was one of the chief contributing causes of his consistently dissatisfied state of mind. Perhaps his having

---

[1] *State Papers—Spanish—Eliz.*, September 10, 1581.
[2] *Ibid.*, October 1, 1581.
[3] *Add. MS.* 15891, f. 61. Printed in Nicolas' *Life of Hatton*, p. 203.

recently taken part in magnificent pageants at the tournament and having been in attendance on a foreign prince may have made more severe demands than usual on his resources. At any rate his angry, half-desperate frame of mind is clearly betrayed in the following letters. On October 10th he wrote to Burghley :

"Yesterday her Majesty, at my taking my leave, said, against that I come up again, she would take some order for me ; I told her Majesty I would beseech your Lordship to have care of me therein. Her Majesty seemed then to like better of some present manner of relief than the expecting the office. Truly, Sir, so do I too. But, being wholly out of comfort, I rather chose to have some token that my friends might see I had not utterly lost my time : so then do I leave it to your Lordship's good favour towards me. My suit is for a £100 a year in impropriations ; if not the one, then the other ; if neither, yet her Majesty's speedy answer will, both in respect of usury and other cumbers, be much better to me than delay[1]."

A month later Sidney wrote a short formal letter to the Queen presenting a cipher which he had devised, and in this letter there is a suggestion that Her Majesty had employed him in some capacity :

" MOST GRACIOUS SOVEREIGN :

This rude piece of paper shall presume, because of your Majesty's commandment, most humbly to present such a cipher as little leisure could afford me. If there come any matter to my knowledge, the importance whereof shall deserve to be so masked, I will not fail, (since your pleasure is my only boldness,) to your own hands to recommend it. In the meantime, I beseech your Majesty will vouchsafe legibly to read my heart in the course of my life ; and though itself be but of a mean worth, yet to esteem it like a poor house well set. I most lowly kiss your hands, and pray to God your enemies may then only have peace when they are weary of knowing your force.

Your Majesty's most humble servant
PHILIP SIDNEY[2].

At Gravesend, the 10th of November,
1581."

[1] Murdin, *Burghley Papers*, p. 364.
[2] *Ibid.* p. 364.

The following letter to Hatton, written from Baynard's Castle on November 14th, doubtless refers to the 'office' mentioned in the letter to Burghley :

" I do here send you my book ready drawn and prepared for her Majesty's signature, in such order as it should be, which I humbly beseech you to get signed accordingly with as much speed as you may conveniently. For the thing of itself in many respects requireth haste, and I find my present case more pitied now than perchance it would be hereafter, when haply resolution either way will be hard to get, and make my suit the more tedious. Mr. Popham thought it would be little or nothing worth unto me, because so many have oftentimes so fruitlessly laboured in it ; and this is the general opinion of all men, which I hope will make it have the easier passage.   But indeed I am assured the thing is of good value, and therefore if it shall please you to pass anything in my book, you shall command it as your own for as much or as little as yourself shall resolve of : it will do me no hurt that seek only to be delivered out of this cumber of debts, and if it may do your Honour pleasure in anything of importance, I shall be heartily glad of it.   I pass nothing by any other instrument than by your own servant, and it shall greatly content me that the suit is of such a nature as I may have means at the least to show how ready I am to requite some part of your favours towards me.   If it be not done before this day seven night I shall be in great fear of it ; for being once known it will be surely crossed and perhaps the time will not be so good as it is at this present, which of all other things putteth me in greatest confidence of good success with the help of your honourable favour.   If you find you cannot prevail I beseech you let me know it as soon as may be, for I will even shamelessly once in my life bring it her Majesty myself. Need obeys no laws and forgets blushing ; nevertheless I shall be much the more happy it if please you indeed to bind me for ever by helping me in these cumbers[1]."

Hatton was accustomed to exacting toll from those whose suits he recommended to the Queen, and even Mendoza purchased his favour on such terms ; we may well wish, however, that Sidney had not been driven to these shifts.   The office, whatever it may have been[2], seems to have been refused him after he had felt sure of securing it ; instead, the Queen offered to give him some of the confiscated possessions of the Catholics against whom more and more severe measures were being

[1] *Add. MS.* 15891, f. 60.   Printed in Nicolas' *Life of Harris*, p. 210.

[2] Mr Fox-Bourne surmises that it was the sinecure worth £120 per year, which some 40 years later was held by George Herbert. (Walton's *Life of Herbert*, ed. 1827, p. 265.)   But Sidney's letter to Hatton would seem to dispose of this possibility.

taken. On December 18th, Sidney wrote once more to Hatton from Salisbury :

"I must ever continue to thank you because you always continue to bind me, and for that I have no other means to acknowledge the band but my humble thanks. Some of my friends counsel me to stand upon her Majesty's offer touching the forfeiture of Papists' goods : truly, Sir, I know not how to be more sure of her Highness in that than I thought myself in this ; but though I were, in truth, it goeth against my heart to prevent a Prince's mercy. My necessity is great ; I beseech you vouchsafe me your honourable care and good advice ; you shall hold a heart from falling that shall be ever yours[1]."

Three days earlier he had written to Leicester in a similar vein. His suit was for £3000 and less would not suit him. As to the source from which it was proposed to draw the money—penalties on Catholics—he declares : "Truly, I like not their persons and much less their religion, but I think my fortune very hard that my fortune must be built upon other men's punishments[2]." It was just two weeks since Campion had been executed, and it would have been strange had Sidney not been troubled as to the foundation on which his new fortunes were to be built.

Sidney probably received the sum he asked for, or some portion of it, though no record of the fact seems to remain[3]. Burghley[4], Leicester and Hatton were powerful advocates and

[1] *Add. MS.* 15891, f. 74*b*. Nicolas, p. 214.

[2] *Appendix to Third Report of Hist. MSS. Com.* MSS. of C. Cottrell Dormer, Esq., Rousham, No. 13.

[3] In the Domestic State Papers under the year 1583 is an undated 'Note of Money leviable upon the Recusants and Clergy with appointment of part of the produce to the Earl of Leicester, Sir Thomas Cecil and Sir Philip Sidney' (vol. CLXV, No. 52). Cecil and Sidney had already received £2000 and they were yet to receive £1000 each. The date of this note should almost certainly be 1586, for in the same collection is a "Note of money received by Robt. Freke for the furniture of certain light horses ; besides the sum of £2000 paid to Sir Tho. Cecill and Sir Phil. Sydney ; which is dated April 20, 1586" (vol. CLXXXVII). See also *State Papers—Dom.—Eliz. Addenda*, vol. XXX, January 1, 1588, for a further reference to sums paid from recusants' fines to Leicester, Cecil and Sidney.

[4] On December 1st a document detailing the extent of the possessions of Sidney was drawn up and signed by Burghley. (*Appendix to Third Report of Hist. MSS. Com.* MSS. of Lord De L'Isle and Dudley.) This document, which should be of great interest, I was, unfortunately, unable to discover at Penshurst.

there is no question of their good-will in the matter ; moreover Sidney was soon occupied once more in foreign travel and plantation projects, and to provide himself for such undertakings he must have found some means of replenishing his empty purse. He was evidently prepared to override his own scruples ; much as he sympathised with the sufferings of individual recusants he probably approved very heartily of the punishments meted out to those whose practices he considered essentially treasonous. He would have agreed with the sentiments expressed by Walsingham in a letter which he wrote at this time to Charles Paget to whom he returned a token which had been sent in the hope of securing his favour.

"You love the Pope," Walsingham wrote, "and I do not hate his person but his calling ; until this impediment be removed we two shall neither agree in religion toward God, nor in true devotion towards our sovereign[1]."

The pressure of increasing debts had rendered Sidney almost desperate, and it must have been a blessed relief to him to be able to visit his sister at Wilton for some weeks. A little daughter had been born to the Countess of Pembroke on October 15th ; Sir Henry had been godfather, and the Countess of Huntingdon, the godmother, had given the child her own name—Katherine[2]. Sidney remained at Wilton for Christmas[3], and the fact that he did not present a New Year's gift to the Queen, and that his name does not appear in the lists of challengers or defenders in the great royal tournament of January 1st which was held in honour of the Duke D'Alençon, makes it probable that he extended his visit into the New Year.

Of the subjects of conversation between brother and sister none, we may be sure, was of more interest than a project of marriage between Sidney and the daughter of his friend Walsingham. The great Secretary's enthusiasm for Sidney had never wavered, and it was now sufficient to overcome the prudential considerations which almost invariably determined Elizabethan marriages. In a letter to him from Wilton

[1] *State Papers—Dom.—Eliz. Add.*, vol. xxvii, A. May 4, 1582.
[2] *Sidney Psalter.*
[3] On December 26th he wrote to Leicester excusing his absence (MSS. of C. Cottrell Dormer, *ut supra*).

W. L. S.

on December 17th to bespeak a kindly reception for a servant
of his brother Robert, Sidney wrote: "The country affords
no other stuff for letters but humble salutations which indeed
humbly and heartily I send to yourself, my good Lady, and my
exceeding like to be good friend." The reference in the last
phrase is certainly to Frances, Walsingham's eldest daughter.
By his first wife Walsingham had no children. She had died
in 1564 and he had married his second wife, Ursula St Barbe,
in 1566; consequently, Frances can now have been hardly
more than fourteen years old. Young ladies were held fit to
be brides, however, at an early age, in Elizabeth's day, and
we may remember that Mary Sidney had become Countess of
Pembroke when she was only fifteen. The project had, indeed,
already been discussed for some months. Among Sidney's
friends was a certain Captain Edward Denny who was related
to Walsingham[1]. Denny had been one of the defendants of
the Fortress of Perfect Beauty, but had proceeded shortly
afterward to a command in Ireland. Sidney's friendship for
him is attested by the following letter which he wrote to Hatton
on October 17th:

"I have spoken with my father touching Powerscourt, which Mr. Denny
sueth for. He tells me assuredly that it is most necessary some English
gentleman should have it, being a place of great importance, and fallen
to her Majesty by the rebellion of the owner. As for him that sueth for
it in the Court, he is indeed a good honest fellow according to the brood
of that nation; but being a bastard he hath no law to recover it, and he
is much too weak to keep it. So that your Honour may do well, if it please
you, to follow this good turn for Mr. Denny, who can and will endeavour
to deserve it of her Majesty[2]."

Now in two of Denny's letters to Walsingham there are references to Sidney which at least read more naturally if we may
assume that his becoming a member of Walsingham's family
was under discussion. On July 16th, Denny wrote from
Dublin, "Above all things, Sir, give me leave to remember you
to love Mr. Sidney, for I know at your hands he is best worthy

---

[1] Walsingham's mother was Joyce, daughter of Sir Edmund Denny of
Cheshunt.

[2] *Add. MS.* 15891, f. 64*b*. Nicolas, p. 206.

love, and to wish my humble duty to your honour and my
Lady[1]." Again on October 6th, writing from Powerscourt,
where he was evidently already in possession, Denny concludes
his letter by

"desiring I may be most humbly commended to my good Lady, and to
my cousin Frances, and I beseech you, good Sir, make a great account
of my matchless Master Mr. Sidney. I speak it the rather for your own
good to hold now to you the most worthy young man in the world[2]."

It is possible, of course, to refuse to find any reference in these
expressions to the marriage plan which was consummated
shortly afterward, but such an attitude would surely be due
to a perversity of scepticism. The point is of interest chiefly
because of its bearing on the time when Sidney was freed from
his passion for Lady Rich. It was possibly in connection with
the marriage settlements that Sir Henry Sidney on January
8, 1582, made his will, by which after leaving to Robert a
Lincolnshire manor and making a similar bequest to Thomas
he bequeathed the whole of the remaining property to Philip[3].

[1] *State Papers—Ireland—Eliz.* vol. LXXXIV, July 16, 1581.
[2] *Ibid.* vol. LXXXVI, October 6, 1581.
[3] Collins, *Mem.*, p. 96.

CHAPTER XV

1582

THE woes of the courtier have been recited by Spenser, Lyly and many minor men of letters, and in the course of the preceding chapters we have seen many illustrations of the hard fate of those who made their abode in Elizabeth's Court, and hoped for favours or employment. One of the chief evils of the Queen's personal government has not been so often emphasized—its failure to provide channels in which the ability and intellect of the country might adequately express themselves. In the case of Sidney we have a man of high purpose, of fine gifts of nature, and of scholarly attainments, a man eminently fitted to do worthy work for his country and filled with a burning desire to be allowed to do such work, but continually checked and thwarted, and forced to recognize the sad fact that his energies were largely dissipated in the performance of tasks merely formal. It is difficult to realize how completely shut out from any honourable career in a large way were all those subjects of Elizabeth who had not attracted her personal interest, and unless we remember this fact we are likely to feel little but impatience with the complaints and reiterated disappointments of those who failed to win her favour. In the few years of Sidney's life which remained before his final departure from England we find him turning now to one scheme, now to another, in the vain hope of discovering some field in which he might perform a man's work. The inevitable result of seeing the years pass in this fashion was a certain bitterness and melancholy which overlaid the buoyant idealism of his youth.

At the beginning of the year 1582 he was employed in a

capacity which can have given him little satisfaction. Once more the Queen had decided that she preferred to purchase the French alliance by marriage rather than by the expenditure of money, and accordingly on November 1st Alençon again reached London without having consulted his brother on the subject. The French King, indeed, was too angry as a result of past experiences and too sceptical of Elizabeth to be enthusiastic about the reopening of negotiations. Three weeks later in the presence of Leicester and Walsingham the Queen told the French ambassador that she intended to marry Alençon, and she confirmed her words by kissing the Duke and presenting him with a ring. Henry III at length sent an envoy to conclude terms and then Elizabeth began to make impossible demands—concluding with the restitution of Calais. The French King was exasperated and threatening, and Burghley, at last despairing of the Queen, could only advise a Spanish alliance. The immediate question was how to persuade Alençon to leave the country. It was represented to him that Parma was winning victory after victory in the Netherlands and that his honour was suffering : he replied that he had never been interested in the Netherlands except as a means to winning Elizabeth's hand, and that he would not go until the marriage had taken place. "The tricks which the Queen is playing," declared Mendoza, "to get rid of Monsieur are more than I can describe." He was finally persuaded to go on condition that the Queen give him a considerable sum of money, promise to marry him a few weeks later, and provide him with a magnificent escort to Holland.

Of this escort, which set out on the first day of February, Sidney was one. It included Lord Howard, the Vice-Admiral, the Earl of Leicester, Hunsdon, Lords Willoughby, Windsor and Sheffield, Sir William Russell, Sir William Drury, Walter Raleigh, Fulke Greville, Edward Dyer, and many others. The whole company consisted of over six hundred persons. The Queen accompanied them to Canterbury by easy stages and there was much feasting and show of grief by the way. At length on February 7th Monsieur departed accompanied by his retinue in fifteen vessels, in one of which Leicester took the precaution to carry with him 50 beeves and 500 muttons. Elizabeth bade Alençon address his letters to his wife the Queen of England[1].

At Flushing they were welcomed by the Prince of Orange, St Aldegonde, the magistrates of the city, and representatives from various parts of the Low Countries. At Middelburg there was much of feasting and bonfires, and everywhere Alençon was hailed as a deliverer. Together with his escort he reached Antwerp on the nineteenth day of the month, where, amid much pageantry and ceremony, he was installed as Duke of Brabant. Then followed a procession through triumphal arches and elaborately decorated streets to the palace. For a week the ordnance of the city boomed and bonfires blazed[2].

Sidney must have been a more or less disgusted witness of all this pomp. The Earl of Leicester is said to have jested at it as an idle illusion. That Orange had approved of the whole scheme is not strange, for he looked upon it as a means of securing the aid of England. No doubt Sidney enjoyed the opportunity of meeting the Prince once more as well as others of his continental friends. But of his short visit[3] to the Low Countries we know no details whatever. The one friend who would have given him a warmer welcome than any other, who would have looked upon his visit as a gift from the gods, was not there to meet him. Languet had died at Antwerp on September 30th of the preceding year, attended in his last days by the kindly ministrations of Mme du Plessis. At his funeral were present a notable company of famous men including the Prince himself. Death probably had few terrors for him. Cut off from almost all those who had been nearest to him, and suffering continually from ill health, his spirits had sunk beneath the spectacle of the power of reaction in Europe, and he had come to take a gloomy view of the prospects of liberty,

---

[1] A poem supposed to have been written by Elizabeth on his departure is preserved in the Ashmolean Museum. In it the Virgin Queen describes herself as "soft and made of melting snow" (Nichols, II, p. 346).

[2] Nichols, II, pp. 343–387.

[3] On February 12th Lord Talbot wrote to his father that the English party was expected to return in about a fortnight.

of Protestantism, and of civilization. A selfish, material Germany, a Laodicean England, his own France distracted by civil wars, seemed to him little calculated to oppose the tyrannical bigotry of Spain, and with many other enlightened observers he feared that the day was not far distant when the Turk would sweep European civilization from the map. His unbounded temperamental idealism was shown nowhere more than in his remarkable, self-forgetting devotion to Sidney. It was a loyalty beyond price which he showered upon a youth to whom he was attracted solely by the perception of qualities akin to his own noblest aspirations. He died after having conquered the respect and admiration of the greatest statesmen and the finest thinkers of his day, and no greater tribute was ever paid to Sidney than the compliment of Languet's friendship.

"In this man," said one of his nearest friends, Du Plessis, "learning contended with piety, knowledge with conscience, art with nature, experience with instruction. No one knew the world better, and from his view of the world he had learned the contempt of it. No one had more opportunities of surveying the manners of men. In that variety of multifarious learning which he possessed the simplicity of his manners was the subject of universal admiration. In short he was in reality what many wished to appear to be : he lived as the best of men desired to die."

What Sidney's thoughts were as he witnessed the pageantry of Antwerp in honour of the foolish, perfidious son of Catherine de' Medici—Antwerp, where a few months before his most devoted friend and one of the noblest of men had breathed his last,—it is easier to imagine than to attempt to describe.

When Sidney returned home, probably early in March, he was more convinced than he had ever been in his life of the futility of hoping that England would render any real assistance to the Netherlands, or adopt any policy whatever that was dictated by higher motives than what he would have called selfish opportunism. His intimate association with Walsingham would only confirm him in this conclusion, but the Queen's discussion of a possible alliance with Spain, her treatment of Don Antonio, and the disgusting course of her relations with Alençon were arguments that needed no confirmation. Accordingly he set himself to casting about for some other field of

action, and within a few months we find him considering
various possibilities. The Dutch, less familiar with the true
state of affairs in England, believed that English assistance
would be forthcoming at once to the Queen's future husband,
and early in April Fremyn wrote to Walsingham of their hope
that "a certain number of cavalry led by some honourable gentlemen recommended by her Majesty" might be sent forthwith.
"It seems to me," he added, "Mr. Philip Sidney would be well
suited for this[1]." A gentleman of Alençon's suite, who had
been on intimate terms with Sidney's circle of friends during
his stay in England, wrote to Greville in similar terms of
expectancy a few days later[2]. But Sidney was under no such
illusions. His first thought seems to have been of service in
Ireland. The aftermath of the Desmond rebellion had been a
sickening slaughter of the natives and a desolating of the
country, with which even Ireland's own annals had nothing to
compare. Lord Grey was an upright honourable man with
less ability and no more profound grasp of the Irish problem
than was possessed by his predecessor. Carnage had only
made the surviving Irish more obstinately determined never
to yield, and to reject the blessings of Protestantism and English
rule. Men now remembered the more peaceful portions of Sir
Henry Sidney's *régime* when there was a semblance of justice
and prosperity in the land, and the desire that he should return
became more and more insistent. Someone—probably Burghley or Walsingham—had approached Sir Henry in the matter,
and, to our amazement, we find him not utterly averse to
considering the possibility. The reasons which operated to
make him willing to think about returning to "that accursed
country" are set forth in "Certain special notes to be imparted
to Mr. Philip Sidney" which are drawn up in Molyneux' handwriting and signed by Sir Henry on April 27th :

"First, that the principal and chief cause that moveth him to fancy or
have any liking to take the charge of the government of Ireland (if the
same be offered him) is the respect he beareth to him. So that if he
will assuredly promise him to go with him hither, and withal will put on a

[1] *State Papers—Foreign—Eliz.*, Antwerp, April 10, 1582.
[2] *Ibid.* Viçose, Sieur d'Alfeyran, Antwerp, April 20, 1582.

determinate mind to remain and continue there after him, and to succeed him in the government (if it may so like her Majesty to allow him) he will then yield his consent to go ; otherwise he will not leave his quiet and contented life at home, considering his years and the defects of nature, that commonly accompany age, to enter into so toilsome a place both of body and mind, but only to leave some memory and worthy mark to his posterity."

Sir Henry's further demands were an unequivocal recognition by the Queen of the value of his past services, such recognition to be evidenced by her bestowing on him a peerage and a grant of land ; he also preferred to have the title of Lieutenant rather than Deputy[1]. How seriously the scheme was discussed we do not know, but at any rate it was dropped. Sir Henry was evidently prepared to undertake a service which he detested, and which the experience of his whole life had proved to be a thankless, hopeless task, in order that he might help to open up a career for his son. We may rejoice that the plan fell through. The Lord Deputy's duty, in the minds of his countrymen, was to coerce the Irish into abandoning their own religion and into accepting the religion and overlordship of England, together with her customs, manners and laws. Woe to the vanquished if they failed to conform to these expectations ! We have no reason whatever to believe that Philip Sidney possessed greater insight into the Irish problem than did his father and Walsingham and Burghley. No one proposed that the Irish should be allowed to worship as they pleased, except when the Queen began to fear that she could not make them do otherwise ; no one suggested that their own laws and customs and tribal organizations should be most carefully preserved, and utilized as the only possible basis for a successful administration of the country. Had any Deputy been mad enough to propose these things he would have been utterly discredited as a sentimentalist in the eyes of those whom even the frightful slaughter of recent years had not taught the futility of a policy of brutal coercion, and who had come to regard the Irish as untamable animals rather than human beings. Sidney's eagerness to secure an Irish forfeiture for one of his friends and his contemptuous rejection of the claims of a bastard—one of the brood of that nation—justify

[1] Collins, I, pp. 295–296.

us in assuming that he had nothing to contribute toward the solution of the Irish problem.

In July Sidney was with his father and he seems to have wished for a time at least to be associated with Sir Henry in the government of Wales. From Hereford he wrote to Moly-neux[1] urging him to solicit Burghley and Hatton to appoint him a member of the Welsh Council. This scheme also came to nothing. In the composing of quarrels and hearing of petty cases—in the internal administration of the principality, he would probably have found little satisfaction. Sir Henry was continually in the midst of petty quarrels. The Bishop of Worcester, Vice-President of the Council, and the Bishop of Hereford were bitterly opposed to him, and they never failed to fortify the recital of their grievances by dwelling upon Sir Henry's extravagances in the use of public moneys—a complaint which was sure to find a favourable hearing with the Queen[2]. Nevertheless his government was to him in reality a haven of peace after the storms of his Irish experiences. The majority of the Council were devoted to him and his zeal for the public good was appreciated. When he visited Shrewsbury School, as he did very frequently[3], both the corporation and the School delighted to do him honour. His chief sorrow was occasioned by the Queen's failure to recognize his past services and by the impoverished condition of his estate. Burghley remained his good friend, and to him Philip, on coming to London, opened his father's mind on various matters. William Wentworth, Burghley's son-in-law, had just died at Theobalds on November 7th: he had been a dear friend of Sidney[4], who was one of his assignees.

[1] Collins, I, p. 296, July 23, 1582.

[2] See a pathetic letter of complaint written by the Bishop of Hereford to Burghley on June 21, 1583 (*Lansdowne MSS.*, vol. XXXVIII, fol. 180).

[3] In 1582, the year in which Thomas Sidney, Philip's brother, entered Shrewsbury, the school was removed to new buildings on the outskirts of the town. Detailed accounts of Sir Henry's visits, and also of the pageants and school celebrations which marked the occasions, are given in Owen and Blakeway's *History*. Lady Sidney accompanied her husband in March, 1583, when the celebration was a notable one (p. 373).

[4] Philip Sidney to Burghley, November 14, 1582 (*Hist. MSS. Com. Reports*, Salisbury MSS.).

"I came up," Sidney wrote to Lord Burghley, "hoping to have been myself a deliverer of the enclosed letters and so to have laid my father's mind and matters in your Lordship's hands, as on whose advice and direction he dependeth.   But finding here the loss your Lordship hath of late had, it made me both at first delay the sending and now the bringing, lest, because we were dear friends and companions together my sight might stir some grief unto your Lordship.   Your Lordship will vouchsafe at your leisure to read them, and command me when you will have me attend your Lordship ; and I beseech your Lordship to hold for assured that the family of my father doth and will hold your Lordship as a patron unto them.   So praying for your long and blessed life, I humbly take my leave[1]."

A fortnight later Sir Henry was able at Ludlow to acknowledge the receipt of Burghley's "kind and loving" reply to his application to the Queen : "if there would any comfort grow in my mind, that letter only might suffice to renew the withered estate of it[2]."   But even the warm, disinterested advocacy of two men like Burghley and Walsingham was unavailing, and Sir Henry accepted Walsingham's announcement of this fact as final, and ceased to trouble the Queen further with requests for a recognition of past services.

Sidney very promptly put aside the thought of possible occupation in Ireland or Wales and turned his attention to another field more closely related to his interest in the Netherlands.   Many of Elizabeth's advisers believed that she could cope with Spain most effectively in America, and to American projects Sidney devoted much of his thought during the next three years.   We have already seen how deep an interest he had taken in Frobisher's voyages, and from that time he had been associated in the public mind almost as much with the plans of the "adventurers" as with the affairs of the Low Countries.   It was partly in recognition of this well-known interest that Hakluyt, his old college friend, dedicated to him in this year his first book—*Divers Voyages touching the Discovery of America and the Islands adjacent unto the same.*

Of those who believed in the greater feasibility of counteracting the power of Spain by English activity in the New

---

[1] Murdin, *Burghley Papers*, p. 372.   Court, November 14, 1582.
[2] Salisbury MSS. (*Hist. MSS. Com. Reports,* November 30, 1582).

World no one was more convinced than Walsingham, and his name appears in connection with most of the numerous schemes that were projected. On March 22, 1574, Sir Humphrey Gilbert, Sir George Peckham, Christopher Carlisle (Walsingham's son-in-law), Sir Richard Grenville and others, petitioned the Queen for a new navigation in South American waters, and in November, 1580, a project was drawn up in Walsingham's hand for establishing a company of such as shall trade beyond the equinoctial line—Sir Francis Drake to be Governor of the Company for life[1]. A month earlier Drake had returned from his voyage around the world, and the intrepidity of the exploit as well as the unknown quantity of treasure which he brought with him made a wonderful appeal to the English imagination.

With the exception of Drake the most prominent English navigator of the time was Sir Humphrey Gilbert. He had seen service in France in 1562, in Ireland where he was knighted by Sir Henry Sidney in 1570, and in the Netherlands in 1572. Since that time he had given his whole attention to seafaring projects, and his famous scheme for an Academy had shown his patriotic desire to have the youth of the English gentry trained in such a way as to enable them to render service to their country. He had known Frobisher well in Ireland, and had been an adventurer in each of his voyages. On June 11, 1578, he secured from the Queen the first letters patent for the planting of an English colony in America. After much difficulty he was able to sail on November 19th with a little fleet, two of the vessels of which were commanded by his half-brothers, Carew, and Walter Raleigh. They returned after a short absence, and there is nothing definitely known either regarding Gilbert's destination or the causes of the failure of his enterprise. For some two years he busied himself cruising about the Irish coast in the hope of falling in with Fitzmaurice, and in July, 1582, £2747 was paid to Gilbert, Denny and some others for this service. Finding extreme difficulty in raising sufficient funds to equip a new American

---

[1] *State Papers—Dom.—Eliz.*, vol. CXLIV.

expedition, and "having nothing tangible left to mortgage," says his biographer, "he evolved the brilliant idea of marketing some of the nebulous rights accorded to him by his Letters Patent[1]." In September, 1580, Dr Dee, the Mortlake astrologer, had purchased from him all the land north of 50 degrees latitude—the Labrador country[2]—and now in the summer of 1582 Gilbert granted to Sir George Peckham and Sir Thomas Gerrard in consideration of certain sums which they had sub-scribed to his expedition, two of four islands which they might discover between Cape Breton and Florida, and also a grant on the mainland of one and one-half million acres. To Sir George Peckham alone he granted another half million acres on the mainland. Both Peckham and Gerrard were prominent Catholics ; both had been imprisoned for their faith, and they were now hoping that they might find an asylum beyond the seas for their co-religionists. Walsingham, whom Gilbert called the patron of his undertaking, looked favourably on this Catholic scheme. Mendoza says, probably inaccurately, that it was Walsingham who approached Peckham and Gerrard for aid in Gilbert's expedition, promising them that

"the Queen in consideration of the service might be asked to allow them to settle there (Florida) in the enjoyment of freedom of conscience and of their property in England, for which purpose they might avail themselves of the intercession of Philip Sidney[3]."

Peckham purchased still more American land from Gilbert and several Catholic ships actually sailed, but no account of their adventures has been preserved.

Sidney's interest in Gilbert's Commonwealth went beyond that of mere intercession with the Queen for Catholic emigrants. Among various schemes for making his expedition possible Sir Humphrey entered into an agreement with the Merchant Adventurers of Southampton toward the end of 1582. In some additions to their articles of agreement it was stipulated that certain knights and gentlemen should have free trade in the

---

[1] Gosling, *Life of Sir Humphrey Gilbert*, p. 184.
[2] *Diary*, p. 8.
[3] *State Papers—Spanish—Eliz.*, July 11, 1582.

countries to be discovered in consideration of their contributions to the expense of the expeditions, and among these knights and gentlemen were Sir Henry Sidney and Philip Sidney[1]. A few months later Philip purchased a portion of Sir Humphrey's lands. By articles of agreement drawn up between them it was covenanted that Sir Humphrey

"for the more speedy execution of her Majesty's said grant, the enlargement of her dominions, and the encouragement of said Sidney and his associates," did grant, "that said Sidney, his heirs, assigns, associates, adventurers, and people shall forever enjoy free liberty to discover anything not before discovered or inhabited by said Sir Humphrey, his heirs or assigns, and to enjoy to their own use such lands so discovered as shall amount unto thirty hundred thousand acres, with power to inhabit, people, and manure the same, together with all jurisdictions, privileges and emoluments whatsoever for governing, peopling etc. the same, holding same of said Sir Humphrey, his heirs and assigns, in free socage....Also the said Sidney etc. to enjoy free liberty to trade, to have the execution of all laws within the precinct of thirty hundred thousand acres of ground, as also upon the sea-coasts so far as said land shall extend....Said Sidney covenants that he shall do his best endeavour to obtain her Majesty's leave that all who adventure with said Sir Humphrey, Sir Thomas Gerrard, Sir George Peckham, the said Philip Sidney or any of them, unto said countries...may freely pass to remain there or return at their pleasure[2]."

Oddly enough, this document is dated July 7th, 1583, some four weeks after Sir Humphrey had sailed, and we can only assume that the plan was not fully matured at his departure, and that he had left power of attorney with some one to represent him. Almost immediately, in this same month of July, Sidney transferred his whole grant to Sir George Peckham[3]. In neither case is the sum paid by the purchaser mentioned, and we can only conclude that Sidney acted as an intermediary to further the enterprise, and to assure the Catholic purchasers of his active good-will. That his interest in their project persisted, however, we have assurance in a letter which he wrote a year later to his friend Sir Edward Stafford, the English ambassador in Paris.

[1] *Calendar of State Papers—Col. Add.* 1574–1674, p. 14.
[2] *Ibid.* p. 22.
[3] *Ibid.* p. 23.

"Her Majesty," he wrote, "seems affected to deal in the Low Country matters, but I think nothing will come of it. We are half persuaded to enter into the journey of Sir Humphrey Gilbert very eagerly, whereunto your Mr Hakluyt hath served for a very good trumpet[1]."

As Sir Humphrey had been drowned in the preceding September, the reference is probably to the venture of Gerrard and Peckham.

It has sometimes been asserted that Sidney was intensely anti-Catholic in his prejudices ; the evidence points strongly in the opposite direction. His relations with Peckham and Gerrard seem to have been those of a trusted mediator between them and the Government. His sympathetic letter to Lady Kitson, and his scruples about "preventing a prince's mercy," tell a similar tale. Vague references in the State Papers frequently suggest that his natural goodness of heart made him glad to mitigate the sufferings of those of whose punishments on political grounds he could not disapprove[2]. At no period of his life are records wanting of acts of gracious kindliness or intercession for those who are distressed. He prefers William Thomas' suit for a bailiwick to Walsingham[3] and that of Bartilmew Newsham for augmenting a lease a certain term of years[4]. When, in 1588, Tarleton the jester lay on his death-bed tortured by the fear that his child of six years and his mother, "a silly old widow of fourscore years," might be defrauded of his small property, he wrote to Walsingham to beg him to protect them, and he knows no stronger argument to use than that his boy is a godson of Sidney and bears his name, Philip[5]. It was to spontaneous acts of humanity like these that Sidney owed in

---

[1] *Sidney Papers*, I, p. 298, July 21, 1584. Sir Edward Stafford was appointed ambassador to the French Court and knighted in October, 1583—a fact which proves that the date of Sidney's letter to him has not been misprinted for that of an earlier year.

[2] For instance, John Aubrey in election to be Sheriff of Brecknock and suspected in religion, in his answer to the untrue exceptions laid against him refers to a quarrel in which he had been engaged which was composed by Sir Henry Sidney and Sir Philip (*State Papers—Dom.—Eliz.*, CLXV, No. 33).

[3] *State Papers—Dom.—Eliz. Add.*, vol. XXX. Wm. Thomas to Sec'y Walsingham : "It is five years since Sir Philip Sidney preferred my suit to you etc." August 29, 1587.

[4] *State Papers—Dom.—Eliz.*, CLXII, August 5, 1583.

[5] *Ibid.* CCXV, September, 1588.

great measure the love and admiration which were poured upon him by all classes of his countrymen as they were shown to no other Englishman of his time.

His financial difficulties and his lack of occupation had made him less scrupulous about pushing his own interests. If the Queen were animated by no high-minded considerations, he seems to have argued, over-delicacy on his part would be misplaced. "Methinks you should do well," he wrote to his friend, Sir Edward Stafford, "to begin betimes to demand something of her Majesty as might be found fit for you. And let folks chafe as well when you ask as when you do not[1]." On New Year's Day, 1583, he presented the usual gift to the Queen—this time "a jewel of gold like a castle, garnished with small diamonds on the one side, being a pot to set flowers in[2]." Eight days later he received the honour of knighthood and became Sir Philip Sidney of Penshurst[3]. He was denied the satisfaction, however, of reflecting that the honour had come to him either as a recognition of merit or as a mark of especial royal favour. Count Casimir was about to be installed as a Knight of the Garter, which honour had been conferred on him during his visit to England with Languet, and as he had named Sidney his proxy, and as no one could act in that capacity below the rank of a knight, Sidney's deficiency was made good. He was present at Windsor on January 10th together with his father, and took his part in the proceedings of the chapter of the most noble order after intricate questions of precedence had been settled[4]. Shortly afterward Sir Philip, as we must now call him, was a candidate for the captaincy of the Isle of Wight. "It is so generally spoken," Dyer wrote to Walsingham, "that Sir Philip Sidney is Captain of the Isle that I know not what to believe[5]." There had been much criticism of Sir Edward

---

[1] *Sidney Papers, ut supra.*   [2] Nichols, II, p. 396.

[3] Wood, *Athenæ*, I, col. 519.

[4] *State Papers—Dom.—Eliz.*, CLVIII, January 13, 1583. Note of certain things to be considered of by the knights of the Noble Order of the Garter : the placing of Duke Casimir and Sir Henry Sidney. "That place Sir Henry Sidney is to take above other knights that are of the Privy Council but not of the Order."

[5] *State Papers—Dom.—Eliz.*, CLIX, March 27, 1583.

Horsey, who now held the post, because of the increase of pirates in the Isle, and the rumour of Sir Philip's appointment may have grown out of this fact, but nothing seems to have come of it. Horsey was actually succeeded somewhat later by Sir George Carey.

In another suit which he now preferred to the Queen he was successful only after the lapse of some two and a half years. Throughout Elizabeth's reign the Earl of Warwick had held the post of Master of the Ordnance; he was now anxious that his nephew be associated with him in the office, and Sir Philip felt that the familiarity which he would acquire with England's means of defence might enable him to busy himself worthily and help to equip himself for better service when the long-delayed day of contest should actually arrive. The following letters to Lord Burghley are self-explanatory :

"I have from my childhood been much bound to your Lordship, which as the means of my fortune keeps me from ability to requite, so gives it me daily cause to make the bond greater by seeking and using your favour towards me.

The Queen, at my Lord of Warwick's request, hath been moved to join me in his office of Ordnance, and, as I learn, her Majesty yields gracious hearing unto it. My suit is, your Lordship will favour and further it, which I truly affirm unto your Lordship I much more desire for the being busied in a thing of some serviceable experience than for any other commodity, which I think is but small, that can arise of it.

I conclude your Lordship's trouble with this, that I have no reason to be thus bold with your Lordship but the presuming of your honourable good-will towards me, which I cannot deserve, but I can and will greatly esteem. I humbly take my leave and pray for your long and prosperous life. At Court, this 27th of January, 1582[1]."

On February 14th Walsingham wrote to the Solicitor-General requesting him to make a patent for the joint-patency, and "that for some considerations you will keep this matter secret, and give especial charge unto your clerk that shall engross the book, to use the same in like sort[2]."

[1] Collins, I, p. 393. The date, 1582, is, of course, old style.
[2] *Egerton Papers* (Camd. Soc.), p. 92.

W. L. S.

A few months later Sir Philip addressed a second letter to
Burghley :

"Without carrying with me any further reason of this boldness than
your well-known goodness unto me, I humbly crave of your Lordship
your good word to her Majesty for the confirming the grant she once made
unto me of joining me in patent with my Lord of Warwick whose desire
is that it should be so.   The larger discoursing hereof I will omit as superfluous to your wisdom ; neither will I use more plenty of words till God
make me able to print them in some serviceable effect toward your Lordship.   In the meantime I will pray for your long and prosperous life, and
so humbly take my leave.   At Ramsbury, this 20th of July, 1583 [1]."

Sir Philip's suit was not granted, but he received some subordinate appointment under Warwick.   During the next two
years, as we shall see, he was very busy in this new capacity.
To certain Orders set down for the government of the office of
the Ordnance by Ambrose, Earl of Warwick, to be observed
by the inferior officers is appended the statement: "In testimony that we think these orders, set down by my Lord of
Warwick, to be very convenient for her Majesty's true and just
service, we do hereunto subscribe."   Then follow the signatures
of Sir Philip Sidney, Sir William Pelham and Jo. Powell[2].
The document is undated but probably belongs to the year
1584.   On July 21, 1585, Sir Philip was appointed joint
master with Warwick "with the salary of 200 marks per annum
allowances for clerks etc. and such perquisites and advantages
as had heretofore belonged to the place[3]."   In the same month
he signs as joint Master various accounts in the office of the
Ordnance, and "notes of the natures of munitions most needful
to be provided" etc.[4]

----

[1] *Lansdowne MSS.*, vol. xxxix, fol. 148.

[2] *State Papers—Dom.—Eliz.*, vol. clxxv, 1584 ?

[3] *Ibid.* clxxx.   Also *State Papers—Dom.—Jas. I*, vol. iii, No. 62—an abstract
of the patents appointing to this office from the time of Edward III to James I.

[4] *State Papers—Dom.—Eliz.* vol. clxxx.   In a document entitled "The
principal officers of the army, 1583," occurs the name of "Sir Philip Sidney,
General of Horse" (*ibid.* clxv, No. 46).   The date should probably be 1585.

CHAPTER XVI

1583

THE great event of Sir Philip's life during the year 1583 was his marriage on Friday, September 21st, to Frances Walsingham[1]. As we have seen, the match had been arranged some two years earlier and was probably delayed on account of the bride's extreme youth. We hear nothing of it in 1582, but on February 10, 1583, Burghley wrote to Walsingham: "I hear of the comfortable purpose toward for your daughter. God bless it; as I would any of my own so is that great hope[2]." Draft articles of agreement had been drawn up between Sir Henry Sidney and Sir Francis Walsingham by which Sir Henry assured certain manors to Sir Philip and his wife, and to her solely in the event of Sir Philip's death, and Walsingham likewise assured to them certain lands. With the exceptions and provisos of the agreement we need not concern ourselves. One rather curious item was to the effect that

"the said Sir Francis is well contented and will undertake to pay or discharge the debts of the said Sir Philip so far as shall amount unto £1500, and will allow to the said Sir Philip and Mrs. Frances and their servants their diet if they will take it with him and in his house.... But this is not meant to be put into the conveyance."

Sir Henry Sidney was smarting under the disappointment of the Queen's final refusal to make him any tangible return for the sums which he had spent in the public service, and on March 1st he addressed to Walsingham the famous letter—his *Apologia pro Vita Sua*—from which we have already

---

[1] *Sidney Psalter.*
[2] *State Papers—Dom.—Eliz.*, vol. CLVIII.

frequently quoted, and which constitutes the most detailed
and reliable account of English rule in Ireland during the first
half of Elizabeth's reign. The letter opens with a reference to
the marriage negotiations and reveals incidentally some very
curious points of view.

"I have understood of late," Sir Henry began, "that coldness is thought
in me in proceeding in the matter of marriage of our children. In truth,
Sir, it is not so, nor so shall it ever be found ; for compremitting the
consideration of the articles to the Earls named by you and to the Earl
of Huntingdon I most willingly agree and protest I joy in the alliance
with all my heart. But since by your letters of the third of January to
my great discomfort I find there is no hope of relief of her Majesty for my
decayed estate in her Highness's service (for since you gave it over I will
never make more means, but say, *Spes et fortuna, valete*) I am the more
careful to keep myself able, by sale of part of that which is left, to ransom
me out of the servitude I live in for my debts ; for as I know, Sir, that
it is the virtue which is, or that you suppose is, in my son that you made
choice of him for your daughter, refusing haply far greater and far richer
matches than he, so was my confidence great that by your good means I
might have obtained some small reasonable suit of her Majesty ; and
therefore I nothing regard any present gain, for if I had, I might have
received a great sum of money for my good-will of my son's marriage,
greatly to the relief of my private, biting necessity. For truly, Sir, I respect
nothing by provision or prevention of that which may come hereafter,
as thus :—I am not so unlusty but that I may be so employed as I may have
occasion to sell land to redeem myself out of prison, nor yet am I so old,
nor my wife so healthy but that she may die and I marry again and get
children, or think I get some. If such a thing should happen God's law
and man's law will that both one and other may be provided for. Many
other accidents of regard might be alleged, but neither the forewritten
nor any that may be thought of to come do I respect, but only to stay
land to sell to acquit me of the thraldom I now live in for my debts."

Sir Henry was at least not open to the charge of having failed
to examine the question from all possible sides.

The course of true love never does run smooth, and perhaps
that was the reason why a very unexpected obstacle to the
marriage now appeared in the fact that the Queen chose to
consider it an 'offence.' Whether her attitude was dictated
by sheer perversity, or by Walsingham's failure formally to
announce the project to her, or simply by her objection to

marriage in general it is difficult to say. On March 19th
Walsingham wrote to Hatton :

"As I think myself infinitely bound unto you for your honourable and
friendly defence of the intended match between my daughter and Mr.
Sidney, so do I find it strange that her Majesty should be offended withal.
It is either to proceed of the matter or of the manner. For the matter,
I hope when her Majesty shall weigh the due circumstances of place,
person and quality, there can grow no just cause of offence. If the manner
be misliked for that her Majesty is not made acquainted withal, I am no
person of that state but that it may be thought a presumption for me
to trouble her Majesty with a private marriage between a free gentleman
of equal calling with my daughter. I had well hoped that my painful and
faithful service done unto her Majesty had merited that grace and favour
at her hands as that she would have countenanced this match with her
gracious and princely good-liking thereof, that thereby the world might
have been a witness of her goodness towards me. As I thought it always
unfit for me to acquaint her Majesty with a matter of so base a subject
as this poor match, so did I never seek to have the matter concealed from
her Majesty, seeing no reason why there should grow any offence thereby.
I pray you, Sir, therefore, if she enter into any further speech of the matter,
let her understand that you learn generally that the match is held for concluded, and withal to let her know how just cause I shall have to find myself
aggrieved if her Majesty shall show her mislike thereof. And so committing
the cause to your friendly and considerate handling I leave you to the protection of the Almighty. At Barn Elms, the 19th of March, 1582 [1583]
Your most assuredly to command, Fra. Walsingham. Postscript;—I will
give orders that my cousin Sidney [Sir Henry] shall be forewarned of
the matter, who, as I suppose, will not be at the Court before the next
week. If her Majesty's mislike should continue, then would I be glad
if I might take knowledge thereof to express my grief unto her by letter,
for that I am forced in respect of the indisposition of my body, to be absent
until the end of this next week, whereof I made her Majesty privy[1]."

It is futile to speculate as to the precise cause of Elizabeth's
displeasure. No wonder that Walsingham was both indignant
and apprehensive. What he felt to be a matter of purely
private concern had become a subject of general discussion in
the Court circle. "I have been with Mr. Secretary," Roger
Manners wrote to his father, the Earl of Rutland, "who is
somewhat troubled that her Majesty conceives no better of
the marriage of his daughter with Sir Philip Sidney, but I

---

[1] *Add. MS.* 15891, fol. 101*b*. Nicolas, p. 327.

hope shortly all will be well[1]." By May 7th he was able to
write, "Her Majesty passes over the offence taken with Mr
Sidney concerning his marriage[2]." Perhaps the Queen's attitude
was responsible for the postponement of the celebration of the
marriage. Walsingham's secretary on May 6th wrote to a
friend :

"Among other matches yet to be solemnized I had forgot to acquaint
you with the full conclusion of that with Sir Philip Sidney and my master's
only daughter and heir, which, I think, shall not be solemnized before
Michaelmas[3]."

To her goodness in overlooking the offence of the marriage the
Queen did not add the virtue of graciousness. An anonymous
correspondent of the Queen of Scots, perhaps Mauvissière, the
French ambassador, in writing that he hoped to persuade
Philip Sidney to become a good servant of hers, added that
Walsingham and Leicester had brought on themselves great
"*jalousie a ceste Reyne*" because of Sir Philip's marriage with
Frances Walsingham[4]. Sir Philip and his wife took up their
residence with his father-in-law, and during the next two
years his letters are written generally from Walsingham House
or Barn Elms, Walsingham's country retreat, a few miles up
the river on the Surrey side. We may well believe that it
was a happy household. Sir Philip's devotion to Walsingham
was equalled by his love and admiration of Lady Walsingham ;
"my best mother," he calls her in a letter written some two years
after his marriage[5]. We may wish that we knew more about
the character of his wife and of her relation to Sir Philip, but
there is no reason whatever for supposing that their marriage

---

[1] *Hist. MSS. Com. Reports*, Belvoir MS., April 20, 1583.

[2] *Ibid.* May 7, 1583.

[3] Nicholas Faunt to Anthony Bacon (*Lambeth MS.*, No. 647). Quoted by
Collier in the *Gentleman's Magazine*, February, 1850, p. 116.

[4] *Hist. MSS. Com. Reports*, Salisbury MSS. The letter is without date,
and is assigned to the year 1585; 1583 would be a more probably correct date.

[5] Sir Philip to Walsingham, December 14, 1585 (*Harley MSS.*, vol. CCLXXXV,
f. 164). Sir William Pelham reckoned Lady Walsingham in the Calendar of
Saints (*State Papers—Irish—Eliz.*, vol. LXXI, Pelham to Walsingham, February
16, 1580). In his will Sir Philip refers to her as "that most honourable lady,
the Lady Walsingham, my good mother-in-law."

was not as truly a successful one as we could wish it to have been[1].

It is probable that Sir Philip's appointment in the Ordnance and his marriage brought him more prominently before the public as a person of consequence. A correspondent of the Queen of Scots, writing to her on June 12th of this year, informs her of the probability of Elizabeth's growing to agreement and accord with her, forgetting all discontents and discords. The writer urges that this will the sooner come to pass if she bestow some favourable message on Mr Secretary and Mr Sidney, who is shortly to be married to his only daughter[2]. At this time, however, we meet his name most frequently in connection

[1] In the Domestic State Papers of Elizabeth's reign (vol. CLVIII) under the year 1583 is a document tentatively assigned to the month of February. It is a petition of a certain John Wickerson addressed to Walsingham. The petitioner has been a prisoner in the Marshalsea for two years by his commitment for his rash contract of matrimony with Mistress Frances which to relinquish would be a perpetual scruple and worm in conscience, and hazard of body and soul. He solicits Walsingham's consent and good-will to the performance of their said contract; otherwise they must live in adultery and be a scornful spectacle and a mocking stock to the world. Walsingham has endorsed the petition: "Desires to be enlarged after his long imprisonment, and that I would not any longer continue my dislike of his contract with Mrs. Frances." The document is very perplexing. It certainly seems to refer to Frances Walsingham. With whom else would Walsingham's dislike of Wickerson's contract of matrimony be so strong that he would imprison the would-be husband for two years? On the other hand, unless we are entirely mistaken as to the date of Walsingham's second marriage, his daughter at the time of this 'contract of matrimony'—1581—could not have been more than 13 years of age, which makes both the story and the language of the petition seem absurd. On her portrait at Penshurst is the inscription, " 1590 Aet. 40," which gives us 1550 as the date of her birth. This is impossible unless Walsingham was an older man than has been believed, and unless Frances was the daughter of his first wife, by whom he is said to have had no children. It may be noted in passing that on November 2, 1579, Sir Henry Wallop, when very ill and in fear of death, wrote to Burghley asking that the wardship of his son be granted to Sir Francis Walsingham in the hope that he would match him to one of his daughters (State Papers—Ireland—Eliz., vol. LXX). Mary, another of Walsingham's daughters, married Christopher Carleill the famous navigator, a son of Walsingham's first wife by a previous marriage, and she was living in 1609. (Yet Nicholas Faunt refers to Frances as 'my master's only daughter' in 1583, and the same language is used by an anonymous correspondent of the Queen of Scots on June 12, 1583 (Salisbury MSS., vol. III). A third daughter of Walsingham died in 1580. (V. letter of condolence from Sir Francis Knollys on July 1st of that year—State Papers—Dom.—Eliz., vol. CXXXIX.)

[2] Hist. MSS. Com. Reports, Salisbury MSS., vol. III, June 12, 1583.

with distinguished foreigners who were visiting England. Those who had at heart the cause of Protestantism or of learning looked to him as the outstanding representative of like-minded Englishmen. Among these was the learned Polish prince Albertus Laski, whose acquaintance Sir Philip had made ten years earlier on the Continent. He reached England about the end of April, and, among other great people, he paid several visits to Dr John Dee—one of them in company with Sir Philip.

"June 15th, about 5 of the clock came the Polonian Prince, Lord Albert Lasky, down from Bisshorn where he had lodged the night before, being returned from Oxford whither he had gone of purpose to see the universities, where he was very honourably used and entertained. He had in his company Lord Russell, Sir Philip Sidney and other gentlemen : he was rowed by the Queen's men, he had the barge covered with the Queen's cloth, the Queen's trumpeters etc. He came of purpose to do me honour, for which God be praised[1]."

Perhaps there was no Englishman living at this time to whom more distinguished visitors resorted for the purpose of doing him honour[2].

The outlook for the Protestant cause had never been more gloomy than during the summer and autumn of 1583. In the Netherlands, after the fiasco of Alençon's duplicity and his dismissal in disgrace to France, the Spaniards had regained town after town. In France the young King of Navarre found it more and more difficult to maintain his position against the Guises, who were roused to new fear by the impending likelihood of both Henry III and Alençon dying early and without children as a result of their profligate lives[3]. In Scotland the Protestant Lords who had accomplished the Raid of Ruthven had once more lost control of James, who had again surrounded himself with the Catholic and pro-French party. In England the elaborate plot which is associated with the name of Throgmorton,

[1] *Diary*, p. 20.

[2] Sidney doubtless believed that "those bodies high rain on the low" (v. *Astrophel and Stella*, Sonnet XXVI).

[3] On August 25th William Cecil wrote to his father from Paris: "Upon St. Bartelmew's day we had here solemn processions and other tokens of triumphs and joy, in remembrance of the slaughter committed this time eleven years past." (Ellis, *Original Letters*, Series II, vol. III, p. 23.)

who eventually confessed to details, was progressing rapidly
although its existence was not even suspected in Elizabeth's
council until a fortunate accident disclosed it towards the
end of the year.   The dimensions of the plot for the invasion
of England by the Duke of Guise in favour of Mary Stuart
amazed while they horrified all loyal subjects.   The Earls of
Arundel and Northumberland had personally made arrangements for the landing-place of Guise ; the Earls of Rutland and
Cumberland were suspected of complicity.   Oddly enough, Sir
Philip wrote a letter at this time to the Earl of Rutland evidently
without knowing that he was under suspicion :

"Her Majesty is well," he wrote, "but troubled with these suspicions
which arise of some ill-minded subjects towards her.   My Lord of Northumberland, I hope, will discharge himself well of those doubts conceived of him.
He is yet kept in his house, but for aught I can learn no matter of moment
laid unto him.   The consideration of removing the Scottish Queen doth
still continue, and I think my Lord of Shrewsbury doth shortly come up.
The ambassadors of Spain and France be noted for great practisers[1]."

A few days after the date of this letter—on January 9th—
Mendoza was expelled from England.

During these months of anxiety and national peril Sir
Philip took an active though subordinate part in the measures
which his father-in-law and Burghley were taking for the
safety of the Queen and of the realm.   In July, Henry of
Navarre had sent his secretary, M. de Ségur, to London to
persuade the Queen to make an open alliance with the French
and Dutch Protestants.   Walsingham promptly foretold that
he would be dismissed with very little satisfaction, and in this
he was right.   M. de Ségur brought with him a letter of introduction to Sir Philip from du Plessis, in which the ambassador
was described as a gentleman full of zeal and piety whose
business would recommend him to everyone having at heart
the common weal of Christendom.

"I wish to know whether you are married or not," the letter concluded.
"I suppose you are, for I have had no letters from you for three months,
and I take it for granted that that could not be were you not busied in
some very special fashion[2]."

----

[1] *Hist. MSS. Com. Reports*, Belvoir MSS., December 20, 1583.
[2] *Mémoires de Messire Philippe de Mornay*, vol. I, p. 232.

Du Plessis was one of the most devoted of Sir Philip's friends, and we may be sure that the latter showed all possible attention to M. de Ségur. A zealous reformer, a trusted friend of Navarre and du Plessis, and a survivor of St Bartholomew, the ambassador would have special claims on Sir Philip's interest. They visited Wilton together toward the end of July, and Sir Philip introduced his guest to Archibald Douglas[1], who was at the English Court in the interest of James of Scotland. This is the first indication we have of the deep interest which Sir Philip took in Scottish politics during the last three years of his life. Perhaps Walsingham had suggested to him the possibility of useful work in this especial field. Of its importance he had a proof on the day of his marriage when Walsingham was not present, having found it impossible to return from a visit which he had made to James at Perth. When, a few months later, the Protestant Lords failed in their attempt again to seize the King, when Gowrie was put to death and Angus and Mar fled to England, we find Sir Philip in closer personal relations with the banished lords than any other Englishman.

The most notable foreigner, however, with whom Sir Philip came into intimate contact at this time was the Italian philosopher, Giordano Bruno, who reached England in the spring of 1583, and remained until near the end of 1585. There is no reason to suppose that Sidney suspected the fact that Bruno was the greatest among contemporary thinkers, and that the sixteenth century was not to produce a more profound or more original student of philosophy. Bruno trod the English earth unguessed at as he had already travelled through Italy and France, but at least his restless spirit was comparatively untroubled during his sojourn in England, and it is pleasant to know from Bruno himself that Sidney was the first Englishman to show him kindness, and was consistently his friend. It is not necessary here to review the events of his stormy life. Early imbued with a conviction that Copernicus had discovered a truth of supreme importance in the history of thought, Bruno had set himself to elaborate his master's ideas and to promulgate

[1] *Hist. MSS. Com. Reports,* Salisbury MSS. M. de Ségur to Archibald Douglas, Ramsbury, July 29, 1583

the doctrines of the new astronomy with all that it implied in philosophic thinking. Scholars had not yet come to the point of treating the Copernican theories as more than a brilliant *jeu d'esprit*, and they were utterly unprepared for Bruno's attack on the Aristotelian-Ptolemaic system with which scholastic philosophy was bound up. His rejection of the doctrine of fixed spheres and of a universe limited in space, his exaltation of mind as he elaborated his own doctrines of infinity, of Nature in which is to be found the illustration of all wisdom and all truth, and of God who manifests Himself everywhere and in all things—these teachings were not likely to recommend Bruno to the learned world of the time. His temperament, moreover, was not calculated to conciliate good-will, for he was irascible, egotistical and captious to a degree. Immediately after his arrival in England he had introduced himself to the Vice-Chancellor of Oxford by a letter in which he describes himself as

"Giordano Bruno of Nola, the God-loving, of the more highly-wrought theology doctor, of the purer and harmless wisdom professor In the chief universities of Europe known, approved, and honourably received as philosopher. Nowhere save among barbarians and the ignoble a stranger. The awakener of sleep.ng souls. The trampler upon presuming and recalcitrant ignorance, who in all his acts proclaims a universal benevolence toward man[1]."

He spent some three months in Oxford giving lectures on the new conception of the universe and its philosophic implications but receiving scant sympathy. He has left an indignant account of his treatment in which he describes the stupid pomposity of the doctors and his own triumphs especially in a disputation before the Polish prince Lasky.

"Hear," he says, "how they could answer his reasonings, and how that unhappy doctor stuck fifteen times, like a chicken in the stubble, amidst the fifteen syllogisms he propounded to us as Coryphaeus of the University on that momentous occasion. Hear how rudely and discourteously that swine went on, and how humanely and patiently spoke that other, showing he was indeed Neapolitan born and reared under a kinder sky[2]."

[1] Quoted by Symonds in *The Renaissance in Italy*, Pt. II, p. 157.
[2] Quoted by Elton, *Modern Studies*, p. 9. Professor Elton's is the fullest and best account of Bruno's visit to England.

From his general condemnation of Oxford dons he excepts Toby Matthew, to whom he may well have carried a letter from Sidney.

With the exception of one or two incidental references we know nothing whatever of Bruno's life in England except what he himself has related.   He lived as a member of the household of Mauvissière, the French ambassador, whose goodness to him he extols, and he wrote and had printed in London seven of his most important works.   In the dedication of the *Cena delle Ceneri* he describes his progess on the river and through the Strand to a supper party at Fulke Greville's house, on the night of Ash Wednesday, February 15, 1584.   It is a vivid picture of the filth and mire of London streets, and of the coarse joviality and hostility to foreigners displayed by the English lower classes.   He was accompanied on this occasion by John Florio, who was to become the translator of Montaigne and the author of *Queen Anna's New World of Words*, and Matthew Gwinne, a Welsh physician, who had written Latin plays and was interested in astronomy.   At the supper-party a knight (possibly Sidney) sat at the head of the table and on each side of him a learned doctor.   The question which they debated with the Nolan was his doctrine that the earth moves, and we have Bruno's own description of their vehemence and ignorance, of their utter discomfiture, and of the courtesy of his host after the debate had been broken up in confusion.   Bruno returned to the ambassador's house in Butcher's Row, "without coming on any of those butting and kicking beasts who had molested our advance."

This story is the only foundation of the legend which has been generally repeated, that Bruno was received into membership in a philosophical club which numbered among its members Sidney, Greville, Dyer, Spenser, Temple, and various other persons, and that they met in Fulke Greville's house to discuss moral, metaphysical, mathematical and natural speculations.   The statement is a mere embroidering upon our scanty information.   We cannot even assert positively that Bruno, Sidney and Greville ever met together on a single occasion.   Of Bruno's relation to Sidney our whole information is derived from the dedications of the two works which Bruno inscribed to his friend—the *Spaccio de la Bestia Triomfante* and the *De Gl' Heroici Furori*.   He had heard of Sidney, he says, when he was in Milan and again during his sojourn in France.   He made his acquaintance immediately after arriving in England, and he pours forth his generous acknowledgments of Sidney's courtesy and his admiration for his nobility of mind in a flood of characteristically impetuous phrases.   Extremely rare, he declares, are such noble spirits either within or without Italy.   To Sidney's name he joins that of Fulke Greville, his intimate friend, who resembles him in the graces both of mind and matter, and Bruno expresses his deep regret that vile, malignant and ignoble persons had done something to alienate from him Greville's good-will[1].

What impression did Bruno's astronomical and philosophic theories make upon Sidney ?   We can only answer that we do not know.   It is generally agreed that in his works there is no trace of Bruno's influence.   This opinion, it is fair to add, has not been held by all students of the subject.

"Who can fail to recognize," says Professor Cook, "the substantial identity of Sidney's reflection on the loveliness of virtue, 'who could see virtue would be wonderfully ravished with the love of her beauty' not only with the common source in Plato but also with the following sentiment taken from Bruno's *Heroic Rapture*....'For I am assured that Nature has endowed me with an inward sense by which I reason from the beauty before my eyes to the light and eminence of more excellent spiritual beauty, which is light, majesty and divinity[2].'"

To the present writer there seems to be no such identity. Sidney is quoting from Plato a commonplace of his doctrines ; the distinctive characteristic of the quotation from Bruno (who was also a Platonist, though with a difference) is his reliance on the "inner light" of Nature, the "natural light"—a doctrine upon which he tells us in the preface to the *Spaccio* he intended to base a system of ethics[3].   It would indeed be an interesting chapter in Sidney's biography if we could give some account

---

[1] *Spaccio de la Bestia Triomfante*, Paris, *i.e.* London, 1584 ; *De Gl' Heroici Furori*, Paris, *i.e.* London, 1585.

[2] *Defence of Poesy*, ed. Cook, p. xiii.

[3] V. Höffding, *History of Modern Philosophy*, I, p. 144.

of his attitude toward various doctrines which were gaining currency and which were to assume great importance in the history of thought. Did he accept, for instance, the fundamental doctrine of his friends Languet and François Hotman, that the sovereign power has been conferred on a ruler only on condition that he fulfil certain duties ? Did he range himself with the Ramists in their attack on the Aristotelian logic ? The dedication to him by Banosius of the works of Ramus[1], and his choice of Temple, the chief of the English Ramists, to be his secretary, would at least suggest an affirmative answer. Did he look with any favour on the increasing strength of the protest of Puritanism ?   Of these things we know nothing.

[1] *V* p. 118.

CHAPTER XVII

1584

MISCELLANEOUS references to Sir Philip abound during the year 1584, as well as much information regarding his increasing activity in public affairs. In February and March he was embroiled in a dispute regarding the goods saved from a vessel which had been wrecked at Havodsporth in Glamorganshire on the night of December 28th. Sir Edward Mansell, upon whose property the wreck had come ashore, complained to the Council of the infamous conduct of the Earl of Pembroke's servant, and declared that an attempt was being made to have the goods sequestered to Sir Philip Sidney; but the petition of Francis Shaxton, merchant of King's Lynn in Norfolk and owner of the vessel, set forth that Pembroke had restored to him all the goods in his possession, but that Sir Edward Mansell refused to deliver the much larger portion which he had secured[1]. We have heard Sir Philip in a letter to his brother deplore his own lack of musical training, and again we have seen him recommending a "poor stranger musician" to Leicester's favour: another proof of his interest in music is furnished by the following extract from a letter written by Sir Arthur Basset to Sir Edward Stradling on February 7th:

"I am hereby to request you to send unto me at any of my houses in Devon your servant, Thomas Richards, by the last day of this instant month, and to cause him to bring with him both his instruments, as well that which is stringed with wire strings, as his harp, both those that he had when he was last in Devon. I have given some commendations of the

---

[1] *State Papers—Dom.—Eliz.*, vol. CLXVIII, February, 1584, and vol. CLXIX, March 7, 1584.

man and his instrument knowledge, but chiefly for the rareness of his instrument with wires, unto sundry of my good friends, namely to my cousin Sir Philip Sidney, who doth expect to have your man at Salisbury before the 7th of March next, where there will be an honourable assembly and receipt of many gentlemen of good calling[1]."

At every period of Sir Philip's life we find him soliciting his influential friends on behalf of those who needed assistance. Of such requests his letters to his father-in-law contain a very large number, and there is no evidence that Walsingham, immersed as he was in affairs of state, ever felt critically toward the son-in-law whose benevolence laid new burdens upon him. Of such letters the following may serve as an example :

"Right honourable Sir : This bearer is the same Captain Goh for whom I have divers times been an humble suitor unto you, and whom, at my parting, you wished I should bid him complain of you to the Queen. I am sure my cousin, my Lady Cheek, condemns me for negligent soliciting of you, but it is no reason so poor a man as I should bear the fault ; it must be between the Queen and you, and indeed, Sir, the gentleman deserves exceeding well and his suits are under the degree of reasonable. I will trouble you no further but with my prayer for your long and happy life. This 6th of March, 1584. Your humble son, Philip Sidney[2]."

Aubrey relates the story that Sir Philip was often wont as he was hunting on the pleasant Salisbury Plains, to take his table-book out of his pocket, and write down his notions as they came into his head, when he was writing his *Arcadia*[3]. The only other reference to his interest in hunting which I have been able to discover is in the following letter addressed to him by Lady Katherine Paget, and here it seems a question rather of procuring a deer than of hunting it :

"Nephew, this 13th of October I received your letter being dated the 23rd of July wherein you require of me a buck in Marybone Park. The delay of your messenger, perhaps not unwillingly has transformed it into a doe, the which Mr. Carye thinketh on you very well bestowed, although

---

[1] *Stradling Correspondence*, ed. J. M. Traherne (London, 1840), p. 239. Also printed in *Sidneiana* (Roxburgh Club Publications). Sir Philip's great-grandmother, Elizabeth, wife of Edmund Dudley, married *en secondes noces* Arthur, Viscount Lisle, a natural son of Edward IV. Their daughter Frances married John Basset of Umberleigh, Devon, and Sir Arthur Basset was their son. He accompanied Leicester to Holland in 1585 and died there in 1586.

[2] *State Papers—Dom.—Eliz.*, vol. CLXIX.

[3] *Brief Lives*, vol. II, p. 247.

in general he be a sparer of that game. This bearer hath received commission to the keeper there to deliver when you shall send. Thus wishing
unto you fortunate success in all your desires, especially in the travails
of my niece, with my commendations unto both, and likewise to my sister
Walsingham, I leave you to God[1]."

Lady Paget's mention of her niece is a reference not to Lady
Sidney but to the Countess of Pembroke. Three days after
the date of Lady Paget's letter her good wishes were realized,
when Lady Pembroke gave birth to her second son, Philip.
The Countess' mother was present to act as godmother and Sir
Philip and Robert Sidney were godfathers[2]. But the family
reunion and the birth of a son can have brought little joy
to Wilton, for on the day before Philip Herbert was born,
Katherine, the elder of the two little daughters of the house,
had died. In the family Psalter Sir Henry Sidney recorded,

"The death of the same Lady Katherine, eldest daughter to the said Harry,
Earl of Pembroke, was at Wilton the XVIth of October, 1584, being three
year old and one day, a child that [3] promised much excellence if she might
have lived, and was buried in Wilton church the seventeenth of the same."

The possibility of a foreign invasion of England was a question that was discussed more or less throughout Elizabeth's reign,
but the Queen regarded the possibility as slight and accordingly
the discussion was more or less academic. The landing of
foreign soldiers in Ireland to assist the Desmond rebellion had
been a feeble enterprise, and the Queen knew Philip of Spain's
procrastinating character well enough to feel assured that he
would not actively resent English indignities or espouse the
cause of the Queen of Scots unless conditions were unusually
favourable. But the revelations of the Throgmorton plot had
shaken the Queen out of her fancied security. That the Duke
of Guise, the sworn brother of King Philip, had brought almost
to maturity his plan of invading England in Mary Stuart's
favour, and that he had secured the active co-operation of
a number of English Catholic noblemen,—this astounding
fact aroused the Queen to the necessity of making elaborate

[1] *Hist. MSS. Com. Reports*—Salisbury MSS., October 13, 1584.
[2] *Sidney Psalter.*
[3] Written 'of' by mistake in the Psalter.

preparations to repel the invading host when it should be led
by the King of Spain. Beginning with the spring of 1584 these
preparations were made on a large scale, and they continued
until the Armada actually appeared. The Ordnance department
was especially busy, as we shall see, about munitions: old
vessels were refitted and new ones built, the entrances to Dover,
Portsmouth and other Channel ports were dredged and protected
by piers, and new fortifications and storehouses were constructed.
The work on the Channel ports was carried on under a commission of which Sir Thomas Scott was president, and Walsingham was in daily communication with him. At every step
the advice of the great seamen of the day was sought, and
Sir Richard Grenville, Sir John Hawkins, Sir George Carey
and many others furnished the Council with elaborate opinions
as to whether the openings to the havens should be protected
with stone or timber, or submitted suggestions regarding the
construction of storehouses and quays. The experts of those,
as of later, days, did not always agree in their opinions, and
storms frequently destroyed the work which had already been
done, but in spite of difficulties much was accomplished[1]. In
all these great undertakings Sir Philip took a considerable
part, whether as an officer of the Ordnance or as the representative of his father-in-law does not appear. On June 8th
Thomas Digges wrote to Walsingham requesting him to write
to Sir Thomas Scott and the rest of the commissioners to meet
Sir Philip Sidney at Dover to consult upon a final resolution
of all the matters which he proceeded to enumerate[2]. Sir
Richard Grenville and Sir George Carey, in reporting their
objections to certain recommendations that had been made
as to the manner in which certain work should be performed,
urged the appointment of some person of ability to superintend
the whole work. They had evidently suggested Sir Philip's
name in this connection, for Walsingham, in announcing the
names of certain gentlemen who were to go down to view the
works, explained that Sir Philip was unable to go[3]. Just what

---

[1] The Domestic State Papers of the time contain hundreds of references to
the varied details of these works.

[2] *State Papers—Dom.—Eliz.*, vol. CLXXI.   [3] *Ibid.*

share he had in these first active preparations for the great conflict we do not know, but we may be sure that he considered it worthy occupation.

He was unable to go to Dover because the Queen had decided to employ him on an embassy which he may well have considered less worthy. Two events of great importance in European politics had recently taken place both of which were a vindication of the wisdom of England's determination to look to her defences. On May 31st the wretched Alençon had died. The significance of his death consisted in the fact that it was an announcement of the impending extinction of the house of Valois. The profligate King, Henry III, was childless and his health had been utterly broken by excesses; there were no more sons of Catherine de' Medici to occupy the French throne, and to behold with comparative indifference the strife between Catholics and Huguenots. Henry of Navarre would be able to take possession of the throne only after defeating Guise and reducing the Catholics of France to subjection, and in this struggle Guise could count upon the whole-hearted support of Spain. In other words, the key-stone of Elizabeth's foreign policy would be gone when the two great Catholic powers were united against her. Moreover, the aspect of affairs in the Netherlands had suddenly changed completely when on June 29th William of Orange fell a victim to an assassin. It was little wonder that the death of the greatest of contemporary statesmen sent a thrill of dismay through Protestant Europe. The fortunes of his compatriots, already in a precarious condition while he yet lived, would, it was believed, be speedily overwhelmed after his death, and St Aldegonde wrote Walsingham that nothing could now save the Netherlands but the assistance of England or France. Under these circumstances the Queen decided to send Sir Philip Sidney to the French Court— ostensibly to condole with the King and Queen-mother on the death of Alençon whom Elizabeth had so entirely loved, but in reality to persuade France to oppose Spain in the Low Countries.

Sidney can have had no great liking for his task. He was intimately acquainted with Mauvissière, the French ambassador in London, and Sir Edward Stafford, English ambassador at

Paris, was his special friend, and either of these men could have told him what he must have known perfectly well in many other ways, that the French Court distrusted Elizabeth and her proposals to the extent of being unwilling to accept her pledged word on any subject. Sir Philip's instructions were drawn on July 8th, and the document[1], which in every line bears the mark of the Queen's own composition, is not more valuable as historical material than for the light it throws on Elizabeth's character and on the character of her diplomacy. Divested of verbiage, Sir Philip's instructions were to persuade the King of France that it was greatly to his advantage that he assist the Netherlands, and to persuade him further to be satisfied with vague generalities if he were insistent as to what assistance England was prepared to give. But the verbiage itself is interesting and even instructive. The first sentence is in Elizabeth's most characteristic style—involved, indirect and profuse.

"After the delivery of our letters and other ordinary ceremonials performed, you shall declare unto the King that though common usage among princes upon like occasions as now most unfortunately happeneth by the death of the Duke, his brother, requireth, both in respect of honour and good-will, that the offices of condoling should be performed, which principally consisteth in the loss of the party taken away and in ministering arguments of comfort to the Prince that is grieved : yet if it be considered how just cause we ourself have of grief having lost so dear a friend as the Duke, his brother, was unto us (whereof no Prince could give more notable and evident arguments to the world of the great and singular good-will and love he bare us) it will then appear that as we are inclined to perform the one, so shall we be found altogether unfit for the other, having more need to receive comfort ourself than apt to comfort others."

There was much of this elaborate condolence for the King, and similarly unimpeachable sentiments were to be expressed to the Queen-mother. The opening of the real business of his visit Sir Philip should delay until a second audience. He should then point out to Henry III and his mother that the death of Orange foreshadowed great danger to France. Unless Henry send succour to

"those poor afflicted people of the Low Countries" who "without some present assistance shall not be able to hold out," the King of Spain will

---

[1] *Cotton MSS. Galba*, E. VI, f. 241.

soon be supreme in Europe, supported as he is by the Pope and various branches of the House of Austria. "What increase of treasure and strength by sea he is grown unto by the possession of the Kingdom of Portugal all men of judgment both see and fear. So as he lacketh only the quiet possession of the Low Countries to make him the most absolute monarch that ever was in this part of the world."

The especial danger to France arising from this situation Sir Philip was to amplify.

If Henry inquired what England was willing to do, Sir Philip "shall then in general words assure him that he shall find us ready to do anything that may stand with our honour, and as due consideration of our future, if he shall show himself so affected to the cause as to proceed therein in such princely sort as appertaineth."

Sir Philip was given no power "to descend into particularities how this Spanish greatness may be prevented"; he might inform the King, should the latter be insistent on this point, that the Queen had found in him such changes and coldness when it should come to a conclusion in the past that she had not thought it reasonable now to send a plenipotentiary. It is almost incredible that she should make such a charge against the brother of Alençon, whom she had treated so outrageously. If the King showed a disposition to proceed effectually in the matter, then Sir Philip should apply to his mistress for fresh instructions and an extension of authority.

Such insincere fencing could not deceive the wily Catherine de' Medici for a moment. She knew Elizabeth well, and she would know that this communication was merely a mechanical repetition of the English Queen's previous attempts to force France to bear the expenses and odium attached to the defence of the Low Countries. Sir Philip was expected to go over to Paris immediately[1]; he had even reached Gravesend when a messenger from Stafford arrived and changed his plans. The official explanation is contained in a letter written by Lord Hunsdon to Davison, the English ambassador to the Scottish King:

"I received lately a letter from Mr. Secretary in the which he writes unto me that Sir Philip Sidney was appointed to go into France to condole for the death of Monsieur, whereof the King was advertised by our

[1] Gilbert Talbot to Lord North, July 8, 1584 (*Add. MS.* 34079, f. 17).

ambassador there. And Mr. Sidney being at Gravesend onward on his
journey, and some of his carriages gone over before, there came letters from
our ambassador that the King was going to Lyons not being accompanied
with such noblemen as was fit to receive an ambassador withal, and
besides he hath given over mourning for his brother, and therefore prayed
the stay of Mr. Sidney which would not be before the latter end of September.
And thereupon Mr. Sidney is returned back again[1]."

As a matter of fact the French Court did not choose to
enter upon insincere negotiations on the subject of the Low
Countries, and accordingly they sent courteous if very uncon-
vincing excuses. Mauvissière was convinced of Elizabeth's
insincerity in an audience which he had just before the arrival
of Stafford's messenger, but he tried to lessen the Queen's
chagrin[2] by conventional excuses—"*pour la contenter*[3]." He
told Sidney that if he went to Paris it would be to his interest
to be frank ; Stafford wrote him that he would not be welcome.
The project was accordingly dropped, and in a few days France
was treating on her own account with deputies from the Low
Countries.

The marriages of the members of the Sidney family seemed
fated to stir the interest of the Court circle to a very unusual
degree, and that of Robert Sidney, which took place in September
of this year, was a topic of even greater speculation and gossip
than had been that of Sir Philip in the preceding year or the
brilliant match of Mary Sidney some six years earlier. The
rather wayward youth had extended his continental tour until
February, 1582, having spent the last six months of the period
in Paris. Cobham, who was English ambassador there, thought
him like his elder brother[4], but, with much spirit and capacity
for action, he had an eye for the main chance which was foreign

---

[1] *Scottish Correspondence,* vol. xxxv, July 28, 1584.

[2] Salisbury MSS., *ut supra.* Mauvissière to Henry III, July, 1584. "Voilà
Sire, encores vostre répétition des termes où nous en estions demeurés quant
elle pensoit que ledict Sieur de Cheidenay [Sidney] deust fere son voyaige,
qui fut incontinent aresté par le retour du courrier, envoye vers le Sieur de
Staffert au grand malcontentment de ladicte Reyne d'Angleterre qui en demeura
fort estonnée."

[3] "Pour estre hors de sayson le voyaige dudict Sieur de Chedenay, après
le deuil fini de mondict Seigneur vostre frère, estant vostre Majesté sur le point
de s'acheminer pour son voyaige de Lion en petite compaignie, etc."

[4] *State Papers—Foreign—Eliz.* Cobham to Walsingham, October 10, 1581.

to Sir Philip. In his famous letter to Walsingham of March
1, 1583, Sir Henry Sidney defined his sons as "one of excellent
good proof, the second of great good proof, and the third not
to be despaired of but very well to be liked." We hear almost
nothing of Robert between the date of his return to England
and that of his marriage except what is contained in a short
note to Molyneux dated "Court, this Sunday, 1582." He asks
his father's secretary to "set down in writing the reasons why
her Majesty should erect the office I sue for. You must do it
in good terms," he adds, "for it is to be showed to her Majesty[1]."
Even this trifle suggests that any statement regarding his
similarity to his elder brother would need to be qualified.

His wife was Barbara Gammage, daughter and sole heir
to John Gammage of the Castle of Cointy in Glamorganshire.
Her great wealth and beauty had attracted many suitors,
chief among them being Herbert Croft, a grandson of Sir James
Croft, Controller of the Household. To Barbara's uncle, Sir
Edward Stradling, Sir James wrote toward the end of 1583
reminding him of the conference they had had at Croft House
regarding the match, and telling him that Sir William Herbert
and Lord Howard approved[2]. Herbert himself wrote Sir
Edward on July 5, 1584, that he had heard that Sir James
Whitney "hath been in your country to gain that which I
would fain have." This danger passed away, however, and
when Herbert Croft visited Glamorganshire toward the end
of August, Sir James wrote to Sir Edward Stradling to thank
him and his wife for their favour in favouring his grandson's
cause[3]. On September 8th John Gammage died, and as his
daughter was of "the age of 22 years and upwards" and therefore
free to dispose of herself as seemed good in her own eyes,
there was great excitement among her suitors. It was some
days before the news of John Gammage's decease reached
London, but when it did arrive Sir Edward Stradling, at whose
house of St Donat's Barbara was residing, was bombarded
with letters. Sir James Croft wrote on September 17th to
remind him that he had his and his wife's handwriting giving

---

[1] Collins, I, p. 296.
[2] *Stradling Correspondence*, p. 39.   [3] *Ibid.* p. 40.

consent and furtherance, and to say he found it very strange
that Sir Edward and Lady Stradling had taken the gentlewoman forcibly from Herbert Croft and detained her as a
prisoner so that he could not have access unto her[1]. On
September 20th Walsingham wrote that

"albeit by late letters from my lords of the Council to the Sheriff of Glamorganshire, Sir William Herbert and others, her Majesty appointed that the
daughter of Mr. Gammage, deceased, should be delivered to remain with
some of them ; yet since the writing of these letters her Majesty for good
causes hath thought it very requisite that the said young gentlewoman be
by you forthwith brought up hither to the Court and to be here delivered
into the custody of the Lord Chamberlain."

Special orders were added that Barbara "be not suffered to
have any such access to her as whereby she may contract or
entangle herself for marriage with any man[2]." Lord Howard
wrote to the same effect the next day, and on September 26th
Walter Raleigh sent a belated letter to the effect that

"Her Majesty hath now thrice caused letters to be written unto you that
you suffer not my kinswoman to be bought and sold in Wales without
her Majesty's privity and the consent and the advice of my Lord Chamberlain and myself, her father's cousin-german, considering she hath not
any nearer kin nor better[3]."

The marriage had already taken place, however, on September
23rd in the presence of the Earl of Pembroke, Sir Edward and
Lady Stradling and many others. Of Robert's wooing we
know nothing. For many years Sir Edward Stradling had
been on terms of intimacy with Sir Henry Sidney and the
Earl of Pembroke, and it is quite possible that Robert and
Barbara had known each other from childhood and had met
at St Donat's, Ludlow or Wilton. The Earl of Pembroke and
Robert Sidney gave a bond for six thousand pounds for the lady's
jointure, and the ceremony was performed two hours before
the arrival of the Queen's message forbidding it. Sir Edward
Stradling probably had few misgivings, for Walsingham had
privately written him that

"being now secretly given to understand that for the good-will you bear
unto the Earl of Pembroke you mean to further what you may young
Mr. Robert Sidney, I cannot but encourage you to proceed therein, for

---

[1] *Stradling Correspondence*, p. 41.   [2] *Ibid.* p. 27.   [3] *Ibid.* p. 22.

that I know her Majesty will no way mislike thereof ; besides, the Lord Chamberlain, Mr. Raleigh, and the rest of the young gentlewoman's kinsfolk do greatly desire it."

And so the prize was won and Robert Sidney had begun to climb the ladder leading to the high fortunes which he was ultimately to attain. Young Mr Croft and his friends made a great bluster about Sir Edward Stradling's contempt of Her Majesty's commands, but a second letter from Walsingham reassured Sir Edward. Congratulations and thanks poured in upon him from friends of the Sidneys, and both Lord Howard and Walter Raleigh declared themselves well pleased. Sir Henry Sidney was especially delighted with the wonderful good fortune which had befallen his son, and his joy was renewed the next year when, through Sir Edward Stradling's influence, Robert was elected to Parliament as Knight of the Shire for Glamorgan.

A new House of Commons had been elected in 1584 and Sir Philip was again a member, probably as Knight of the Shire for Kent. The writs were issued in October and Parliament met on November 23rd. A large number of Sir Philip's nearest friends had seats,—Greville, Drake, Hawkins, Grenville, Raleigh, Bodley, Arthur Atye, Edward Wotton, Henry Neville, Sir George Carey, Lord Russell, Sir William Herbert, besides the members of the Council. Other members who were destined to fame for various reasons were Francis Bacon, Robert Cecil and Sir Thomas Lucy. Sir Walter Mildmay, the Chancellor of the Exchequer, reminded the members of the Commons that if they had been called very suddenly and at an unseasonable time of the year it was for very urgent and necessary causes. What these causes were no member of the House needed to be reminded. The assassination of the Prince of Orange and the amazing revelations of the Throgmorton plot for the invasion of England and the assassination of Elizabeth, had caused a panic fear to spread through the nation both for the present safety of the Queen and because of the chaos that would inevitably follow her death. To anticipate such a catastrophe the Bond of Association had been drawn up and circulated a few weeks before, and Parliament had assembled

for the express purpose of confirming the intent of the Bond—
"for the disabling of such as, pretending title to the Crown,
should seek to disturb her Majesty's possession during her
life." A bill embodying these objects was eventually passed,
but the Queen managed once more to evade the necessity of
having her successor definitely named.

One very dramatic incident occurred which furnished a
striking demonstration of how real and how near the peril was.
A bill against Jesuits, seminary priests and such-like disobedient
subjects, ordering them on pain of death to leave the country,
had reached its third reading and was about to be passed
unanimously, when Dr Parry, a member of the House, in very
insolent terms denounced the whole bill as "full of blood,
danger, despair and terror or dread to the English subjects of
this realm." He was committed to the custody of the Serjeant,
but, on the Queen's interceding for him, he was allowed after a
humble submission to resume his seat. This was on December
18th, and three days later the House adjourned until February
4th. In January, Neville, an accomplice of Parry, accused
him of a plot to kill the Queen. Parry confessed, was tried on
February 25th, and five days later was executed. The Commons
had already expelled him, and Sir Thomas Lucy proposed that
some form of execution be devised fit for this most terrible
kind of treason. The bill against Jesuits was passed after a
conference with the Lords by a committee of which Sir Philip
was a member[1].

Although called for a special purpose, Parliament passed
many bills of a miscellaneous character, and Sir Philip must
have been very busy while they were in the committee stage.
He was a member of the committees to which were referred
bills for the preservation of timber in the county of Sussex,
for confirmation of letters patent made unto Mr Walter Raleigh
for the discovery of foreign countries, for the maintenance of
Rochester bridge, for preservation of woods near the town of
Cranbrook in Kent, the bill touching the curriers of London,
and the bill for subsidy. When Sir Philip's servant, John
Pepler, was made a prisoner for debt in the Counter, a warrant

[1] D'Ewes, *Journals*, p. 352.

for a writ of privilege was awarded setting him free, though a similar favour was denied the servant of another member, as it appeared that he had procured himself to be received into the service of the said member to escape from arrests.

This House of Commons, in spite of the Queen's having forbidden all dealing with spiritual matters, was bitterly condemnatory of the episcopacy. Besides bills for the better and more reverent observing of the Sabbath, and for the liberty of godly preachers who were oppressed by their superiors, they presented to the Lords in the form of "humble petitions" their complaints. In brief, these complaints dealt with the appointment of illiterate ministers, with the evils of pluralities and non-residence, and with the petty tyranny exercised over godly ministers by the ecclesiastical commissioners. The Lords found their suggestions either unnecessary or already provided for, and the Archbishop of York "utterly disallowed" the great majority of them. The Queen, however, in her speech at the conclusion of Parliament, admitted that there might be some faults and negligence, and that if any schisms or errors heretical were suffered it could not be excused. "All which, if you my Lords of the Clergy do not amend, I mean to depose you. Look ye therefore well to your charges. This may be amended without heedless or open exclamations." She did not wish her words to be interpreted, however, as animating Romanists or tolerating "new-fangleness."

"I mean to guide them both," she declared, "by God's holy true rule. In both parts be perils, and of the latter I must pronounce them dangerous to a kingly rule, to have every man according to his own censure to make a doom of the validity and privity of his Prince's government with a common veil and cover of God's word, whose followers must not be judged but by private men's exposition. God defend you from such a ruler that so evil will guide you!"

Elizabeth was too well acquainted with the history of the relation of the Kirk to kingly power in Scotland to give any encouragement to the growth of "new-fangleness" on English soil.

CHAPTER XVIII

1585

Toward the end of this year 1585 Sir Philip left England, and the few remaining months of his life were spent in aiding the Netherlanders in their struggle against Spain. And yet, oddly enough, at the beginning of this last year which he was to spend in his native land, he had come to the conclusion that this project, in which for years he had been eager to engage, was not the most effective means of warding off the blow which all men now believed Spain would soon aim against England. Some of the most remarkable chapters of Fulke Greville's account of Sidney's life[1] are those in which he details at length the views of his friend, expressed to him in conversation, on the political situation of the day. Sir Philip had studied the subject himself for too many years, and he had come into too close relations with men like William of Orange, Walsingham and Burghley, to have any doubt that the growing power of Spain constituted a supreme menace to the liberties of Europe in general and of England in particular. Moreover, he was convinced, as were these statesmen, that this menace could be confronted more successfully in an offensive than in a defensive war. His impatience with the policies of "that blessed Lady which then governed over us," who was more ambitious of balancing neighbour princes from invading one another than under any pretence of title or revenge apt to question or conquer upon foreign princes' possessions, was neither greater nor less than that of Burghley or Walsingham. We cannot give here even a full synopsis of his views concerning each of the European states : in brief, however, his opinion was as follows. The

---

[1] Chapters VIII, IX and X.

greatness of Spain could be coped with successfully only by
a general league among free princes.   Half-hearted support of
the Netherlanders would avail little; "while Spain had peace,
a Pope, money or credit, and the world men, necessity or
humours, the war could hardly be determined upon this Low
Country stage." Spain was actually better prepared to resist
attack in Flanders than anywhere else in her vast dominions,
and her powerful armies and fortified cities would resist all attacks
made on them at least for a long time.   Sir Philip's plan was
"to carry war into the bowels of Spain, and by the assistance
of the Netherlands burn his shipping in all havens as they passed
along, and in that passage surprise some well chosen place for
wealth and strength, easy to be taken and possible to be kept
by us."   A strong fleet thus engaged would be immediately
available for purposes of defence as well.   If such a design
should be considered too dangerous or costly, at least England
should keep "a strong successive fleet all seasonable times
of the year" upon the narrow seas, that birthright of hers,
and should enter into an alliance with the Protestant party in
France which might result in a perfect reconciliation between
these anciently allied kingdoms.   He even questioned whether
Italian hatred of Spanish tyranny would not make welcome a
revival of our old rights in the kingdom of Sicily ; nay, so far
did his enthusiasm carry him, that he was inclined to believe
that the Pope himself would not be ill-pleased by such a
moderating of the over-greatness of the Spanish monarchy.
But if this plan, too, were rejected, he fell back upon one, of
the feasibility of which he had not the slightest doubt, namely,
to follow Drake's example and strike at the Spaniard where he
was weakest.   From Peru and Mexico he drew his sinews of
war, and Sir Philip determined to bend all his strength to
attacking him there, having become convinced of the impossibility of persuading the Queen to effective action elsewhere.
The feasibility of the scheme he based on what Englishmen had
already accomplished in Spanish America, on Spanish lack of
discipline and on the appeal which the prospect of great wealth
would make to enterprising spirits in England.   He foretold
the happy conjunction of England, Ireland and Scotland, and

declared that their increasing populations could only become a source of strength provided that manufacturing were developed at home and an opportunity afforded for employment in English colonies.

To putting such a plan into execution Sir Philip had bent all his energies, and, though we know little of the details except what Greville tells us, we know enough to see how largely his design was conceived, and how far it was advanced when the Queen appointed him to a command in the Low Countries. He had secured a promise from the Netherlands to second an English fleet under his charge with one of their own, and thirty English gentlemen had agreed to contribute one hundred pounds each to fit out another. His intention was first to seize Nombre de Dios or some other Spanish haven near it to serve as a base for fighting operations, and he hoped to establish a colony which should be "an Emporium for the confluence of all nations that love or profess any kind of virtue, or Commerce." What the success of this voyage would have meant lies hid, as Greville says, in God's secret judgments, but had the Queen not been forced at this particular juncture to depart from her established policy in relation to the Low Countries, the name of Sir Philip Sidney might be known to-day chiefly as one of England's great navigators and a founder of her Colonial Empire.

Raleigh's first expedition under Captains Amadas and Barlow had discovered Virginia in the preceding year, and they had fired the enthusiasm of their countrymen with their accounts of the riches of the new land and the friendly character of the natives. When the second expedition was fitted out in the spring of 1585 it was half expected that Sir Philip would go in command. "Had Sidney gone," says Professor Raleigh, "it is possible that the whole course of the history of Virginia and of North America might have been changed[1]." Sir Richard Grenville was substituted in his stead, and after braving the Spaniards in St John and Hispaniola he went on to Virginia, where he subjected the natives to the most cruel treatment. Ralph Lane, who had long been a friend of the Sidneys, was

[1] *Hakluyt's Principal Navigations*, vol. XII, p. 41.

left as Governor of the Colony, and a letter which he sent
to Sir Philip in August shows how warmly he had entered into
the latter's plans.

"My most noble General : Albeit in the midst of infinite business, as
having, amongst savages, the charge of wild men of mine own nation... nevertheless I would not omit to write these few lines of duty and affection unto
you....If her Majesty at any time find herself burthened with the King of
Spain, we have by our dwelling upon the island of St. John and Hispaniola
for the space of five weeks so discovered the forces thereof, with the infinite
riches of the same, as that I find it an attempt most honourable, feasible
and profitable, and only fit for yourself to be chief commander in....To
conclude : finding by mine own view his forces at land to be so mean,
and his terror made too great amongst us in England, considering that
the reputation thereof doth altogether grow from the mines of his treasure,
and the same in places which we see here are so easy both to be taken
and kept by any small force sent by her Majesty, I could not but write
these ill-fashioned lines unto you, and to exhort you, my noble general,
by occasion not to refuse the good opportunity of such a service to the
Church of Christ, of great relief from many calamities that this treasure
in Spaniards' hands doth inflict unto the members thereof, very honourable
and profitable for her Majesty and our country, and most commendable
and fit for yourself to be the enterpriser of. And even so for this time
ceasing further to trouble you, with my humble commendations to my
lady your wife, I commit you, my noble general, to the mercy of the
Almighty."

At this time no project against the Spaniard seemed so feasible
to Sir Philip[1].

In the meantime he was by no means unoccupied. His
work at the Ordnance Office seems to have been of the most
painstaking, and he was in frequent conference with the Queen
regarding the state of the national defences. Something of the
increase of poise which he was gaining is reflected in a letter
to Burghley[2] in which he very humbly justifies himself for
having spoken quite plainly to Her Majesty regarding the
deficiency of stores in the Ordnance. Elizabeth was attracted,
as was everyone else, by his enthusiasm and devotion to his

[1] For some years Sidney's interest in Terra Florida was generally recognized.
Le Moine, the survivor of Ribaut's Huguenot colony, dedicated to Lady Sidney
his collection of drawings of the flora and fauna of the new world. See Lee,
The French Renaissance in England, pp. 306–307.

[2] *State Papers—Dom.—Eliz.*, May 15, 1585.

ideals, but she was always more or less suspicious of devotion
and ideals. She called him 'her Philip'—to distinguish him
from the King of Spain, and at some undetermined date she
presented to him a lock of her hair which is still preserved
at Wilton.

Sir Philip was probably able to visit Penshurst more frequently during these months. Sir Henry, who in 1579 had added
to the noble pile of buildings the Gatehouse, and the whole
north and west façade, was now engaged in erecting a stone
tablet over the Porch of the Gatehouse on which he recorded
the gift of the house and manor to his father by Edward VI.
Sir Philip's interest in such work we may take for granted.
Walsingham, however, furnished him with his most serious
occupation during this summer—acting as intermediary between
the Queen and the banished Scottish lords. After the failure
of the Protestant noblemen to seize James in the spring of
the preceding year, the leaders—Mar, Angus and Glamis—
had fled to England, and the King had again fallen under the
control of the Earl of Arran, an unprincipled adventurer, who
had managed to possess himself of the wealth of Hamiltons
and Protestant noblemen alike. In December he had sent up
the Master of Grey to London to demand the expulsion of the
exiled lords, but it soon appeared that the ambassador was willing to play a very different part, viz. to urge on Elizabeth a
league with James for the preservation of Protestantism and
for mutual defence. James wished to secure a pension, to
shut off all recognition of his mother's claims to be associated
with him in the government of the kingdom, and, if possible,
to be recognized by Elizabeth as her successor : Elizabeth
wished to secure the friendship of Scotland—a consideration
vital to the safety of England as long as Spaniards or Guises
meditated an English invasion. The Master of Grey gave
assurances that Arran's star was waning and that James, who
was about to try his experiment in Episcopacy for Scotland,
wished for nothing more than to be guided by his "good sister."
In April Edward Wotton was sent as ambassador to Edinburgh
to negotiate the treaty, but of course there was much suspicion
of motives and haggling over terms to be overcome before the

goal could be reached.   The good-will both of Arran and the
Master of Grey was cultivated by the English Court.

In all these matters Sir Philip took a very important share.
He seems never to have suspected the actual baseness of
character of the Master of Grey, and their relations were of the
most intimate sort.   He was in continual correspondence with
Wotton and seems to have been practically responsible for the
entertainment of the exiled nobles.   To his straightforward
way of thinking it was incredible that Elizabeth should haggle
over the £5000 annual pension to James which she had promised
to the Master of Grey, when its effect would be to strengthen
Protestantism in Scotland and checkmate the plans of England's
continental enemies.   To the securing of the pension he bent
all his efforts, and he and Walsingham seem to have determined
to raise the sum among their friends if the Queen held out.
On May 23rd Walsingham wrote to Wotton :

"The writing of the enclosed that you shall receive from Sir Philip Sidney,
which he hath prayed me to peruse, groweth upon an advice delivered
unto him by Mr. Douglas touching the offer of a pension which you are
directed to make unto the king[1]."

A few weeks later, however, he had to write :

"We are grown here to such an extreme kind of nearness as I see no hope
to get the Master of Grey any relief from hence.   I have already furnished
him with £2100, delivered unto him, notwithstanding, as a thing proceeding
from her Majesty, for that otherwise he would not have accepted thereof.
Sir Philip Sidney hath moved the Earl of Leicester to be content to yield
some present support until her Majesty may be wrought to make more
accompt of the matter than presently she doth, but he yieldeth a deaf
ear[2]."

It was discouraging work.   By September, Walsingham had to
report that he could not persuade the Queen to write to the
Master of Grey nor to give James the pension, and he concludes
that all his work to cement the unity with Scotland has been
for nothing.   "Sir Philip Sidney is little at the court, and all
men, as it seemeth, weary.... The poor Earl of Angus and
Earl of Mar," he added, "receive here little comfort otherwise
than from poor Sir Philip Sidney, so as our course is to alienate

---

[1] *The Hamilton Papers*, vol. II.   [2] *Ibid.* June 18th.

all the world from us!" And again: "The burden of the charges of entertaining the Scottish lords will light upon Sir Philip Sidney[1]." In other letters to Wotton, Walsingham refers to the letters which Sidney has written to his friend giving him instructions from the Queen or Council.

In all references to Scottish affairs during this year Sir Philip's name is prominent[2]. We do not know that he ever visited Edinburgh or met the Scottish king, although the references to their relation to each other suggest personal acquaintance. Fulke Greville says that Sidney's service was affectionately devoted to James, from whom he received many pledges of love and favour. "Your king, whom indeed I love," is an expression taken from one of Sidney's letters to the Master of Grey[3]. One who had an interview with James immediately after the news of Zutphen reached Edinburgh reported that

"the hurt of Sir Philip Sidney is greatly lamented here and chiefly by the king himself, who greatly lamenteth, and so heartily sorry as I never saw him for any man. To-morrow his Majesty is determined to write to him[4]."

The first elegy in the memorial volume published by the University of Cambridge was by James. Writing to Queen Elizabeth a short time afterward, the King referred to Sir Philip as one "to whom I was so far beholden[5]." Years afterward James commended Sir Philip Sidney for the best and sweetest writer that ever he knew—"surely it seemeth he loved him much[6]." It is somewhat disturbing, especially if we have placed Sidney on a pinnacle of perfection, to reflect on the warmth of feeling and admiration which he gave to men like James VI, the Master of Grey, and Sir Christopher Hatton. Though of course our knowledge of his relations with them is limited, we may fairly infer that in the case of Grey and Hatton at least, Sir

---

[1] *The Hamilton Papers*, vol. II, August 26th, September 4th, September 10th.

[2] See, for example, two letters written by 'Yours Knawin' to Archibald Douglas on June 3rd and August 21st (*Salisbury MSS.*).

[3] Murdin, *op. cit.* p. 557.

[4] Roger Aston to Archibald Douglas, October 24, 1586 (*Salisbury MSS.*).

[5] *Letters of Elizabeth and James VI*, p. 54.

[6] *Declaration by Henry Leigh*, etc. (*Calendar of Border Papers*, vol. I), 1600, c. April 12th.

Philip had no real conception of the fact that they were in truth poor creatures raised by the accident of a monarch's favour into temporary prominence. Grey, contemptible time-server though he was, felt real affection for Sidney, and Hatton seems to have been unusually willing to serve him[1]. The truth is that Sir Philip's judgment of men was by no means profound. He was himself so generous and free from all contriving that he was little apt to suspect baseness except when it appeared in its darkest colours. He could never have hoped to emulate the practical worldly wisdom of his father-in-law or Burghley, and one wonders if Walsingham must not have sometimes found his son-in-law's detached, idealistic attitude to men and problems of State rather perplexing.

We may here conveniently notice several of Sir Philip's minor literary works, most of which probably date from the last two years which he spent in England and at least two of which were certainly written within a few months of his sailing for Holland. In Greville's letter to Walsingham mention is made, among other works of Sidney's, to "40 of the Psalms translated into myter." They remained in manuscript until 1823, when they were printed from "a copy of the original manuscript transcribed by John Davies of Hereford"—a member of the Countess of Pembroke's literary circle. In this manuscript the translation is described as "begun by the noble and learned gent., Sir Philip Sidney, Knt. and finished by the right honourable the Countess of Pembroke." Grosart's edition is printed from a Bodleian manuscript which the editor believes to have been "taken from a MS. of a scribe who copied under the superintendence of Sir Philip Sidney himself[2]." In the Bodleian MS. at the end of Psalm xliii. is written "Thus far Sir Philip Sidney." We have no clue as to the date of composition. There is no reason to suppose, as Mr Fox-Bourne does, that the brother and sister occupied themselves with the work during Sidney's long visit at Wilton : indeed Greville's silence regarding that portion of

---

[1] See letters of Walsingham to Hatton on April 26th and May 1st of this year, *Add. MSS.* 1589, fol. 153*b*.

[2] *Works*, vol. III, p. 72. Grosart also includes occasional readings from a MS. in Trinity College, Cambridge.

the translation which was done by the Countess suggests that it dates from a period subsequent to her brother's death[1]. Moreover, there is something incongruous in the idea of Sidney's being engaged on a translation of the Psalms during the months when he was producing his love sonnets and his *Arcadia*. It is more reasonable to assume, while other evidence is lacking, that his translations of religious works all date from the same general period, and there is good reason to believe that this was several years later, as we shall see.

Translations of the Psalms had appeared in large numbers, especially since the beginning of the Reformation in England. Christopher Tye, musical preceptor to Edward VI, had versified the *Acts of the Apostles*, and in dedicating it to his royal master he says :

> "Your grace may note, from tyme to tyme
> That some doth undertake :
> Upon the Psalmes to wryte in ryme
> The verse pleasaunt to make[2]."

No great measure of success crowned any of these efforts. Warton contemptuously refers to their authors as "the mob of religious rhymers who, from principles of the most unfeigned piety, devoutly laboured to darken the lustre, and enervate the force of the divine pages." The version of Sternhold and Hopkins, published in 1562, bad as it is, was by far the best known, but such eminent names as those of Sir Thomas Smith, Archbishop Parker, and Stanyhurst are in the list of translators. Of Sidney's rendering the best we can say is that it never falls to the level of the worst of his predecessors : in no case does it reach the level attained by him in many of his sonnets and songs. He probably undertook the work rather as a duty than in obedience to a poetic impulse. His admiration of the Psalms as literature is evidenced in several places in his *Apologie for Poetrie*, and he had come to reflect on the vanity of songs and sonnets, and on how much more worthily poetic ability might be employed "in singing the praises of the immortal beauty,

---

[1] Babington, chaplain to the Earl of Pembroke, is said to have assisted the Countess (Wood, *Athenæ*, II, col. 816).

[2] Quoted by Warton (*Hist. Eng. Poetry*, vol. IV, p. 149).

the immortal goodness of that God who giveth us hands to write and wits to conceive." His intimacy with many of the greatest contemporary men of letters in France suggests the possibility of his indebtedness to the version of Marot and Beza, but there is no similarity either in the form of stanzas or in phraseology.

The list of Sidney's acquaintances among French literary men is a long one. Languet, Estienne, Hotman, Pibrac, Ramus, L'Hôpital, Du Plessis, Le Moine—of these we know definitely, and there is good reason to suppose that Ronsard and Du Bartas should be added to the number. The latter paid to Sidney a compliment which in his own time was esteemed more highly than it is since Du Bartas' name has fallen from its high estate. In his second *Sepmaine* he eulogizes Sir Thomas More, Sir Nicholas Bacon and Sidney as the firm pillars of the English tongue :

> "Et le Milor Sydne, qui Cygne doux chantant
> Va les flots orgueilleux de Tamise flatant,
> Ce fleuue gros d'honneur emporte sa faconde
> Dans le sein de Thetis & Thetis par le monde[1]."

So boundless was the enthusiasm for Du Bartas' epic that something of the lustre of his name was reflected on Joshua Sylvester, the English translator of his works. Even Ben Jonson declared that " Bartas doth wish thy English now were his." In an address 'Lectoribus,' versified in pyramidal form, Sylvester announced that "England's Apelles (rather our Apollo) World's wonder Sidney, that rare more-than-man, This lovely Venus first to limn began, with such a pencil as no pen dares follow[2]." Florio says that he had seen Sidney's rendering of the first septmane of that arch-poet Du Bartas[3], and Ponsonby, the publisher, when he secured a licence to print the *Arcadia*, was at the same time licensed to print "A translation

---

[1] Edition of 1616, p. 484.

[2] Sylvester's *Bartas, His Devine Weekes and Workes Translated*, appeared in 1605.

[3] In the dedication of the second book of his *Montaigne* to Lady Rutland, Sidney's daughter, and Lady Rich (1603). He beseeches them to publish the translation.

of Salust de Bartas done by ye same Sir P. in the Englishe[1]."
It is also mentioned by Greville in his letter to Walsingham.
There is no record of its ever having been published, the
manuscript is not now known to exist, and we do not know
when Sidney did the work. In 1584 James VI of Scotland
had published his translation of Du Bartas' *Uranie*, and in
the same year Thomas Hudson under James' patronage published his version of the *Judith*. It is possible that acquaintance
with Sidney's work was one reason for the unusual favour which
James showed him.

Another French work the translation of which Sir Philip began
was his friend Du Plessis' *De la Vérité de la Religion Chrétienne*.
A complete English version was published a few months after
his death by Arthur Golding, and in the dedication[2] to Leicester,
Golding says that Sir Philip had "proceeded certain chapters"
in the work. "Being thus determined to follow the affairs of
Chivalry it was his pleasure to commit the performance of this
piece of service which he had intended to the Muses, or rather
to Christ's church and his native country, unto my charge."
How much of the work was done by Sir Philip has not been
determined. Mme Du Plessis simply says that he did her
husband the honour of translating the work into English[3].
Greville was evidently unaware of any arrangement between
Sir Philip and Golding. In the letter to Walsingham, from which
we have already quoted, he says :

"Besides he hath most excellently translated, among divers other notable
works, Monsieur Du Plessis' book against Atheism, which is since done
by an other ; so as both in respect of love between Plessis and him, besides
other affinities in their courses, but especially Sir Philip's uncomparable
judgment, I think fit there be made stay of that mercenary book, so that
Sir Philip might have all those religious works which are worthily due to
his life and death."

There would seem to be no solid grounds for Greville's suspicion
as to Golding's good faith, as there are none for the oft-repeated
statement that Golding was a "near friend" of Sidney. Greville

---

[1] Arber's *Stationers' Register*, II, p. 496.
[2] Dated May 13, 1587.   [3] *Mémoires*, p. 117.

was naturally jealous for his friend's reputation, and had not been informed by Sir Philip that he had requested Golding to complete his labours.

Another translation of Sir Philip's, the existence of which has been entirely forgotten, consisted of the first two books of Aristotle's *Rhetoric*. The fact that he actually translated it is preserved in John Hoskins' *Figures of Rhetoric*, where the writer declares that

"the understanding of Aristotle's *Rhetoric* is the directest means of skill to describe, to move, to appease or to prevent any mood whatsoever. Whereunto, whosoever can fit his speech shall be truly eloquent. This was my opinion ever, and Sir Philip Sidney betrayed his knowledge in this book of Aristotle to me before ever I knew that he had translated any part of it, for I found the 2 first books englished by him in the hands of the noble, studious Henry Wotton but lately."

It was probably never published. From what we know of Sir Philip's acquaintance with Greek it is not likely that his translation was made directly from the original. Sir Henry Wotton had no doubt become possessed of the manuscript through his elder brother, Edward, the friend of Sidney. Greville refers to "many other works" of Sir Philip than those which are now known, and it is not improbable that if we were acquainted with the whole *corpus* of his work we should have to modify our ideas both as to the extent of his literary activity and as to the breadth of his literary interests.

Perhaps the last piece of formal writing done by Sir Philip was *A Discourse in Defence of the Earl of Leicester*[1], in answer to an anonymous libel on the Earl, entitled *A Dialogue between a Scholar, a Gentleman and a Lawyer*. The authorship of this book was generally ascribed at the time to Parsons, the Jesuit, and was popularly known as *Father Parsons' Green Coat*, in allusion to the colour of the leaves. It gave a detailed account of all the crimes which the Earl had ever committed or been said to commit, and he was portrayed as the real governor of England which had become in effect Leicester's Commonwealth[2].

---

[1] First printed by Collins—*Memoirs*, pp. 62–68.
[2] Under this title the book was twice reprinted in 1641.

The book was printed abroad in 1584 and a French translation appeared in the following year.

The Council, by letters sent into all parts of the realm, ordered the immediate suppression of the libel, the Queen in her own clear knowledge declaring and testifying Leicester's innocency to all the world[1]. In his attack upon the unknown author Sir Philip passes lightly over the crimes wherewith his uncle was charged, and confines himself largely to the accusation that Leicester was of low birth.

"He hath not ancient nobility," the libel declared, "as other of our Realme have, whereby men's affections are greatly moved. His father, John Dudley, was the first noble of his line who raised and made himself big by supplanting of other and by setting debate among the nobility; as also his grandfather, Edmund, a most wicked promoter and wretched pettifogger enriched himself by other men's ruins, both of them condemned traitors....So that from his ancestors this Lord receiveth neither honour nor honesty but only succession of treason and infamy[2]."

Acknowledging himself proud that he was a Dudley in blood, Sir Philip recites the glories of his ancestors—Greys, Talbots, Beauchamps and Berkeleys,—and concludes by sending a challenge to the libeller, who, he declares, "lies in his throat." The reply was evidently written with the intention of publishing it, but its only effectiveness is of sound and fury, and Sir Philip may have been dissuaded from his first purpose.

Occupied as he was during this year with literary work, the Scottish business, and his duties in the Ordnance, Sir Philip probably knew that a larger field of activity was to be open to him at any moment. When in March the Dutch envoys received their definite repulse from Henry III, to whom they had offered the sovereignty of their country, and at whose Court they had spent weary months awaiting a reply, English statesmen were aware that the significance of their repulse was hardly less for England than for the Netherlands. Henry III and Catherine de' Medici were unwillingly forced to recognize that the power of the Guises and the Holy League was too great to allow France to assume the rôle of a protector of Protestants

[1] *State Papers—Dom.—Eliz.* Privy Council to Lord Mayor of London, June 26, 1585.

[2] P. 176 (1641 edition).

and a confessed enemy of Spain. For England this meant that the corner stone of her foreign policy during a quarter of a century was gone: in other words, if a Catholic continental league was imminent England must put herself at the head of a Protestant league. Accordingly, negotiations were at once begun, looking to England's definitely assuming the part of the champion of Dutch liberties. Ortel, the Dutch envoy in London, was in conference almost from day to day with Walsingham, Leicester, Burghley and the Queen, and in these negotiations Sidney was frequently an intermediary. According to the wont of Elizabeth's diplomacy there was prolonged haggling over the terms on which assistance was to be given. A formal deputation arrived from the Netherlands, the coming of which Elizabeth had arranged, and once more offered to her the sovereignty of their country. This offer she once more refused, but she promised to send men and money, demanding in return that the important coast towns of Flushing and Brill be temporarily handed over to the English as 'cautionary towns.' Ostensibly they were to be held by Elizabeth as security for the repayment of whatever sums of money she might advance ; nevertheless, the Dutch hesitated, feeling vaguely uneasy as to the Queen's real motives. As a result, England affected coolness, and the Dutch likewise pretended that they might possibly choose another course if their present offers were refused.

For a time it looked as if there might be no actual alliance after all.

"As for the news here," Lord Talbot wrote to his father from the Court at the middle of July, "they are more uncertain than the weather, and it is not possible your Lordship should know anything but doubtfulness of the proceedings in the Low Country matters as yet, but within a very few days they will be resolved, and in the meantime every one may guess as he list, and I for my poor part believe that some five or six thousand footmen shall be sent, and no horsemen, although Sir Philip Sidney be so far prepared to take the charge of five hundred[1]."

Walsingham was ill in his house at Barn Elms and Sir Philip was in constant conference with Ortel. It was generally assumed that he would take an important command in the

[1] *Belvoir MSS.*, July 14, 1585.

English army when it should be sent, and Leicester had already
assured the Dutch envoys that he was ready, if her Majesty
chose to make use of him, to go over in person, and place life,
property and all the assistance he could gain from his friends,
upon the issue. The handing over of Flushing was the great
obstacle. By August 26th, however, Walsingham was able to
write to Wotton :

"Mr. Davison was yesterday despatched from the Court unto them of
Holland and Zealand to assure them that her Majesty will furnish them
with five thousand footmen and one thousand horse, according to their
own demand, and that a nobleman shall be sent over unto them—all
which is to be performed presently, when her Majesty shall understand that
they are content to deliver into her hands the towns of Flushing and Brill,
whereof it is thought they will make no difficulty, if my Lord of Leicester
may have the charge of the army and Sir Philip Sidney of Flushing[1]."

While the petty bargaining thus went on Antwerp was lost—
an event of such importance that in the judgment of many
well-informed observers of events it marked the close of serious
opposition to Spanish dominion in the Low Countries. The
Dutch now accepted all of Elizabeth's conditions, only to find
her still irresolute. She insisted that the garrisons of Flushing
and Brill should be included in the number of troops which
she had promised to furnish, and on this point too the Dutch
yielded. The Queen still hesitated for some weeks as to her
choice of officers for the expedition. At first it was taken
for granted that Leicester should go. Then Lord Grey was
proposed. Even late in September Leicester wrote Walsingham that the Queen was desirous that he should remain
in England. She was doubtful of herself by reason of her
often disease and last night worst of all. She used very pitiful
words to him and feared she should not live and would not
have him from her. A few days later she was resolved on his
going[2].

Elizabeth's irresolution regarding a choice of Governor for
Flushing seems to have been even harder to overcome, and led
Sir Philip to take a desperate resolution.

---

[1] *The Hamilton Papers*, August 26, 1585.
[2] *State Papers—Dom.—Eliz.*, vol. CLXXXII, September 21st, September 24th.

"Sir Philip hath taken a very hard resolution," Walsingham wrote to Davison, the English ambassador in the Netherlands, "to accompany Sir Francis Drake in this voyage, moved thereto for that he saw her Majesty disposed to commit the charge of Flushing unto some other; which he reputed would fall out greatly to his disgrace, to see another preferred before him, both for birth and judgment inferior unto him. The despair thereof and the disgrace that he doubted he should receive have carried him into a different course[1]."

Greville says that Drake's expedition was of Sir Philip's own projecting, that they had agreed that both should equally be governors when they had left the shore of England, but that while things were preparing at home Sir Francis was to bear the name, and by the credit of Sir Philip have all particulars abundantly supplied. We must assume that Greville's affection for his friend caused his memory to play him false here, when we remember the short time that intervened between Sir Philip's first confident expectation that he should go to Flushing and the date of Walsingham's letter quoted above. According to a pre-arranged plan Drake sent a letter post for Sir Philip informing him that the fleet was at Plymouth and awaited only him and a fair wind. Sir Philip set out at once under colour of going to meet Don Antonio, who was expected to land at Plymouth. But the real cause of his going had been noised about. A correspondent of the Earl of Rutland wrote him from the Court:

"Sir Philip Sidney's departing with Sir Francis Drake was so fully advertised her Majesty as it pleased her to command Mr. Vice-Chamberlain to write three letters, one to himself to command his immediate return, the other to Sir Francis to forbid him the receiving of him in his fleet, the third to the Mayor of Plymouth to write him to see this performed accordingly; and that if they were already gone some bark should be sent after with the letters. This messenger was one Hyts whom I think your Lordship knows, one serving my Lady Drury, who was despatched accordingly, and when he was within 4 miles of Plymouth he was surprised by four mariners and his letters taken from him; the which being opened and read were sent him again. Since when, one Prynne, who attendeth Don Antonio, is come from thence with letters from his master and Sir Philip, and now it is said Sir Philip never meant to go, but stayeth there

[1] *State Papers—Dom.—Eliz.*, September 13, 1585.

to see the ships set forth. Yet the bruit runneth on stilts in London and amongst many courtiers that Sir Francis is gone and Sir Philip too[1]."

The story is amplified for us by Fulke Greville, who had accompanied Sir Philip to Plymouth in the expectation of sailing with him. Drake received them with much pomp and feasting, but Greville perceived that their presence was embarrassing to him. He declares that Drake made many excuses for not sailing and in the meantime sent a post to the Queen. The mariners who intercepted her messenger were in the pay of Sir Philip, to whom they brought the letters. A second messenger to him was a peer of the realm, who delivered to him a more imperial mandate "carrying with it in the one hand grace, the other, thunder." The grace had to do with his appointment as Governor of Flushing. So magnanimous was Sir Philip that, overlooking Drake's duplicity toward himself, he made a plausible address to Drake's sailors with the object of preserving untarnished their leader's reputation and insuring the success of the voyage.

Such is Fulke Greville's account. On September 21st the same correspondent of the Earl of Rutland wrote him: "This day Sir Philip Sidney was with her Majesty who receiveth it for a truth from himself that he never meant to go[2]." We must reconcile this statement as best we can with what information we already possess. Sir Philip had probably little difficulty in making his peace under the circumstances ; the Queen could easily forgive those whom she thwarted. She was highly amused by a letter from Don Antonio confessing that he too had planned to sail with Drake in order to bear Sir Philip company[3].

There was no further question made regarding Sidney's appointment although the letters patent were not issued until November 9th[4]. Throughout September and October he

[1] *Belvoir MSS.* John Stanhope to Earl of Rutland, Nonsuch, September 12, 1585.

[2] *Belvoir MSS., ut supra.*

[3] *Spanish State Papers* (1580–1586), October 8, 1585. Mendoza to King Philip.

[4] Minutes of the letters patent which were to be made, are in the *Holland Correspondence*, vol. v, fols. 4 and 5 (uncalendared). By the erasures in this draft it appears that Thomas Cecil was Sir Philip's rival for the Flushing

was much busied in preparing for his departure, in conferences
with Leicester and Walsingham, and in levying a company of
soldiers in Wales. On November 10th he was at Gravesend,
whence he sent to the Queen a cipher alphabet in accordance
with Her Majesty's command. It is, he writes, such as little
leisure would afford him[1]. Her Majesty bestowed on him a
final mark of favour by consenting to become the godmother
of his little daughter, but the christening ceremony was for
some reason delayed until two days after Sir Philip had reached
Flushing. In the register of baptisms in St Olave's, Hart
Street, is the entry: "1585, November 20, the daughter of Sir
Philip Sidney, Knight[2]." In an account book of expenses of
the royal household we have two items referring to the event:

"Item.—Paid to Richard Brackenbury, one of the ordinary gentlemen
ushers of her Majesty's chamber, to be by him distributed and given
by way of her Majesty's reward to the nurse and midwife, at the christening
of Sir Philip Sidney his daughter, to whom her Majesty was godmother,
the sum of 100s.

Item.—Paid to Richard Brackenbury, one of the ordinary gentlemen
ushers of her Majesty's chamber, for the allowance of himself, one groom
of the chamber, and one groom of the wardrobe, for riding from the court
at Richmond to London, to make ready for her Majesty, against the christening of Sir Philip Sidney his daughter, by the space of four days, mensis
Novem. 1585, as appeareth by a bill signed by the Lord Chamberlain,
66s. 8d.[3]"

The child was of course named Elizabeth. The exact date of
her birth has not been discovered. Hunter has a note to the
effect that

"the date of her birth is very precisely fixed by the Inq. on her father's
death which sets forth that at time of his death, October 17, 1586, she
was aged 2 years, 8 months and 18 days, according to which she would
be born January 31, 1583/4[4]."

governorship and that Sir Philip was to be given Brill. The appointments
were finally made of Sidney to Flushing and Cecil to Brill. Sidney's letters
patent are on folio 39.

[1] *Salisbury MSS.* (*Hist. MSS. Com. Reports*).

[2] *Collectanea Topographica et Genealogica*, vol. ii, p. 311.

[3] *Harleian MS.* 1641. On the same folio are similar items referring to
the baptisms of the son of the French ambassador in March and the son of
Mr William Howard in October.

[4] *Chorus Vatum*, p. 18 (*Add. MS.* 24490).

This is manifestly incorrect, but it has been generally accepted as the correct date[1].   How the error arose it is difficult to see, but the matter is settled by a letter written to Sir Robert Sidney by his highly intelligent agent Rowland Whyte on March 3, 1599, *i.e.* 1600, when Elizabeth Sidney had become Countess of Rutland.   Whyte has heard that the Duke intends to sell his wife's lands.

"Your Lordship," he writes "may do well to have an eye unto it, and suffer not yourself to be persuaded to confirm any act of your niece's, for until she be XXI (which will not be yet these 6 years) no act of hers is good, and you the assured heir in remainder[2]."

Since a legal point is involved, we may be sure that Whyte would be particularly accurate in his statement, and we may accept his letter as proof that Elizabeth Sidney was born in 1585.   In that year Scipio Gentili, the great jurist and Oxford Professor of Law published in London a poem on her birth— *Nereus, sive de natali Elizabethae illustriss. Phillippi Sydnaei filiae.*

Before leaving England Sir Philip chose as his private secretary Mr William Temple, a well-known enthusiast for the Ramist logic, who had published in 1584 at the University Press, Cambridge, an annotated edition of Ramus's *Dialectica* in the original Latin.   The book was dedicated to Sir Philip. Temple afterward became provost of Trinity College, Dublin, and he increased his claim to be remembered by becoming the grandfather of the famous Sir William Temple.

[1] See, for example, Sir Sidney Lee's article on Sidney in the *Dictionary of National Biography*.

[2] *Sidney Papers*, vol. II. 7, 174.   See also pp. 83 and 120.

CHAPTER XIX

THE NETHERLANDS

WHAT was Elizabeth's real object in sending her troops to the Netherlands ? On our answer to this question depends our interpretation of the whole course of the war. It is essential that we remember how far she was from sympathizing with the aspirations of the revolted provinces to be free from the domination of Spain. To Elizabeth they were rebels whose undoubtedly rightful master was Philip of Spain, and of this fact she never lost sight. She was willing to assist them to extort from Spain such a measure of toleration as she accorded to her own Catholic subjects—no more. Should Spain at any moment show her willingness to conclude the war on these terms there is not the slightest doubt that Elizabeth would have promptly withdrawn her troops from the Netherlands. Not without hope of reaching such a solution she intended to send her troops, but she intended no less to paralyze their activity, once they had arrived, by sending them neither money nor supplies except in driblets. Perhaps their effectiveness was paralyzed even more completely by the constant rumours that England and Spain were negotiating a treaty of peace and that the Dutch would be left to their fate. Nor were such rumours entirely without foundation. Walsingham, in a letter of October 26th to Burghley, referred to the evil consequences of the Queen's irresolution in the whole affair, and pointed out that Her Majesty might compose matters with Spain with greater advantage now that she had Flushing and Brill[1]. There is little doubt that this consideration was present to the mind of Her Majesty when she insisted on being given possession of the cautionary towns, and she was prepared to equivocate in

[1] *State Papers—Dom.—Eliz.*, October 26, 1585.

her interpretation of that article in the contract which defined the conditions under which peace might be made. Furthermore, agents of the Duke of Parma were actually for some time in London seeking to find the basis of an agreement with Elizabeth, until Walsingham discovered their presence and made impossible the continuance of this kind of negotiation.

In sending assistance to the Netherlands Elizabeth and her ministers were well aware that their action was tantamount to a declaration of war with Spain. To avoid such a war, or at least to postpone it as long as possible, had been the most fundamental principle of the Queen's foreign policy for a quarter of a century, but it had now become obvious that for a number of reasons the inevitable struggle was near at hand. Diplomatic relations between the two Courts had long been strained to the very point of breaking; they had not been formally broken off, only because Philip wished to have done with his troubles in the Low Countries before undertaking the English enterprise, and because Elizabeth counted as gain each year that elapsed before the final contest. If Philip failed to give her satisfaction for the wrongs inflicted on Englishmen within the domains of Spain, she knew how to indemnify herself in less formal fashion. She openly encouraged what was fast becoming one of the most popular of English games—that of singeing the King of Spain's beard, nor did she take much trouble to conceal the fact that she was personally the chief stockholder in such piratical expeditions. When in November, 1583, she discovered that Mendoza was the directing spirit of the Throgmorton plot, and expelled him with scant ceremony, Philip showed no more resentment than did Elizabeth when Mendoza was at once appointed Spanish ambassador at Paris. Nevertheless it was impossible that such a relationship between the two countries should continue indefinitely. Elizabeth knew that for the past twenty years Spain had meditated a descent on England in favour of the English Catholics and Mary Stuart, and although she hated war she knew that sooner or later such an attack was inevitable. Moreover she now felt able to meet it, and she was probably not ignorant of the fact that Philip, goaded to desperation by the insults and injuries to which

England had subjected him, had at last overcome his constitutional inertia to the point of drawing up a very definite scheme for the conquest of England, whereby Elizabeth was to be disposed of in some vague way, Mary Stuart was to ascend the throne as the wife of the Prince of Parma, and no religion but Catholicism was to be tolerated. In this plot for the future government of England Philip's reputation for far-sightedness finds its justification, for he even went into the question of the succession to the English throne in the event of no children being born to Parma and Mary Stuart.

When Elizabeth finally decided to send assistance to Philip's rebellious subjects it must not be supposed that she was actuated by any love of liberty or Protestantism or by any special sympathy for a brave people who were seeking to shake off the grasp of the tyrant. She considered the Netherlanders and their master equally absurd in their magnifying of the religious question into a position of such importance, and her active sympathy, such as it was, she reserved for England. She had as little interest in fanatical quarrels as she had in altruistic projects. She did not want to send troops into Holland, and the sovereignty of the Netherlands she consistently rejected. Sovereignty was likely to prove a mere excuse for draining England's resources, and even the sending of troops would cost money which it might be hard to collect from the Netherlanders. Elizabeth had approved of the Duke of Alençon's assuming the sovereignty, for by his instrumentality France might be persuaded to bear the cost of keeping Philip occupied in the Netherlands ; she had later favoured a joint protectorate of England and France, trusting in such an arrangement to be able to place upon the shoulders of Henry III a considerable part of the burden of maintaining the war. When this latter scheme failed she had even viewed with considerable equanimity the embassy which had gone to Paris to offer the sovereignty of the revolted provinces to the French King. When, after months of hesitation, Henry at length recognized that the strength of the Holy League in France would make it impossible for him to assume the protection of rebellious Protestants, Elizabeth felt that she was practically forced to do the work

herself. Otherwise Spain would soon be unhampered in her
projected invasion of England.

The momentous character of the decision was fully realized
by the Queen and her ministers, and they had published in
English, Dutch, French and Italian *A Declaration of the Causes
moving the Queen of England to give aid to the defence of the people
afflicted and oppressed in the Low Countries*. The 'Declaration'
reads as if it were the Queen's own composition :

> "Although Kings and princes sovereign owing their homage and service
> only unto the Almighty God, the King of all Kings, are in that respect
> not bound to yield account or render the reasons of their actions unto
> any others but to God, their only sovereign Lord : yet (though amongst
> the most ancient and Christian monarchs the same Lord God having
> committed to us the sovereignty of this Realm of England and other our
> dominions, which we hold immediately of the same Almighty Lord, and
> so thereby accountable only to his Divine Majesty) we are notwithstanding
> this our prerogative at this time specially moved for divers reasons here-
> after briefly remembered, to publish not only to our own natural loving
> subjects but also to all others our neighbours," etc., etc.

The close friendship that had long existed between the Low
Countries and England, witnessed in many commercial treaties,
is rehearsed. The liberties of those countries had been destroyed
by the Spaniards, at first on the pretext of suppressing Protestantism. Later, however, Catholics had been persecuted
almost as much; witness the execution of Egmond, the very
glory of that country. The French King would have given
aid to the Netherlanders had it not been for the growing power
of the house of Guise. Elizabeth had made many friendly
representations on the subject to the King of Spain "as a good
loving sister to him," but Spain was evidently bent on the
utter destruction of Dutch liberties. How King Philip had
repaid the friendly offices of his good, loving sister might be
seen in the fact of his having sent troops into Ireland a few years
since. Mendoza's intimate connection with the Throgmorton
plot is recounted in detail.

In sending English troops into the Low Countries the Queen
declared that her object was threefold,—to secure "the end of
wars with restitution of the Low Countries to their ancient
liberties, surety from invasion of her own realm, and renewing

of the mutual traffic between the countries." She had taken over the cautionary towns to secure "sure access and recess of our people and soldiers in safety." The document was virtually a declaration of war against Spain. Henceforward there was no pretence of keeping up the formal relations which subsist between friendly powers.

Elated as Sir Philip doubtless was with his appointment and the prospect it held out of an opportunity to fight for the cause he loved, we may imagine that the sinister rumours which were in circulation must have been disquieting enough. He was gratified to know that Count Maurice, the son of William the Silent, had concurred in the temporary transfer to the English, of Flushing, a town of which he was hereditary seignor and proprietor, and before sailing he received a message from the generous-hearted boy (he was now eighteen years old) in which he begged Sir Philip to consider him as his brother and companion in arms. The news from Holland on the whole, however, was not reassuring. St Aldegonde, late burgomaster of Antwerp, was suspected and not without cause, for the devotion of a life-time was insufficient in the eyes of his country-men to atone for his present error of judgment in believing that Spain might be persuaded to grant toleration, and the Provinces return to their allegiance. He was living in his house near Middelburg and by many was held to be a traitor. Since the death of the Prince of Orange he was the only man capable of leading the States as a whole, and their present leaderless condition had resulted in much disorder. Then there were clashes between the Dutch and English authorities, and among the English authorities themselves. Two days before Sir Philip reached Flushing, Davison, her Majesty's resident ambassador in that town, wrote to him the following letter[1]:

"Your long stay doth very much amaze and trouble us, and the more in that we can hear nothing in the meantime of y [our proceedings][2]. It is a shame to think how things are handled. Of three or four months the companies have been here they have not had above one month's pay,

[1] *Holland Correspondence*, vol. v, fol. 75. Davison's wife was descended from the Guildfords, on account of which relationship Sir Philip usually addressed him as 'Cousin.'

[2] The letter is injured by damp.

many of them are already wasted with hunger's miseries, and but for the straining of mine own poor credit had been at this time utterly broken and disordered. At our coming into this town I found mean to pay these garrisons for an outgo which already spent and the poor men in want I am driven off now by the Treasurer's stay to try my poor credit for some £1400 or £1500 more to relieve both them and others. The charge of the Rammekins I committed to Captain Huntley (a gentleman I knew you loved and trusted well) till your coming. Mr Edward Norris [........] in the place hath procured warrant brought hither to dislodge him which I would not suffer till your coming. The charge of this burgh in the meantime left to myself by her Majesty's express commandment and warrant. This is the beginning of a faction which your presence will soon determine. If you make no other choice of captains and officers than you shall find here you shall do wrong to your own honour and her Majesty's service. Captain Williams hath tarried here these ten or twelve days in a hope and longing to see you. St Aldegonde continueth at his house yet unmolested. Colonel Maurice is to be here within two or three days to attend my Lord of Leicester. He is newly confirmed in his government of Holland and Zealand[1] before [........] The General remaineth before Nimeguen having fortified upon the river and against it, from whence he [.....] into the town. The bruit is they should be in part with him ; I pray you that be not also the manner of Zutphen. The force is not above 5000 strong. The enemy is gone thitherward with eight or nine thousand footmen and eight or ten cornets of horse, resolved to attack them if that be possible. We are afraid my Lord of Leicester's journey be cooled if his Lordship do not follow you all the sooner. I hope at your coming to make a start home. Praying therefore to God so much the rather for your happy and speedy passage, etc."

Sir Philip could not have received this letter before leaving England, for it was written only on the day that he sailed, but some five days earlier Davison had written a similar account to Walsingham, and we may therefore be sure that Sir Philip was familiar with the details of the quarrel. As soon as Davison had appointed Captain Huntley to take charge of the Rammekins General Norris sent to the Captain the following warrant :

"Whereas I am given to understand that my Lord Ambassador hath appointed you to remain in the Rammekins contrary to his instructions from her Majesty and the agreement that was between his Lordship and myself : These be therefore to will and require you to receive into the said castle of the Rammekins Captain Edward Norris and his company, and that you yourself with the company make your present repair unto

[1] *i.e.* as permanent Stadtholder.

Flushing there to accomplish such direction as the said Edward Norris shall give you. And this fail ye not to do as you will answer to the contrary at your peril. From the camp this 2nd of November anno 1585, *stylo Anglico*. John Norris[1]."

Huntley, not knowing whom to obey, wrote to Walsingham that he was commanded one thing by the General, but "my Lord Ambassador commands me in her Majesty's name to stay and answer for the place until Sir Philip Sidney's arrival. I know not what they mean, the General offering me great wrong undeserved[2]." Edward Norris also wrote wishing that Sir Philip and Sir Thomas Cecil (who had been appointed to the governorship of Brill) "might have the hearing of these things and advertise your honour of the truth." "I have so many controllers of my doings at this time," he complained, "that I must yield to their opinions attending the coming of the Earl of Leicester which must reform our doings or else we shall have little credit by them." Here was a state of anarchy indeed, and Sir Philip may well have had misgivings as to whether his presence would have the magical effect foretold by Davison.

On November 16th Sir Philip, leaving his wife and little daughter in the household of his father-in-law, sailed for Flushing. With him were his brother Robert and a small party of his friends and attendants: his company of 200 soldiers, which was being levied in the counties of South Wales[3], was not yet complete and did not reach the Netherlands until a month later. In the work of furnishing his cornet of lances many of his friends—the Earl of Rutland[4], Sir Moyle Finch[5], Sir Edward Stradling[6] and others—had come to his assistance by contributing each a good horse from his stable. After a

---

[1] *Holland Correspondence*, vol. v, November 16, 1585.

[2] *Ibid.* November 13, 1585.

[3] *Add. MSS.* 5753, f. 276. Fulke Greville had been appointed by Leicester to the command of a cornet, but at the last moment the Queen forbade him to go.

[4] *Belvoir MSS.* Roger Manners to Earl of Rutland, November 10, 1585 (*Hist. Man. Com. Reports*).

[5] Sir Philip to Sir Moyle Finch. *Penshurst MS.*—a copy of *Finch MS.*

[6] Walsingham to Sir Edward Stradling, January 11, 1586. *Stradling Correspondence*, ed. J. M. Traherne, London, 1840.

rough passage Sir Philip reached Walcheren on Thursday, November 18th, but owing to the stress of weather he was compelled to land at the Rammekins and proceed to Flushing on foot.   He was " the welcomer that he brought money[1]."   He

"was not so entertained and received," wrote William Borlas to Walsingham, "as I think he should have been if the weather had not fallen out so foul, by means whereof he was constrained to land three miles beyond the town and come afoot from the Rammekins hither which is almost four miles from this place. And so the Captains with their soldiers and the rest of the town received him in such manner as the time would permit. Upon Sunday, the 21st of this present, the Governor dined at the State House, where he was very honourably entertained according to their country's manner, where he took his oath, and the 22nd of this present he went to the State House again, where they in like manner took their oaths unto her Majesty and to him as Governor. And thus he hath from time to time very carefully employed himself in looking into the state of the town, which he doth find in some place to be very weak and the garrison to be very small for so great a town, for that there is almost 200 of the soldiers sick in the hospital, and I think 1000 to be too few for so great a town[2]."

Sir Philip took up his residence with M. Gelee, a citizen of the town and " one of good reckoning among the inhabitants," for both officers and soldiers lodged with the burghers as there were no barracks. Mindful of the strange hesitations and shiftings which had recently characterized the Queen's policy, he did not enter on his task as light-heartedly as he might otherwise have done ; nevertheless, he realised that he had had committed to his care a city the strategic importance of which was not surpassed by that of any other in the Netherlands, and he set to work at once to put his charge into as good order as possible. Situated at the mouth of the Scheldt, Flushing commanded the water commerce of Antwerp and the other Scheldt cities ; it was " the key to the navigation of the north Seas," and that its safety should be absolutely beyond question was of the highest importance. Naturally this was the first question to which the new Governor gave his attention, and he was soon immersed in the multifarious business of his office. Four days after landing he wrote to Leicester an account of

[1] Doyley to Walsingham (Wright, II, 270).
[2] *Holland Correspondence*, vol. v, November 23, 1585.

the situation as he found it, in which is revealed his eagerness to accomplish some worthy work, as also his resourcefulness and capacity.

"Right honourable, my singular good Lord: Upon Thursday we came into this town, driven to land at Rammekins because the wind began to rise in such sort as our masters durst not enter before the town, and from thence came with as dirty a walk as ever poor governor entered his charge withal. I find the people very glad of me, and promise myself as much surety in keeping the town as [the] popular good-will gotten by light hopes and [....] by [....] as slight conceits may breed me, for indeed the garrison is far too weak to command by authority which is pity, for how great a jew[el] this is to the Crown of England and the queen's safety I need not write it to your Lordship who knows it so well. Yet I must needs say the better I know it the more I find the preciousness of it. I have sent to Mr Norris for my cousin Scot's company, for Colonel Morgan's, and my brother's (which I mean to put in the Rammekins), but I doubt I shall but change and not increase the ensigns by any more than mine own company, for fear of breeding jealousies in the people which is carried more by shows than substance. And therefore the way must be rather to increase the number of men in each company than the companies, and that may be done easily enough with their good liking. But I mean to innovate as little as may be till your Lordship's coming, which is here longed for as Messias is of the Jews. But indeed most necessary it is that your Lordship make great speed to reform both the Dutch and English abuses. I am more and more persuaded that with that proportion which her Majesty alloweth, the country is fully able to maintain the wars, if what they do be well ordered and not abused as it is by the States, and that they look for at your Lordship's hands, it being sh[own] that the people show themselves far more careful than the governors in all things touching the public.

The taking of the sconces by Mr Norris was of good moment, but now his lying before Nymegen is greatly feared will both waste his men (besides the danger of the enemy who very strongly marcheth that way) and little prevail, there being a great riv[er] between him and the city. But the great sufficiency of the gentleman may overweigh other conjectures. Mr Edward Norris delivered the companies here unto me whom he had very well and soldierly governed, but the companies indeed very sickly and miserable. Good my Lord, haste away if you do come, for, all things considered, I had rather you came n[ot] at all than came not quickly, for only by yo[ur] own presence those courses may be stopped whic[h] if they run on will be past remedy.

Here is [St] Aldegonde, a man greatly suspected but by no man charged. He lives restrained to his [own] house, and, for aught I can find, deals with[h] nothing, only desiring to have his ca[use] wholly reserved to your Lordship. And therefore with t[he] best heed I can to his proceedings I will leave h[im] to his clearing or condemning when your Lordship sha[ll] hear him.

I think truly if my coming ha[d] been longer delayed some alteration would ha[ve] followed, for the truth is the people is weary [of] war, and if they do not see such a course taken as may be likely to defend them the[y] will in a sudden give over the cause. They have newly made Count Maurice Governor of Holla[nd] and Zealand, which only grew by the delays of your Lordship's coming, but I cannot perceive a[ny] meaning of either diminishing or crossing your Lordship's authority, but rather that the Count means wholly to depend upon your Lordship's authority.

With £3000 charges I could find means so to lodge myself and soldiers in this town as would [in] an extremity command it, where now we are at their mercies. [The] enemy threatens divers places as Ostend, Sluys, [B]ergen and Bornel, but yet we have no certain news what he will attempt, but whatsoever it be there is great likelihood he will endanger it, the soldiers are so evil paid and provided of everything that is necessary. I have dealt earnestly with the States of Zealand for the relief of Ostend, but yet can obtain nothing but delays. I conclude all will be lost if government be not presently used.

Mr Davison is here, very careful in her Majesty's causes and in your Lordship's; he takes great pains therein and goes to great charges for it. I am yet so new here that I cannot write so important matters as perhaps hereafter I shall, and therefore I will not any further triflingly trouble your Lordship, but humbly leave you to the blessed protection of the Almighty. At Flushing this 22nd of November, 1585.

Your Lordship's most humble and obedient nephew,
PHILIP SIDNEY.

Edward Norris, as [li]kewise his brother, put great [ho]pe in your Lordship, which I have thought good to nourish because I think it fit for your Lordship's service. Mr Edward would fain have charge of horses, and for that cause will seek to erect a company here. I am beholding to this bearer, Captain Fenton[1]."

The Flushing garrison consisted of the companies of Captain Edward Norris, Captain Willford, Captain Wingfield, and Captain Huntley, and to these was now added that of Sir Philip, while Robert Sidney's company was stationed in the Rammekins[2]. They were described by the treasurer Huddlestone

---

[1] *Cotton MSS.* Galba, C. VIII, 213. The *lacunæ* are owing to the fact that the edge of the MS. has been burned.

[2] The companies of Captain Errington and Captain Hender were shortly after added to the Flushing garrison. *Holland Correspondence*, vol. v, f. 309.

in a letter to Burghley as "the worst accommodated of all our soldiers, amongst a people of a froward and perverse disposition. At the Brill," he added, "they are far more tractable and willing to obey[1]." Nearly two hundred of the soldiers were sick in the hospital, and none of the bands had their full complement of men. The muster-master described them as "weak, bad-furnished, ill-armed and worse-trained[2]." The great strategic importance of the town and the inhospitable attitude of the burghers made the weakness of the garrison a matter of the gravest concern. "If anything should fall out between the townsmen and us," wrote Burnham to Walsingham, "we are likelier to be governed than that Sir Philip should govern them. To prevent the practices of such as stand ill-affected it were good to reinforce it[3]."

Nor was the inadequate garrison Sir Philip's only concern in his new government; the defences of the town were in an even more disheartening condition. The muster-master reported to Walsingham

"that surely the rampiers and bulwarks were delivered in very bad case, the barriers in many places fallen to ground, the sentinel and *cours de garde* house badly repaired and most beastly defiled in most loathsome manner, by whose fault I will not say, the ordinary in very bad case having neither good caring nor platforms. But I hope," he continued, "that by the good orders and laws that shall shortly be established by the Governor many of these defaults shall be mended and the town kept in other state than it is at this present."

As an expert on fortification he gave it as his opinion that it was "utterly impossible with this garrison to hold it (Flushing) against any royal force,"—and this in spite of Sir Philip's excellent qualifications[4]. In a more detailed report to Sir Philip himself he pointed out that the chief strength of the town consisted in its situation, the ground round about for a great distance being so low that it might every spring-tide be drowned by the sea. Yet he would not wish too

---

[1] *Holland Correspondence*, vol. VI, January 21, 1586.
[2] *Ibid.* January 2, 1586, Thos. Digges to Walsingham.
[3] *Ibid.* December 27, 1585.
[4] *Ibid.* vol. V, November 23, 1585.

much security reposed on that natural strength. He advises that

"all the platforms for the ordnance be well repaired, the carriages amended, the ordnance well-mounted, and some convenient number of gunners appointed to give their attendance on their pieces....Then so soon as the season of the year will permit that the barriers and ruinate rampiers be re-edified and well sanded round, that the soldiers may march dry upon them. The *Corps du garde* and sentinels also to be repaired, and some severe orders to keep them clean and sweet, and not in such loathsome manner as at this present they are."

He concluded, however, that a much more radical and costly 'plot' for strengthening the town was highly desirable[1].

Here was work sufficient, one would suppose, to engage the attention of the governor for some time, but almost immediately he was called away to other duties. He had been in Flushing only three or four days when an advertisement came that the veteran La Motte, Governor of Gravelines, with 27 ensigns of foot and three or four cornets of horse had arrived at Blankenburg, a town situated on the sea-side mid-way between Ostend and Sluys, and that his object was to capture Ostend. At the same time Sir Philip received letters from Captain Errington, the Governor of Ostend—now an old man and one of Sir Philip's warmest friends—that he suspected some practice for the enemy within the town, where a majority of the inhabitants were Catholics, and where both munitions and food were very short. Sir Philip at once dispatched a messenger to Count Hohenlo, the general of the Dutch forces, and to the States of Zealand, urging them to send munitions and another agent into Holland to buy armour. He then sent his brother, Captain Willford, Captain Hungate and Captain Wingfield to meet the enemy. The next day Sir Philip learned that La Motte had marched to Ostend and laid siege to the town, but the danger passed within a few days when La Motte changed his mind and withdrew[2]. That the danger had been real, however, no one could doubt, for the town—one of the most important remaining in the hands of the patriots—was as ill able to resist an attack

---

[1] *Ibid.* vol. v, f. 150 and f. 141.
[2] *Ibid.* vol. v, Digges to Walsingham, December 2, 1585.

as was Flushing. So great was Captain Errington's fear of internal treachery that he had refused permission to any of his English companies to pass the gates for the purpose of meeting the enemy.

"This garrison hath so spoiled the country hereabouts," wrote Robert Sidney to Leicester, "that almost for twenty miles riding every way there is never a house standing nor never a man out of a walled town to be seen....Here is want of all things—no victuals in store for above twenty days ; if a soldier should break his pike or his halbert not any here to furnish him ; of powder not 12,000 weight whereof five is not serviceable, all our victual must come from Flushing and out of Holland, and that is very dear....The men of war of Dunkirk lie so up and down here as without danger no small bark can pass."

For four months the garrison had received no pay, with the result that "there cannot be more hate conceived than the Governor and Dutch captains here bear the States. Your Lordship's coming," Robert concluded, "is wonderfully looked and wished for everywhere[1]." Until Leicester should arrive— an event which it was popularly hoped would work wonders— Sir Philip was occupied in trying to improve the condition of his garrison. He was in consultation with Edward Norris and Davison as to the best way of mustering and paying the companies conformably to the order of the English Council[2], and was forced to borrow £300 'at usance' to relieve their most immediate necessities[3]. He found General Norris rather difficult to persuade to his point of view regarding the strengthening of the Flushing garrison by adding to it Colonel Morgan's regiment, but in Davison he had a good friend, and Count Hohenlo approved of the young governor's plans[4].

On Friday, December 10th, Leicester reached Flushing, after a favourable one day passage from Harwich. He was accompanied by a large number of young English knights and noblemen—Lord North, the Earl of Essex, Lord Audeley, Lord Willoughby, Sir William Russell, and many others, including Thomas Sidney ; they had crossed in two parties—

---

[1] *Ibid.* November 29, 1585.
[2] *Ibid.*, Norris to Walsingham, November 28, 1585.
[3] *Harleian MSS.* Sir Philip to Walsingham, December 9, 1585.
[4] *Ibid.* Sir Philip to Davison, December 7, 1585.

one from Harwich, the other from Gravesend, in some fifty vessels. There were probably 3000 soldiers all told, but according to contemporary Spanish reports Sir William Stanley and Sir Henry Harrington had each 1500 men from Ireland, the Master of Grey 600 from Scotland, and altogether the Queen of England had sent a mighty force to check the Prince of Parma's victorious career[1]. In Flushing they were received by Count Maurice and Sir Philip, and Leicester was escorted to his lodgings with a very considerable amount of civil and military pomp. He remained in the town only one day—" to inform himself thoroughly of the state of the garrison and to give such direction to his nephew Sidney for the supply and reinforcing thereof as he deemed expedient"—to quote the words of his report to the Council. On the evening of his arrival Count Maurice with others of the States Council visited the Earl to convey to him the congratulations of the General Estates.

The next afternoon he left Flushing and, accompanied by Sir Philip, passed the Rammekins and reached Middelburg. Here began the series of wonderful banquets and entertainments which the loyal Netherlanders had devised as a fitting welcome for their champion.

"Pigs served on their feet, pheasants in their feathers, and baked swans with their necks thrust through gigantic pie-crust; crystal castles of confectionery with silver streams flowing at their base, and fair virgins leaning from the battlements, looking for their new English champion, 'wine in abundance, variety of all sorts and wonderful welcomes'—such was the bill of fare[2]."

The Lieutenant General proceeded by way of Dort, Rotterdam and Delft to the Hague, and honest Burnham wrote Walsingham that it was thought that when Charles V made his entry into those towns there were not greater ceremonies. Leicester was delighted with the fertility and wealth of the country and the cordiality of his reception, and the Hollanders were amazed at the splendour and magnificence of their deliverer's dress. Since the death of William the Silent the difficulty of

---

[1] *State Papers—Spanish*, December, 1585.
[2] Motley, *The United Netherlands*, I, 351.

securing united action among the Netherland provinces had been one of the chief sources of their ill-success. Count Maurice was merely a boy ; St Aldegonde, the only other man who might conceivably have united the discordant elements in the States, was too deeply suspected at present to have any unifying influence. Everyone who had at heart the success of the Netherlands was anxious to end the prevailing anarchy, and accordingly on January 1st, the States-General determined to offer to Leicester the Governor-Generalship of all the provinces. Leicester appeared coy at first, but in the ensuing negotiations he showed himself restive regarding the degree of authority which the States proposed to retain. All difficulties were overcome, however, and on January 14th he accepted the Governor-Generalship. In military matters he was supreme, as also in matters political and civil according to the customs prevalent in the reign of the Emperor Charles V. He might summon the States-General when and where he would, though they were also competent to meet on their own initiative. Leicester was addressed by the title 'Your Excellency[1].'

The step which Leicester had taken was universally approved in the Netherlands—by the Dutch and by the resident English officers as well. It also commended itself to the judgment of the English Council. But it was in direct opposition to Her Majesty's instructions. Leicester had been appointed lieutenant-general of the English forces in the Low Countries and adviser of the States-General. Elizabeth had been entirely unwilling to assume any closer relationship to the revolted provinces, and in her published 'Declaration' she had disclaimed any such intention. In his 'Instructions' Leicester was commanded

"To let the states understand that, where by their commissioners they made offer unto her majesty, first, of the sovereignty of those countries, which for sundry respects she did not accept, secondly unto her protection, offering to be absolutely governed by such as her majesty would appoint and send over to be her lieutenant. That her majesty, although she would not take so much upon her as to command them in such absolute sort yet unless they should show themselves forward to use the advice

[1] Motley, I, pp. 384–385.

of her Majesty to be delivered unto them by her lieutenant, to work amongst them a fair unity and concurrence for their own defence...her majesty would think her favours unworthily bestowed upon them."

"To offer all his lordship's travail, care and endeavour, to understand their estates, and to give them advice, from time to time, in that which may be for the surety of their estate and her Majesty's honour[1]."

These were the last two items in Leicester's formal instructions, and his action in accepting the absolute governorship, as it was called, was an unequivocal violation of them. Moreover, the Queen had amplified her meaning in private conversation with the Earl. That he had clearly understood the limits of his charge seems hardly possible, however, for in a 'minute' which he set down before leaving England as to the powers which he should exercise in his new capacity, he is of the opinion that he should have as much authority as the Prince of Orange had or any other governor or captain-general hath had heretofore[2]. Dazzled by the magnificence of his new station Leicester yielded to his own inclinations which coincided perfectly with those of everyone by whom he was surrounded. Sidney and Davison were probably not aware that his act was one which had been specifically forbidden by the Queen. Nothing in Leicester's whole career more perfectly convicts him of a lack of judgment which amounted to folly, for no one in England had had greater opportunities of acquainting himself with the character of Elizabeth.

The first news of the proposed change in Leicester's position which reached England was contained in a letter written by Lord North to Burghley on January 2nd[3]. He referred to the action of the States-General almost incidentally. "I do not see his Lordship minded as yet to accept it," he wrote, "or if he do I suppose he will have laid down plainly and certainly how and which way this liberal offer may have performance." Lord North expected prolonged negotiations—these States walk so slowly and surely. One cannot but feel that an attempt is being made to minimise the importance of the news. Leicester did not refer the question to the Queen or her Council, and

---

[1] *Leycester Correspondence*, ed. Bruce (Camden Soc.), 1844.
[2] *Ibid.* p. 20.
[3] *Holland Correspondence*, vol. VI, fol. 3.

made no mention of the matter until the day of his acceptance, when he wrote Walsingham how the governorship had been forced on him : he would send Davison at once to explain in detail why he had accepted.

For some unexplained reason Leicester did not send Davison for some weeks : he reached London on February 13th. In the meantime the Earl seems to have been unconscious of the storm that was about to break. He wrote Walsingham begging for money and men, he regrets the Queen's unwillingness to send him certain Irish soldiers and to send Sir William Pelham, a military expert who was in temporary disgrace with Her Majesty : he fears that Parma's tales about Elizabeth's intended peace with Spain will work much harm. Finally he hears that the Queen mislikes his having assumed the title of 'Excellency'; he justifies himself, and declares boastfully that he might have had a much higher title had he chosen[1]. When at length he learned from Walsingham of the Queen's great mislike of his proceedings and of her intention to disavow them wholly he was grieved to the heart, and professed himself anxious only to withdraw into some out-corner of the world where he might languish out the rest of his few, too many, days, praying ever for Her majesty's long and prosperous life[2].

Meanwhile Burghley and Walsingham were engaged in a futile attempt to modify the Queen's wrath and indignation. Leicester had flatly disobeyed her, he had not consulted her previous to taking the momentous step, he delayed sending Davison over, he still addressed no letter to her. The cup of his iniquities was indeed full to overflowing. She determined to humble him by insisting on a public resignation of his new office. When Davison arrived he was able to accomplish no more than might have been expected. There was no possibility of condoning Leicester's disobedience, nor could it be denied that his act violated the spirit of the Queen's public 'Declaration' of her intentions. These were capital sins in her eyes, and the practical considerations which made her advisers willing to overlook them did not appeal to her. She had been

[1] *Leycester Correspondence*, p. 94.   [2] *Ibid*. p. 98.

infuriated by a report that the Countess was about to join her husband and to set up a more magnificent court than that of the English Queen. Had Leicester thrown himself on her mercy, had he made a direct appeal, something might have been done, but his silence was suicidal. The Queen sent him the following letter by Sir Thomas Heneage, a letter which for terseness and vigour has seldom been surpassed :

"How contemptuously we conceive ourself to have been used by you, you shall by this bearer understand, whom we have expressly sent unto you to charge you withall. We could never have imagined, had we not seen it fall out in experience, that a man raised up by ourself, and extraordinarily favoured by us above any other subject of this land, would have in so contemptible a sort broken our commandment in a cause that so greatly toucheth us in honour ; whereof, although you have showed yourself to make but little accompt, in most undutiful a sort, you may not therefore think that we have so little care of the reparation thereof as we mind to pass so great a wrong in silence unredressed ; and, therefore, our express pleasure and commandment is, that, all delays and excuses laid apart, you do presently, upon the duty of your allegiance, obey and fulfil whatsoever the bearer hereof shall direct you to do in our name : whereof fail you not, as you will answer the contrary at your uttermost peril[1]."

Fortunately Heneage was delayed by contrary winds for a fortnight, and, after Burghley had tendered his resignation and the whole Council had stood firm in approving of Leicester, Heneage's instructions were slightly modified. After some weeks the Queen was at length willing that the Earl should continue in his new office. But, as Leicester himself phrased it, his credit in the Netherlands was cracked. The States-General became less and less willing to divest themselves of the power which at first they had eagerly conferred on the Earl, and his relations with their leading men became more and more strained. Elizabeth's refusal to send money to her own ragged, starving troops lent colour to the rumours that she proposed to make a treaty with Spain on her own account and to sacrifice the Netherlands. It was rumoured that Leicester was considered a poor creature even by the English Queen, who had never intended to prosecute the war seriously. Had

[1] *Leycester Correspondence*, p. 110.

Leicester been a much more competent general than he actually was, the affair of the absolute governorship would have almost nullified his chances of success.

Sir Philip, too, had to bear his share of the royal disfavour. When Davison reached London Walsingham informed him that the Queen "had threatened Sir Philip Sidney and myself as principal actors and persuaders thereof[1]." Leicester had shown little sense of personal dignity in the whole matter, and assured both the Queen and Council that he had been over-persuaded by Davison and others to yield to the desire of the States. He also found himself deeply aggrieved by what he considered Davison's inadequate defence of his case before the Queen. Davison's answer was that Leicester had needed no great persuasion—"let Sir Philip Sidney and others witness"—and that Leicester alone was aware that the Queen had expressly forbidden his acceptation of any such office.

It was a wretchedly difficult position in which Sir Philip found himself. Toward him the Queen "had put on a very hard conceit," and Walsingham hinted that she might decide to remove him from his governorship of Flushing. Davison confidently called upon him to justify his course in relation to the Earl, and however clearly Sir Philip may have perceived the merits of the case, it was embarrassing to be expected publicly to condemn his uncle who was also his commanding officer. His embarrassment is evidenced in the following letter to Davison :

"Cousin : My lord thinks great unkindness in you, being advertised from thence that you greatly disclaim from his defence, which now your absence from Court seems much to confirm, but of your faith I will make no doubt while I live. Only, I think you answered not the point of her Majesty's mislike, for you answered only upon the necessity, but should have argued withal upon the nature, which is not absolute as her Majesty took it. Well, a great blow is stricken ; things went on beyond expectation —I doubt me hardly to be redressed. And so I commit you to God, my good cousin, with hearty commendations to my cousin your wife. At Amsterdam this 19th of March, 1586.
                                        Your loving cousin,
                                              PH. SIDNEY[2]."

[1] Davison to Leicester, Bruce, p. 118.
[2] *Harleian MSS.* vol. CCLXXXV, f. 293.

Davison probably understood this letter perfectly. Sir Philip approved of him thoroughly, but he must not at least formally condemn his uncle. Sir Philip could hardly have meant seriously that Davison's fault consisted in his not having explained to the Queen that the absolute governorship was not absolute. Davison was especially anxious that Sir Thomas Heneage should hear Sir Philip's version of the story immediately on his arrival in Holland, for he knew that he could trust him thoroughly[1]. " For yourself, cousin," Sir Philip wrote him a little later, " assure yourself anyway that I can testify my assured friendship toward you. I will ground upon it for I will not fail you[2]."

It was a weary winter for Sir Philip. His health seems to have improved in spite of, or perhaps because of, his strenuous life, but the miserable condition of his troops, unrelieved by the most necessary supplies from England, the continual rumours that Parma was treating with Elizabeth for peace, the long-drawn-out business of the absolute governorship, and the inactivity of the English forces, preyed on his spirits. " Sir Philip is in good health," Burnham wrote Walsingham, " and hath been so ever since his coming, God be thanked,—but not without melancholy[3]." From everyone he gained golden opinions. " My nephew Sidney," declared Leicester, " is notably esteemed, and I think within a few months shall be able to do her Majesty here other manner of service than may well be looked for[4]." " Sir Philip doth apply himself with care that all things may be carried with the honour and surety of her Majesty[5]," wrote Davison to Walsingham. He was in constant communication with his father-in-law and the Council, now recommending some Englishman who was returning, now asking for the removal of some grievance under which his Flushing subjects were labouring, and always begging for means to relieve the indescribable poverty of his troops. His

---

[1] Wright, II, p. 284. Bruce, p. 142.
[2] *Harleian MSS*. vol. CCLXXXV, f. 243.
[3] *Holland Correspondence*, f. 200, December 12, 1585.
[4] Bruce, p. 70.
[5] *Holland Correspondence*, vol. VI, f. 69.

own credit he seems to have pledged almost recklessly. Whenever he could absent himself from Flushing he was with Leicester consulting tirelessly regarding details and travelling from one part of the country to the other to carry out his uncle's plans. When not with Leicester he wrote him frequent letters, in which he went into the minutest details of the service. Sometimes his impatience regarding their do-nothing policy breaks out : he probably did not know that Leicester's instructions enjoined on him a purely defensive campaign. " Here are no news in Rotterdam," he wrote on February 12th, " but that your band is of very handsome men, but merry and unarmed, spending money and time to no purpose[1]." " The enemy," he wrote to Leicester in another letter, " stirs of every side, and your side must not be idle, for if it be, it quickly loseth reputation[2]." Leicester had appointed him to the colonelcy of a Zealand regiment, and there was talk of his being made Governor of all the Isles[3] ; he was eager to undertake some exploit that would justify the good opinions conceived of him, and he wrote to Leicester on February 2nd begging that he be allowed to besiege Steenberg. Parma was besieging Grave, and Sir Philip felt that either the English forces would be able to capture Steenberg or at least force the Spaniards to raise the siege of Grave. Lant, the engraver of his funeral roll, says that Sir Philip would have prevailed had it not been for a sudden thaw[4].

The increasing lack of harmony between Leicester and the chief representatives of the States was illustrated in the opposition which developed to Sir Philip's being given the Zealand

---

[1] *Cotton MSS. Galba*, C, xi, fol. 265.

[2] *Ibid. Galba*, C, ix, f. 93.

[3] *Holland Correspondence*, vol. vi, f. 128.   Captain Willford to Walsingham, January 26th, 1586.

[4] Thomas Doyley reported to Burghley that "News came that Sir Philip Sidney's enterprise against Steenbergen failed, having had a 1000 men out of Berghes-op-Zoom for the execution thereof. Notwithstanding that Monsieur Marbois, Capt. of Wow Castle held his correspondency and killed La Fergie, the Governor of Steenbergen, by training him to the castle under pretence to resign it " (*Holland Correspondence*, vol. vi, fol. 228). This is the only reference I have found to the attack. Motley says that Sidney was overruled in his desire to undertake the project.

regiment. Count Hohenlo, Paul Buys, and Barneveldt were especially jealous of the Dutch honours being conferred on Englishmen.

"Upon my having the Zealand regiment," wrote Sir Philip to Davison, "which you know was more your persuasion than any design in me, the Count Hollock (*i.e.* Hohenlo) caused a many-handed supplication to be made that no stranger might have any regiment, but presently after, with all the same hands, protested they meant it not by me, to whom they wished all honour, etc. The Count Maurice showed himself constantly kind to me therein, but Mr Paul Bus hath too many busses in his head— such as you will find he will be to God and man, about one pitch[1]."

It was probably due to this opposition that Leicester did not carry out his purpose of appointing his nephew Governor of the province.

It was to the defences of Flushing and the care of his own garrison, however, that Sir Philip gave most attention. Impressed with a sense of the momentous importance of the stronghold which had been committed to his care, he was amazed and sickened by the spectacle of his half-filled companies, ragged, sick, starving and on the verge of mutiny, abandoned, it would seem, by the English Queen who had sent them to do her work. The States-General raised £20,000 per month for the maintenance of the Dutch and English forces, but from this provision the garrisons of the cautionary towns were excluded, and their condition was universally recognized as one of extreme wretchedness. Sir Philip had written to the Council urging the erection of barracks to prevent the frequent clashes between townsmen and soldiers. Her Majesty approved, but thought that the burghers should be persuaded to build some new houses or rent vacant ones to free themselves of the imposition of the soldiers upon them. He should confer with Leicester who must finance the scheme as "her Majesty's charges do daily increase beyond her expectation." If he and Leicester cannot possibly squeeze the cost out of the burghers perhaps Her Majesty might yield some portion for the accomplishment of so necessary a service. This last statement appeared in

---

[1] *Cotton MSS. Galba*, C, x, f. 75, February 24, 1586.

the draft letter written to Sir Philip by the lords of the Council, but was struck out in the final copy[1].

It seemed as if England were willing to abandon her own soldiers to a wretched fate. There were dangerous mutinies of English troops at Bergen-op-Zoom and at Dort, and Sir Philip dared not think of the consequences, should the discontent at Flushing take a similar form. He wrote to Burghley begging his aid,—

"for truly, my Lord, else there will some terrible accident follow, particularly to the cautionary towns if her Majesty mean to have them cautions. . . .I cry only for Flushing, and crave your favour which I will deserve with my service[2]."

Perhaps one of the chief weaknesses of Sir Philip's temperament was a certain impatience with the world of things as they are, a tendency to waste his energies in criticism and exasperation rather than to husband them for more constructive work. It is the weakness of the idealist who learns hardly the lesson of compromise between what ought to be and what may be. It is owing to no desire to discover imaginary perfections in Sir Philip, however, that we recognize, especially in this last year of his life, the strides which he had taken toward attaining a poise and self-possession which promised much for the future. Both Leicester and Walsingham have left on record their unqualified admiration of his good judgment and general capacity in the high office which he had been called to fill, and many of the letters which he wrote during these months bear witness to his greater maturity. Nor was it at the expense of his high ideals of conduct that he developed a spirit of greater tolerance and forbearance. One of his letters to Walsingham, written toward the end of March[3], will illustrate the point as well as give Sir Philip's view of the general situation :

"Right Honourable : I receive divers letters from you full of the discomfort which I see, and am sorry to see, you daily meet with at home, and I think such is the good-will it pleaseth you to bear me that my part

[1] *Holland Correspondence*, vol. VII, Draft copy fol. 1, March 2nd. Final copy fol. 3, March 10th.

[2] *Ibid.*, f. 76, March 18, 1586.

[3] *Harleian MSS.* vol. CCLXXXVII, f. 1, Utrecht, March 24, 1586.

of the trouble is something that troubles you. But, I beseech you, let it not. I had before cast my count of danger, want, and disgrace, and before God, sir, it is true in my heart the love of the cause doth so far overbalance them all that with God's grace they shall never make me weary of my resolution. If her Majesty were the fountain, I should fear, considering what I daily find, that we should wax dry. But she is but a means whom God useth, and I know not whether I am deceived but I am faithfully persuaded that if she should withdraw herself other springs would rise to help this action. For I think I see the great work indeed in hand against the abusers of the world, wherein it is no greater fault to have confidence in man's power than it is too hastily to despair of God's work. I think a wise and constant man ought never to grieve while he doth play, as a man may say, his own part truly, though others be out, but if himself leave his hold because other mariners will be idle he will hardly forgive himself his own fault. For me, I cannot promise of my own course, no nor of the [....]¹, because I know there is a higher power that must uphold me or else I shall fall, but certainly I trust I shall not by other men's wants be drawn from myself. Therefore, good sir, to whom for my particular I am more bound than to all men besides, be not troubled with my troubles, for I have seen the worst in my judgment beforehand, and worse than that cannot be. If the Queen pay not her soldiers she must lose her garrison : there is no doubt thereof. But no man living shall be able to say the fault is in me. What relief I can do them I will, I will spare no danger if occasion serve, I am sure no creature shall be able to lay injustice to my charge, and for further doubts, truly, I stand not upon them. I have written by Adams to the Council plainly thereof : let them determine. It hath been a costly beginning unto me, this war, by reason I had nothing proportioned unto it, my servants inexperienced, and myself everyway unfurnished, and no helps but hereafter. If the war continue I shall [....] much better through with it.

For Berghen-op-Zome I delighted in it I confess because it was near the enemy, but especially having a very fair house in it and an excellent air, I destined it for my wife, but finding how you deal there, and that ill-payment in my absence thence might bring forth some mischief, and considering how apt the Queen is to interpret everything to my disadvantage, I have resigned it to my Lord Willoughby, my very friend, and indeed a valiant and frank gentleman and fit for that place. Therefore, I pray you, know that so much of my regality is fallen. I understand I am called very ambitious and proud at home, but certainly if they knew my heart they would not altogether so judge me.

I wrote to you a letter by Will, my Lord of Leicester's jesting player²,

---

¹ The manuscript is injured by damp.
² Probably Will Kemp, the famous jester. *V.* John Tucker Murray, *English Dramatic Companies*, vol. I, p. 35.

enclosed in a letter to my wife, and I never had answer thereof   It contained something to [from ?] my lord of Leicester and counsel that some way might be taken to stay my Lady[1] there.   I since divers times have writ to know whether you had received them, but you never answered me the point.   I since find that the knave delivered the letters to my lady of Leicester, but whether she sent them you or no I know not, but earnestly desire to do, because I doubt there is more [....] interpreted thereof.

Mr Erington is with me at Flushing, and therefore I think myself at the more rest having a man of his reputation, but assure you, sir, in good earnest, I find Burlay another manner of man than he is tak[en for or] I expected.   I would to God Burn[am] obtained his suit : he is honest but somewhat discouraged with consideration of his estate.   Turner was goo[d] for nothing, and worst with the sound of the [....].   We shall have a sore war upon us this summer, wherein if appointment had been kept, and these disgraces forborne which have greatly weakened us, we had been victorious.   I can say no more at this time, but pray for your long and happy life.   At Utrecht, this 24th of March, 1586.

Your humble son,
PH. SIDNEY.

I know not what to say to my wife's coming till you resolve better, for if you run a strange course I may take such a one here as will not be fit for any of the feminine gender.   I pray you make much of [....].   I have [been] vilely deceived for armours for my horsemen : if you could speedily spare me any of your armoury I will send them you [again] as soon as my own be finished.   There was never so good a father had a more troublesome son.   Send Sir William Pelham, good sir, and let him have Clerk's place for we need no clerks and it is most necessary to have such a man in the Council.

In this letter we feel that we come into closer touch with Sir Philip than in almost any other of his writings which has survived, and the irresistible charm of his character which compelled admiration from all sorts and conditions of men who were his contemporaries seems easier of comprehension. The transparency of his motives, the absence of self-consciousness, the unquestioning devotion of himself to what he conceived to be right, the mildly playful spirit, the pensive seriousness— all are here combined where we have seen them but singly elsewhere.

Throughout the spring the procrastinating policy continued, and there is not much to record in Sir Philip's life.   At the end of

---

[1] *V.* page 352.

March he spent some time in Germany "to draw some from thence to assist the Hueguenots[1]." On April 22nd Walsingham sent him a letter for the States of Zealand : "her Majesty's pleasure is that you yourself do deliver unto the States of Zealand the enclosed letter[2]." He was probably at Utrecht on April 23rd when Leicester kept the Feast of St George with magnificent celebrations. On April 29th he wrote to a Mr Mills in Edinburgh who had sent him a long account of Scottish affairs and had communicated to him the Master of Grey's desire to take a body of troops into the Low Countries. Sir Philip rather discourages the plan. "For I cannot, considering how things stand here, wish any friend of mine whom I love, as I have reason to love him, to embark himself in these matters until we be assured of better harbour." "You know," he added in a postscript, "it should evil become me to disgrace our own wars, but, considering how we are backed, I rather wish some other than he found the hardness of it[3]." A few weeks later he wrote to the Master of Grey, himself, in a similar vein[4]. On May 25th he wrote Walsingham :

"I humbly beseech you that express commandment be given to Mr Treasurer from her Majesty that as soon as the treasure lands at Flushing, the garrisons of the cautionary towns be paid with the service money due to the two companies above her Majesty's proportion. My Lord [Leicester] would have the treasure all brought hither [Arnheim] first, but truly, herein for the great importance of the places and churlishness of the people's humours, especially of Flushing, I must needs crave that they be first looked to[5]."

Meanwhile Sir Philip had suffered an overwhelming blow in the death of his father. Not yet 57 years of age, Sir Henry died on May 5th at the Bishop's palace in Worcester, "of a kind of cold palsy" according to the faithful Molyneux, "by reason of an extreme cold he took upon the water in his passage and remove by barge between Bewdley and Worcester not

---

[1] Thos. Morgan to Queen of Scots (*Salisbury MSS.* March 31, 1586).
[2] *Cotton MSS. Galba,* C, IX, 185.
[3] *Holland Correspondence,* vol. VII, f. 244.
[4] *Salisbury MSS.* May 17th, 1586.
[5] *Holland Correspondence,* vol. VIII, f. 97.

long after he had been purged[1]." According to the custom of
the time, his heart, enclosed in a small leaden urn[2], was taken
to Ludlow and buried in the little oratory of the parish church,
where Sir Henry had raised a monument to his daughter
Ambrosia ; the entrails were buried in the Dean's Chapel of
Worcester Cathedral, and preparations were made to convey
the body to Penshurst. The funeral procession of one hundred
and forty horsemen, members of the Welsh Council, and friends,
kinsmen, and servants of Sir Henry, set out on June 15th and
travelled for six days by way of Chipping Norton, Oxford and
Kingston to Penshurst[3]. He was buried in Penshurst Church
on June 21st.

"Surely," said the preacher of the funeral sermon, "his name deserves
with us a pillar of gold, which had and held so many offices and so great,
nay, which bare them so long, and wielded them so well, who, truly, as a
candle consumed himself in yielding light to other men[4]."

There are few Elizabethans whose career it is possible to
review with greater satisfaction than that of Sir Henry Sidney.
He was a type of the best manhood of England in the sixteenth
century. Not a brilliant man intellectually, he left a record of
lasting achievement which many a brilliant man might envy.
His one ambition was to serve the State in worthy fashion, and
to inspire his sons with similar ideals. Like the eldest of these
sons he was too uncompromising, too simply upright, to attract
the special favour of Elizabeth, though she was by no means
lacking in a real appreciation of his worth. As Lord Deputy
of Ireland he made the mistakes which were made by every

[1] Holinshed's *Chronicles*, vol. III, p. 1548.

[2] Nichols records, without explanation, the discovery about a century ago
of this leaden urn in the garden of Edward Coleman, Esq., of Leominster, in
Herefordshire. On it was rudely carved :

Her. Lih. The.
Hart. of Syr.
Henry. Sydny. L.P. Anno.
Domini. 1586.

[3] An interesting and very detailed account of the "Charges and Expenses
in fetching of the corpse of Sir H. Sydney, Knight of the Order, deceased, from
the City of Worcester to his Manor of Penshurst," is contained in the *Lansdowne
MSS.* (vol. L, fol. 197 +).

[4] *A Goodlie Sermon, etc.* By Thomas White, professor in Divinity, London
1586, B.L. White was the founder of Sion College.

other English statesman of the day, but his military ability, his honesty, and his true love of order and fair dealing enabled him to achieve a partial success far greater than that of any other Lord Deputy. It is a notable fact that the Irish themselves regarded him with something like affection, and the appreciation of his services in Wales was a constant source of satisfaction to him[1]. Among his contemporaries he was famous for his knowledge of history, genealogy, heraldry and antiquities. Science, he would declare, was to be honoured in whomsoever it was to be found, and many a young scholar found in him a generous patron. Holinshed dedicated to him his *Chronicles of Ireland*, and Stanyhurst his *Description* of that country. His library of rare books was widely known, and Wood justly calls him "a great lover of learning[2]."

His love of antiquities and of enduring works of architecture, Sir Henry carried into his administrations. He re-edified Dublin Castle and the bridge over the Shannon at Athlone. He first caused the Irish statutes to be printed; he had the Irish records arranged and housed in a suitable building, and appointed a salaried Master to supervise the collection. It was a bitter disappointment to him that he was unable to persuade the Irish parliament to carry out his plans for establishing an Irish university. He rebuilt a great part of Ludlow Castle, one tower of which was devoted to the housing of the ancient Welsh records, and had a famous conduit constructed for supplying the town and castle with water.

His diligence in business and his ability to compose private quarrels were proverbial. "Is not this easier than going to London or Ludlow?" he would exclaim to would-be litigants who had listened to reason. Continually one meets with references to his activities of this kind. His grave, dignified exterior covered a warm, generous heart, and his love of justice attached

[1] The Bishop of Hereford, however, had been able to find neither security nor quietness under the Lord President during 23 years. See his letter to Burghley, June 21, 1583 (*Lansdowne MSS*. vol. xxxviii, f. 180).

[2] I have not found his name, however, in any list of the members of the Elizabethan Society of Antiquaries, to which his eldest son and his friend Archbishop Parker both belonged.

the common people to him in an unusual degree. To his
servants he was a kind of second father. The death of one of
them, he writes to Burghley, has made him almost incapable
of attending to public business ; he writes to Leicester, in the
midst of harassing cares, to beg that he procure for him a litter
on which another of his servants may be carried, for he is
" grievously sick of consumption of the lungs, and yet not without hope of recovery if he were at London." It was this large
humanitarianism and simplicity of nature which impressed all
men with whom he came in contact. Few governors have
been more clear in their great offices or have borne their
faculties more meekly.

Lady Mary survived her husband only three months. She
died in London on August 9th and was buried in the same
tomb with her husband in Penshurst Church[1]. During her
later years she lived 'solitarily' to quote the phrase used by
Sir Henry, but she sometimes accompanied him on his journeys
about his principality, and was sometimes at Wilton[2]. For
many years she had been an invalid, and sorrow and ill-health
had made her old before her time. It is sad to think of her
last days when, mourning the husband to whom she had been
entirely devoted, she was deprived of the solace of having any
of her three sons with her. Molyneux has written an account
of " the godly and pious end of the most noble, worthy, benefi-
cent and bounteous lady," and has recorded her

"apt and ready conceit, excellency of wit, and notable eloquent delivery,
for none could match her and few or none come near her either in the
good conceipt and frame of orderly writing, indicting and speedy dispatching, or facility of gallant, sweet, delectable and courtly speaking[3]."

[1] In the Registers of St Olave's, Hart Street, under Burials for 1586, is the
following entry : " August 22—The oulde Ladye Sydney, widdowe, named
Mary, was carried from hence to be buried at Penshurst in Kente by Sr. Henry
hir husbande, but pd all dutyes here, both to the pson, the pishe, and the
officers of the churche." (*Coll. Top. et Gen.* vol. II, p. 315.)

[2] Together with Sir Henry she visited Shrewsbury for about ten days in
March, 1583, when the Corporation presented her with £10. 18s. 11d. Thomas
Sidney was then one of the scholars (Owen and Blakeway, *op. cit.* p. 373).
In October, 1584, she was godmother to Philip Herbert when her sons, Sir
Philip and Robert, were godfathers.

[2] Holinshed's *Chronicles*, vol. III, p. 1553.

In her high birth, her great ability and her noble character, her early life was full of the promise of happiness, but the bright morning was succeeded by tempest and storm, and her life was one of vexation and buffetings. We may hope that her last days were comforted by her daughter and sister, whose town houses were near her own, and by the many warm friends whose kindness went far to alleviate the sorrows which came to her.

CHAPTER XX

MILITARY OPERATIONS

THE sudden death of his father, for which he can have been in no wise prepared, must have been a terrible shock to Sir Philip. The news reached him some eight days after Sir Henry's death[1], and it was generally assumed that he would return at once to England. Arrangements for his father's funeral had to be made, and many business matters demanded attention ; his mother was lying desperately ill in London. Sir Philip at once applied earnestly to the Queen for leave of absence from his charge. Meanwhile he was writing to Walsingham, asking that certain horses which had been Sir Henry's might be sent over to supply the full number of his cornet[2]. But he was not to leave the Netherlands. To all his entreaties the Queen turned a deaf ear[3]; his worth seemed much greater in her eyes when he wished to resign his post. As soon as it was obvious that he must remain in the Netherlands his wife prepared to join him. She reached Flushing in the latter part of June[4].

With the opening of spring active military operations began. The possession of the fortified towns, which commanded the commerce of the five great rivers of the country, was the

[1] Thos. Doyley to Burghley, May 24th, 1586, Arnheim (*Holland Correspondence*, vol. VIII, f. 93).

[2] *Holland Correspondence*, vol. VIII, f. 110.

[3] *State Papers—Spanish* (1580–1586), June 24th, 1586, Unsigned Advices from London.

[4] Sir Philip to Walsingham, Utrecht, June 28th (*Holland Correspondence*, vol. VIII, f. 316). "I am presently going toward Flushing where I hear that your daughter is very well and merry."

aim of Parma and of Leicester alike. The situation at the opening of the campaign is thus summarized by Motley :

"Antwerp, with the other Scheldt cities, had fallen into Parma's power, but Flushing, which controlled them all, was held by Philip Sidney for the Queen and States. On the Meuse, Maastricht and Dermond were Spanish, but Venloo, Grave, Meghem and other towns held for the commonwealth. On the Waal the town of Nymegen had, through the dexterity of Martin Schenk, been recently transferred to the royalists, while the rest of that river's course was true to the republic. The Rhine, strictly so called, from its entrance into Netherland, belonged to the rebels. Upon its elder branch, the Yssel, Zutphen was in Parma's hands, while, a little below, Deventer had been recently and adroitly saved by Leicester and Count Meurs from falling into the same dangerous grasp[1]."

Another summary of the situation is given by an anonymous writer who served under Leicester :

"In Holland, Zealand and Utrecht the enemy had clearly nothing ; in Friesland also nothing saving that the city of Groningen and that part of the country called Omelands were wholly his : in Gelderland and Zutphen he had a good part : in Brabant the Estates had but Berghen-op-Zome, St. Ghertrudenburg, Huesden, Grave and Wowe Castle with the fort of Liilo : in Flanders they had Sluice and Ostend and the forts of Terneuse, the Dole, Lyskenshooke and St. Anthony's Hook; all the rest were the enemy's together with all the other of the seventeen provinces[2]."

Parma's first object was the reduction of Grave ; the English force was encamped before Nimeguen—to prevent supplies being sent in, and, if possible, to recapture it. After early April, Sir Philip was almost constantly in camp, and visited Flushing only from time to time as his presence was required.

The campaign had opened with an action of most happy augury. Leicester had commissioned Sir John Norris and Count Hohenlo to relieve Grave, and in a brilliant encounter with the best Spanish troops they had won a great victory ; on April 6th, five hundred additional soldiers were added to the garrison and provisions sufficient to last a year. Leicester was so much elated that he seems to have believed that within two or three months he would be able to drive the Spaniards from the country. "If the Spaniard have such a May as he has had an

---

[1] *The United Netherlands*, vol. II, p. 1.

[2] *A Briefe Report of the Militarie Services done in the Low Countries by the Earl of Leicester*, London, 1587, B.L.

April," wrote the young Lord North to Burghley, "it will put water in his wine."

By the middle of May, however, Parma had renewed active operations against the town, and he refused to be drawn off by English demonstrations against Nimeguen. Several assaults by Parma were repulsed—the last on May 30th ; a few hours later, to the amazement of besiegers and besieged alike, the young Governor Hemart surrendered.

"The best fortified place thoroughly of all these provinces," wrote Leicester to Walsingham, "none like it, being full manned, victualled, and stored with all manner of artillery and munition, having but three hours battery laid to it, and a show of an assault upon Thursday last in the morning gave it up at afternoon[1]."

The cause of Hemart's action is difficult to decide. " The best that can be made of it," said Lord North, " was most vile cowardice mixed with such negligence as is unspeakable in the time of that siege[2]." He was tried at Utrecht on June 17th by a court-martial of which Sir Philip was a member[3], and the next day he and several of his captains were beheaded.

Parma promptly besieged Venlo, and Leicester determined to make a bold attempt to enter the town. The terrible Martin Schenk and the brave Welshman, Roger Williams, were entrusted with the task. Accompanied by only 150 lances they reached Parma's camp at midnight, killed the sentinels and the very guards of Parma's tent, and it was even rumoured that Schenk had struck down Parma with the butt of his pistol. " While night lasted," says Lord North, " they were Kings in the camp and did what they would[4]." They were pursued by 2000 horsemen and lost in killed and wounded about 50 men. " A notable enterprise and most marvellous scape," is Lord North's comment. It was one of those feats of incredibly reckless bravery which characterized the whole campaign, but which usually lacked real significance as far as the general

---

[1] *Leycester Correspondence*, p. 284.

[2] To Burghley, June 16th. *Holland Correspondence*, vol. viii, f. 216.

[3] Thos. Doyley to Burghley, June 24th. *Holland Correspondence*, vol. viii, f. 279.

[4] *Ibid.*

fortunes of the war were concerned. On June 19th Venlo capitulated to Parma.

Meanwhile Elizabeth's only concern seemed to be regarding the cutting down of 'charges.' During July Parma besieged Neusz on the Rhine, and when after a siege of about a month he captured the city almost every soul, garrison and citizens alike, was put to the sword. Elizabeth, apparently unaffected by this series of military disgraces, was sending dispatches to Leicester to the effect that she hoped he would be able through his good care and diligence to spend somewhat less than the sums formerly agreed on, especially since she was content to yield to a toleration of the authority conferred upon him by the States-General. His lordship should give present order that the two bands of the governors of Flushing and Brill should be reduced to be part of the 5000 footmen comprised in the contract between her Majesty and the States. There was much more of this scheming to load expenses on to the States and thereby lighten the burden of Her Majesty[1]. When one reads the accounts of the savagery that characterized the slaughter of the brave defenders of Neusz, it is difficult to read these English dispatches without indignation, for Leicester made no attempt to relieve the town, and lack of supplies was unquestionably one of the chief causes of his impotence.

The incapacity of the commander-in-chief was, however, the greatest cause of his failure to accomplish anything worthy of the hopes that had been reposed in him. As time passed he failed more and more to inspire confidence and to organize the friends of Dutch freedom into a united force. Prince Maurice was antagonized, and had spent the spring months at Middelburg with St Aldegonde upon whose loyalty dark clouds of suspicion still lay. Sir John Norris, the highly capable general of the English troops, was at bitter enmity with Leicester, and was consistently humiliated or ignored by him. Norris constantly urged an aggressive campaign, and took small pains to hide his contempt for the do-nothing policy of lying in garrison. Sir William Pelham finally arrived on July 13th and

---

[1] *Holland Correspondence*, vol. VIII, f. 263. A memorial for Mr Atye, June 20th.

was given the equivocal title of Lord Marshal; this kindled anew the jealousy of Norris and of Count Hohenlo as well. The Netherlanders looked more and more coldly on the man who seemed chiefly concerned in the apportionment of important commands to his favourites, and who was allowing the prestige of the patriot arms to sink lower every day. The ragged, half-fed troops were infuriated by rumours that such money as was sent from England was being misappropriated, and the general suspicion was confirmed when the muster-master, Digges, laid a formal charge against the treasurer, accusing him of an attempt " to defraud or defeat her Majesty of treasure due, exacting intolerably upon the poor soldiers and abusing the Earl of Leicester[1]."

"Our affairs here be such," wrote Thomas Cecil to his father, "as that which we conclude over night is broken in the morning. We agree not one with another but we are divided in many factions, so as if the enemy were as strong as we are factious and unresolute I think we should make shipwreck of the cause this summer[2]."

Doyley reported to Burghley that Leicester was about to take the field, "but," he added, " I know not how the Count Hollock, the Lord Marshal, or Sir John Norris...can brook one to command or be commanded of the other[3]." The constant fear of mutiny among the soldiers gave a last touch to the picture of approaching anarchy.

In the midst of this utter discouragement Sir Philip was able to perform some feats of bravery which tended to revive the spirits of the English and Dutch forces. On the last day of June, Count Hohenlo, Sir Philip, Robert Sidney and some other captains overthrew a cornet of horse belonging to Breda, and Hohenlo and Robert Sidney captured the mercenary Captain Walsh and 30 horsemen who were in the service of the governor of the town[4]. Leicester ordered that Walsh be instantly hanged, but spared him on Sir Philip's intercession[5]. An event of really serious importance was the surprise and capture of the town of Axel. " The enterprise was imparted first unto me

---

[1] *Holland Correspondence*, vol. IX, f. 17, July 7th.   [2] *Ibid.* f. 102.
[3] *Ibid.* f. 166.   [4] Stow, *Annals*, p. 731.
[5] *Sadler Letters*, vol. II, p. 231.

W. L. S.

by the Count Maurice," says Leicester[1]; and in another letter he adds that Sir Philip "with his bands had the leading and entering the town[2]." The details of the scheme were worked out between Count Maurice and Sir Philip. On the night of July 6th Sir Philip with his Zealand regiment joined Lord Willoughby with about 500 men at Flushing. They rowed up the Scheldt to a point within about three miles of the town, where Count Maurice joined them. Stow tells us how Sir Philip, when they were within a mile of the town, addressed his soldiers, reminding them of the great cause for which they were fighting, and exhorting them to acquit themselves like Englishmen. "Which oration of his did so link the minds of the people that they desired rather to die in that service than to live in the contrary." They reached Axel shortly after midnight; 30 or 40 soldiers swam the moat, overpowered the guards, and opened the gates. Sir Philip placed a guard in the market-place, while the English and Dutch soldiers literally exterminated the garrison. The invading force lost not a single man, and but one was wounded. Four sconces in the neighbourhood were also captured, and a garrison of 800 men under Colonel Pyron was left in the town. Count Maurice had pierced the dykes, with the result that a vast amount of property was destroyed. This invasion of Flanders was the first really aggressive blow that had been aimed at Parma in the territory where he was master[3].

The successful attempt on Axel did something to restore the spirits of the army.

"The victory," Thomas Cecil told his father, "I assure your Lordship happened in good time, for since the loss of Grave and Venlo your Lordship will not think with what faces they looked upon us. This hath made us somewhat to lift up our heads."

---

[1] *Holland Correspondence*, vol. IX, f. 31. Leicester to Burghley, July 19th.

[2] *Leycester Correspondence*, p. 337. Leicester to Walsingham, July 8th.

[3] The accounts of the taking of Axel—as also of the battle of Zutphen—are hopelessly at variance in matters of detail. Greville, Holinshed and Sadler give to Sir Philip the whole credit both of the planning and of the achievement. Thomas Cecil says that "the plot was laid as I understand by Monsieur Byrd, Governor of Turneux, not far off Axel," and that it was he who first entered the town (*Holland Correspondence*, July 13th). Cecil adds that the garrison consisted of 150 men; Stow says there were 300; Leicester says there were 600 'as I hear.'

Leicester was highly elated. "This town of Axel," he declared, "is of very great importance; we shall have way to get at Antwerp and Bruges by it[1]."

Another expedition which Sir Philip made out of Flushing was less successful. Some Walloon captains informed him that by bribery and promises of preferment they had corrupted a sergeant, a corporal, and several of their friends in the garrison of Gravelines, and that they had promised to hand the town over to Sir Philip[2]. Gravelines was commanded by La Motte, a veteran soldier, and Sir Philip might well be wary. Captain Nicholas Marchaunt, who had conceived the plan, spent some 14 days in the town, ostensibly to win over as many as possible of the garrison. On July 16th Sir Philip cast anchor before the town. Prearranged signals were exchanged, and Sir Philip awaited the coming of the hostages whom Marchaunt was engaged to deliver. Instead, a corporal and a servant of Marchaunt alone approached, bearing a letter which contained plausible explanations, and assured Sir Philip that the town and castle were at his devotion. He sent one of his captains to investigate and received from him an assurance that all was well. He then sent a party of 26 men, and after them Lieutenant Browne with 50 more. The garrison now threw off the mask, fell upon the Englishmen and, with the help of the castle ordnance, pursued them to the water side. The fleeing soldiers fell into an ambuscade of horsemen, and although assisted by the fire from Sir Philip's vessel 44 of them lost their lives in the encounter[3]. It was a bitter disappointment to Sir Philip. "The long practice of Graveling which was brought unto us is proved a flat treason I think even in them that dealt with us," he wrote to Davison. He was given credit, however, for having shown great discretion in the whole matter, and for having refused to risk the lives of more than a small body of his troops.

[1] *Leycester Correspondence*, p. 346.

[2] This account is taken largely from *A Discourse of the enterprise of Graveling*, 23rd July, 1586, an anonymous manuscript in the *Holland Correspondence*, vol. IX, f. 104. See also Greville's *Life*, pp. 121–125.

[3] Doyley to Burghley, August 8th. *Holland Correspondence*, vol. IX, f. 166.

Great discretion has not ordinarily been associated with the name of Sidney, and yet it is possible to cite instance after instance of the maturity of his judgment and the wisdom of his attitude during these months. In the matter of conflicting personal interests among Leicester's officers, Sir Philip, incredible as it may seem, was able to hold the good-will and the confidence of them all. Count Hohenlo quarrelled continually with Leicester, with Pelham and with Sir John Norris : against Sir Philip he had a peculiar grievance in regard to the Zealand regiment, but it was Sir Philip who finally reconciled him to Leicester[1]. Norris resented bitterly the treatment which he received from Leicester, Pelham and the Count ; one of his chief grievances was that Leicester continually showed favouritism to kinsmen and friends, but regarding Sir Philip he declared that "he had given and received from me a full assurance of our continual love and friendship[2]." Sir William Pelham had long been and continued to the end one of Sir Philip's warmest friends. They all recognized his unselfish devotion to the cause, and his love of justice and fair dealing. On one occasion he carried a challenge from Edward Norris to Hohenlo, when he believed that the Count and Sir William Pelham had wantonly insulted Norris[3]. How disgusted he must have been with these drunken quarrels it is easy to imagine. Leicester might well acknowledge that it was through his nephew that he was able to uphold the honour of his casual authority. The reports of his services which reached the Queen made little impression on her, however. She chose to believe that Hohenlo's disaffection sprang entirely from Sir Philip's having supplanted him in the colonelcy of the Zealand regiment, and that Sir Philip's ambitious seeking should be curbed. "I see her Majesty very apt," wrote Walsingham to Leicester, "upon every light occasion to find fault with him[4]."

Elizabeth probably knew the value of Sir Philip's services, but she was antagonized by his plain downright dealing and

[1] Greville, p. 126.
[2] Norris to Walsingham. *Holland Correspondence*, vol. x, f. 190.
[3] Motley, II, pp. 87–94.
[4] *Leycester Correspondence*, p. 345.

his inability to practise the arts of the successful courtier. She could allege his absence from the Ordnance Office as a sufficient reason for refusing to allow Sir William Pelham to leave England, but his plain speaking regarding the situation in the Netherlands and especially in Flushing merely irritated her. He seriously doubted the possibility of holding Flushing against an attack by the enemy, so wretchedly was it provided with munitions, and he had exhausted every device to secure additional supplies.

"These States," he wrote to the Council, "I have tried to the uttermost, but partly with the opinion it more toucheth her Majesty because it is her pawn, but principally because they have ever present occasion to employ both all they have, and indeed much more, upon the places nearest to the enemy, we in this town, and, as I think, Brill, shall still demand, and still go without[1]."

On the same day he wrote to Walsingham :

"I assure you, Sir, this night we were at a fair plunge to have lost all for want of it [money]. We are now four months behind, a thing unsupportable in this place. To complain of my Lord of Leicester you know I may not, but this is the case : if once the soldiers fall to a thorough mutiny this town is lost in all likelihood. I did never think our nation had been so apt to go to the enemy as I find them. If this place might possibly have some peculiar care of it, it should well deserve it, for, in fine, this island if once her Majesty would make herself sure of it is well worth all the charge her Majesty hath ever been at in this cause, and all the King of Spain's force should never be able to recover it though all the rest were lost, and without it should be never able to invade England[2]."

How little Sir Philip was to blame for the danger in which Flushing stood may be gathered from the fact that the Burgomaster and Council of the city esteemed him one of their best friends and an ideal governor[3], and the oldest of his captains was able to declare, "I never doubted the obedience of the people here as long as he lived, though he were never so long absent, the love and zeal of all men had him in such reverence[4]."

After the fall of Neusz, Parma besieged Berck on the Rhine. During the greater part of August Leicester was massing his forces for the purpose of engaging Parma in a pitched battle.

---

[1] *Holland Correspondence*, vol. IX, f. 217. [2] *Ibid.* vol. IX, f. 219.
[3] *Ibid.* vol. XI, f. 7. [4] *Ibid.* vol. X, f. 209.

At the last moment, however, he decided that his force was inadequate, and he suddenly decided to invest the town of Doesburg in the hope that Parma would be compelled to raise the siege of Berck, where some 1200 English and 800 Dutch under Martin Schenk and Morgan constituted the garrison. On August 30th Leicester reached the neighbourhood of Doesburg. The next night, while he and Sir William Pelham were inspecting the trenches, a bullet from the town struck Pelham in the stomach, but the wound, fortunately, did not prove to be serious. On September 2nd, after a battery of some ten hours, two breaches in the walls were made. Sir Philip had taken an active part in the operations from the beginning of the attack on the town, and now he and several others besought Leicester to allow them to lead the assault. Leicester assigned one breach to Hohenlo, however, and the other to Sir John Norris. Just as they were about to enter, the town capitulated. In spite of Leicester's peremptory orders the soldiers pillaged the town, Sir William Stanley's men being the chief offenders. Norris' efforts to restrain them were hotly resented by Stanley, and the victory illustrated once more the lack of discipline which characterized Leicester's army.

When it was too late Parma had decided to attempt the relief of Doesburg but had fallen back at once on Berck. In order again to draw him from the city, and also, if possible, to gain possession of the whole course of the Yssel, Leicester moved his camp on September 13th to within a mile of the strong city of Zutphen, some six or seven miles north of Doesburg and an equal distance from Deventer, the other strong place on the Yssel. Zutphen stands on the east or right bank of the river; on the opposite side were two forts known as the forts of Zutphen, which were so strong as to be accounted impregnable. Two years earlier they had been besieged by Count Hohenlo for some ten months with 11,000 foot and 3000 horse, but to no avail. Taxis, one of the best of Parma's soldiers, was now in command. Leicester decided to lay siege to both town and forts, and accordingly threw a bridge of boats across the river to preserve communications between the two parts of his force. Sir John Norris strongly established his camp in

a churchyard on the land side of the town, which he proceeded
to invest. With him were Sir Philip and Count Lewis William of
Nassau. Leicester pitched his own camp on the Veluwe or 'bad
meadow' side of the river to attempt the reduction of the forts.

Parma at once determined at all hazards to thwart Leicester's
plans. He was able to send the veteran Verdugo into Zutphen,
and he himself hastily collected an enormous quantity of provisions which he hoped to get into the town. The rather
equivocal allegiance of Deventer to the States caused Leicester
some concern, and while trenches were being thrown up about
Zutphen and the forts, he made a visit to the town accompanied
by Sir Philip and Robert Sidney with their cornets of horse
and 400 footmen. They had been in Deventer only two days
when they learned that Parma had come into the neighbourhood
of Zutphen. Leaving both the foot and cavalry in Deventer,
Leicester and his nephews returned at once to the camp[1].

Of Sir Philip's occupation after his return from Deventer on
Tuesday our only record is a letter which he addressed to
Walsingham. It is dated September 22nd, but this is surely
an error ; it was probably written on September 21st or possibly
on September 20th, when Leicester wrote Walsingham on the
same subject. The matter is not important but it is highly
characteristic of the writer :

"RIGHT HONOURABLE :
    This bearer, Richard Smyth, her Majesty's old servant, hath my
Lord Leicester, his letters, directed unto you in his favour for his suit to
her Majesty, and therewithal requesteth mine, hoping your Lordship will
the rather help him. I beseech you, therefore, the rather at my request,
to help him, and be the good mean for the poor man's preferment, having
so long served, and now being aged and weak, hath such need of this or
such other good mean for his relief, as, without it, he may rest, as I fear,
in more misery than the desert of so long service requireth. I commend
him and his cause to your Lordship's good favour and help, and so I humbly
take my leave. From the Camp at Zutphen, this 22 Sept., 1586.
                                            Your humble son,
                                                PH. SIDNEY[2]."

---

[1] *Brief Report*, etc.

[2] *Holland Correspondence*, vol. x, f. 50. Only the subscription and his
name are in Sir Philip's own handwriting. The body of the letter and the
endorsement are in a secretary's hand.

Neither weighty business nor preoccupation with his own affairs ever made Sir Philip deaf to the pleas of the poor and the distressed.

Wednesday, September 21st, was spent in completing the trenches about Zutphen. Toward evening a Spanish trooper was captured while attempting to make his way into the town, and from him Parma's plan for sending a convoy of provisions into Zutphen early the next morning was learned. Leicester supposed that only a comparatively small force of Spaniards would accompany the provision waggons; he had evidently no scouting service which gave him any more accurate information. Accordingly, he ordered Sir John Norris, who had entrenched his camp in Warnsfeld churchyard, about a mile from Zutphen, to prepare an ambuscade for the convoy. Sir John had about 200 horsemen and Sir William Stanley's bands of 300 foot, and this was considered ample provision. The main body was, of course, in the camp on the other side of the river, and no arrangement was made for having reinforcements sent to aid Norris should his force prove inadequate to their task.

It was known that the Spaniards expected to reach Warnsfeld at dawn and that Verdugo was to attempt a sally from the town to assist them should their efforts to throw in the provisions be opposed. The young noblemen and gentlemen in Leicester's camp were ill-pleased with the programme which compelled them to inaction when blows were being exchanged. A number of them—the flower of the army—accompanied by a few followers, determined to be present at the action, and about 50 or 60 men crossed the river with Leicester before daybreak[1]. The mist was so thick that they had difficulty in finding their way to Norris' camp, where they were warmly welcomed.

The little band of not more than 550 men all told was unconsciously preparing to encounter an army of 3000 foot and 1500 horse under the command of the Marquis del Vasto, who had approached with the utmost caution, and had thrown up

---

[1] Writing to Burghley, Leicester says they were at the battle "unwares to me." (*Holland Correspondence*, vol. x, f. 58.) To Walsingham he wrote: "I was the appointer myself of all that went forth." (*Leycester Correspondence*, p. 416.)

entrenchments while awaiting Verdugo's expected sally from the Zutphen gates. They constituted a strong, well-disciplined army under the most competent leadership. But neither their numbers nor their position was known to the little company that was waiting to intercept them. When the fog suddenly lifted Englishmen and Spaniards beheld each other almost within striking distance, and the disparity in their numbers was revealed to both sides.

Few as they were, the Englishmen saw in the situation only a greater opportunity to win glory and "do the Queen service." Perhaps in no battle before or since did the 'men of name' constitute so large a proportion of the combatants. Under Leicester and Norris were such soldiers as Sir William Stanley, the Earl of Essex, Sir William Russell, Sir William Pelham, Lord Willoughby, Sir Philip Sidney and his brother Robert, Sir Henry Unton, Sir William Hatton, Sir Thomas Perrot, Edward and Henry Norris[1]. This morning they seemed inspired by the noblest traditions of the days of chivalry ; they felt themselves to be the representatives of England and the cause of freedom, and the zeal of service for their country possessed them. Sir John Norris overtook Stanley as they were about to engage the enemy : "There hath been," said he, "some words of displeasure between you and me, but let all pass, for this day we both are employed to serve her Majesty. Let us be friends, and let us die together in her Majesty's cause." Stanley replied, "If you see me not this day by God's grace serve my prince with a valiant and faithful courage, account me for ever a coward, and if need be I will die by you in friendship[2]." Sir Philip, in complete armour, met his old friend Sir William Pelham less fully equipped, and with quixotic magnanimity threw away his own cuisses[3]. Lord North had been wounded in the leg a day or two before during a skirmish : hearing of the engagement, he had himself placed on a horse and, wearing but one boot, led some of his followers into the battle[4].

---

[1] The names of some of their followers have been preserved by Whetstone in his *Sir Philip Sidney, his honourable life*, etc.

[2] Stow's *Annals* (1615 ed.), p. 736.

[3] Greville's *Life*, p. 128.   [4] *Leycester Correspondence*, p. 417.

Without a moment's hesitation the English horsemen charged the lines of Spanish cavalry, and with such fury that they drove them back upon their line of supporting pikemen and over their own trenches, from which a volley of musket shot caused the Englishmen to retreat. Quickly reforming their ranks, they charged a second time ; again they drove the Spaniards to seek safety behind their musketry, and again they were forced to retreat before the deadly fire. The wonderful feats of reckless daring are too numerous to be recorded. Sir William Stanley's horse was shot eight times but his rider was unhurt. Sir Thomas Perrot at one blow mortally wounded Count Hannibal Gonzago ; Lord Willoughby—"of courage fierce and fell"—unhorsed the famous Albanian cavalry leader, Captain George Crescia, and took him prisoner. " The smallest fear was held that day a shame," Whetstone tells us. The action was as brilliant as it was hopeless. A third time the English horse rode through the Spanish ranks, utterly disorganizing their cavalry, but the rain of bullets from the trenches could not be faced. Fulke Greville says they were also subjected to the great shot that played from the ramparts of Zutphen, though it is difficult to see how this could have been possible. From an hour and a half to two hours the battle raged, but when Verdugo with 2000 additional troops issued from the Zutphen gate the English retired across the river. They had lost only 22 foot soldiers and 12 or 13 of the cavalry. Between 250 and 350 Spaniards had fallen.

Wherever the battle had raged most fiercely there Sir Philip had been present, fighting with a bravery which called forth the admiration of what was, perhaps, as brave a group of English soldiers as had ever been gathered together. In the second charge his horse was killed under him, but he secured another, and in the third charge rode right through the Spanish lines. Just as he turned to retreat a musket-ball from the trenches struck him about three fingers above the left knee, and shattered the bone in pieces. His quixotic act in throwing away his cuisses was to cost him his life. Noticing the difficulty with which Sir Philip was able to control his horse, a trooper named Udall dismounted to lead the animal, but Sir Philip

ordered him to desist lest the Spaniards should learn that he
had been wounded.　He was able to keep his seat in the saddle
and rode off the field unassisted.　Fulke Greville's account of
a historic incident should be given in his own words :

"The horse he rode upon was rather furiously choleric than bravely
proud, and so forced him to forsake the field, but not his back, as the noblest
and fittest bier to carry a martial commander to his grave.　In which sad
progress, passing along by the rest of the army, where his uncle the general
was, and being thirsty with excess of bleeding, he called for drink which
was presently brought him ; but as he was putting the bottle to his mouth,
he saw a poor soldier carried along, who had eaten his last at the same feast,
ghastly casting up his eyes at the bottle.　Which Sir Philip perceiving,
took it from his head before he drank, and delivered it to the poor man
with these words, *Thy necessity is yet greater than mine.*　And when he
had pledged this poor soldier, he was presently carried to Arnheim."

The heroes of the day crowded about him overmastered by
sorrow and admiration.　No one had acquitted himself more
worthily than Sir William Russell.　He

"charged so terribly," an eye-witness relates, "that after he had broke
his lance, he with his curtle-axe so played his part that the enemy reported
him to be a devil and not a man, for where he saw 6 or 7 of the enemies
together thither would he, and so behave himself with his curtle-axe that
he would separate their friendship[1]."

Russell was overwhelmed by the fate that had befallen his
friend.　Coming up to him, he kissed his hand and said with
tears, "O noble Sir Philip, there was never man attained hurt
more honourably than ye have done, nor any served like unto
you."　The mingled pride and humility of the wounded man
touched all beholders.　Unflinchingly he bade the surgeons do
their work and do it thoroughly while yet his mind was clear
and his body free from fever.　Not for a moment did his self-
control fail him, and he appeared much more concerned to
comfort his friends than to receive comfort from them.　He
bade Leicester take courage and consider the battle as a good
omen of their future success.　But the joy of the whole camp
was turned into sorrow because of the price at which the
victory had been bought.

[1] Stow, p. 736.

CHAPTER XXI

THE END

NEVER in his whole life did Leicester appear to better advantage than in his attitude to his nephew at this time. On the afternoon of the fatal day of battle he sent Sir Philip up the river to Arnheim, some twenty miles distant, and there the sufferer found comfortable quarters in the house of a lady named Mlle Gruithueissens, where the best available physicians and surgeons exercised their crude art upon him. But the bullet had glanced upward, shattering the whole thigh bone, and all their probing to find it was in vain. At first his friends were filled with the darkest forebodings as to the outcome. Writing to Heneage on the day after the battle, Leicester referred to the slight losses sustained by the English, and added :

"Albeit I must say it was too much loss for me, for this young man he was my greatest comfort, next her Majesty, of all the world, and if I could buy his life with all I have to my shirt I would give it. How God will dispose of him I know not, but fear I must needs greatly the worst ; the blow in so dangerous a place and so great ; yet did I never hear of any man that did abide the dressing and setting his bones better than he did. And he was carried afterwards in my barge to Arnheim, and I hear this day he is still of good heart and comforteth all about him as much as may be. God of his mercy grant me his life which I cannot but doubt of greatly. I was abroad that time in the field giving some order to supply that business which did endure almost two hours in continual fight, and meeting Philip coming upon his horseback not a little to my grief. But I would you had stood by to hear his most loyal speeches to her Majesty, his constant mind to the cause, his loving care over me, and his most resolute determination for death, not one jot appalled for his blow, which is the most grievous that ever I saw with such a bullet ; riding so a long mile and a half upon his horse ere he came to the camp ; not ceasing to speak still of her Majesty ; being glad if his hurt and death might any way honour her Majesty, for hers he was whilst he lived and God's he was sure to be if he died ; prayed all men to think that the cause was as well her Majesty's as the Countries', and not to be discouraged, for you have seen such success as may encourage us all, and this my hurt is the ordinance of God by the hap of the war. Well, I pray God, if it be his will, save me his life, even as well for her Majesty's service' sake as for mine own comfort[1]."

The deep sincerity of Leicester's concern in this letter is only heightened by the slight incoherence of the form. As the days passed and favourable reports came from Arnheim, the general fear gave way to confident expectation that Sir Philip's life was to be spared, and a sense of relief and gratitude breathes through the many extant references to his illness. Some of them are as follows :

Leicester to Burghley, September—

"A particular grief to myself is happened by the hurt of my dear nephew, Sir Ph. Sidney, in a skirmish upon Thursday last in the morning with a musket shot upon his thigh three fingers above his knee,—a very dangerous wound, the bone being broken in pieces. But yet he is of good comfort, and the surgeons are in good hope of his life if no ill accident come. As yet there is not : he slept this last night 4 hours together, and did eat with good appetite afterward. I pray God save his life and I care not how lame he be[2]."

Sir William Pelham to Walsingham, September 26th :

"How unhappily the hurt did light upon your son-in-law, in which as I hope the danger is past so hath his noble courage won him (in the face of our enemies) a name of continuing honour, which I pray God to increase and to send him a speedy recovery[3]."

Leicester to Burghley, September 27th :

"I received letters even now from the surgeons about my nephew that they have very good hope of him. He had this last night a fever and was very ill, and this morning he took very great rest 2 or 3 hours together, after which he found his self very well and his fever clean gone from him, and was dressed, and they find his wound as well and with all the good signs they could wish. I thank God for it and will hope the best[4]."

Leicester to Walsingham, September 27th :

"My grief was so great for the hurt of your son, my dear nephew and son also, as I would not increase yours by the discomfort thereof ; but seeing this is the VIth day after his hurt, and having received from the surgeons

---

[1] Collins, *Memoirs*, p. 104.   [2] *Holland Correspondence*, vol. x, fol. 58.
[3] *Ibid.* fol. 65.   [4] *Ibid.* fol. 71.

a most comfortable letter of their very good hope they have now of him, albeit yester-evening he grew heavy and into a fever, about 11 o'clock he fell to exceeding good rest, and after his sleep found himself very well, and free from any ague at all, and was dressed, and did find much more ease than at any time since he was hurt, and his wound very fair, with the greatest amendment that is possible for the time, and with as good tokens. I do but beg his life of God, beseeching for his mercy's sake to grant it. My hope is now very good[1]."

Leicester to Walsingham, September 28th :

"I have received great comfort and hope from time to time specially this day, being the 7th day, from his surgeons and physicians...the Lord giveth me good cause to hope of his merciful dealing in granting life to our dear son to remain with us, for he hath all good accidents that may be wished[2]."

Leicester to Walsingham, October 2nd :

"I trust now you shall have longer enjoying of your son, for all the worst days be past, as both surgeons and physicians have informed me, and he amends as well as is possible in this time, and himself finds it, for he sleeps and rests well, and hath a good stomach to eat, without feare [fever ?] or any distemper at all.   I thank God for it[3]."

Leicester to Walsingham, October 6th :

"Lastly, and that will not like you least, your son and mine is well amending as ever any man hath done for so short time. He feeleth no grief now but his long lying, which he must suffer. His wife is with him, and I to-morrow am going to him for a start[4]."

Two weeks had passed since Sir Philip had received his wound, and it was generally believed that he was now out of danger.   In the last letter from which we have quoted Leicester gave a glowing account of the successful attack on the Zutphen forts, and of Edward Stanley's incredible valour in scaling the walls.   He had never been better pleased with the course of events since he had come to the Netherlands.   He had managed to visit Arnheim several times, as had Robert and Thomas Sidney ; Lady Sidney was continually by her husband's bedside, and the uncomplaining fortitude of the sufferer and his anxiety to buoy up the spirits of those about him had deceived them all.   They had allowed themselves to believe what they

---

[1] *Leycester Correspondence*, p. 414.   [2] *Ibid.* p. 415.
[3] *Ibid.* p. 422.   [4] *Ibid,* p. 429.

hoped. But Sir Philip was not deceived. After the first week had passed he became convinced that he was not to recover, and, grateful that he was to have an opportunity to prepare his mind for death, and to put his worldly affairs into order, he devoted himself to these objects in a truly heroic fashion. His shoulder-bones had broken through the skin and he suffered acutely, but physical pain could not conquer the steadfastness of his mind.

On the last day of September he made his will[1]—a document which bears eloquent witness to his character. Lady Sidney was appointed sole executrix, and to her Sir Philip bequeathed for the term of her natural life one-half of all his lands and revenues. To his brother Robert he left the remainder of his property and the reversion of the lands left to Lady Sidney ; should Robert die without male heirs the property was to go to Thomas Sidney and his heirs. Lady Sidney was pregnant, and Sir Philip's bequest of the bulk of his property to Robert is conditional on Lady Sidney's not giving birth to a son. In that event the bequest to Robert Sidney is cancelled. To his daughter Elizabeth and to the daughter who may possibly be born after her father's death Robert Sidney is to pay a total sum of £5000 for their portion : this money is to be invested " by purchase of land or lease, or other good and godly use, but in no case to let it out for any usury at all." Robert Sidney must assume responsibility for the payment of many outstanding obligations and many annuities. In the first place he is to sell at once a sufficient amount of land to discharge all the debts left by Sir Philip and his father. Walsingham already held Sir Philip's letter of attorney for this purpose. Sir Philip confirms and ratifies this letter, and authorizes Walsingham and Robert Sidney, jointly or singly, to proceed in the matter—" beseeching them to hasten the same, and to pay the creditors with all possible speed." They were also to assign to Thomas Sidney lands of the value of £100 per year.

To his uncles of Leicester and Warwick Sir Philip gave £100 each as a remembrance of his duty and great love to them, and to his sister his best jewel. There were jewels also for the

---

[1] Printed in Collins' *Memoirs*, pp. 109–113.

Countesses of Huntingdon, Warwick and Leicester. Sir William Russell was to have his best gilted armour; his dear friends Dyer and Greville were to have all his books. Edward Wotton was to have a buck yearly from Penshurst Park. One hundred pounds each was left to Walsingham and Lady Walsingham "to bestow in jewels or other things as pleaseth them to wear for my remembrance." A jewel of £100 value was also to be given to Her Majesty and one of £50 value to Sir Thomas Heneage. Further bequests were made to Dr James "for his pains taken with me in this my hurt," and to each of the five surgeons who were in attendance.

Some nine or ten of his oldest servants were mentioned by name, and annuities apportioned to each of them. Smaller sums were to be given to each of his servants in ordinary and to each of his yeomen, both those who came over with him from England and those who had joined him since. Special provision was made for several of his servants to whom he felt especially indebted, and particularly for "my servant, Stephen, now prisoner in Dunkirk," for whose release he begs Walsingham to have a care, the same Stephen "having lain so long in misery[1]."

This document alone should give the quietus to the assumption of those writers who assure us that Sir Philip's relations with Lady Rich continued after his own marriage, and preclude the possibility of that marriage having been primarily a love-match. This much is certain: everything that we know of the relations of Sir Philip and Lady Sidney to each other suggests warm affection and whole-hearted devotion. For the carrying out of the spirit of his will Sir Philip evidently placed more reliance on the character and good judgment of his wife than on any one else. He bequeathed to her a life interest in one-half of his lands, and after devising the remainder of his lands to his brother, he adds: "the rest of all my goods, moveable

---

[1] In the *Holland Correspondence* (vol. XI, fol. 1) is a manly letter written to Sir Philip by Stephen Lesieur "from the woful prisons of Dunkirk." He was evidently a man of sterling character who knew how to meet adversity. One-third of his whole letter is taken up with suggesting means for the release of William Chaping, a Margate captain, whose acquaintance Lesieur had first made in the prison and who had long been tortured by the Spaniards. The letter is dated November 1st—more than a fortnight after Sir Philip's death.

and immoveable, and all my chattels, I give and bequeath to
my most dear and loving wife." He made her sole executrix.
Moreover, he appointed that she should actually disburse all
the moneys named in his various annuities to servants, after
having received the same from Robert Sidney: should his
brother fail to pay to her these sums of money, Walsingham
was authorized to sell a sufficient portion of the lands bequeathed
to Robert Sidney to meet these demands, and to convey the
sum total to Lady Sidney. Then follows a most significant
sentence: "I pray mine executrix to be good, and to give so
much money, as to her discretion shall seem good, to those
mine old servants, to whom by name particularly I have given
nothing to, referring it to her as she shall think good." In the
absence of all evidence it is gratuitous and absurd to assume
that Sir Philip's relation to his wife was other than we would
wish it had been.

On the same day on which he made his will Sir Philip sent
for Mr Gifford, a learned preacher of the time, who was in the
camp[1]. Once convinced that he was to die he wished only to
prepare himself for death. He had made the religion he professed, Fulke Greville tells us, the firm basis of his life, and the
simplicity and sincerity of his religious convictions were never
more in evidence than now. His wound he looked upon as a
direct summons from God, and God was all-wise and all-loving.
He submitted himself without repining to God's will, but he
was troubled by the thought of his own sins and of God's
righteous judgment. With Gifford and other learned men he
discussed the attitude of the Greeks and of the Hebrew writers
to the question of immortality. He spent much time in prayer
and in the reading and discussing of passages from the Bible.
All the strangeness of the human lot oppressed him, and especially he pondered "the design of God in afflicting the children
of men." Throughout his life he had never engaged in worldly
affairs without being conscious of a sense of their unreality, and

---

[1] Gifford has left a very detailed and rather over-wrought account of Sir
Philip's last days. The manuscript is in the Cottonian collection (Vitell. C.
XVII, 382) and has been much injured by fire and damp. The greater part of
it was printed by Zouch.

W. L. S.

now it was not difficult for him to detach himself from them.
Continually he expressed his sense of the wretchedness of man—
"a poor worm." He marvelled that any man at the point of
death should be buoyed up by the memory of what was good
in his past life; for himself, "he had walked in a vague course."
He is said to have asked that after his death the *Arcadia* be
suppressed[1]. We hear nothing of any interest which he showed
in the events of the war. When Leicester and Robert Sidney
visited him on October 7th he would hear the wonderful story
of the capture of the Zutphen forts, and he would learn that
Robert had won his spurs on the fateful morning of September
22nd, but of his interest in these things there is no record.
The world and its affairs had receded to an immeasurable
distance, and his only concern was that his mind should remain
clear and unconquered by pain in the one fight more which he
must face.

There were times when his desire to comfort those about
him broke in upon this preoccupation, and his light-heartedness
returned. Like Sir Thomas More, to whose character his own
bore a striking resemblance in many points, he could even jest
about his own fate. He composed a poem on *La Cuisse Rompue*,
and had it set to music to be sung to him. Molyneux tells us
that he also

"wrote a large epistle to Belerius, a learned divine, in very pure and
eloquent Latin...the copy whereof was not long after, for the excellence
of the phrase and pithiness of the matter brought to her Majesty's view."

Neither of these compositions has survived.

At length it became obvious to everyone about him that
blood-poisoning had set in and that he could not recover, and
the news caused general consternation in the camp. Count
Hohenlo was lying ill at the time, having received a musket
wound in the throat, but he had sent his own surgeon to
attend Sir Philip. When the Count inquired for his friend,
the surgeon, with a sad countenance, answered that Sir
Philip was not well. "Away, villain," exclaimed the Count;
"never see my face again till thou bring better news of that
man's recovery, for whose redemption many such as I were

[1] Edward Leigh, *A Treatise of Religion and Learning* (1656), p. 324.

happily lost." On October 16th a last access of hope sprang up in the heart of the dying man, and with his own hand he wrote the following letter to John Wyer, the distinguished physician, who had long been resident at the Court of William, Duke of Cleves: "Mi Wiere, veni, veni. De vita periclitor et te cupio. Nec vivus, nec mortuus, ero ingratus. Plura non possum, sed obnixe oro ut festines. Vale, Tuus Ph. Sidney." The letter was to be forwarded by Gisbert Enerwitz, a nephew of Wyer, who at the same time wrote to his uncle as follows[1] :

"I was this morning early, as well as before within these three days, sent for by his Excellency's nearest attendant on Mr. Sidney who is lying here in the house of Madlle Gruitthueissens, wounded in his thigh by a shot received from the enemy, about three weeks since, before Zutphen, which wound has hitherto done tolerably well. But in the course of the last three days the good gentleman has been attacked by fever, and is become on that account a little weaker. He [the General] has therefore urgently besought me, as have also the other gentlemen, that I would write to you, my uncle, and make it my own request that you would be pleased to visit him in his illness, and thereby impart to him all that consolation which you have been wont to afford, and which may prove serviceable to him in his weak state. And although I have caused the good gentleman to be informed that you are yourself labouring under indisposition (and have shown the letter which you sent me) yet he has, nevertheless, expressed his full persuasion that if you should not have had any accession of illness you will come and pay him a visit. He has also in his bed and with his own hand written the above to you, and desired me to write therewith, which I could not refuse to him and the other gentlemen : and I do, therefore, hereby most earnestly entreat you that if it be possible you will come and visit him, a favour which will ever be remembered by him. Colonel Martin Schmick [Schenk] has also written in his behalf to the captain of the fort at Grave, and to the ships of war there lying, to bring you hither with a convoy of yachts or ships ; or in case you should prefer to take your passage by land Captain Schmick is to provide you a sufficient escort. His Excellency arrived here this night, and Councillor Leoning would also have written to you but the post would not wait long enough. We must therefore do the best we can in the matter....My thoughts are now and then whether Mr. Sidney will live. At Arnheim the 26 [16] October, 1586.

Your obedient nephew,
GISBERT ENERWITZ."

---

[1] *Archaeologia*, vol. XXVIII, pp. 27–37. The translation from the Dutch original is by G. F. Beltz, *Lancaster Herald*.

During the succeeding night Sir Philip knew that his strength was failing. In the morning he added a codicil to his will in which he made bequests of money to Mr Temple, his Secretary, and to several of the surgeons and ministers, and his swords to the Earl of Essex and Lord Willoughby. Unable to endure the emotional strain of his brothers' presence, he bade them farewell with the words :

"Love my memory, cherish my friends ; their faith to me may assure you they are honest. But above all govern your will and affections by the will and word of your Creator ; in me beholding the end of this world, with all her vanities." "All thing in my former life," he protested to those about him, "have been vain, vain, vain."

As death approached his mind became very peaceful, and he whispered to Gifford that he would not change his joy for the empire of the world. He retained perfect consciousness until almost the last moment. He passed away between two and three o'clock in the afternoon.

No definite news of the battle of Zutphen reached England until more than three weeks after the event. Leicester's messenger, whom he had dispatched the day after the battle, was prevented by contrary winds from reaching London until October 12th. The whole nation was in the throes of excitement caused by the revelation of the Babington conspiracy, and Walsingham and the other commissioners had just reached Fotheringay, where on October 11th the trial of Mary Stuart for complicity in the plot had begun. Davison conveyed to the Queen at Windsor the news of the battle and of Sir Philip's wound, "which doth appear much to trouble her," he wrote to Walsingham, "albeit the messenger do assure us from my Lord that there is no danger or doubt of his leg, much less of his life[1]." The Queen at once wrote a letter to Sir Philip and dispatched Burnham with it, with orders that he return immediately to report Sir Philip's condition. Lady Walsingham was thrown into an agony of fear, but Davison and Heneage persuaded her that her fears were groundless, and Elizabeth also wrote her reassuringly. No further news reached England until November

[1] *State Papers—Dom.—Eliz.*, cxciv, October 12th.

2nd—more than two weeks after Sir Philip's death. For more
than 20 days no boat had been able to leave Flushing for England[1], with the result that no one was in any way prepared for
the blow which fell upon them with such startling suddenness.
The announcement of Sidney's death was received as the news
of a great national calamity. The Queen, Davison declares
in several letters written on the days succeeding the arrival
of the Flushing post, was so afflicted with sorrow that she
could not transact public business. Accustomed though he
was to the slippery turns of the world, Walsingham was
stunned by the blow. "Her Majesty," he could only say,
"hath lost a rare servant, and the realm a worthy member[2]."
The records of the period abound in references to Sidney's
death, and in all, the writers have felt impelled to pronounce
a eulogy and to record their sense of the greatness of England's
loss. It may not be unfitting to set down here extracts from
some of these letters :

Burghley to Walsingham :

"Sir, I know it unseasonable to send you any matter to take care
thereof considering how otherwise your mind is burdened." After referring
to the loss of his own well-beloved son-in-law and of his daughter, he
continues: "Divinity and moral Philosophy ought to instruct us to exercise
fortitude and patience, but surely nothing shall more ease a thoughtful
mind than to be drawn by colloquies of familiar friends to other cogitations."
He fears lest one result be that Walsingham find himself seriously embarrassed financially : "Until I hear more certainly hereof I shall remain
very careful for your estate." "You do very well to provide as much
comfort as you can for the young lady, your daughter, considering that,
as I hear, she is with child, which I hope may prove to be a son for so much
diminution of all your own grief. God comfort you and my lady your
wife, as I would have wished for me and mine, and this I write in simplicity's words from my house late this 2 of Nov. of 1586 with my prayer
for your comfort.

                                                    W. BURGHLEY.

I cannot in my haste forget the Godly precept, *Mementote afflictionem
qua fuistis afflicti*[3]."

---

[1] *Holland Correspondence*. Captain Errington to Walsingham, vol. x
p. 209.

[2] *Lansdowne MSS.*, 982, f. 69.

[3] *State Papers—Dom.—Eliz.*, vol. cxcv.

Buckhurst to Leicester :

"With great grief do I write these lines unto you being thereby forced to renew to your remembrance the decease of that noble gentleman your nephew, by whose death not only your Lordship and all other his friends and kinsfolk, but even her Majesty and the whole realm besides do suffer no small loss and detriment. Nevertheless, it may not bring the least comfort unto you that as he hath both lived and died in fame of honour and reputation to his name in the worthy service of his prince and country, and with as great love in his life and with as many tears for his death as ever any had, so hath he also by his good and godly end so greatly testified the assurance of God's infinite mercy towards him as there is no doubt but that he now liveth with immortality free from the cares and calamities of mortal misery[1]."

Fulke Greville to Archibald Douglas :

"I go no whither, therefore I beseech you pardon me that I visit you not. The only question I now study is whether weeping sorrow or speaking sorrow may most honour his memory that I think death is sorry for. What he was to God, his friends and country, fame hath told, though his expectation went beyond her good. My lord, give me leave to join with you in praising and lamenting him, the name of whose friendship carried me above my own worth, and I fear hath left me to play the ill poet in my own part[2]."

Du Plessis to Walsingham :

"Monsieur J'ai sçeu la triste nouvelle de la mort de M. de Sidney. J'ai eu des travaux et des traverses en ce miserable temps, mais rien qui m'ai tant pesé, ni tant percé le coeur, rien qui m'ai plus vivement touché ni en particulier, ni en publiq. Je l'ai ressentie en moi pour vous et pour moi mesmes. Je le pleure encor et le regrette, non pour l'Angleterre seulement, mais pour la Chrestienté....C'est ce qui me fait desesperer de mieux, quand le bon s'en va, et la lie nous demeure. Et c'est trop aussi en une année d'en avoir perdu deux; je dis feu M. le Comte de Laval et M. de Sidney, tels en leurs personnes, tels a leurs amis, tels au publiq. Desormais je suis tenté ou de n'aimer personne, ou de haïr moi mesmes. Toutesfois je me resouls enfin de les aimer et honorer en tout ce qui les touche, et veux redoubler particulierement vers vous en affection, en honneur, en service. Faites moi, donq., cest honneur, Monsieur, de faire estat de moi de plus en plus; et concluons par ce mot, La Volonté de Dieu soit faite, lequel je supplie[3]."

---

[1] Collins, vol. I, p. 393.
[2] *Hist. Man. Com. Reports, Salisbury MSS.*, vol. III, November, 1586.
[3] *Mémoires*, January, 1587.

Ortel (the Dutch envoy in London) to Walsingham:

"I cannot express my grief for the lamentable fate which has overtaken M. de Sidney, nor do I dare to present myself before your honour for fear of renewing your sorrow, realizing very well how much this country, your honour and his friends on the one side, and we on the other have lost in a man so universally loved and of whom such great expectations were cherished."

If Walsingham will suggest any way in which the States can be of service to him or Lady Sidney he will find that it is not in words only that they would express themselves[1].

The Burgomaster and Council of the City of Flushing wrote to Walsingham to offer their sympathy. They referred to Sir Philip's kindly attitude toward them, his vigorous guarding of them from 'outrage,' their sense of indebtedness to him and to his wife. They were persuaded, they said, that they would never again have such a Governor[2]. Even Mendoza, when he heard the news of Sir Philip's death, declared that

"he could not but lament to see Christendom deprived of so rare a light in these cloudy times, and bewail poor widow England, that having been many years in breeding one eminent spirit, was in a moment bereaved of him[3]."

The States of Zealand made application to Leicester that they might have the honour of burying Sir Philip at the expense of their Government. If their request were granted, they added, they would undertake to erect to his memory as fair a monument as any prince had in Christendom, even though it should cost half a ton of gold to build it. But the request could not be considered. On October 23rd Sir Philip's body was brought by water from Arnheim to Flushing, where it lay in state for eight days. On November 1st

"he was brought from his house in Flushing to the sea-side by the English garrison, which were 1200, marching by three and three, the shot hanging down their pieces, the halbert, pikes and ensigns trailing along the ground, drums and fifes playing very softly. The body was covered with a pall of velvet; the burghers of the town followed, mourning, and as soon as he was

[1] *Holland Correspondence*, vol. XI, f. 5
[2] *Ibid.* fol. 7.
[3] Greville, p. 32.

embarked the small shot gave him a triple volley; then all the great ordnance about the walls were discharged twice, and so took their leave of their well-beloved Governor[1]."

In *The Black Pinnance*, a vessel which had belonged to Sir Philip, and of which the sails, tackling and all the furnishings were black[2], the body was conveyed to London accompanied by a convoy of other vessels. On November 5th it was landed at Tower Hill and carried to the Minories, a church without Aldgate.

The funeral, however, was to be delayed for many weeks. During the year which he had spent in the Netherlands Sir Philip's zeal for the cause and his pity for the wretchedness of his garrison had impelled him to pledge his credit in an almost reckless fashion. He believed firmly that he had arranged for paying all the debts he had incurred by giving his father-in-law a letter of attorney authorizing him to sell certain lands. But it proved otherwise.

"I have paid and must pay for him above £6000," wrote Walsingham to Leicester, "which I do assure your Lordship hath brought me into a most hard and desperate state, which I weigh nothing in respect of the loss of the gentleman who was my chief worldly comfort." "I have caused Sir Philip Sidney's will to be considered of," he continued, "by certain learned in the laws, and I find the same imperfect touching the sale of his land for the satisfying of his poor creditors, which I do assure your Lordship doth greatly afflict me, that a gentleman that hath lived so unspotted a reputation, and had so great care to see all men satisfied, should be so exposed to the outcry of his creditors. His goods will not suffice to answer a third part of his debts already known. This hard estate of this noble gentleman maketh me stay to take order for his burial until your lordship return.

---

[1] *The Funeral of Sir Philip Sidney*, by Thomas Lant—an introduction to the remarkable funeral roll designed by Lant, who styles himself servant to Sir Philip Sidney, and engraved by Derick Theodor de Brü (London, 1587). The roll, which is 7¾ inches wide and something more than 38 feet in length, consists of 28 plates containing 344 figures. Upon it is based exclusively our detailed knowledge of Sir Philip's funeral. There is a copy in the British Museum and another at Penshurst.

[2] Reference to the black trappings of the vessel is made in the last poem contained in the memorial volume published by the University of Cambridge :

"Cur atra sim quaeris ? Sidneii ad sydera rapti,
En veho per tumidas nobile corpus aquas.
Parcite jam fluctus, adversi parcite venti.
Nobilius corpus num tulit ulla ratis ? "

I do not see how the same can be performed with that solemnity that appertaineth without the utter undoing of his creditors which is to be weighed in conscience[1]."

Burghley's fears were only too well grounded. Walsingham's determination that Sir Philip's memory should be free from any stain was to bring about his own financial ruin. It would seem that the greater part of the property was entailed, of which fact Sir Philip was not aware, and only fee-simple land was available for satisfying creditors[2]. Leicester was not eager to come to Walsingham's rescue or could not do so, and Robert Sidney was chiefly occupied in securing his own rights. Sir Philip's debts had been incurred in the service of the State; Walsingham, who had made himself responsible for paying them, was perhaps that one of her councillors to whose foresight Elizabeth was most indebted. Burghley at once determined to point out to the Queen in their proper light the obligations which lay upon her, and at first he was hopeful of success. But eventually she refused to do anything, and Walsingham, sick with grief and indignation, retired to Barn Elms. His patriotism and Burghley's persuasions at length brought him back to give to Elizabeth's service the few remaining years of his life. When he died and was laid beside his son-in-law he was buried at night to save the expense of a public funeral, and Lady Walsingham could be described as "a widow that is poor and friendless[3]."

The months immediately following Sir Philip's death must have been the bitterest of Walsingham's life. He had just saved his Queen and country from one of the greatest dangers that had ever threatened them, and his reward was black ingratitude. He was mourning the death of the young man who had been his chief worldly comfort, and he was harassed

---

[1] *Leycester Correspondence*, pp. 454 and 456.

[2] See *Questions touching the Execution of Sir Philip Sidney's Will* (*Lansdowne MSS.*, vol. L, fol. 197). Much information on what proved to be a very complex problem can be found in *Lansdowne MSS.*, vol. LIV, fol. 88; *Add. MSS.* 17520. fol. 1, and in *Sidneiana* (Memorial of Thomas Nevitt). Many years later, when Sir Philip's widow had become the wife of the Earl of Clanricarde, her law-suit with Sir Robert Sidney was still undecided. V. *Hist. Man. Com. Reports*, 8th Report, Part III, vol. x, p. 23.

[3] Ellis, *Original Letters*, series II, vol. III, p. 164. Essex to Burghley.

by insoluble financial problems. Moreover, the state of his daughter's health was a source of great anxiety.

"Your sorrowful daughter and mine," Leicester had written him a week after Sir Philip's death, "is here with me at Utrecht, till she may recover some strength, for she is wonderfully overthrown through her long care since the beginning of her husband's hurt, and I am the more careful that she should be in some strength or she take her journey into England, for that she is with child, which I pray God send to be a son, if it be his will; but whether son or daughter they shall be my children too[1]."

Toward the end of December Lady Sidney was very seriously ill, and we may assume that she was confined prematurely[2]. The only ray of comfort that can have crossed the dark path of Walsingham and his wife during these bitter months must have been their knowledge that their sorrow for Sir Philip was shared by the whole nation. "It was accounted a sin," a contemporary writer informs us, "for any gentleman of quality, for many months after, to appear at Court or City in any light or gaudy apparel[3]."

Meanwhile Walsingham had determined that Sir Philip's funeral should be celebrated in what seemed to him a fitting manner and "spared not any cost to have this funeral well performed[4]." No subject of an English sovereign had ever been interred with comparable magnificence. Whatever we may think of Walsingham's wisdom in this respect it must be recognized that in the eyes of his contemporaries it was but a just expression of the esteem in which Sir Philip was held in the hearts of Englishmen of all ranks of society. The funeral took place on February 16th. The cortége was ordered by Robert Cooke, Clarenceux king-at-arms, and consisted of some 700 persons who proceeded from the Minories by way of the principal streets of the city to St Paul's Cathedral. The streets, Lant tells us,

"were so thronged with people that the mourners had scarcely room to pass; the houses likewise were as full as they might be, of which great multitude there were few or none that shed not some tears as the corpse passed by them."

[1] *Leycester Correspondence*, p. 446.
[2] *Ibid.* pp. 480–481.
[3] John Phillips, *The Life and Death of Sir Philip Sidney.*   [4] Lant.

At the head of the procession were two 'conductors to the poor,' followed by 32 poor men, one to represent each year of Sir Philip's life. Then came six representatives of the officers of his foot in the Low Countries, and a youth trailing an ensign which bore the motto *Semper eadem*; these were followed by an equal number of officers of his horse and another youth trailing a guerdon with the inscription *Pulchrum propter se*. His standard, decorated with porcupines and bearing the inscription, twice repeated, *Vix ea nostra voco*, was preceded by two 'conductors to his servants,' and then came 60 of his gentlemen and yeomen servants, Dr James and William Kelle, his chief physician and surgeon, and Griffin Maddox, who had served him from boyhood. These were followed by 60 esquires of his kindred and friends and 14 knights, among whom were Sir William Hatton, Sir William Knowles, Sir Thomas Perrot, and Sir Francis Drake. Next came the preacher and two chaplains, and then a richly decorated pennon of Sir Philip's arms followed by his war horse, which was ridden by a youth, Henry Danvers[1], trailing a broken lance. The barbed horse which followed was magnificently caparisoned in cloth of gold, and was likewise led by a footman and ridden by a page who carried a battle-axe, the head downward. The heralds " carrying the hatchments and dignity of his knighthood" were preceded by two yeomen ushers and by Henry White carrying the great banner. Portcullis bore the spurs, Bluemantle the gloves, Rougedragon the helmet surmounted by the porcupine, Richmond the shield, and Somerset the escutcheon. They all wore capes ornamented with the Sidney coat of arms, as did also Clarenceux, who came last. The coffin was preceded by a gentleman usher. It was covered with rich velvet ornamented with the Sidney arms and carried by 14 of Sir Philip's yeomen. The corners of the pall were held by Thomas Dudley, Fulke Greville, Edward Wotton and Edward Dyer, and the banneroles were carried by four kinsmen of Sir Philip—Henry Sidney, Edmund Packenham, Edmund Walsingham and William Sidney. Immediately behind the coffin came Sir Robert Sidney as chief

---

[1] Afterwards Earl of Danby (1573–1644). Aubrey says he was page to Sir Philip. V. *Brief Lives*, I, p. 193, and II, p. 247.

mourner, and then Sir William Fitzwilliam, Sir John Harrington, Sir Henry Harrington, Sir Henry Goodyear, Thomas Sidney his brother, and Thomas West, as mourners' assistants.   Two gentlemen ushers preceded the noblemen who rode two and two, Huntingdon and Leicester, Pembroke and Essex, Lord Willoughby and Lord North.   Then came representatives of the States of Holland, among them Menyn, Valke and Ortel, who had all known Sir Philip intimately.   They were followed by the Lord Mayor of London, Sir George Barnes, in his purple robes[1], preceded by a Sheriff of the City of London, eight alderman knights, and eight other aldermen.   Next came 120 members of the Company of Grocers[2] in their liveries, walking two and two.   The procession was concluded by about 300 citizens of London practised in arms, who marched three and three.

The procession entered the cathedral by the great west door, which was kept by some of her Majesty's guard, and proceeded to the choir, where the Windsor and Chester heralds placed the noblemen and others according to their degrees. The coffin was placed on a beautiful hearse covered with velvet, which was adorned with escutcheons of the Sidney arms and inscribed with the motto *Beati mortui qui in Domino moriuntur.* The whole cathedral was hung with black cloth.   When the sermon was ended the body was carried from the choir and interred in the upper north-east end of the aisle above the choir by the second pillar.   The soldiers in the churchyard did then by a double volley "give unto his famous life and death a martial 'Vale.'"

It is one of the strange anomalies of our national history that no monument has ever been erected to the memory of Sir Philip Sidney.   Perhaps it was deemed superfluous to record in brass or marble the virtues of one whose memory Englishmen

[1] Kennet, in his *Additions to Anthony à Wood* (*Lansdowne MSS.*, 982, ol. 69), says that Sir Woolston Dixey was Lord Mayor.

[2] Lant says that Sir Philip was 'free' of the Company, but Mr Somers-Smith, now Clerk of the Company, who very kindly caused a careful search of the Company's Records to be made, has not been able to find that Sir Philip was a member.   The Quires of the Warden's Accounts record payments to the beadle for wine, sugar and bread for the Company on the day of the funeral, and for the hiring and carrying of three graven armours for three young men who served as pikemen on the occasion.

would always treasure as a national possession ; in the words
of the elegy written by King James,

> "he doth in bed of honour rest
> And evermore of him shall live the best."

More probably the poverty, which was the lot of Lady Sidney
and her parents after Sir Philip's death, furnishes a sufficient
explanation. A tablet inscribed with some doggerel verses in
praise of Sir Philip by an unknown author was at one time
fastened to a pillar near the place where he was buried[1]. There
was also a project to erect worthy inscriptions to his memory
and to that of his father-in-law, who was buried beside him,
and a beautifully printed copy of these remains among the
Cottonian manuscripts[2]. They are in Latin, dignified and
fitting, and we may perhaps ascribe the pious intention to
Lady Walsingham or the Countess of Pembroke. With the
burning of St Paul's in the Great Fire the exact place of Sir
Philip's interment ceased to be known[3].

A word should be added regarding the remaining members
of the Sidney family. Lady Sidney became the wife of the
Earl of Essex in 1590, and after his death she married, in 1603,
the Earl of Clanricarde. She died before 1635. Sir Philip's
only daughter, Elizabeth, became Countess of Rutland when
fifteen years of age, and died without issue on September 1,
1612. The lives of the Countess of Pembroke and of Robert
Sidney, who became Earl of Leicester, are too well known to
need rehearsing here. Of Thomas Sidney's life little is known.
In May, 1589, he was with Drake at Corunna, and is described
as one of the bravest of those who led the assault on the city[4].
In July of the same year he was in command of two or three
ships off Dartmouth[5]. He is mentioned in Peele's *Polyhymnia*
as a combatant in jousts in 1591[6]. It was probably in this
year or early in 1592 that he married Margaret Dakins, the

---

[1] Quoted by Collins in his *Memoirs*, p. 109.

[2] *Vespasian*, C, xiv, fol. 206.

[3] Aubrey gives us the rather gruesome information that after the fire he
himself saw the leaden coffin in which Sir Philip had been buried.

[4] Hume, *The Year after the Armada*, p. 38.

[5] *State Papers—Spanish—Eliz.* Paris Archives, July 21, 1589.

[6] *V.* Shuckburgh's edition of Sidney's *Apologie*, p. xvii.

widow of Walter Devereux, younger brother of the Earl of Essex[1]. He died without issue in July, 1595, and was buried at Kingston-upon-Hull. He was an especial favourite of the Earl and Countess of Huntingdon; the Earl advised him in money matters, and the Sidney Papers contain several references to the grief of the Countess at his untimely death.

The outpouring of elegiac poetry occasioned by the death of Sidney is unique in English literature; a mere list of the authors and the titles of their poems would fill many pages. Some of the better known names are those of Constable, Daniel, Drayton, Greville, Breton, Watson, Spenser, Raleigh, Ben Jonson, Carew, Baxter, Davies, Fraunce. Brief biographical memorials in verse, or prose, or both, were published by Whetstone, Churchyard, Robert Waldegrave, Angel Day, John Philips, Sir William Herbert, and Sir James Perrot. During the year succeeding Sir Philip's death two memorial volumes were published at Oxford—*Exequiae Illustrissimi Equitis D. Philippi Sidnaei*, dedicated to Leicester, and *Peplus Illustrissimi viri D. Philippi Sidnaei*, written entirely by members of New College, and dedicated to Pembroke. In the same year appeared *Academiae Cantabrigiensis Lachrymae Tumulo Nobilissimi Equitis D. Philippi Sidneii Sacratae*. Most of the contributions are in Latin, many in Greek, and one each in Hebrew and English—the latter being King James' sonnet, which is also given in a Latin version. A volume not so well known as these should also be noted here as testifying to the interest shown by continental scholars—*Epitaphia in Mortem Nobilissimi et Fortissimi Viri D. Philippi Sidneii, etc.* Lugduni Batavorum. Ex Officina Joannis Poetsii, 1587. It contains twelve pages of Latin eulogies. "The universities abroad and at home," Fulke Greville tells us, "accompted him a general Maecenas of learning," and now both learning and literature bewailed the loss of one

[1] Devereux died in September, 1591, and immediately a warm contest for the hand of his widow began between Thomas Sidney and Mr Posthumus Hoby. Hoby's suit was supported by Lord Burghley, his mother, Lady Russell, and Lady Perrot, but Sidney had the support of the Earl and Countess of Huntingdon and was successful. Mr Hoby became the lady's third husband in 1596 (*V.* MSS. of G. M. Fortescue in *Hist. Man. Com. Reports*; also *Devereux Earls of Essex*, I, p. 264).

whom they accounted foremost among their patrons and defenders.

"Gentle Sir Philip Sidney!" exclaimed Nash, "thou knewest what belonged to a scholar, thou knewest what pains, what toils, what travail conduct to perfection. Well couldst thou give every virtue his encouragement, every wit his due, every writer his desert, 'cause none more virtuous, witty or learned than thyself. But thou art dead in thy grave, and hast left too few successors of thy glory, too few to cherish the sons of the muses, or water with their plenty those budding hopes which thy bounty erst planted."

But Sir Philip's contemporaries did not only bewail their loss : he had left them something which they could not lose, and in their sorrow they were conscious of that purgation of spirit which a great tragedy always effects. They were proud to be Englishmen because Sir Philip was an Englishman, and their exaltation of mind is fittingly voiced in Camden's tribute to his dead friend :

"Rest then in peace, O Sidney, (if I may be allowed this address). We will not celebrate your memory with tears but admiration. Whatever we loved in you, whatever we admired in you still continues and will continue in the memories of men, the revolutions of ages, and the annals of time. Many, as inglorious and ignoble, are buried in oblivion, but Sidney shall live to all posterity. For as the Grecian poet has it, *Virtue's beyond the reach of fate.*"

POSTSCRIPT

THE dead past buries its dead so effectively that it is impossible that we of to-day should come into really living touch with him who died 300 years ago. The society in which he moved, the intellectual and moral atmosphere which he breathed, differed from that of our own time in subtle ways which our imagination is only half successful in re-creating. The details of his life which have survived deal too largely with external things, or at best give us glimpses of a whole which is never completely revealed. For these reasons we are inclined, in estimating the men of past ages, to assign them to various well-recognized types.

Sir Philip Sidney with the passing of the centuries has become an embodiment of mythical perfections—a kind of King Arthur, so perfect as to be unreal. To deliver him from the body of this death should be the first impulse of his biographer. And yet, no one can have familiarized himself with the details of Sidney's life without realizing what a large measure of truth there is in the popular conception of his character. His contemporaries saw in his life a daily beauty which called forth their love and admiration for him as for no other man of his day. Men of all classes, from Princes and Secretaries of State to the humblest of his servants, loved him and sorrowed for him after his death as if a great light had gone out in the world. This is the phenomenon which we must explain to ourselves if we would know Sidney in any real sense.

Personal charm or magnetism can never be made to yield up its mystery by enumerating its ingredients. At best we may hope to indicate something of its nature. In Sidney's case it was not due to any alleged perfection or lack of faults.

Of his faults we could sum up a formidable list were it worth while to do so. He was foolishly extravagant in the spending of money, and was sometimes forced to seek to improve his financial position by means which were at least not dignified. He was somewhat arrogant and hot-headed. He was inclined to be egotistical. But all of these tell us nothing of the man ; they are almost lost sight of in the consideration of his dominant characteristics. In the first place he was essentially high-minded. Practical affairs tending to his personal aggrandizement could never have absorbed more than a small part of his interest. He lived in an age when great commercial enterprizes were beginning to exercise their fascination over the minds of Englishmen ; he was the prospective heir to vast material wealth ; but these things never took captive his imagination. He never forgot that at best they could be only subsidiary, and that the things which are unseen are real. His deep, consistent piety, his fervent love of country and his unswerving loyalty to his friends were the spontaneous expression of this high-mindedness. His life was governed by his love of beauty, whether it were the beauty of holiness, or of serving one's country, or of an artistically conceived, well-ordered life. To follow this ideal cost him less of effort than it costs most good men. In him love would seem almost to have become an unerring light and joy its own security.

To us there appears something strangely simple in Sidney's attitude toward most of life's problems. It is scarcely possible that he had been seriously touched by the philosophic and scientific stirrings of his time. His religious beliefs were as simple as those of a little child. None of the daring speculations of Bruno or the scepticism of the intellectuals of his day finds utterance in his writings. His only religious doubts had to do with his failure to be obedient to the God who was his heavenly Father. His political creed could hardly have been more simple. The enemies of England and of Protestantism were his enemies; like Milton he believed that God looked upon his Englishmen as a chosen people to whom he entrusted the carrying out of his purposes. Regarding the social structure of English society, as far as we can know, he had no misgivings ;

W. L. S.

we have no reason to think that the radical reconstructions of More would have appealed to him as other than poetic dreaming. Instinctively he loved all men, and he never failed in offices of kindliness and helpfulness to the lowly and the unfortunate,— not in a spirit of condescension, but because the brotherhood of man and the fatherhood of God were the fundamental tenets of his creed. But he probably had no question in his mind as to whether the present constitution of society were favourable or otherwise to the realization of this ideal.

In this simplicity and serenity of outlook upon life consists, without doubt, much of the charm which Sidney's life and character possess for us. It is due, however, in much greater measure to his utter unworldliness. Like Sir Thomas More he was constantly possessed by a double sense of the reality on the one hand, and on the other of the unreality of all human striving. He threw himself into the religious and political activity of his age intensely and unreservedly, and yet he was never free from the consciousness that he was primarily a spectator of these things rather than an actor in them. *Vix ea nostra voco* was his favourite motto—a most felicitous expression of his real attitude to the golden life that flowed about him. Few, even of his contemporaries, knew the zest of living more keenly than he ; he was eager to touch experience at as many points as possible ; but all the time he remembered that his chief business was to preserve the integrity of his soul. Chivalry had come to be looked upon as the rather *naïf* ideal of a bygone age ; it was soon to be laughed off the stage of modern life ; but to Sidney its counsels of perfection were forever valid for him who had once caught a vision of the beauty of holiness.

If we understand Sidney aright we shall understand better the Gilberts and Drakes, the Essexes and Raleighs of his day. One and all they recognized in him the flower of Elizabethan life, the highest expression of England's real Renaissance period. It is difficult not to believe that Shakespeare had him in mind when he wrote his greatest play. His versatility, his intense aversion from that which was evil, his intense enthusiasm for that which was good, his courtesy and kindliness toward

inferiors, his generosity, his mingled humility, pride and haughtiness, his self-assurance, his loyalty to friends, his tendency to
dwell in the ideal, his love of generalization—all remind us of
Hamlet. Like Hamlet, too, he was loved by the distracted
multitude. His servants, his soldiers, his colleagues, his friends,
all delighted to confess the compelling charm of his character.
A love of justice and of liberality Molyneux considered his most
marked characteristics. . To do some worthy service for Queen
and country was his highest aim—to translate his ideals into
noble action. These were the aims, though often mixed with
baser matter, of his greatest contemporaries, and they shone the
more brilliantly against the background of selfishness, world-
liness and sycophancy which were equally characteristic of the
period. Nothing of what was best in humanism was alien to
Sidney's spirit, and his countrymen hailed him as the president
of noblesse and of chivalry.

Mr Morley has said that it is a weightier and a rarer privilege
for a man to give a stirring impulse to the moral activity of a
generation than to write in classic style, and to have impressed
the spirit of his own personality deeply upon the minds of
multitudes of men than to have composed most of those works
which the world is said not willingly to let die. This privilege
was Sidney's. His greatness is not in his works but in his
life. He gave a stirring impulse to the moral activity of the
society to which he belonged, which left his country richer in
all that makes for the highest civilization, and he impressed the
spirit of his personality so deeply upon his contemporaries that
their posterity have continued to delight in doing him honour.

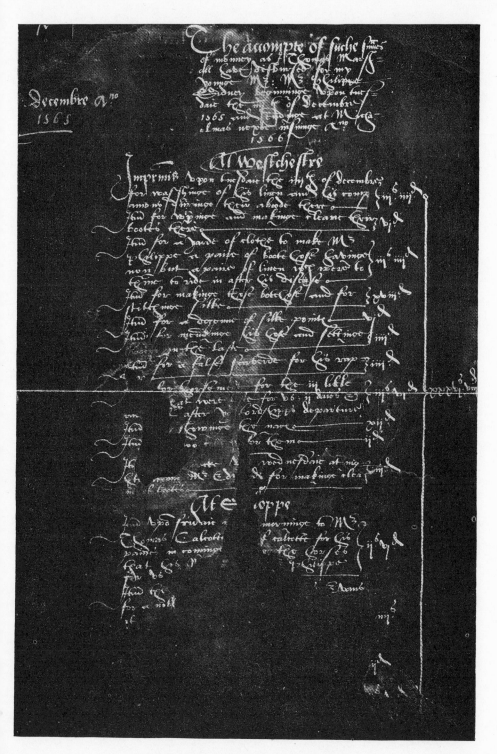

Facsimile page of Marshall's manuscript

APPENDIX I

[[On Front Cover]]

The Accompte of Mr Philippe Sidneys expenses since the iiith of Decembre 1565 untill the Feast of St Michael the Archangel 1566.

[[Page 1]]   SUMMES OF MONNEY RECEIUEDE
by me Thomas Marshall yowre
Lordshippes humble servaunte to the
vse of my younge M^r. Mr Philippe
Sidney since yowre honnors departure withe my Lady frome weste-
chestre towardes Irelande namelie
Mundaie the iiith of Decembre 1565
vntill Michaelmas next insuinge
a^{no} 1566.

IMPRIMIS Receued of my felowe Rafe Knight
by yowre Lordeshipps ordre at westchestre
the suṁe of twentie nobles amonthe ϶.......... } vi^{li}: xiii^s. iiii^d.

Itm the xxiiiith of Julie Rd of Mr George
Lighe owre ost in Saloppe at M^r
Philipps firste goinge to his uncle of
Lecestre at Killingworthe ϶ ...... six poundes ..... } vi^{li}

Itm for his charges in the iourney thether
and hether againe as by Mr Lighes
bill ϶..................................... } xLvi^s. iiii^d.

Itm upon Saturdaie the xviith of Au
guste borowed of Sr Richarde Newporte
at Coventre ϶............................. } iii^{li}. i^s.

Itm the xixth daie receued at Killingw
orthe frome my felowe Rafe Knighte
fortie shillinges that upõ discresio[n]
he sente to Mr Phillippe heare [   ]
his georney thether the seconde [   ] } xL^s.

Itm upon fridaie [   ]th of S[eptem]bre
receued more at [Ox]forde of [my Lord] of
Lecestre for M^r [Phil]ipps charg[es as] by
a bill of my han[de de]livered of the same } iii^{li}. xx^d.

Itm receaued of [M^r] Astone that the
Earle gave h[im the]re and spente
thereof as case [require]d ϶ .... } iii^{li}. vi^s. viii^d.

T[HESE RECEI]PTS amonthe
[to twentie six] pounds
[nine shillings] .... } xxvi^{li}. ix^s. ϶ .....
[   ] ....

THE ACCOMPTE OF SUCHE sum̃es
of monney as I Thomas Marshall have disbursed for my
younge M^r: Mr Philippe
Sidney beginninge vpon tues
daie the iiiith of Decembre
1565 and endinge at Micha
elmas nexte insuinge a^{no}
1566

AT WESTCHESTRE

IMPRIMIS vpon tuesdaie the iiiith of Decembre
for wasshinge of his linen and his comp
anions during their abode there ୭ ....   } iii^s. iiii^d.

Itm for wipinge and makinge cleane their
bootes there ୭ ....   } vi^d.

Itm for a yarde of clothe to make M^r
Philippe a paire of boote hose havinge
non but a paire of linen wch were to
thine to ride in after his disease ୭............   } iii^s. iiii^d.

Itm for makinge these botehose and for
stitchinge silke ୭ ....   } xviii^d.

Itm for a dozenne of silke point*es* ....   vi^d.

Itm for mendinge his hose and settinge
bootes on the laste ୭ ....   } iiii^d.

Itm for a false scaberde for his rap
[ie]r ୭.................................   } iiii^d.

I[tm] for horse meate for the iii litle
[nags t]hat were left for vs ii daies &
an [half]e after yor Lordshipps departure   } iii^s. 6^d.

Itm [for] showinge the nag*es* ୭ ....   xii^d.

Itm [for t]oo coll[ars] for them ୭ ....   ii^d.

It[m at C]hirke [upon] wednesdaie at nig
ht at one M^r Ed[war]ds for making clea
ne of bootes ୭............................   } iiii^d.

} xxxvi^s. viii^d.

AT S[AL]OPPE

Itm upō fridaie [in the] morninge to M^r
Thomas Calcotte [   ]f calcotte for his
paines in cominge [with] the horses
that his [   ] Philippe   } ii^s. vi^d.
for us [   ] ୭ ......

Itm the [   ] Evans
for a nobl
at

iiii^s.
iii^d.

AT SALOPPE

[DECEMBRE] Aᵓᵒ ITM upon Mundaie the xᵗʰ daie for the
1565   mendinge of the locke of Mʳ Philipps
     cofre and for an yron bolte for his
     chambre dore ꝫ .... } xiiᵈ.

Itm upõ thursdaie the xiiiᵗʰ daie for blacke silke buttons ~~for blacke silke~~ viiiᵈ.
for quil*es* iiᵈ for a blacke silke lace iiᵈ ꝫ .... } xiiᵈ.

Itm for gomme gall and coparase to
make yncke and a potte for the same ꝫ .... } viᵈ.

Itm for a penne and ynckhorne and
sealinge wax ꝫ .... } viᵈ.

Itm for two skaines of blacke and white
silke to mende his shirt*es* iiiiᵈ and two
skaines of white and blacke threde and
nedles to mende apparell ꝫ ......ⁱⁱⁱᵈ...... } viiᵈ.

Itm for two quier of paper for examp
le bookes, frases, and sentences in la-
tyne and frenche ꝫ .... } viiiᵈ.

Itm for wax sises to burne in the
scoole amorninges before daie ꝫ .... } iiiiᵈ.

Itm for mendinge a glasse windowe in
his chambre ꝫ .... } iiiiᵈ.

Itm for a silke gyrdle for Mr Philippe ..... xiiiiᵈ.

Itm the xxiᵗʰ daie for three example
bookes for the secretarie hande for
the younge gentlemen ꝫ .... } xiiᵈ.

Itm to the barber for polinge them
againste Xỹmas ꝫ .... } xiiᵈ.

Itm upon Xỹmas [da]ie for three dozẽ
of silke pointes fo[r]him ꝫ .... } xviiiᵈ.

Itm for certaine b[yrd b]oltes for to showte
at byrds ꝫ .... } viiiᵈ.

Itm payd for a [yar]de and a quarter
of fyne blacke [   ] to make him a
coate to waire [with] his cape againste
Xỹmas not h[avinge any] fitte garmẽt
to go in at [   ]de ꝫ .... } xxˢ.

Itm for [   ] duble
tafeta co[   ] .... } iiˢ. viᵈ.

Itm for tw[   ] no
to lyne the fac[e   ].. } xviiiᵈ.

Itm for xꝇiiii
for the same ꝫ

Itm for halfe an
[s]kaines to sewe
     for two dozen
nd for m
d au
for two

} xꝇvˢ. ixᵈ.

[[Page 4]]   AT SALOPPE

[DECEMBRE A]ᴺᴼ   Itm for a paire of showes for Randall ⎫
    1565   Calcotte who attendethe on Mr   ⎪
                 Philippe withe me who since he   ⎬ xiiᵈ.
                 came hathe not put yowre Lordeship ⎪
                 greatlie to further charges beside ⎪
                 his dyete, showes and wasshinge ⎭

               SUMMA DECEMBRIS ⎫ ∽........iiiiˡⁱ. iiiˢ. vᵈ.
                  foure pounds iiiˢ. vᵈ. ⎭

JANUARIE ANᵒ IMPRIMIS the ~~viii~~ seconde daie for mendinge ⎫ iiiiᵈ.   ⎫
   1565   his dagger shethe ∽...................... ⎭   ⎪

         Itm at Eton Sr Richardė Newport*es*   ⎫ viiiᵈ. ⎪
         for wasshinge of s[h]irt*es* ∽.....^{in rewarde}.... ⎭   ⎪

         Itm for makinge c[lea]ne of bootes ∽........ iiiiᵈ.   ⎪

         Itm the ixᵗʰ daie for a quier of paper   ⎫ iiiiᵈ.   ⎪
         at Saloppe ∽........................... ⎭   ⎪

         Itm the said daie [pa]ide to Edmonde   ⎫   ⎪
         woodall cordnere of [S]aloppe for showes ⎪   ⎪
         and bootes delive[red] to John Tassell ⎬ viiˢ. iiiᵈ. ⎪ xiiiiˢ. iⁱ.
         for Mr Philippe [   ] James Turkefelde ⎪   ⎪
         wᶜʰ was lefte [   ] as by a bill ⎭   ⎬

         Itm for h[   ]e bolonia ⎫ iiˢ. viiiᵈ.   ⎪
         sarce[net   ⎭   ⎪
         hose   ⎪

         It[m   lande to ⎫ viiiᵈ.   ⎪
                                .... ⎭   ⎪

                            makinge of ⎫ viiiᵈ.   ⎪
                                .... ⎭   ⎪

                  cha]ngeable silke nighte ⎫viiiᵈ.   ⎪
                                  .... ⎭   ⎪

                               paire viᵈ.   ⎪
                         nether stock*es* .... ⎭

[[Page 5]]   AT SALOPPE

[JANUARIE] A^{no}   ITEM the xith daie for an oz of oile of roses ⎱
1565   and an other of camomell to suppell his knee ⎰ vi^d.
                   that he coulde not plie or bende ∋ . . . . ⎰

                   Item the xiith daie for a paire of knitte hose   xviii^d.

                   Itm the xvith daie for a written booke being ⎱
                   an abstracte of Mr Astons doinge of tullies ⎰ iii^s.
                   offices and lodouicus diologue wise ∋ . . . . ⎰

                   Itm the xixth daie for iii yards of frese ⎱ iii^s.iiii^d.
                   to make him a coate ∋ . . . . ⎰

                   Itm for ii yards & qr of cotton for lininge ∋ .. xvi^d.

                   Itm for two dozen of buttons therto ∋ . . . . vi^d.

                   Itm for the makinge of the said coate   viii^d.

                       SUMMA JANUARII ⎱
                         twentie iiii^s. xi^d. ⎰ . . . . .xxiiii^s. xi^d.

FFEBRUARIE A^{no}   IMPRIMIS the xvith daie for a paire of ⎱
1565   knitte hose for Mr Philippe ∋ . . . . ⎰ xviii^d.

                   Itm for a paire of showes for him ∋ . . . . x^d.

                   Itm for a paire for Randall Calcotte ∋ . . . . . xii^d

                   Itm the xxiiiith daie for a quier of paper ∋ .. iiii^d.

                   Itm for wax thred and quil*es* ∋ . . . . vi^d.

                   Itm the xxvith for the barber to trim thẽ all xii^d.

                   Itm for a Virgile for Mr Philipp ∋ . . . . xx^d.

                   Itm for Calvines chatachisme ∋ . . . . iiii^d.

                   Itm the xxviiith daie for a paire of ⎱
                   knitte hose for him ∋ . . . . ⎰ xviii^d.

                       S[U]MMA FEBRUARII ⎱
                         [E]ight shillings viii^d. ⎰ ∋ . . . . .viii^s. viii^d.

MARCHE A^{no}   IMPRIMIS the vi[th daie] for a paire of ⎱
1565   showes for [Mr Philippe ∋] . . . . ⎰ x^d.

                   Itm for [a paire for Randall Cal]cote ∋ . . . . . xii^d.

                   Itm the [   ] buttons ⎱
                   for his sh[   ] gowne ⎰ xiiii^d.
                   at the han[

                   Itm for a
                   coller of
Suṁe payd   mendinge t
28^s. 10^d.   Itm paid
                   [wa]sshinge M

[[Page 6]]   AT SALOPPE

[MARCHE] A^{NO}   ITM for Randall Calcotte*s* wasshinge   } ii^s. vi^d.
1565   since the same tyme ⊃ .... }

                 Itm for Radolpho Gualtero Tigurino de   } viii<sup>d</sup.   } iiii^s. i^d.
                 sylabarum et carminum ratione ⊃ .... }

                 Itm for silke buttons iiii^d for thred
                 buttons ii^d for thred point*es* iiii^d for a } xi^d.
                 lace for his knives ⊃ ....^{id}...... }

                      SUMMA MENSIS ⊃..................... } xiii^s. v^d.
                      MARTII thretten^s. v^d. ⊃ .... }

APRILE A^{NO}   IMPRIMIS the firste daie for a girdle   } xiiii^d.
1566   of silke for Mr Philippe ⊃................... }

                 Itm for yncke and quil*es* ⊃ .... iiii^d.

                 Itm the xiith daie for a quier of paper ⊃....... iiii^d.

                 Itm for a paire of knitte hose for   } xviii^d.
                 Mr Philippe ⊃........................... }

                 Itm the xiiith daie for a paire of   } vi^d.   } vi^s.
                 gloves for him ⊃ .... }

                 Itm the xiiiith daie beinge Ester   } x^d.
                 for a paire of showes for him ⊃............... }

                 Itm for a paire of showes for Rand   } xii^d.
                 all Calcotte ⊃............................ }

                 Itm for buttons for the blacke ierkine   } iiii^d.
                 that Robt wrighte sent frome Ludloo   }

                      SUMMA MENSIS APRILIS ⊃................. } vi^s.
                      SYX SHILLINGS ⊃...................... }

MAIE A^{NO}   IMPRIMIS the iii[i]th of Maie for a quier } iiii^d.
1566   of fine paper ⊃ .... }

                 Itm for makinge of [a] paire of boothose for } iiii^d.
                 Randall Calcott[e ⊃]...................... }

                 Itm the xth d[aie for] yncke ⊃ .... iiii^d.

                 Itm the xxx[th daie] for his barber ⊃.......... iiii^d.

                 Itm for [   ] when we   }
                 wente [to visit at the house of] Sr And-   } iiii^d.
                 rue C[orbett and that of S^r] Richarde   }
                 Newpo[rte when the scholar]s were sicke   }

                 Itm for [   ] eringe his   } iiii^d.
                      ....   }

                      [SUMMA] MENSIS ⊃... }
                      [MAII T]WO SHILLI͂GS }.............. } ii^s.

[[Page 7]]   AT SALOPPE

[JUNII A]NNO   IMPRIMIS the xxith daie for a Sa </br> 1566   luste for him ⱶ........................ } xiiii^d.

Itm for perfumes to ayre the chambre </br> withe when we came furthe of the </br> countree after the yownge gentlemen </br> were recovered ⱶ..................... } xii^d.

Itm geven to the Lawndresse to bye </br> sylke to mende his shirt*es* ⱶ .... } iiii^d.

Itm for mendinge of his dagger ⱶ .... ii^d.

Itm for two dozen of large thred </br> point*es* ⱶ............................. } vi^d.

Itm for threde, nedles, and buttons ⱶ....... xii^d.

Itm for a paire of gloves for him ⱶ .... vi^d.

Itm for a lace for his penne and </br> ynckehorne ⱶ.......................... } i^d.

Itm the xxvth daie for makinge of his </br> grene coate whereof the clothe came </br> frome my felowe knighte ⱶ .... } ii^s.

Itm for a quarter of grene sarcenette </br> for the coller and to face it ⱶ............. } xiiii^d.

Itm for a yarde of fustiane to line the </br> bodie of the same ⱶ .... } x^d.

Itm for a yarde and an halfe of cottõ </br> to line the skirtes ⱶ .... } xii^d.

Itm for buttons therto ⱶ .... viii^d.

Suᷤe payd } </br> 13^s. 4^d. }   Itm for xiiii yards of lace to compase </br> it abowte ⱶ............................ } xxii^d.

Itm for iiii skaines of silke ⱶ.............. viii^d.

Itm for canvas fo[r] the coller ⱶ .... i^d.

Itm for a quier o[f] paper ⱶ .... iiii^d.

} xiii^s. iiii^d.

S[UM]MA MENSIS JUNII ⱶ .... </br> [t]hretten shilling*es* iiii^d. ⱶ........... } xiii^s. iiii^d.

[[Page 8]]

[JULII A^{NO}]
1566

IMPRIMIS vpō thursdaie the xith daie
at the Christeninge of a sonne of M^r
Leighs who berethe his name geven to
the midwife xx^d and to the nurse   } iii^s. iiii^d.
xx^d and more monney was offered
to the mother but it wolde not be take
nne Ͽ .... _{my Ladie Newporte being godmother} ....

Itm the xxiiiith daie goinge towards
my Lorde of Lecestre at Killingworthe
the firste tyme for showinge the red   } x^d.
nagge Ͽ...........................

Itm for his meat in stable beinge taken } xii^d.
vp a daie before we wente Ͽ...........

Itm for trimminge of his rapier } xii^d.
and false scaberde Ͽ..................

Itm to the barber Ͽ .... iiii^d.

Itm for white buttons for a dublette of } iii^d.
his Ͽ ....

Itm for browne paper Ͽ.............. ii^d.

Itm for two dozenne of silke point*es* Ͽ.. xii^d.

Itm for thred to make shirte laces Ͽ.... i^d.

Itm for a quier of paper Ͽ............ iiii^d.

Itm the charges of a newe sadle for
the nag that my Lorde Vicounte gave
him as folowethe Imprimis for a   } xiiii^s.
remmante of blacke velvette betwixt
a yarde and thre quarters for the seate

Itm for two frenche skynnes for the } iii^s. viii^d.
coveringe Ͽ........................

Itm for two onces of fringe to cōpasse } iiii^s.
the seate Ͽ........................

Itm for fowr skaines of silke to stitche } viii^d.
the same Ͽ........................

Itm for the stuffe that the sadler } x^s.
founde and the makinge Ͽ............

Itm for two girth[es] and a surcingle Ͽ.. xvi^d.

Itm for a pair[e of st]yrrops withe the } xviii^d.
leatheringe Ͽ......................

Itm for the [   ]   xx^d.

Itm for [   ] .... viii^d.

Itm [   ] .... x^d.

Itm f[or   ] .... xiiii^d.

[   ] shirte of } vi^d.
[   ] ....

[   ] ruffes Ͽ ... vi^d.

[   ] and silke Ͽ .. ii^s.

[   ] .... viii^d.

[   ]

} lii^s. x^d.

[[Page 9]] AT SALOPPE

[JULII A^NO] 1566	ITM paid to the Lawndres for the laste quarter for Mr Philippe and Randall Calcotte wch was due the vi^th of June	vii^s. vi^d.	
	Itm for thre paire of showes for Mr Philippe since Ester ꝯ	ii^s. vi^d.	
	Itm for two paire for randall since the same tyme ꝯ	ii^s.	
	Itm for two canvas alam bag*es* to put showes and bookes in that were caried with vs in the cloke bag ꝯ..........	iiii^d.	
	Itm a paire of velvette overstock*es* that I made him of his olde shorte blacke velvette gowne the charges whereof folowethe, imprimis for a yarde of duble sarcenette to line them with ꝯ..........	vi^s.	
	Itm for two yards two neyles and an halfe of saten of Bruges to lyne the paynes of his hose ꝯ..........	v^s. vii^d.	
	Itm for halfe a yarde of whighte lininge and halfe a q^ter ꝯ..........	viii^d.	
	Itm for a yarde of cottone for an vtter lininge ꝯ	xii^d.	
	Itm for halfe a yarde and a naile of Holande to line the hose inwardelie	viii^d.	lii^s. iiii^d.
	Itm for a q^ter d. of jene fustian for two pockett*es* in his hose ꝯ..........	iiii^d.	
	Itm for fyve onces of lace and a yarde for the paines of his hose ꝯ..........	xi^s. vii^d.	
	Itm for an once and a pennie waighte of silke to sowe theme ꝯ	xii^d.	
	Itm for the makinge of them ꝯ	iiii^s.	
	Itm for two dozen[ne] of silke pointes ꝯ	xii^d.	
	Itm for dowlas for [a] paire of bootehose for him ꝯ	xv^d.	
	Itm for a border [for] them	viii^d.	
	Itm for the m[akinge] of theme ꝯ	iiii^d.	
	Itm for halfe [a yarde] and a naile of Hollande [to make him a] paire of hose of [ ]	vii^d.	
	Itm for [ ]	iiii^d.	
	Itm the c[harges for makinge of a can]vas dublette for imprimis for		
Sume [ ]	[ ] fine canvas		
[ ]	[ ] yarde		

[[Page 10]]

[JULII A^{NO}] ITM for a q^{ter} of whighte sarcenette for ⎫ xiii^d. ꝧ ....
1566   to line the coller and to face it afore ⎭

Itm for a q^{ter} of bombaste for the sleves   iiii^d.

Itm for two dozenne of buttons ꝧ ....   viii^d.

Itm for the makinge of his dublette ⎫ ii^s.
beinge pincked ꝧ .... ⎭

Itm for the makinge of a whighte leather ⎫
ierkine whereof the skinne came frõ   ⎪
my felowe knighte ꝧ .... ⎬ ii^s.
and makinge of a paire of velvette   ⎪
showes ꝧ .... ⎭

Itm for a dozenne of buttons to it ꝧ ......   iiii^d.

          Itm here folowethe the charges of the ⎫
          iourney to Killingwoorthe and home   ⎪
          againe amontinge to xlvi^s. iiii^d. disb- ⎪
          ursed by Mr Lighe wherewith I haue ⎪
          charged my selfe in the page of   ⎪
          recept*es* we beinge in nombre as a   ⎪
          fore I haue written to yowre Lordship ⎪
          Imprimis my yowng M^r, M^r Ed-   ⎪
Mr Aston warde Onsloo, Mr George Lieghe   ⎬ xv^d.   ⎫
          Thomas Marshall Randall calcotte   ⎪   ⎪
          Mr Onsloos two men, Mr Lighe one ⎪   ⎪
          man and Mr Astone one man, M^r ⎪   ⎬ xl^s. v^d.
          Onsloo paide for his horsemeate   ⎪   ⎪
          and the reste was at yowre   ⎪   ⎪
          Lordships charges.   Upon wednesdaie   ⎪   ⎪
          the xxiiiith of this presente at Shi- ⎪   ⎪
          fnole at after none drinckinge   ⎪   ⎪
          there ꝧ .... ⎭   ⎪

Itm the same nighte for supper ⎫ vi^s. iiii^d.   ⎪
at wollerhampton ꝧ .... ⎭   ⎪

Itm for horsemea[te] there ꝧ ....   iiii^s. iiii^d. ⎪

Itm vpõ thursdai[e] the xxvth daie ⎫ vii^s. iiii^d.   ⎪
for dynner at Brimigeame ꝧ .... ⎭   ⎪

Itm for horsemea[te t]here ꝧ ....   ii^s. ii^d.   ⎪

Itm at Ham[pton on] the Hill drin ⎫ iiii^d.   ⎪
ckinge t[here ꝧ ....].............. ⎭   ⎪

Itm v[pon fridaie the xxv]ith daie ⎫ v^s. x^d.   ⎪
for [   ] orthe ꝧ .. ⎭   ⎪

Itm a [   ] drinck ⎫ vi^d.   ⎪
[inge there   ] .... ⎭   ⎪

[su]pper at ⎫ v^s. iiii^d.   ⎪
[   ] ꝧ .... ⎭   ⎪

[Ra]ndall*es* spurre ꝧ ...   i^d.   ⎪

[   ] nag ꝧ ....   iiii^d.   ⎪

[   ] Mr Astones sadle   iiii^d.   ⎭

[[Page 11]]   AT SALOPPE

[JULII A^{NO}]   ITM for a girthe for Mr Lighe ɘ.............   ii^d. ....

[1566]   Itm for horsemeate there ɘ.................   iii^s. x^d.

Itm vpon saturdaie the xxviith daie ⎫
at Boningall an ynne v miles on   ⎬ vi^s.
this side wollerhamptone for dynner   ⎭

Itm for horsemete there ɘ ....   ii^s. iiii^d.

Itm the same nighte at Saloppe ɘ ....   ∝

Itm vpo Mundaie the xxixth daie for ⎫
a yarde of Hollande for two paire of   ⎪
linen hose for Mr Philippe after   ⎬ xviii^d.   xix^s. viii^d
he came frome Killingworthe bycawse   ⎪   xvi^s. x^d.
of his meriegall*es* ɘ.. and breking furth throughe heat ⎭

Itm for the makinge of theme ɘ............   iiii^d.

Itm for cuttinge less*e* Randall*es* blew   ⎫ vi^d.
coate ɘ ....   ⎭

Itm for pesinge his other coate sider   ⎫ ii^d.
in the waste ɘ.........................   ⎭

Itm for a box of ointemente for   ⎫
his meriegall*es* and after that for   ⎪
an other to have with vs to Killin   ⎬ ii^s.
gworth yf the like sholde happe ɘ .... ⎭
          ɘ ....

          SUMMA MENSIS JULII ɘ...... ⎫
                  two   v   ⎬ viii^{li}. v^s. iiii^d.
          Eighte pounds ƒyve shilling*es* iiid. ɘ ⎭ ii^s. v^d.

AUGUSTE A^{NO}   IMPRIMIS Expe[n]ded for my younge   ⎫
    1566   M^r and his train[e], beinge besides him- ⎪
                selfe, Mr Asto[ne] Thomas Marshall   ⎪
                Davie Longe M[^r A]stons man and   ⎪
                Randall Calco[tte g]oinge the seconde   ⎪
                tyme to t[he Erle of Lecestre his] uncle aga- ⎬ x^d.   ⎫
                inste the [   ] to kill   ⎪   ⎪
                ingwort[he   re]torne   ⎪   ⎪
                to Sa[loppe   as folo]wethe   ⎪   ⎬ ii^s. x^d.
                viz. vp[õ wednesdaie the x]iiiith daie ⎪   ⎪
                for show[es   ] for ⎭   ⎪
                Randall   ⎪
                                                                   ⎪
                Itm for   ⎪
Sum̃e [   ]   beinge   ⎪
22^s. [d   ]   ⎭

[[Page 12]]   AT ARCOOLE

[A]UGUSTE A^{NO}
1566

Itm the said xiiiith daie at nighte
w^t Sr Richarde Newporte at his
house at Arcoole ꝰ .... } ∝ ....

Itm vpõ thursdaie at nighte the xvth
for supper at wollerhamptone ꝰ........ } iii^s.

Itm for horsemeate there ꝰ........... xx^d.

Itm vpõ fridaie the xvith daie
for owre dynner at Brumegeame } iii^s.

Itm for horsemeate there ꝰ........... xii^d.

Itm at Hamptone on the Hill drin
ckinge there ꝰ...................... } vi^d.

                    AT COUENTRIE

Itm vpõ saturdaie the xviith daie
for horsemeate there ꝰ............... } iiii^s.

Itm for seruant*es* diete there ꝰ........ xii^d.

                AT KILLINGWORTHE

Itm for my horse meat and davies
vpon sundaie the xviiith daie
ridinge frome Killingworth to Coven
trie to speke with my Lorde
of Lecestre for the knowledge of
Mr Philipps apparell ꝰ .... } viii^d.   } xxxii^s. viii^d.

Itm for thre dozenne of silke
point*es* for Mr Philipps hose ꝰ .... } xviii^d.

Itm vpon wednesdaie the xxith daie
geven in rewarde [to] Mr Spilsberie a
ᴧfrĕch   i̶n̶ ̶r̶e̶ ᴧfor his gen[tle]nes showed at
crowne   all tymes to M^r [P]hilipp and his
M^r and all yo[wr]e Lordshipps ꞅeru
aunt*es* that the[re w]ere attendinge
on him as my [selfe] sterrie whitton
Pope & Pavie [there be]inge no place
elles with [   ] to plante
his fo[a]bode there } vi^s.

Itm for [   ] at }
go‿dwi[fe   ] of } ii^s.

....

al]ꞅo for o^r }
iiii^d. } viii^s. iiii^d. }

W. L. S.

AT KYLLINGWORTHE

[AUGUSTE Aᴺᴼ]   ITM for servaunt*es* dyete at the ynne at ⎫ xxiᵈ.
      1566   some tymes where the horses wente   ⎭

                   Itm for makinge cleane bootes ꝫ....... iiiiᵈ.

                   Itm the same daie at nighte by my   ⎫
                   Lorde of Lecestres appointmente in   ⎪
                   the waie towards Oxforde conducted   ⎬ ∝
                   by doctor wilsonne at supper at   ⎪
                   one Mʳ Raules beyonde Warwike   ⎭

                   Itm to the musicians there ꝫ......... xiiᵈ.

                   Itm vpõ fridaie the xxiiiᵗʰ for dy   ⎫ iiˢ. viᵈ.
                   nner at Tuddingtone ꝫ................⎭

                   Itm for horsemeate there ꝫ........... iiˢ.

                          AT OXFORDE

                   IMPRIMIS the saide fridaie at nighte ⎫ viiˢ. viᵈ.
                   for supper there at the ynne   ⎭

                   Itm vpõ saturdaie the xxiiiiᵗʰ daie ⎫
                   for servaunt*es* dynner, there beinge⎬ xxᵈ.
                   also Mʳ doctors men ꝫ................⎭

                   Itm for Mʳ Philipps supper there   iiiˢ. iiiiᵈ.

                   Itm for servaunt*es* dynner there vpon⎫ xviiiᵈ.
                   sundaie the xxvᵗʰ daie ꝫ ....⎭

                   Itm the same daie at nighte, supper ⎫   ⎫
                   at Lincolne Colledge with Mʳ Brid-   ⎪   ⎪
                   gwater one of my Lorde of Lecestres ⎪   ⎪
                   Chaplaines and rector of the same   ⎪   ⎬ xxxˢ. iᵈ.
                   colledge and so continued at his   ⎪   ⎪
                   table duringe oʳ aboode there, withe ⎪   ⎪
                   the whole traine, and partlie lodg- ⎬ ∝   ⎭
                   ed there also, the space of xv daies ⎪
                   viz. frome the saide sundaie at   ⎪
                   supper inclusive vntill the viiiᵗʰ   ⎪
                   of Septembre beinge sundaie at   ⎪
                   after dynner ꝫ...................... ⎭

                   Itm for mendinge [M]ʳ Phillipps velvette ⎫ iiᵈ.
                   girdle and a buc[kle] for the same   ⎭

                   Itm for show[inge cer]taine of owre ⎫ iiˢ.
                   horses there ꝫ..[..........] ....⎭

                   Itm for mend[inge sadles] and bridles⎫ xviᵈ.
                   there ꝫ.........[.............] ... ⎭

                   Itm for [sarce]nette⎫
                   to make [Mʳ Philipp a pai]re of   ⎬ iiˢ. xᵈ.
                   skalinge [hose bycause of cer]taine   ⎪
                   merieg[alles   ] .... ⎭

                   I[tm

Sum̃e [
  30ˢ. 1ᵈ.

[[Page 14]]

AUGUSTE A^{no}
1566

ITM for silke to sowe them and the skalinghose ꝯ...................... } ii^d.

Itm for makinge of these and garters   xvi^d.

Itm for a paire of duble solde showes for Mr Philippe and an other for Randall ꝯ........................ } xx^d.

Itm for mendinge Mr Philipps duble taffeta coate and for makinge his blewe streked canvas dublette mete for him ꝯ .... } xvi^d.

Itm for a lace to drawe his scalinge hose together benethe knee ꝯ .... } i^d.

Itm for a quier of paper ꝯ...........   iiii^d.

Itm for Yncke ꝯ...................   i^d

Itm for thred to sowe with ꝯ ....   ii^d.

Itm to the currier for licoringe and blakinge his bootes ꝯ.............. } iiii^d.

Itm vpõ saturdaie the laste of Auguste for iiii of owre horses at grasse since the xxiiiith of the same beinge vii daies inclusive at vi^d. apece daie and nighte ꝯ .... } xiiii^s.

Itm for thre of owre horses kepte in the stable frome the saide saturdaie the laste of Auguste vntill sundaie at after none the viii of septembre the daie of owre departinge frome Oxforde ꝯ .... } xxii^s. vi^d.

Itm for two horses at grasse du-ringe the said tyme whiche was viii daies ꝯ .... } vi^s. viii^d.

Itm for servaun*tes* dyete some tyme at the ynne ꝯ.................... } ii^s. vi^d.

Itm gevenne by Mr Philippe to one Oliver a frenchman preferred to yowre Lord[shipp]s service by therle of war[wike] who was at the Cowrte [   ]inge a sute w̃ yowre Lord[shipp   ]ie on his backe a [   ]......... } ii^s.

Itm gev[en by M^r] Philipps comãnd-ment [and on Mr Astone]s advise t[o certaine of therle of Lece]sters men [   ] of them } vi^s.

} iii^s. xx^d.

} iij^{li}. iiij^s. vii^d.

[[Page 15]]

[AUGUSTE A^{NO}]
1566

ITM for a sadle ether to carie a troncke on or to ride in, withe girthes surcingle leathering*es* and Warwike staffe the whiche was boughte to carie Mr Philipps apparell vpon that therle of Lecestre vouchsaved to bestowe on him the catalogue whereof ens- uethe ɔ .... } xiiii^s.

Imprimis a shorte damaske gowne garded withe velvette and laide on withe lace } ∝

Itm a duble tafeta coate garded thro- ughe owt withe the same, and covered with Lace ɔ.......................... } ∝

Itm a crimsen saten dublette cutte ɔ..... ∝

Itm a gren taffeta dublette cutte ɔ .... ∝

Itm a canvas dublette streked with blewe ∝

Itm a canvas dublette streked withe ɔ.... red and silver ɔ...................... } ∝

Mr Elise tooke paines abowte this apparell and to sende it frome London.

Itm a plaine canvas dublette not yet rece aved wch is to be sente hether by Whittell therles tealer .... } ∝

Itm a paire of crimson velvette hose withe silke netherstock*es* ɔ.............. } ∝

Itm a paire of hose of stamell of carnatione couler withe nether stock*es* of the same ɔ........................ } ∝

Itm a paire of blewe leather laid on with lace and nether stock*es* of crule } ∝

Itm a paire of grene leather laide on with lace and nether stock*es* of cruele ɔ............................. } ∝

Itm a white leat[her] Jerckine compas ed with parchm[ent] lace of goulde ɔ ..... } ∝

Itm a red leat[her] Jerckine ɔ .... ∝

Itm a black leat[her Je]rckine ɔ .... ∝

Itm vi paire of [duble so]lde showes two white, [two blacke and] two blewe } ∝

Itm a shir[te   ] blacke silke and silv[er   ] .... } ∝

Itm a sh[irte   b]lacke silke ∝

Itm tw[o   ] and } ∝

Sum̃e
14^s.

[[Page 16]]   JOURNEINGE TOWARDES SALOPPE

~~AUGUSTE A~~ꬴꝺ
1566
SEPTEMBRE

IMPRIMIS vpon sundaie the viiith of Septembre at after none for a collatione at Woodstocke ꝺ . . . .   xviii^d.

Itm the same nighte at Chippinge Nortõ for owre supper there and greg with vs to bringe Mr Philippe vnto his father Sheldone ꝺ . . . .   vi^s. viii^d.

Itm for vii horses in the stable viz. v. of those that we broughte furthe and one that Mr Yates of Glostre shier lente Mr Philipp to carie his apparell vpon and Greg*es* ꝺ . . . .   vi^s. viii^d.

Itm for buckles for the troncke sadle the firste beinge broken ꝺ . . . .   iiii^d.

Itm geve*n*ne by Mr Philipps commandmente to a blinde harper who is Sr Willm̃ Holles man of Notinghm̃ shier ꝺ . . . .   xii^d.

Itm vpon Mundaie the ixth of septembre for dynner at Stratforde vpõ Havon ꝺ . . . .   ii^s. viii^d.

Itm for horsmeate there ꝺ . . . .   ii^s. vi^d.

Itm for the smithe ꝺ . . . .   vi^d.

Itm for the sadler ꝺ . . . .   vi^d.

Itm for ale and cakes by the waie thence to belie ꝺ . . . .   iiii^d.

Itm the same nighte at Mr Sheldons at Belie ꝺ . . . .   ∝

Itm tuesdaie the xth daie all daie there   ∝

Itm vpõ wednesdaie the xith daie at dynner at Mr Blunt*es* at Kittermaster and there remain[e]d all nighte ꝺ . . . .   ∝

Itm for owre hors[es] at the ynne ꝺ . . . . . .   v^s.

Itm to the smit[he ꝺ] . . . .   vi^d.

Itm to the sadl[er ꝺ] . . . .   iiii^d.

Itm vpon th[ursdaie at] dynner at Bewdlie w[ith Sr Geor]ge Blunte   ∝

Itm for [   ]even ꝺ . .   ii^s.

Itm in [m]y Ladie . . . .   ∝

Sr George   ∝

xxxi^s. iiii^d.

[[Page 17]]

[SEPTEMBRE A^{No}]
  [156]6

IMPRIMIS vpon Mundaie the xvith daie
for the hier of one to sende home
Mr Yates his horse by that he lente
Mr Philippe at Oxfordde to carie
his apparell on and for the horses
charges ꝰ .... } iii^s. iiii^d. }

Itm the same daie for certaine
of owre horses in the stable at the
ynne and certaine at grasse
vntill we sente them to their
~~honours~~ owners and eles where } iii^s. vi^d.

Itm vpon saturdaie the xxi daie for
a yarde and a naile of howswives clothe
to make him iiii paire of sockes ꝰ ...... } xiiii^d.

Itm for makinge the said sockes ꝰ...... iiii^d.

Itm for two yards and an halfe of
shopp clothe to make him ten hand
cerchers ꝰ.......................... } v^s.

Itm for the makinge of them ꝰ .... xii^d.

Itm the xxiiiith daie for two quier
of paper ꝰ.......................... } viii^d.

Itm for a Cato his former being
loste ꝰ............... and a french gramer ... } xii^d.

Itm for yncke ꝰ...................... iiii^d.

Itm to the furrier for mendinge
his gowne of changeable taffeta .... } xii^d.

Itm for a silke ribande to hange
his tablette at ꝰ .... } iiii^d.

Itm for a stopper for his ynckhorne   i^d.

Itm vpon Michalmes daie for a
paire of showes for him ꝰ .... } x^d.

Itm for a paire for Randall ꝰ ....
Calcotte ꝰ,.......................... } xii^d.

Itm the same [daie] paide to the
Laundres for [was]shinge Mr Phi
lippe and R[andall] Calcotte since
the vith [of June ꝰ......].............. } vii^s. vi^d.

Itm for [for]mer being
loste in [ꝰ ....] .... } xvi^d.

Itm for [   ] for him ꝰ...   xvi^d.

Itm fo[r   ]s for } x[^d].

} xxxi^s. v^d.

Suṁe payd }
  31^s. 5^d. }

[[Page 18]]   AT SALOPPE

SEPTEM—   ITM for a lace for his penne and yncke ⎱ i^d.
BRE   A^{NO} 1566   horne ꝰ.......................... ⎰

Itm for blacke and white silke buttons ⎱ viii^d.
for the reparinge of his apparell ⎰

Itm for thred ꝰ .... iiii^d.

Itm for nedles ꝰ .... i^d.   ⎱ v^s. ii^d.

Itm for a paire of newe bootes for ⎱ iiii^s.
him ꝰ .... ⎰

Itm for a paire of new gloves ꝰ .... ⎱ vi^d.
for him ꝰ .... ⎰

Suṁe payd   Itm for two dozenne of thred pointes   vi^d.
5^s. 2^d.   ꝰ ....

SUMMA MENSIS SEP ꝰ...... ⎱
      TEMBRIS thre pounds   ⎰ iii^{li}: vii^s: xi^d.
seven shillinges xi^d. ꝰ...... ⎰
        ꝰ ....

SUMMA TOTIUS that hathe bene
expended to the use of my yownge
Mr Mr Philippe Sidney ~~frome~~
since the daie of yowr Lordshipps
departure withe my Ladie frome
Westchestre towards her Mties Real
me of Irelande viz. frome the iiiith vi^s
daie of decembre 1565 inclusive   ⎱ xxvi^{li}. i̶x̶$^s̶$. iii^d.
vntill Michalmas daie nexte in-
suinge that date, also inclusive A^{no}
            and valewe
1566 amontethe to the suṁe ∧ of
         vi^s.
twentie six pounds ~~nyne~~ shillinges
    thre
and ~~a~~ pennies ꝰ.................

          ] Lordshipp ⎱ ii^s. ix^d.

APPENDIX II

NOTES ON EXTANT PORTRAITS OF SIR PHILIP SIDNEY

	Owner	Locality	Painter	Description	Notes
A.	Lord De L'Isle and Dudley	Penshurst	?	Sir Philip and his brother Sir Robert, whole length figures, arms entwined	A. Exhibited at Portrait Exhibition, 1866, No. 301, and at Tudor Exhibition, 1890, No. 388. Reproduced in Fox-Bourne's *Life* in Heroes of the Nation Series
B, 1.	Duke of Bedford	Woburn	Zuccaro ?	Life-size to below waist. Youthful, bare-headed, clean-shaven; close ruff, steel gorget, face three-quarters right, yellow dress, black trunk hose, his right hand on hip, his left holding sword hilt	B, 1. Engraved by E. Scriven for Lodge's *Portraits*. Enamel by H. Bone, R.A., Original drawing in National Portrait Gallery. See Woburn Catalogue by G. Scharf, No. 34, p. 27
2.	Marquis of Bath	Longleat			2. Similar to B, 1
3.	Earl of Warwick	Warwick Castle			3. Do. Exhibited Portrait Exhibition, 1866, No. 274. Reproduced in Grosart's *Poems*
4.	Sir Brownlow Sherrard (d. 1748)	Penshurst		Probably the same picture	4. Do. Engraved by Houbraken for Birch's *Lives*. Also reproduced in Fox-Bourne's *Life*
5.	Lord De L'Isle and Dudley				5. Do. Exhibited Portrait Exhibition, 1866, and Tudor Exhibition, 1890
6.	Viscount Dillon	Ditchley		Canvas 45½ inches by 35¾ inches	

C, 1.	H.M. The King	Windsor	J. Oliver	Miniature, wearing hat, seated under tree, clean-shaven face	C. 1. Formerly belonged to Dr Mead. Engraved by G. Vertue for Collins' *Sidney Papers*. Exhibited R.A. Old Masters, 1879, and at Tudor Exhibition, 1890. Reproduced in Lord R. Gower's *Historic Galleries*; *Art Journal*, 1896. p. 139; Foster's *British Miniature Painters*; Bishop Creighton's *Queen Elizabeth*
2.	Duke of Portland	Welbeck	J. Oliver?	Copy of C, 1	
D.	Marquis of Lothian	Blickling	?	Life-size, half length in armour, holding a baton, bare-headed. Face three-quarters left, moustaches, small tuft below lip, no beard, very wide ruff. Helmet on table to left	D Exhibited at Portrait Exhibition, 1866, No. 275
E.	Earl of Darnley	Cobham Hall	?	Life-size bust. Wearing hat. Moustaches and beard	E. Exhibited at Tudor Exhibition, 1890, No. 427
F, 1.	Earl of Chesterfield			Life-size panel to waist. Face three-quarters left. Wide ruff. Moustaches and beard	F, 1. Sketched by Sir G. Scharf at Chesterfield House, Berkeley Square, 1869
2.	Engraved in *Heroologia*, 1620			To waist. Head three-quarters right in wide ruff. Cloak opened to show doublet. Moustaches and slight beard	2. Sir G. Scharf says that F, 1 is the original of the *Heroologia* engraving which was copied by Vertue
G.	Duke of Buccleugh		Hilliard? Oliver?	Bust slightly to left. Moustaches and slight chin tuft. Wide, turned-over lace collar open at the neck	G. Reproduced in *Historic Portrait Miniatures*, 1863, p. 53. Also in Pears' *Letters*

INDEX

DUE